Ascription and Labor Markets

Race and Sex Differences in Earnings

QUANTITATIVE STUDIES IN SOCIAL RELATIONS

Consulting Editor: Peter H. Rossi

UNIVERSITY OF MASSACHUSETTS
AMHERST, MASSACHUSETTS

The list of titles in this series continues on the last page of this volume

Ascription
and Labor Markets

RACE AND SEX DIFFERENCES
IN EARNINGS

TOBY L. PARCEL

CHARLES W. MUELLER

DEPARTMENT OF SOCIOLOGY
UNIVERSITY OF IOWA
IOWA CITY, IOWA

1983

ACADEMIC PRESS

A Subsidiary of Harcourt Brace Jovanovich, Publishers

New York   London
Paris   San Diego   San Francisco   São Paulo   Sydney   Tokyo   Toronto

ACADEMIC PRESS, INC.
111 Fifth Avenue, New York, New York 10003

United Kingdom Edition published by
ACADEMIC PRESS, INC. (LONDON) LTD.
24/28 Oval Road, London NW1 7DX

Library of Congress Cataloging in Publication Data

Parcel, Toby L.
  Ascription and labor markets.

  Includes bibliographical references and index.
  1. Discrimination in employment. 2. Sex
discrimination in employment. 3. Wages. I. Mueller,
Charles W. II. Title. III. Title: Race and sex
differences in earnings.
HD4903.P37 1983   331.2'2   82-22741
ISBN 0-12-545020-6

To
John Wood Gerber
and
Elizabeth and Rachel

Contents

Foreword

It is a pleasure to welcome the work reported in this volume to the expanding literature on the institutional, industrial, and organizational factors that shape the earnings and employment experience of labor market participants. Although earlier work by economists and sociologists on human capital formation and status attainment, respectively, has enriched our understanding of the contributions of labor force participants' own attributes to the determination of their fates, it is only recently that significant numbers of investigators have turned to the large unexplained residuals of conventional studies and to the construction of tests that permit us to examine factors on the demand side of exchanges occurring in labor markets.

Professors Parcel and Mueller have managed to work with a larger number of structural factors in their research than have other researchers in reports that have been published to date. This volume will help to fill a number of lacunae that have limited us in our ability to stake out a satisfactory theoretical apparatus, that is, an apparatus that simultaneously deals with demand and supply. One's confidence is enhanced by the fact that the authors of the present report have relied a good deal less slavishly on sectoral typologies in favor of direct analyses of market characteristics; their efforts will thus surely help us to get beyond some of the well-recognized difficulties in sectoral analyses.

Professors Parcel and Mueller have turned to factor analyses rather than to a developed set of logics in some of their efforts to pinpoint and to assign priorities to the characteristics they have used as the independent variables in their analysis of market structures. But that too is helpful because their selection of specific variables for factor analytic treatment is informed by persuasive arguments, arguments that can be compared to those offered by others who have worked with multiple indicators of structures and who have also sought to assign priorities with the help of factor analytic techniques. The fact that many of these investigators are exploiting survey data as well as ecological data will further help us to sharpen our theoretical conceptualizations.

Professors Parcel and Mueller's report will also be of interest to investigators whose preoccupations are not essentially those of students of labor and labor markets. Indeed, their data concerning the differences between sex and race discrimination will be of great interest to students of discrimination per se and to the growing number of students of the benefits and costs of public policy alternatives. In addition, the authors offer both findings and insights concerning these findings that permit more sensitive assessments of phenomena pertaining to processes of social selection; whereas students of social stratification generally recognize that there are indeed issues in this area, this research addresses several of them more directly. It accordingly helps us to join the issues in more imaginative and, one strongly suspects, in what will be more productive ways.

Prior to the recent pursuit of labor market and related structural variables, progress in understanding the circumstances of labor force participants was marked, but uneven. Indeed, the most unfortunate participants in the labor force could too easily be blamed for their lots in studies that focused exclusively on the differential attributes of "winners" and "losers." In the more recent investigations, we begin to perceive that the attributes of industry structures, market structures, and organizational structures play telling roles in the determination of successes and failures in the world of work. Public policies, we may now safely conclude, are misguided precisely to the degree that they target almost entirely workers' and would-be workers' traits. Clearly, there are large margins for the application of incentives and disincentives to employers as well as to labor force members. It also appears to be clear that these applications need not be as inflationary as was so often suggested in the tall pile of research reports that consigned most unemployed Americans to a population conceived to be unemployable. A great many of those who are unemployed in one setting, it turns out, have traits in common with peers who fare far better in other differently "structured" contexts. It must be added, though, that we will need further studies before we can urge that one or another particular policy lever be pulled; the authors' evidence demonstrates that activating the usual array of policies has differential effects on the members of different race–sex groups, which points to the need for more data, more analyses, and more caution. It is to the authors' great credit that they designed their investigation such that they could uncover some very essential facts on this vexed and vexing matter. Professors Parcel and

Mueller thus added to the probabilities that public policy debates will be more thoughtful even as they help us move a step ahead in straightforward scientific terms.

IVAR BERG
UNIVERSITY OF PENNSYLVANIA

Preface

In this book we report analysis of earnings attainment as a function of both personal and structural characteristics, for workers who vary by race and sex. The project is motivated by two major concerns. First, we believe it important to understand more fully the impact of labor market characteristics on individual workers' earnings. We also believe it important that such analysis be undertaken within the context of previous research concerning personal investment and socialization determinants of earnings attainment. Thus, we seek theoretically and empirically to integrate traditions featuring discussion of labor market structures with those concerned with individual earnings attainment. Second, we believe that analysis of race and sex differences in inequality will benefit from incorporation of both structural and individual perspectives. Previous research conducted by each of us suggested that a better understanding of ascriptive status differences in earnings attainment could be achieved by explicit and systematic consideration of these traditions, which generally have been treated as distinct and occasionally as competitive.

The particular labor market contexts that we investigate in this volume include local labor markets, industrial labor markets (or economic sectors), and occupational labor markets, as well as measures of workers' class/authority positions. In Chapter 1 we review literature relevant to these contexts, as well as literature describing sex and race differences in earnings attainment based on human capital and status attainment perspectives. In Chapter 2 we describe the data sources, measurement strategy, and analytic techniques used in the book. This chapter also reports the results of a series of factor analyses aimed at describing local, industrial, and occupational labor market differentiation. These pictures of market differentiation are of theoretical interest by themselves; they also suggest dimensions of labor market structures that could influence individual workers' earnings.

Chapters 3 through 5 are devoted to assessing the extent to which these dimensions of markets are associated with earnings, net of human capital and socialization factors. The analysis of covariance models are presented for status groups that vary by race and sex; the models for women workers are further divided by marital status. In Chapter 3 we focus on local labor markets; in Chapter 4 we add indicators describing industrial market differentiation; and Chapter 5 incorporates measures of occupational market differentiation as well as indicators of class/authority position. Thus, in these chapters we present models that cumulatively evaluate the impact of structural as well as personal determinants of earnings. In addition, in each chapter we bring evidence to bear on the issue of race and sex discrimination by exploring possible changes in race–sex earnings differences due to changes in access to and/or efficacy of resources.

In Chapters 6 and 7 we consider three additional issues. In Chapter 6 we incorporate additional controls for family background and social psychological factors so as to provide conservative estimates of the effects of labor market characteristics on earnings. We also consider the issue of social selection in earnings attainment. We present estimates of the extent to which the several status groups are nonrandomly allocated to labor market contexts according to their personal characteristics. Chapter 7 considers questions involving interaction effects in earnings attainment. Whereas the bulk of the analysis presents additive effects, in this chapter we evaluate several hypotheses concerning differences in returns to earnings determinants depending on factors such as age/cohort and key labor market characteristics. Chapter 8 presents a general summary of findings plus implications for theory, policy, and future research.

This volume is intended for those interested in structural explanations of inequality. It is also intended for those concerned with race and sex differences in socioeconomic outcomes. The work should therefore be of interest to economists and sociologists with these substantive interests and to those additional readers concerned with poverty, education, and quantitative methods. More generally, we hope that readers, regardless of their particular substantive orientation, will find the integration of structurally and individually oriented perspectives useful not only in the study of inequality, but also for investigation of other social phenomena.

Acknowledgments

We gratefully acknowledge support of this project from the National Science Foundation, Grant #SOC-7825566. Without this support, any research that we might have undertaken for this project would have been far narrower in scope. We also appreciate additional support from the University of Iowa in the form of an Old Gold Summer Fellowship to the first coauthor and a Developmental Assignment Award to the second coauthor, as well as additional computer funds from the University of Iowa Graduate College. Neither the university nor the National Science Foundation bears any responsibility for the conclusions expressed herein.

Survey data used in the analysis were provided by the Michigan Survey Research Center, University of Michigan. This organization bears no responsibility for the conclusions stated in this volume. Help in data production and data management was provided by the University of Iowa Laboratory for Political Research directed by G. R. Boynton and formerly directed by William Welsh. Chia-Hsing Lu, John Kolp, and Jim Grifhorst from that office were particularly helpful. Larry Haffner capably created and managed numerous data files used throughout the analysis. Doug Black, Dalene Stangl, Sarah Enticknap, Martha Morris, and Bill Montgomery provided additional research support.

Numerous colleagues provided reactions to our ideas throughout this project. We particularly appreciate comments on all or parts of this volume provided by Ivar Berg, Robert Althauser, Glen Elder, Linda Waite, Robert Kaufman, Fred Pampel, and Jim Price. Other colleagues who provided comments on work related to the project or who provided general support included Robert Szafran, E. M. Beck, Patrick Horan, Samuel Preston, Barbara Reskin, and Kathryn Ward.

Manuscript typing was handled by Janet Wood, Joyce Ridout, and Gail Chadwick; the Department of Sociology secretarial staff at the University of Iowa under the direction of Mary Smith provided additional secretarial support. Assistance in proofreading was provided by Tom Ford, Rebecca Ford, Kazuko Odani, and Dung-Ju Yang.

Finally, we very much appreciate support from the staff at Academic Press throughout the publication process.

None of those acknowledged herein bears any responsibility for conclusions stated or defects present in this volume. The authors retain full responsibility for these features of the work.

CHAPTER 1

The Problem and Theoretical Foundations

Introduction

Analysis of socioeconomic inequality continues to occupy the attention of policymakers as well as academicians. In a society committed to equal opportunity, the study of inequality provides guidance in formulating policy aimed at promoting equal access to avenues of economic success as well as facilitating scientific understanding of our stratification system. A central problem in the study of inequality is understanding why members of certain groups, including blacks and women, achieve socioeconomic outcomes that are lower than those of majority groups. In this research we study the *labor market* determinants of such differentials in earnings.

It is important to realize that despite the prevalence of labor market explanations of inequality reflected in certain economic conceptualizations and in popular thinking, such explanations have only recently become of interest to sociologists. The status attainment and human capital traditions, for example, have emphasized socialization and investment explanations for inequality. Although interest in discrimination against economic minorities (racial groups and women) often motivated such analyses, inferences concerning discrimination were indirect. In this monograph new evidence will be provided concerning forms of discrimination that occur in labor markets to hinder the economic status attainment of these workers.

The conceptualization of the labor market that we find most useful to this analysis of inequality is one that allows for differentiation of labor markets along regional, industrial, and occupational bases.[1] We find uninteresting

[1]We use the term "industrial labor markets" to refer to the economic sectors suggested by the dual economy literature that we discuss later.

statements declaring that *the* labor market is tight for blacks and women, since such notions provide no explanation of tightness except for global discrimination against economic minorities. Because such statements allow for no variation in the structural processes that influence achievement, *the* labor market becomes a constant. In contrast, other popularized notions of labor markets are more closely aligned with the conceptualization we present. News media proclaim that workers in the steel industry face wage cutbacks or increased unemployment due to decreased demand and that residents of economically depressed local labor markets face little prospect of better employment opportunities in the coming year. Such statements allow for variation in structural processes across occupational, industrial, or regional boundaries. It is this variation that we believe is essential to understanding variation in achievement and in particular, variation in achievement by ascriptive status.

It is the case that labor markets are differentiated along a variety of lines. In a recent review, Althauser and Kalleberg (1981) catalog several types of labor market differentiation including primary and secondary (Piore, 1971), internal and external (Kerr, 1954), and urban (Rees and Schultz, 1970). Althauser and Kalleberg also reference several typologies specific to occupational labor markets (Form and Huber, 1976) and acknowledge additional formulations of labor market differentiation (D. Gordon, 1972; Bibb and Form, 1977). We argue, however, that areal, occupational, and industrial differentiation are among the more important dimensions of labor market differentiation to the study of inequality based upon ascription. It is for these dimensions that the maximum amount of theoretical guidance for formulating this analysis is available, and as will be demonstrated, it is for these dimensions that it is possible to fashion the closest fit between theory and data. In addition, known differences in the distribution of economically disadvantaged workers by occupation, industry, and area raise questions concerning how this differential distribution may be functioning to create and maintain our stratification system.

In order to clarify terms, we adopt for this analysis Althauser and Kalleberg's definition of labor markets as "arenas (Freedman, 1976) in which one or more of the following are similarly structured: employment, movement between jobs, development and differentiation of job skills, or wages (1981:121)." This definition suggests that within given occupations, industries, or areas, there is similarity in the status attainment process due to structural mechanisms that operate with uniformity across persons. We recognize, however, that many structural mechanisms fail to operate uniformly when persons vary by ascribed status. Theoretical analyses of institutional discrimination suggest that the handicaps economic minority groups face are external to the human capital or background characteristics they embody and instead are a function of institutional arrangements that operate to their disadvantage. This analysis directly incorporates into models of attainment *indicators of structural mechanisms* specific to occupational, areal, and industrial labor markets, which theory and past research suggest are important in producing variation in attainment by status.

It is important to recognize how such a strategy differs from those previously utilized. Since many analyses have focused on microlevel explanations of inequality, measurement of concepts appropriately has been confined to the individual level. Theories that argue for the importance of family origins, mental ability, years of schooling, and job training have spawned studies where the individual was selected as the unit of analysis and measurement of individual characteristics utilized as a matter of course. Additional studies of inequality have been produced where *ecological analysis* is utilized. As will be shown later, such studies of occupations or of urban areas are motivated by macrolevel (or structural) explanations of inequality, some of which feature labor markets as explanatory concepts. One goal of our analysis is to incorporate the advantages while avoiding the disadvantages of each approach. For example, treatment of structural determinants of attainment in individual-level analyses has often been accomplished through using sets of dummy variables to represent affiliation with various geographical areas (Blinder, 1973; Mueller, 1974; Lane, 1968), industries (Wachtel and Betsey, 1972; Harrison, 1972), and sometimes jobs (Wachtel and Betsey, 1972). Although knowledge that such sets of dummy variables are statistically significant determinants of economic status may be an important first step in ascertaining whether additional analysis is needed (Hauser, 1974), such findings do not tell us *why* variation in categorical membership is important. Ecological analyses of inequality evidence a complementary deficiency. Although characteristics of institutions and/or labor markets are incorporated into the analyses, thus permitting direct inferences concerning characteristics of institutions associated with inequality, measurement of individual-level characteristics is necessarily incomplete (Spilerman and Miller, 1976; Masters, 1975; Wallace and Kalleberg, 1981). This defect is a particularly serious one given that both the human capital and status attainment traditions have provided clear evidence of the importance of individual investments and socialization experiences as determinants of economic outcomes.

Our solution to these problems is to perform a *contextual analysis* in which the individual is retained as the unit of analysis and independent variables are measured at both the individual level and at higher levels of aggregation (Valkonen, 1969; Farkas, 1974; Boyd and Iverson, 1979; see Spilerman and Miller, 1976, for another approach). Earnings and individual determinants of outcomes (education, mental ability, weeks worked) are measured at the individual level; characteristics of occupational, areal, and industrial labor markets are measured via global variables (Lazarsfeld and

Menzel, 1969) at those levels of aggregation. Studies by Alexander and his colleagues (e.g., Alexander and Eckland, 1975) have used a similar strategy to investigate the role of school characteristics on student educational outcomes. Classic analyses by Lazarsfeld, Berelson, and Gaudet (1968) and Lipset, Trow, and Coleman (1962) were also concerned with the effects of group or organizational characteristics on individual outcomes. Thus, this strategy is not a new one. As indicated, however, application of this approach to analysis of labor market effects on individual earnings solves problems evident in previous research, as well as providing a means to evaluate theory. Hence the analysis proposed will move beyond studies that indicate that categorical membership "makes a difference" by providing estimates of the extent to which theoretically suggested characteristics of labor markets do influence the economic status of individuals.

It is clearly the case that interest in discrimination has motivated prior analyses of differential achievement by ascriptive status, and such concern motivates this research as well. Although many researchers have utilzed statistical decompositions in order to draw inferences concerning the extent to which the achievement process varies by status (Althauser and Wigler, 1972; Iams and Thornton, 1975; O. Duncan, 1969; Blum, 1972; Coleman, Blum, Sorensen, and Rossi, 1972; R. Hall and Kasten, 1973; Reskin and Hargens, 1980), we believe that use of such techniques is *most* fruitful in conjunction with the measurement strategy proposed. That is, we see as primarily important the direct incorporation of indicators of institutions (in this case, characteristics of labor markets) into the analyses of individual outcomes. Although sociologists traditionally proclaim interest in the relationship between social structure and the individual, our analytic strategy takes on additional promise within the context of analysis of discrimination. If one takes seriously the precept that an important part of understanding economic discrimination lies in analysis of social structure and that promotion of equal opportunity may be effectively facilitated by manipulating characteristics of the institutions within which individuals function, then analysis of the relationship between structural characteristics and individual outcomes should be of high priority.

Most of the material in this monograph will provide evidence concerning the extent to which labor market characteristics influence the economic status attainment of individuals. Our focus will be upon the prediction of individual labor earnings. We recognize that earnings forms only one component of economic status, although for most workers it is the most important. In addition to earnings, however, most people receive some amount in fringe benefits as part of employment and also accumulate assets during their careers. We expect that the models developed in this analysis may also be useful in the study of these other components of socioeconomic status.

Several specific questions guide this analysis. We are interested in understanding, for example, whether characteristics of industrial labor markets differentially affect earnings attainment for blacks and whites. We also ask, Does the economic productivity of an areal labor market as a whole influence a woman's chances of economic success, independent of her particular skills and other labor market characteristics? Evidence relevant to these questions can be used to assess the impact that changes in labor market institutions would have upon the individuals who function within them. Hence, empirical evidence concerning the issues we raise could provide guidance for policy, as well as new evidence concerning ascription and the stratification system.

In addition, descriptive data will be produced that provide evidence concerning differential access to institutional resources by economic groups. We know, for example, that blacks attain fewer years of schooling than do whites, evidence lower status origins (e.g., in terms of father's occupational background), and, in families, produce greater numbers of children. We know comparatively little, however, concerning individual access to ecological resources. Do blacks evidence reduced access to industrial resources relative to whites? Is women workers' access to occupational resources less than men's? As will be indicated, answers to these questions are inextricably linked to the answers to the analytical questions posed.

This book aims at a fruitful intermarriage of concern for structural explanations of inequality with careful considerations of previous work within the research traditions of status attainment and human capital. That is, we take seriously the production of cumulative findings in science, and as the subsequent literature review indicates, this research is formulated to evaluate to what extent labor market explanations can add to our understanding of inequality. Although we believe that much previous research has neglected to evaluate the structural explanations of economic status attainment that we propose to test, many studies *have* provided well-developed analyses of individual determinants of economic outcomes. Thus, they provide a firm basis by which to evaluate the propositions to be tested. The next section summarizes this previous research.

Status Attainment and Human Capital
Approaches to Inequality

The status attainment tradition within sociology (Blau and Duncan, 1967; O. Duncan, Featherman, and Duncan, 1972; Sewell and Hauser, 1972; Haller and Portes, 1973; Sewell, Hauser, and Featherman, 1976; Featherman and Hauser, 1978) and the human capital perspective within economics (Becker, 1964; Becker and Chiswick, 1966; Thurow, 1969; Schultz, 1962; Mincer, 1970, 1974; Blaug, 1976) have provided their respective disciplines with durable and fertile paradigms for the study of inequality. Within both traditions, the emphasis to date has been on characteristics of individuals rather than labor market factors as determinants of socioeconomic status.

Studies of status attainment emphasize the role of familial origins, educational attainment, and additional indicators of socialization experiences as determinants of occupational status and, more recently, of earnings. Although additional analyses do consider some structural explanations of achievement under the label of "school effects" (see Alexander and Eckland, 1975, for a review), even these explanations are largely confined to the preadult period of socialization. In recent analyses, Featherman (1976) and Trieman (1976) both suggest that one of the most important contributions of the tradition has been the demonstration that the American educational system serves as an important mechanism of social mobility that introduces variation in socioeconomic achievement independent of familial origins.

Another important contribution of this research tradition is the statement of causal ordering among the variables in the status attainment process. Based on assumptions about events in each individual's life course from childhood through adulthood, it has been possible to estimate both direct and indirect effects of the various life-cycle variables. Recently, Hogan (1978, 1980) has assessed the appropriateness of these assumptions by determining the degree of conformity to the assumed normative ordering of events. In testing whether those who order their transition events in a normative way are disadvantaged socioeconomically, he found no effect on occupational attainments but did find that they received lower earnings returns to their education and lower earnings in general. This is supported by the replication of the Blau and Duncan classic (1967) study by Featherman and Hauser (1978), who document two complementary trends: (a) declining status ascription, as measured by the influence of status origin variables on socioeconomic outcomes (occupation and earnings); and (b) increasing status allocation on the basis of universalistic criteria such as educational attainment.

Human capital analyses emphasize the importance of "investment" in human capital as a means of yielding subsequent "returns" in earnings. With reference to wage attainment, the theory suggests that individual income may be increased by investments in wealth (or human capital) where that wealth is multiplied by the implicit interest rate (i.e., rate of return) to yield income. Those who invest to increase the quantity or quality of human capital can expect greater incomes because those investments presumably cause increases in marginal productivity. Investments may take a variety of forms, and researchers have argued that education (Becker, 1964; Hansen, 1963), job experience (Mincer, 1974), training (Mincer, 1974), improved health (Weisbrod, 1966), migration (Sjaasted, 1962; Bowles, 1970), and job information (Stigler, 1962) function as investments in human capital. The theory's devotees recognize that these investments may be affected by structural factors. For example, variations in labor market productivity affect migration; availability of government loans affects educational investment. However, the investments themselves are clearly characteristics of individuals, and structural factors are not included in the models.

RACE AND SEX DIFFERENCES IN SOCIOECONOMIC STATUS: SOCIALIZATION AND INVESTMENT EXPLANATIONS

Both of these traditions have advanced our understanding of the effect of ascription upon inequality beyond the descriptive level. Analyses of racial inequality compatible with the status attainment tradition have emphasized racial differences in access to individual resources, differential effectiveness of such resources, and discrimination as sources of differential outcomes (Coleman, Blum, Sorenson, and Rossi, 1972). O. Duncan (1969) argues that the "culture of poverty" explanation is ineffective in understanding black–white income differences and that educational attainment and job status are of major importance. Coleman and his colleagues (Coleman, Blum, Sorenson, and Rossi, 1972; Blum, 1972; Coleman, Berry, and Blum, 1972) analyze both first job and first earnings, and Blum finds that educational attainment is the most important determinant of earnings for both races. Featherman and Hauser (1978) find that blacks must rely almost exclusively on education for social mobility, whereas the white population relies also on differentials in their status origins. In addition, they find that the occupational returns to schooling for blacks are lower than for whites at the precollege level; the returns to college training are more comparable for the two races, however. From the human capital tradition we learn that both blacks and whites obtain returns to age, education, and region of current residence (Weiss and Williamson, 1972) and that school resources and familial origins exercise indirect effects upon earnings through years of schooling attained (Morgenstern, 1973). Blinder (1973) also relies heavily upon socialization and investment variables in his analysis of black–white earnings attainment.

Sociologists and economists have followed similar models in studying sex differences in earnings.[2] Although several studies of occupational attainment have indicated essential similarity by sex (Treiman and Terrell, 1975; Mc-Clendon, 1976; Featherman and Hauser, 1976a), analyses of earnings attainment suggest that the process of earning income varies by sex. Suter and Miller (1973) and Treiman and Terrell (1975) indicate that years of schooling is a less effective resource for women than for men. Featherman and Hauser (1976a) also conclude that it is in the process of earnings attainment, as opposed to educational or occupational achievement, that sex differences are the greatest. More recent analyses by Spaeth (1979) and others have begun to suggest explanations for this difference, and these arguments will be reviewed shortly.

The human capital approach to sex differences in earnings manifests fidelity to human capital theory by suggesting that earnings attainment processes may differ by sex due to women's roles in the family. Although the sexes are equal with regard to IQ and nearly equal in education, women are not viewed as perfectly substitutable for men. Women accumulate less human capital primarily because their family responsibilities lead to different patterns of labor force participation. Women spend fewer years in the labor force than men, which leads to quality of labor differentials that in turn result in productivity differentials (Mincer and Polachek, 1974). The woman's decision to forego the accumulation of large amounts of human capital (by not working for wages continuously) is seen as a rational decision, given her role in the family (Becker, 1965, 1973; Mincer, 1962). Research compatible with the basic human capital tradition has shown the unadjusted male–female wage differential to be 50–80%, with control variables such as experience, education, training, and marital status accounting for about half of this gross differential (Fuchs, 1971; Cohen, 1971; Oaxaca, 1973). Polachek (1975:466), relying entirely on the human capital model, obtains an *estimate* of "post-school human capital investment," which results in an equation accounting for over 90% of the male–female earnings gap. It must be emphasized, however, that these postschool factors are not measured empirically. Hence, this study cannot be used to invalidate previous studies on the

[2]Sociologists have used three other forms of analysis including: (*a*) the examination of male–female differences in intergenerational occupational mobility (DeJong, Brewer, and Robin, 1971; Tyree and Treas, 1974; Featherman and Hauser, 1974; Rosenfeld, 1978); (*b*) the study of female mobility through marriage (Glenn, Ross, and Tully, 1974; Chase, 1975; Taylor and Glenn, 1976; Mueller and Campbell, 1977; Mueller and Pope, 1980); and (*c*) the study of the relationship between female labor force participation and various demographic and social psychological variables (Sweet, 1973; Oppenheimer, 1973; Waite, 1976; Waite and Stolzenberg, 1976). Although these bodies of research have been useful at a descriptive level, they have not been as informative as the status attainment strategy for unraveling sex differences in the processes whereby earnings are achieved. For this reason they are minimally useful to the development of our arguments and hence are not reviewed here.

significance of occupational segregation or theories that argue for structural effects.

STRUCTURAL INFERENCES: HOW CLEAR?

The emphasis in the previously mentioned and related studies has been on individual-level attainment processes. This phenomenon is due to the theoretical bases of the human capital and status attainment perspectives, which are rooted in neoclassical economics and functionalism, respectively (see Blaug, 1976 and Horan, 1978 for relevant arguments). Since these perspectives do not suggest the importance of structural determinants of socioeconomic status, empirical analyses emanating from these traditions have not devoted much attention to incorporation of structural factors. Despite this emphasis, however, inferences concerning the role of social structure in attainment are sometimes presented. One of the most common strategies used to produce such inferences consists of using dummy variables to represent respondents' affiliations with and participation in various contexts. Very commonly researchers will include a variable that represents whether the respondent lives in a given region (e.g., North) or not (Blum, 1972); dummy coding schemes including both region and city size are also used (Weiss and Williamson, 1972; Mueller, 1977). Alternatively researchers have created separate dummies representing specific local labor markets (Mueller, 1974). These analyses allow investigation of whether residence in grossly defined types of local labor markets promotes or hinders earnings attainment or whether residence in particular markets promotes or hinders attainment. Interpretations of such findings are often phrased in terms of characteristics of the areas or in terms of the people who live there. So when Blum (1972) finds that northern residence contributes positively to earnings attainment for blacks and whites, she interprets this in terms of North–South differentials in racial discrimination. In his analysis of city size effects, Mueller (1977) argues that since larger cities have a more complex and specialized division of labor, more universalistic criteria will be used in the screening, selecting, promoting, and rewarding of employees. Based on this he hypothesizes, but does not find, that racial discrimination will decrease monotonically with city size.

In the analyses by Wachtel and Betsey (1972) and Harrison (1972), occupational, industrial, and areal dummies are used to measure the key variables of interest—structural determinants of earnings. In Harrison's (1972) analysis, for example, his discussion concerning "good" versus "bad" jobs and the "primary" versus "secondary" sectors is operationalized with two variables: (a) occupational prestige; and (b) dummy variables representing industrial affiliation, although dummies representing unionization and location are also included. Wachtel and Betsey's (1972) analysis was similar; they utilized categorical variables representing occupation and industry of current employment, region of employment, city size, and union membership as indicators of "structural" factors affecting wage attainment. Both studies are interpreted to suggest that the structural factors do influence workers' earnings, independent of controls for human capital variables. Use of this strategy, however, does not allow us to understand the operation of structural characteristics underlying these categories as they influence earnings. Such inferences remain indirect.

Another way in which previous analyses have made structural inferences is by default. Given that not every factor can be taken into account in every study, researchers within the status attainment and human capital traditions have sometimes attributed part of the unexplained variance to structural factors. For example, when O. Duncan (1969) discusses the findings from his regression standardization procedure, 38% of the variance is attributed to discrimination and structural factors omitted from the analysis; Blum (1972) follows a similar strategy. Clearly, this practice does not allow us to ascertain anything specific concerning the effects of structure upon individuals.

Given the limitations of these previous approaches, the intent in this analysis is to move beyond such indirect inferences. In order to accomplish this, however, a theory must be formulated specifying which dimensions of the several contexts should influence individual earnings attainment. These dimensions can then be measured and incorporated into analysis. Both theoretical and empirical analyses performed at the ecological level are relevant. That is, we draw upon previous theories and studies concerning local labor markets, industrial labor markets or sector differentiation, and occupational labor markets. We also review literature concerning class/authority relations within the firm. The studies reviewed later tend to focus on one or two of these contexts, and these analyses concerning the respective structures are important in their own right.

Due to the interrelationships that exist among these structures, however, a complete picture of ascriptive status differences in earnings attainments as a function of labor market characteristics must incorporate the four contexts we delineate. Literature suggests that there are predictable relationships among local markets, industrial sectors, occupational markets (or the primary–secondary labor market), and the authority structures of firms. Local labor markets vary in their industrial composition, which in turn implies differing distributions of jobs across local markets (Thompson, 1965:69–70). Viewing this argument in terms of the dual economy and dual labor market perspectives, the dual economy is not equally distributed across all local labor markets. Assuming some degree of correspondence between the dual economy and the dual labor market, we would expect an uneven distribution of "good" jobs across locales, with some areas having a higher proportion than others. This uneven distribution of "good" (and therefore "bad") jobs across communities implies differential distribution of job characteristics including complexity of work tasks, pleasantness of working conditions, and the nature of job skills required. Such differential distribution also implies that access to authority positions within firms is uneven across local markets. Given these expected interrelationships, conducting the analysis in terms of one or two of these contexts could produce misleading inferences regarding the impact of any one type of context. In addition, given our interest in ascriptive status differences in the effects of labor market characteristics, the use of several contexts allows us to present a more complete picture of these differences by status group than would be the case in a more limited analysis.

In order to accomplish our goal of understanding the relationship between macro structures and individual outcomes, we first must understand something of the respective macro structures themselves. Therefore, initially we address questions such as: How do sociologists and economists describe urban labor markets? What is the dual economy? What types of jobs comprise primary and secondary labor markets? Second, we discuss how the operation of these structures affects the earnings of individual workers. This involves translation of the theories and concepts specified at the ecological level into hypotheses that can be tested via contextual analysis. Finally, where possible, we hypothesize how various race–sex groups may be differentially affected by the relevant labor market characteristics we describe. In the following sections, each of these questions for three types of labor markets of interest is addressed.

Local Labor Markets

ECONOMIC ORGANIZATION

We begin with the local labor market. At a descriptive level, urban economists and sociologists identify several types of local labor markets depending upon their dominant form of economic activity. Thompson (1965), who is interested in urban growth, suggests that cities may be classified as being in one of four stages of development. In the first stage, that of "export specialization," the local economy is largely a function of a single industry or firm that provides goods for export, and therefore supports local service and retail businesses through its income. In the second stage, the "export complex," the export sector is more developed. Development may occur by achieving industrial vertical integration if the area contains suppliers for the major manufacturing firm(s) and/or if the products of that firm are further utilized in the production processes of other firms. Development may also occur if firms produce additional products. In the third stage, that of "economic maturation," the local economy can largely rely upon the goods produced locally instead of importing from other locales as is characteristic of the two earlier stages. In addition, the scope and quality of local business and consumer services increases. Finally, the stage of the "regional metropolis" may be reached when adjacent areas depend upon the city for services it provides and when the city exercises regional economic dominance. In sum, in the early stages of urban development, the economic organization of cities is heavily dependent upon those firms and industries that produce goods for export and is often characterized by the nature of the product(s) these businesses produce. In the more advanced stages of urban growth, cities become increasingly self-sufficient in terms of producing needed goods and services and eventually export services as well as goods to surrounding communities.

O. Duncan and Reiss (1956) provide another scheme for characterizing local labor markets. They also utilize the notion of an export base, in this case to suggest that urban communities differ in the nature and extent of functional specialization. Specialization is defined in terms of whether there exists an export function for the economic activity in question. Local labor markets can specialize in manufacturing, wholesale and/or retail trade, higher education, public administration, transportation, military–national defense, and entertainment and recreation, where each of these economic goods or services can be conceptualized as being exported to nonresidents and thus providing income for the exporting community. They describe manufacturing centers, for example, as having a high proportion of over-21-year-olds, more likely to be located in the North, having higher male, but not female, labor force participation rates, having lower specialization in trade, and being of higher income levels but lower socioeconomic (i.e., educational and job status) levels than nonmanufacturing centers (O. Duncan and Reiss, 1956:272–273). Those areas with retail trade specialization have slightly higher rates of female labor force participation, greater proportions of white collar workers, and somewhat higher levels of educational attainment than those areas specializing in (a) wholesale trade; (b) trade devoted to maintenance functions for the local populations; or (c) other nontrade activities (O. Duncan and Reiss, 1956:297). Similar ideas are noted by Form and Miller (1960:Chapter 2).

This descriptive analysis of city types forms the basis for theoretical analysis concerning the impact of local labor market economic functioning upon workers' earnings. Thompson (1965) argues that local labor market organization affects workers' earnings independent of labor supply. He argues that the higher wage levels in the "export base," which is composed of the major firms in the manufacturing sector, influence wages for other jobs in that labor market through competition for labor. Thus an "intra-area wage roll-out" effect occurs. He suggests, for example, that the local service sector must offer wages that are at least partially competitive with the dominant export sector industries or they will face problems in recruiting workers. Thus, a high-wage export industry directly enriches its own workers by paying them high wages and indirectly enriches other workers by raising wages in the local service sector through intraarea competition (Thompson, 1965:73). This hypothesis assumes that the local labor market is at least partially autonomous and that migration between labor market areas is sluggish. Thompson juxtaposes the influence of national occupational labor markets with those of regional labor markets by posing the illustrative question: "Do the wage rates of medical technologists and retail clerks in Detroit reflect more the national demand and supply for these skills or the pay scales in the nearby automobile factories? (1965:74–75)." We will return to this particular issue later.

Thompson also utilizes his theory to analyze income inequality. He argues that a high-wage export sector will tend to decrease income inequality because a narrower range of skills is required for blue-collar as opposed to white-collar work, there is less risk-taking in a high-wage export sector (i.e., fewer small businesses in an area dominated by larger firms), and the service sector, which lacks a counterpart to the egalitarian-oriented labor unions present in the dominant export sector, is comparatively small. He summarizes:

> a strong union leads to an aggressive wage policy; large plants, oligopoly, and firm control over price enables local firms to buy industrial peace with product price increase without sacrificing profits; industrial specialization narrows the range of occupations, and unionization further constricts wage differentials on ideological grounds; absentee ownership reduces the role of property income as a local source of income—a kind of income usually disproportionately realized by the upper income groups. All of this combines to produce an economy which has a higher average income and a very low degree of income inequality (1965:183).

Concerning income stability, Thompson argues that the greater the dependence upon export base firms, the greater the amplitude of local economic swings. For example, Detroit is a market heavily concentrated in one type of goods, automobiles. Given a drop in demand for this export sector product, workers in the automobile industry itself, those supplying that industry, and those service, wholesale, and retail firms depending upon automobile workers' incomes will be hurt to some extent. These workers experience corresponding prosperity during times of high demand. In a local labor market where the industrial base is more diversified, a decrease in demand for one product affects a smaller proportion of workers initially, and produces small roll-out effects to other firms, thus maximizing stability of earnings over time.

In terms of empirical support for Thompson's theory, Parcel (1981) has demonstrated that there are intraarea wage roll-out effects between manufacturing and the service, wholesale, and retail sectors in most time periods between 1947 and 1972 for the 100 largest SMSAs and that characteristics of the manufacturing sector may have had even more pervasive effects upon the economic functioning of other sectors than Thompson suggests. Economists have also conducted analyses based on the perspective.[3] Mattila (1973) illustrates the usefulness of the theory for understanding economic functioning within a specific local labor market, while Mattila and Thompson (1968) develop a cross-sectional econometric model of development for urban economics. Concerning its relevance for this analysis, Thompson's theory alerts us to the importance of viewing local labor market economic organization in terms of industrial composition and in terms of the health or prosperity of respective sectors. We view as important the economic size and functioning of manufacturing activity as well as that in services, retail, and wholesale trade. If his theory is correct, then we should find that wage levels in manufacturing are positively associated with workers' earnings independent of workers' personal characteristics. Previous work by Parcel (1979) has suggested that this hypothesis is supported for males. As will be indicated in Chapter 2, in this analysis several dimensions of local labor market economic organization are operationalized and used to further evaluate this hypothesis.

We are also concerned with how export sector functioning affects race and sex differences in earnings. Thompson argues that local economies with dominant export sectors will evidence reduced racial income inequality as compared with more diversified local labor markets, and several researchers have provided evidence consistent with this idea. Reder (1955), for example, suggests that a high proportion of manufacturing in an urban area will reduce

---

[3]Economists have also criticized Thompson's theory. Heilbrun (1974), for example, argues that the dichotomy of basic–nonbasic economic activities is overly simplistic. He suggests that such aggregation fails to capture the complexity of relationships among industries and will probably produce inaccurate estimates concerning responses of specific industries to increases or decreases in export base activity. He suggests that attempts to calculate multiplier effects to assess the magnitude of shortrun economic changes have been disappointing and that use of the basic–nonbasic analysis for making long-run economic forecasts is infeasible, due in part to the multitude of other variables that operate in the long run (Heilbrun, 1974:150–152). Other researchers have highlighted the difficulty of assesssing what proportion of an SMSA's goods and services are consumed locally and what proportion are exported (0. Duncan, Scott, Lieberson, B. Duncan, and Winsborough, 1960; Hirsch, 1973).

wage differentials. He reasons that since manufacturing demands a high proportion of semiskilled labor (and since such demand allows greater competition between workers), if blacks are in predominantly low-skilled jobs, they should have substantial access to manufacturing positions. Analyses by Turner (1951) and Masters (1975) support the notion that "proportion manufacturing" is associated with greater racial income equality and Spilerman and Miller (1976) echo this conclusion.[4] Additional evidence supports Thompson's notion that urban manufacturing provides the only substantial source of high-wage employment for blacks. Franklin (1968) suggests that urban economies characterized by capital-intensive production processes are associated with large establishments in which production is not technically conducive to racial discrimination. Jobs in such industries generally require repetitive usage of machines by one person and a minimum of social interaction that would require blacks to exercise authority over whites. Nor are the managers of such enterprises directly accountable to the public for a justification of the race of the workers whose labor produced the product, as might be the case in small establishments. Thus the motivations for racial discrimination in hiring blacks are weaker in the manufacturing sector than in service-oriented positions in which consumer contact is paramount and authority relations play a large role in the production process.

In addition, we wish to understand how export base activity affects sex inequality in earnings. There has been little attention addressed to this topic, with the exception of descriptive analysis by Bluestone, Murphy, and Stevenson (1973). These authors argue that "the structure of product markets (i.e., the structure of industries) in a region has a definite impact on the wages of different race–sex groups" (1973:106–107). They indicate that although wage inequality is reduced in the north central region for white males and blacks of both sexes, white women fare poorly there. They attribute this to the north central area's emphasis on durable manufacturing industries, which employ relatively few white women. In contrast, white women do well in the Northeast where there is substantial white-collar employment. They note that these findings are in part a function of industrial distribution and of race–sex barriers to employment in given labor market positions. This reasoning emphasizes the interrelation among area, occupation, and industry in determining earnings.

In addition to considering the *distribution* of these structural resources, there remains the question of *equality of returns* to whatever distribution of resources does exist. For example, in more detailed analysis Bluestone and his colleagues indicate that among cities, Houston has the third highest

---

[4]Methodological criticisms of these findings have been advanced by Stolzenberg and D'Amico (1977). These concerns do not, however, negate the validity of this hypothesis.

average wages for white males, yet the very lowest average wages for black males. Can this entire mean wage difference ($2.46/hr according to the data these authors use) be attributed to differences in access to structural and human capital resources? It seems likely that at least part of the discrepancy is due to differential returns to the structural resources. Other examples cited by Bluestone *et al.* include white women doing well in Washington, D.C., San Francisco, and New York, whereas black women did best in Los Angeles, Detroit, and San Francisco. White women's wages in these cities are a function of white-collar employment there, whereas economic growth rates in the West and black female employment in the automobile industry account for the findings among black women. They argue that in cities without durable manufacturing opportunities, black women are often found in private household jobs and other poorly paid service positions. If these ideas are correct, we should observe weaker returns among women to manufacturing characteristics than we find among men, independent of these workers' personal characteristics.

SOCIAL ORGANIZATION

Our discussion of local labor market social organization is more limited than that of economic organization. Certainly researchers have realized that local markets vary according to characteristics such as availability and cost of housing, government expenditures on services, crime rate, and other social characteristics. Hadden and Borgatta (1965) provide a factor analysis of U. S. city characteristics that suggests that urban areas vary along dimensions such as percentage of non-whites, age composition, foreign-born concentration, total population, and population density. They then use these and other characteristics to present profiles of U. S. cities. Although their analysis is useful in outlining salient characteristics of local labor market social organization, two limitations come to mind. First, their factor analytic solutions include within single factors both social organization and economic outcome variables. For example, the nonwhite factor includes both the percentage of nonwhites as well as the percentage of families with incomes under $3,000. In our analysis we wish to understand how urban social organization *affects* individual economic outcomes. Hence we do not directly incorporate their findings into our analysis. Second, some of the factors combine a wide range of variables, thus making it difficult to derive specific hypotheses concerning the effects of the factors upon earnings of different status groups. Work by D. Smith (1973) on territorial social indicators also reveals advantages and disadvantages. He suggests ways of measuring quality of life in urban areas, but the data that would be needed to operationalize some of the concepts are not always available for a wide cross section of areas.

Since the goal is to evaluate whether aspects of local labor market social organization influence earnings of respective status groups, additional research traditions specific to racial inequality become relevant. In particular, considerable attention has been devoted to analysis of the implications of residential segregation for levels of black earnings. Theoretical arguments such as those by Kain and Persky (1969) have guided studies that seek to uncover the extent to which black employment opportunities are limited by residential segregation. They argue that segregation is pervasive, that there are employment opportunities blacks miss because the sheer size of metropolitan areas constitutes an obstacle both in acquiring information concerning jobs and to reaching places of employment once jobs have been secured. The trend towards "suburbanization" of employment has removed and will continue to remove jobs from the central cities where the majority of blacks live, thus exacerbating the problem. Although several authors present empirical evidence consistent with the Kain–Persky hypothesis (Mooney, 1969; Kain, 1968), other research (Masters, 1975) reports negative findings. Parcel (1979), however, reports for *both* blacks and whites negative partial slopes of earnings regressed on an indicator of residential segregation (although the magnitude of the slope is larger for blacks), thus suggesting that both black and white workers suffer from residential segregation to some extent.

A second aspect of labor market social organization that researchers have argued is important to understanding inequality is racial competition within the local labor market. Blalock (1967) suggests that there may be a positive relationship between minority percentage and discrimination if that minority percentage results or is perceived to result in competition for scarce resources. He finds some empirical support for suggesting that high percentages of nonwhites are associated with several indices of discrimination, although the relationship may be confined to southern SMSAs (Blalock, 1956, 1957). Thompson (1965) finds that the percentage of blacks is positively associated with racial income inequality, and Jiobu and Marshall (1971) produce compatible findings. Parcel (1979) reports that local labor market percentage of blacks is positively associated with white males' earnings, but negatively associated with black males' earnings.

This analysis will provide additional tests concerning how racial competition operates for several groups of workers who vary by ascriptive status. On the basis of theory, we would expect blacks to suffer from residence in residentially segregated and crowded markets, but that whites would benefit from such crowding. No prediction is offered concerning the effects of residential segregation on white earnings. In addition, there is a paucity of theoretical guidance concerning how these characteristics as well as other dimensions of social organization affect women's earnings. In this analysis we investigate whether residential segregation and racial crowding operate similarly by sex. Investigation of the effects of other dimensions of local labor market social organization must await future analysis.

Economic Sectors and Occupational Labor Markets

A major portion of the recent interest in inequality has concerned the existence and location of economic sectors and occupational structures. Guiding theoretical analyses include Averitt's (1968) discussion in *The Dual Economy*, O'Connor's (1973) *The Fiscal Crisis of the State*, and Edwards' (1975) analysis of the relationship between economic production processes and work organization. Our discussion of these issues will be in two parts. First, we will outline dual economy theory and indicate the types of empirical studies researchers have used to evaluate it. Second, we will discuss the connections between the organization of the production process and the structure of jobs that individual workers hold. These latter ideas by Edwards and others writing about the dual labor market form a connection between economic structure and individual outcomes that is important to the contextual models we test.

THE DUAL ECONOMY

The dual economy thesis suggests that the United States economy is divided into distinct sectors. The primary sector, or core of the economy, is composed of firms that are oligopolistic, or concentrated.[5] That is, a few firms are able to control the bulk of production for a given product and operate as quasi-monopolies. Examples of concentrated firms are those in automobile or aircraft manufacturing and in large-scale computer equipment. Firms in the core of the economy are also large, partly as a function of their oligopoly power. The ability to dominate markets means the few firms have a competitive advantage that enables them to expand both in terms of

---

[5]Different writers use different terminology in discussing these ideas. For example, Averitt refers to "center" and "periphery" firms, whereas O'Connor uses the terms "monopoly" and "competitive" sectors. In this discussion we adopt the "core" and "periphery" terminology used by Beck, Horan, and Tolbert (1978). Despite differing usage, the arguments are conceptually similar.

capital growth as well as in personnel. Accumulation of capital tends to produce a high degree of capital intensity in these firms. Thus, not only are workers using modernized capital, but the capital–labor ratio is high. This produces high rates of productivity and profitability. Core, or center, firms tend to produce a variety of products and also to sell to national or international as opposed to local markets. Finally, core firms are characterized by vertical integration. That is, they control many steps of the production and sales processes, such as the purchase of raw materials and the transportation of finished goods, as well as actual production.

A minority of center firms may be described as conglomerates (Averitt, 1968). These firms are not identified primarily by a single product line but instead control production and service enterprises that span several industries. Examples include Litton Industries and F.M.C. Such firms are decentralized, thus leaving lower-level management in charge of decisions specific to the divisions and allowing corporate management freedom to manage capital. These (and certain other center firms that are not conglomerates) receive a substantial proportion of their income from international operations (Averitt, 1968:58–61).

Firms on the periphery present a contrasting picture. They are not concentrated and thus do not control an appreciable share of market production. This means that their economic organization more closely resembles that of competitive capitalism than that of monopoly capitalism. These firms are smaller than core firms, with fewer assets and smaller numbers of employees. The firms are less capital-intensive and what capital is used may be antiquated, thus keeping productivity and profitability relatively low. The firms may focus on producing only a few products that are sold to local or regional markets and are unlikely to be vertically integrated, which again suggests that these firms are more subject to the forces of competition in the production and sales processes than are firms in the economic core. We can see that the economic situations of core and periphery firms are quite different on a number of dimensions.[6]

Concerning empirical evidence for this theory, some of the recent sociological interest in the dualist perspective has focused on ascertaining the structure of the U. S. economy. Wallace and Kalleberg (1981) perform an exploratory factor analysis of U. S. industrial characteristics that suggests that several factors underlie the concepts implied by dual economy theory,

---

[6]O'Connor (1973), Hodson (1978), and others differentiate the state from both core and periphery since it clearly differs in terms of productivity and because of its special relationship to the other two sectors in providing basic services and regulating those sectors' production activities. Since our analysis does not rest on defining a distinct number of segments, but rather on identifying the dimensions of differentiation, we will not elaborate further on the nature of the state sector.

as opposed to the single factor that the perspective would imply.[7] Kaufman, Hodson, and Fligstein (1981) address more directly the issue of the number of sectors into which the economy is divided. Using a combination of factor and cluster analysis, they argue that the dichotomy implied by dual economy theory is inadequate and that a multidimensional view more closely represents U. S. industrial economic organization. In contrast to the dualist notion that portrays alignment of mulitple dimensions such that high and low values on relevant dimensions group together, they portray the complexity of U. S. industrial structure by describing the differences among industrial groups. Both sets of authors agree, however, that the concepts specified as relevant by the dualist perspective are important to the understanding of the economic system.

Economists such as Scherer (1980) and Oster (1979) have also provided analyses of these issues. Oster's factor analytic test of dual economy theory derives dimensions of industrial differentiation consistent with dualist arguments. Scherer provides a wealth of information concerning industrial organization that is useful in understanding contemporary business functioning. In general, then, these sources suggest characteristics of industries or firms that differentiate these units from one another.

DUAL LABOR MARKET THEORY

Dual economy theory as described by Averitt (1968) is not at all concerned with individuals. It is conceptualized entirely at the level of the firm; economic characteristics of firms are interrelated, as previously discussed, without mention of how these characteristics affect individual employees. The most pertinent question for our analysis, however, is how does this economic structure impact workers' earnings? To address this, we introduce an additional perspective that is closely related to that of the dual economy and that takes as its premise that there are two types of jobs. Dual labor market theory (Wachter, 1974; Doeringer and Piore, 1971) argues that there are "good" jobs (that comprise the primary labor market) that pay well and have safe, often pleasant working conditions. Employment in the primary labor

---

[7]Although theorists often phrase arguments regarding the dual economy in terms of the *firm* as the unit of analysis, operationally, when a cross-sectional analysis is planned it is far easier to obtain data by *industry*. Such a situation produces a discrepancy between the data analyzed and the inferences the researcher wishes to make. Therefore, although Wallace and Kalleberg's (1981) conclusions are stated in terms of firms, their analysis is not conducted on that basis. They argue that there are forces that tend toward intraindustry homogeneity, but such arguments await empirical demonstration. Research by Baron and Bielby (1980), for example, should be useful in assessing the validity of this assumption.

market is relatively stable and unlikely to be affected if there is a drop in demand. These jobs are part of internal labor markets or job ladders that afford opportunities for upward mobility within the firm. They also are characterized by equity and due process in the enforcement of work rules that are formalized and explicit within the organization.

Piore (1975) has argued that the primary labor market is divided into an upper and a lower tier. Jobs in the upper tier are professional and managerial jobs. They have higher prestige than other white-collar jobs and command the highest pay. They have long job ladders, and educational credentials are important to obtaining the entry level positions from which upward mobility occurs. Workers in these positions rely largely upon internalized codes of performance (e.g., a doctor's code of ethics) in completing job duties, as opposed to sole dependence upon written rules. These jobs also entail variety in work. Jobs in the lower tier of the primary labor market are the craft and skilled blue-collar jobs. They are lower in status than the professional jobs but still pay well and are part of moderately long job ladders. Educational credentials are less important to obtaining these positions than those in the upper tier (although a high school diploma is probably demanded for most of them), but they require specialized skills such as knowledge of plumbing or electrical work. Work rules for these positions are formalized (e.g., union rules) but not internalized as are those in the upper tier. There is less variety in work than in the upper tier, but jobs are not strictly routinized. Workers are likely to be unionized, which provides some job security.

Jobs in the secondary labor market, or the "bad jobs," are divergent on each of these dimensions. They have low wages and undesirable, often unsafe working conditions. Work is routinized and repetitive. There are no internal labor markets in the secondary labor market, which is largely composed of entry-level positions; hence chances for advancement are few. There is uncertainty concerning job stability since positions are often cut when demand drops. There is arbitrary enforcement of work rules that are generally only informally defined. These conditions promote job turnover, with workers moving among secondary labor market jobs and between employment and unemployment in this labor market over time.

Predictions concerning the impact of industrial and occupational structures on workers' earnings can be readily derived from this discussion. We expect that workers will obtain positive returns to job characteristics that differentiate the primary market from the secondary market; the higher the skill level, the greater the variety in work, and the better the working conditions, the higher the individual earnings. Concerning race-and sex-specific hypotheses, we make use of a major tenet of dual labor market theory that suggests that blacks and women are more likely to occupy secondary labor market positions than are white males, who hold most of the "good" jobs. This notion suggests that blacks and women will obtain lower returns than white males to job characteristics such as skill level, variety in work, etc.[8]

We also expect that workers located in the core of the economy will obtain positive returns in earnings to the characteristics associated with those positions. The more profitable the firm, the more concentrated the industry, and the larger the firm, the higher the workers' earnings. The basis for this hypothesis is complex. In part, the hypothesis is derived from the general expectation that more profitable firms will pay workers higher wages. In addition, it derives from the expectation that there will be some coincidence between primary labor market jobs and the core of the economy, as well as some coincidence between the secondary labor market and the periphery of the economy. Although writers do not expect that the relationship between economic sectors and labor markets will be perfect (although Bluestone's (1970) early work assumed essential correspondence between economic sectors and labor market segments), some degree of positive relationship is expected (Hodson, 1978; Wallace and Kalleberg, 1981). For example, the fact that firms in the core of the economy are oligopolistic and often in a position to shape demand means that workers can be assured of job stability, a characteristic of primary labor market jobs. The higher rates of profitability characteristic of core positions mean that jobs are more highly paid, again a characteristic of the "good" jobs. Edwards' (1975) arguments concerning causal relationships between economic production processes and work organization are relevant here as well. Edwards sees features such as internal labor markets, bureaucratic control, and formalized definitions of work tasks as deriving from growth in firm size under the development of monopoly capitalism. For these reasons, then, we expect correspondence between, for example, characteristics of the core and of the primary labor market.

Empirical analyses, however, have not supported the idea that this overlap is particularly strong. Wallace and Kalleberg (1981) suggest that there is only a weak relationship between the economic organization of firms and

---

[8]It should be clear that the dualist perspectives contrast in emphasis with those of human capital and, to a large extent, status attainment. As Wachter (1974) indicates, the crucial distinction in the dual labor market perspective is between good and bad jobs, not between skilled and unskilled workers, as the human capital approach suggests. Since the potential for economic productivity and attendant high wages adheres to jobs as opposed to workers, programs designed to train workers (programs inspired by the human capital perspective) would not necessarily solve the problem of underemployment since there would be no restructuring of jobs to accommodate the more highly skilled work force. We see, then, that the debate between the dualist and human capital perspectives has important practical as well as theoretical implications.

occupational structure, which implies that the dimensions of industrial structure discussed earlier may have effects on earnings independent of workers' job characteristics. Hodson (1978) finds that although the monopoly sector (core) consists of 80% primary and 20% secondary labor market jobs, the jobs in the competitive sector are also more likely to be "good" jobs (63%) than "bad" jobs (38%). These particular percentages and findings are, of course, dependent upon operationalizations of sectors and labor markets. Despite this negative evidence, the hypothesis of overlap between economic sectors and segments of the labor market is a reasonable one.

Two types of hypotheses are suggested by this discussion. One is a structural hypothesis and concerns the degree of overlap between economic sectors and labor market segments. It follows that the greater the overlap between the core of the economy and the primary labor market, the less independence we will observe between the economic sector characteristics and primary–secondary labor market characteristics. In this analysis we will be able to evaluate whether this overlap varies in strength across status groups. The second type of hypothesis concerns the effects of the economic sector and labor market characteristics on earnings. As implied, we expect that firm (industry) characteristics such as profitability, concentration and size, and job characteristics such as skill level, degree of variety in work, and working conditions should be positively associated with earnings and that white males will obtain higher returns to these characteristics than will blacks and women. In addition, these two types of hypotheses are related. If there is substantial overlap between economic sector and labor market or job characteristics, then we should find that introduction of the job characteristics adds little independent explanation to earnings over and above that attributed to economic sector variables.

OCCUPATIONAL LABOR MARKETS

In this section, the question of primary interest is: What occupational characteristics account for race and sex differences in earnings? First, however, we wish to understand something about occupational labor markets as structures and second how the key characteristics of these markets affect workers generally. Two lines of argument are useful in thinking about occupational labor markets as structures. Stolzenberg (1975) argues that labor markets tend to be segmented along occupational lines, since there are prestige and monetary incentives for workers to occupy the positions for which they were trained. He presents evidence that suggests that workers obtain lower wages and lower job prestige when they enter occupations different from those for which they have obtained specific training. He then suggests that the supply and demand of job skills and abilities and the social organization of work vary by occupation. Spenner's (1979) analysis of job skill, defined as "mental, interpersonal, and manipulative complexity" operationalized as relationships to data, people, and things, is also compatible with this orientation. Later we indicate how job skills and abilities and characteristics of the social organization of work influence workers' earnings directly.

Additional work by Spaeth (1979) has provided an analysis of occupational differentiation that suggests that occupations can be ranked on the vertical dimensions of authority, complexity, and prestige. His theoretical argument suggests that as the division of labor within a society becomes more complex, occupational specialization increases the variation in job complexity. In industrialized societies, some jobs are highly repetitive and routinized, and others consist of complex professional and/or scientific work applied to narrow subfields. Thus especially in societies with complex divisions of labor, job complexity becomes a dimension along which occupations vary (Spaeth, 1979:748). Increases in the complexity of division of labor also increase the need for supervision of workers, since the smaller segments of work must be coordinated. Supervision in the workplace, or occupational authority, becomes an additional dimension along which occupations may be ranked. Using confirmatory factor analysis, Spaeth empirically demonstrates that authority, complexity, and prestige are related but may be viewed as distinct vertical dimensions on which occupations vary. Kohn (1969), Kohn and Schooler (1978), and Temme (1975) also give priority to occupational complexity as an important dimension of work task differentiation.

These two analyses suggest several sets of characteristics along which occupations vary and that therefore potentially influence workers' earnings. The first set consists of task and job characteristics such as skills, abilities, and working conditions. Following Stolzenberg's discussion of task characteristics and Spaeth's discussion of job complexity, we recognize that numerous task and skill characteristics differentiate occupations. Some jobs involve social interaction with others, as opposed to relating to inanimate objects. Service occupations, such as nurse's aide, waiter or waitress, and police officer require a strong "people" orientation, whereas engineers must relate well to objects and be able to make decisions according to objective criteria. Jobs also vary according to the type of skills required. Physical abilities such as strength, climbing, and manual dexterity are important in construction and building trades positions, and white-collar positions require various combinations of intellectual abilities such as verbal competency, numerical aptitude, and spatial ability. Jobs vary in terms of whether incumbents work under hazardous and/or undesirable conditions or in pleasant and/or safe environments. They also vary in complexity and repetitiveness.

Since there are potentially many job characteristics involved here, it is cumbersome to specify how each may affect workers' earnings. We therefore defer specification of hypotheses until Chapter 5. In general, however, given that earnings levels for occupations vary depending on the combination of these task and skill characteristics and that blacks and women experience limited access to particular occupations, we would expect these task and skill characteristics to partly account for race and sex earnings differentials. We also expect that the efficacy of the resources they do possess for producing earnings will be less than that of majority workers.

The second category of criteria along which occupations vary is that of social organization. An important dimension of occupational social organization is that of race and sex competition and segregation (see Blaxall and Reagan, 1976; Hodge and Hodge, 1965; Taeuber, Taeuber and Cain, 1966, for discussion of these issues). The arguments are analogous to those advanced in the discussion of racial competition in local labor markets. At a structural level, occupations vary in the extent to which they are occupied by white males or members of some economic minority group. Occupations such as physician, dentist, lawyer, and many managerial jobs are disproportionately occupied by white males. Jobs such as waitress, nursing home attendant, and janitor are disproportionately occupied by blacks and/or women. Concerning how such segregation affects workers' earnings, the theories indicate that increases in the percentage of economic minorities within an occupation many result in competition for jobs between majority and minority workers, which results in depressed wage levels for all incumbents of an occupation, or in segregation of minorities into low-paying occupations thus reserving high-paying jobs for majority workers.

Findings produced within this tradition have been conflicting. Bergmann (1971) suggests that crowding (i.e., segregation) of blacks into a few occupations lowers black marginal productivity and thus wages within those jobs, as well as resulting in lower wages for blacks in "white" occupations. Snyder and Hudis (1976) indicate that segregation of blacks into low-paying jobs contributes to the explanation of the negative correlation between the minority percentage and white male income. In contrast, a study by Flanagan (1973) yields equivocal results concerning distinct income gains or losses for whites as a function of the percentage of blacks in the occupation, and work by Szymanski (1976) also suggests that minimal gains accrue to whites due to blacks' economic disadvantage. The findings for women appear to be somewhat more consistent, with evidence suggesting competition between white males and women workers (Snyder and Hudis, 1976). Our analysis will provide an additional test concerning the influence of a concentration of economic minority workers on majority group earnings. Although we expect such concentration to adversely affect minority earnings, we do not advance a prediction concerning the direction of the effect for majority group workers.[9]

The third category along which occupations may be differentiated is the extent to which a job involves the exercise of authority. Certainly the authority dimension is related to task complexity (job characteristics), as both are derived from the division of labor (Spaeth, 1979). The authority level of a job may also be related to the social organization of work since the exercise of authority over subordinates is clearly an important mechanism through which work relations are arranged within organizations. However, we view the authority dimension as differing from other task characteristics since it is clearly a function of a particular job within a firm (organization) and not of the occupational task generally. We also view it as differing from occupational social organization since it is a firm and organization-specific phenomenon, not an occupation-specific one. As evidence for this idea, analysis of U. S. Census occupational categories reveals that net of firm and industry affiliations, there are predictable differences in authority exercised by incumbents *within* occupations in categories such as professional and technical, managerial and supervisory, clerical and sales, crafts, operative, farm and unskilled labor. Spaeth's work, which indicates that authority operates independently of job status, also supports this conceptualization.

There now exists substantial evidence that an individual's class/authority position is important in understanding earnings differences.[10] In their study

[9]Because the theory is conceptualized to address race–sex earnings inequality, it makes no sense to suggest more general hypotheses applied to workers undifferentiated by ascribed statuses.

[10]As discussed by Robinson and Kelley (1979) and Aldrich and Weiss (1981), there have been both conceptual and empirical ambiguities in the study of class/authority influences on earnings. These problems arise in part because researchers wish to remain true to a Marxian conception and at the same time incorporate neo-Marxist theory to capture the realities of modern capitalism. This problem is especially apparent in the various attempts to distinguish between the social class dimension and the authority dimension. For example, most of the recent research has argued for the importance of social class as defined by control (not ownership) over the means of production. This typically has resulted in differentiating employer, manager, and worker classes. Obviously, however, this is confounded with the authority hierarchy since the distinction between worker and manager is almost always based on who supervises and who does not. Although lack of conceptual clarity is partly at fault, this problem undoubtedly also is a function of the data available for this kind of research. The survey questions typically asked do not allow operationalizing either the class or the authority dimension as theory would direct. However, even with the ambiguities in determining whether the effect is class or authority or some combination of the two, there is sufficient evidence that these positional characteristics are quite important in understanding earnings differences.

of employer, manager, and worker categories, Wright and Perrone (1977) control for age, job tenure, occupational status, and education and find that earnings monotonically increase from worker to manager to employer. Similarly, categorizing authority (class) position as employer, manager, or worker, Kalleberg and Griffin (1980) find that for white males, employers receive greater earnings even when numerous personal characteristics and several occupational measures are controlled. Their analysis does show, as they hypothesized, that class position and occupational position operate largely independently of each other in their influence on earnings. Several other studies support this general finding of a positive relationship between authority position and earnings and are also valuable in providing data about race and sex differences in earnings.

Wright and Perrone (1977) find that the returns to education are greater for members of the managerial class than for the working class, and these differences vary by race and sex. Within class (authority) categories, however, the returns to education across race and sex categories are very similar. This suggests that class (authority) membership operates to homogenize individuals of different ascriptive status to produce similar rates of return to education. In another paper on race differences, Wright (1978) finds that the commonly observed racial difference in returns to education is primarily a function of the differential distribution of racial groups across class (authority) categories; when regression equations are run within class (authority) categories, the education coefficients for black and white males are very similar. Robinson and Kelley (1979), who examine both Marxian class categories and position in the authority hierarchy, compare the earnings of U. S. men and women. They find that for men, position in the class/authority structure substantially increases the explained variance in earnings over that explained by basic human capital and status attainment variables. For women, however, the additional explained variance is quite small. Using regression standardization, the authors conclude that this difference accounts for a large part of the male–female earnings gap. Kluegel (1978), who examines authority hierarchy rather than class position, finds that not only are black males generally in lower authority positions than white males, but also that blacks receive a lower income return to authority than do whites. Based on these findings and additional analysis, he concludes that a substantial portion of the black–white earnings gap is due to the operation of the authority variable.

In sum, we would expect to find from these studies that authority has a strong influence on earnings that operates essentially independently of important human capital and status attainment variables. In addition, we would expect to find that sex and race earnings differences are in part explained by the differential sex and race distributions across authority categories. Finally, we would expect to find that returns to certain human capital variables differ depending on class/authority position.

Two concluding points concerning occupations and authority relations are of interest here. First, the previous discussion of occupational labor markets and authority relations underscores the fact that there are occupational characteristics in addition to prestige or socioeconomic status that may influence workers' earnings. Although investigations have suggested that differential returns to prestige and socioeconomic status account for part of the racial earnings gap (O. Duncan, 1968; Blum, 1972), sex differences in earnings are not a partial function of differing degrees of prestige and occupational status effectiveness (Treiman and Terrell, 1975; Featherman and Hauser, 1976a). Most of the past research has relied on measuring only this dimension of occupations. Although the prestige and socioeconomic status dimension of occupational differentiation is still incorporated into our model, we do not rely on it as the only occupational characteristic of interest.

Second, we note that the foregoing discussion of occupational task characteristics, social organization, and authority levels overlaps with the discussion of the dual labor market. For example, the dualists argue that workers in the secondary labor market often occupy positions with hazardous or unpleasant working conditions. These "bad" jobs are also frequently repetitive. Skills such as verbal competency or working with data are more likely to be required in "good" white-collar jobs than in the secondary labor market positions.[11] It also follows that those jobs that are segregated by sex may also be classified as either "good" or "bad." Jobs such as doctor, engineer, and lawyer are clearly primary labor market jobs, and as we have indicated, they are disproportionately occupied by white males. Similarly, jobs such as waitress, janitor, and porter are "bad" jobs and are disproportionately occupied by economic minorities. Although the coincidence of occupational segregation by race and sex and the good job–bad job distinction is imperfect, there remains a noticeable empirical relationship between the two constructs. The connection is also featured prominently in dual labor market theory itself.

Similarly, we recognize that there is overlap between our discussion of authority relations and that of the dual labor market. According to Piore (1975) the upper tier of the primary labor market contains professional and managerial jobs with long job ladders that coincide with the authority hierarchies within those organizations. In the lower tier of the primary market

---

[11]Others of these characteristics differentiate among jobs but are not specified by the dualists as properties of one or the other type of position. For example, it is likely that jobs from both the "good" and "bad" ends of the continuum may demand skill in relating to people, motor coordination, or spatial ability.

are the skilled and blue-collar jobs that have moderately sized job ladders and thus may involve the exercise of some authority. The secondary labor market is composed of entry-level positions from which advancement is unlikely. These "bad" jobs involve no exericse of authority. This distinction may be summarized by saying that lengthy and well-specified authority hierarchies characterize the primary labor market, whereas very limited authority hierarchies are found in the secondary market. We would expect that the earnings gap between "good" and "bad" jobs is to be explained by differences in authority structures as well as by the differences in task characteristics noted earlier.

Summary and Plan of the Book

This chapter has provided the theoretical foundation for the analysis of labor market determinants of earnings. Human capital and status attainment approaches to the analysis of earnings attainment were reviewed, as were findings relevant to race and sex differences in earnings. Inadequacies of previous approaches to the analysis of structural determinants of earnings were noted, and arguments were presented concerning which dimensions of local, industrial, and occupational labor markets should affect workers' earnings. In particular, hypotheses suggest that males' returns to local labor market manufacturing sector characteristics should exceed those of females and that black workers' earnings levels would suffer due to crowding and residential segregation in local markets. Workers should obtain positive returns to industrial labor market characteristics associated with the core of the economy such as firm oligopoly (power concentration), profitability, and size, as well as to job characteristics associated with the primary labor market, such as complexity, diversity in work activities, and pleasant working conditions. We also indicated that women and blacks, who are less likely to obtain positions in the primary labor market, would obtain weaker returns to characteristics associated with these positions than would white male workers. We then indicated that a variety of occupational task characteristics and occupational segregation and competition were also associated with earnings. Finally, we suggested that race and sex earnings differences should also be affected by authority differentials present within incumbents' organizations.

In the following chapters we bring evidence to bear on these ideas. In Chapter 2 we discuss the data and methods used in analysis; we also interpret the results of factor analyses of data describing areas, industries, and occupations in terms of the structures of these respective markets. In each case we describe the dimensions of market differentiation and indicate the extent that these dimensions are interrelated. By analyzing the structures at their respective macrolevels, we form the basis for our analysis of these structures' effects on individual workers' earnings. In Chapters 3 through 5 we address this latter issue. The models presented in these chapters are both additive and cumulative in their explanation of earnings attainment. For each model we present separate estimates by race–sex group, with females further divided by marital status. In Chapter 3 we investigate the effects of local labor market characteristics on earnings. We find that although characteristics of local labor market economic organization affect earnings for most workers, the strongest effects are observed for black males. The effect of racial crowding on earnings attainment is also limited to black males.

In Chapter 4 we find that characteristics that differentiate economic sectors are statistically significant predictors of earnings for several status groups, independent of local labor market characteristics. These affects are absent among white males but particularly strong for female workers. In Chapter 5 indicators of occupational labor market characteristics and class/authority are added to the model. We find that occupational complexity and class/authority position are particularly important predictors of earnings for white males and of varying importance for the remaining groups. In these three chapters we also address policy questions relating to inequality by comparing how changes in the levels of access to resources and the effectiveness of resources would affect race and sex inequality. We find that the processes of race and sex discrimination are sufficiently distinct to argue that given policies could have very different effects on sex as opposed to race inequality.

In later chapters we present data to extend and refine the conclusions discussed in the first chapters. In Chapter 6 we incorporate several social psychological variables theoretically relevant to status attainment and evaluate their role empirically as compared with the labor market factors found to be relevant in Chapters 3–5. Findings here suggest that controlling for social psychological variables does not affect the general pattern of labor market effects discussed in Chapters 3–5, although returns to schooling are reduced for several subgroups. We then provide evidence concerning the role of social selection in earnings attainment. We wish to understand the extent of "matching" between workers' personal characteristics and the characteristics of the labor markets in which they work. Our findings suggest that this selection is usually positive; that is, the workers with the highest personal potential for productivity are located in the most favorable markets, and the magnitude of selection is strong, particularly for women and blacks.

In Chapter 7 we address the matter of statistical interaction. Although we regard this issue as peripheral to our main goal of investigating additive effects, both theory and previous research suggest several nonadditive hypotheses that we evaluate in order to present a more refined picture of labor market effects on earnings. Our findings suggest that the number of statistically significant interactions is small, and these interactions are more likely to be present for blacks than whites. Thus although these findings suggest some minor revisions to the conclusions discussed in Chapters 3–5, the bulk of those inferences remain undisturbed.

In Chapter 8 we provide conclusions from the entire analysis. We point out the ascriptive status differences in the magnitudes of the labor market effects we have studied and discuss these differences in terms of the several labor market theories on which the analysis is based. We comment on the implications of our findings for ideas on universalism and discrimination in the earnings attainment process. We also provide additional discussion of how policies affecting the distribution and/or efficacy of resources would have very different effects on race versus sex inequality.

CHAPTER 2

Data, Methods, and Labor Markets' Structures

Introduction

In this chapter we have several goals. First, the methods used to produce the findings discussed in subsequent chapters will be described. The study analyzes files composed of individual respondents from selected surveys to which have been added ecological data describing their local, industrial, and occupational labor market affiliations. This chapter will describe the survey source used, sources of ecological data, and general data production procedures. Second, the findings will be presented from the factor analyses performed for the areal, industrial, and occupational labor market data. These findings will then be used as the basis for creating composite measures for subsequent analysis. The factor analysis results are also of substantive interest since they present a descriptive picture of the structure of each type of labor market. In addition, the measurement strategies and methods of analysis to be used in subsequent chapters will be outlined. To that end, we begin with a discussion of one key strategy, the use of contextual analysis.

Contextual Analysis: Pro and Con

Contextual analysis has been the subject of some controversy within sociology and related disciplines.[1] Early formulations emphasized its useful-

---

[1]"Contextual analysis" is used in the most general sense to refer to multivariate explanatory models that include variables that measure characteristics of individuals *and* variables that measure group or context characteristics. The literature (described later) on contextual analysis

ness as a tool for ascertaining the impact of social structural characteristics upon individual behavior (Merton and Kitt, 1950; Lazarsfeld *et al.*, 1968; Lipset *et al.*, 1962; Davis, 1966; Barton, 1968, 1970). The method was and is extensively employed in the analysis of school effects upon achievement (Campbell and Alexander, 1965; Coleman, Campbell, Hobson, McPartland, Mood, Weinfeld, and York, 1966; McDill, Rigsby, and Meyers, 1969; Meyer, 1970; Drew and Astin, 1972; Alexander and Eckland, 1975). Following Lazarsfeld and Menzel (1969), we distinguish three types of contextual variables: (*a*) analytic properties (derived by performing a mathematical operation on data derived from each member of a collective); (*b*) structural properties (derived by performing a mathematical operation on the interrelations among members); and (*c*) global properties (indicators of emergent properties of the collectivity, not derived as functions of data provided by individual group members). Although the bulk of contextual variables that have been utilized are analytic properties, such as mean IQ score or mean socioeconomic status rating for a school, the contextual variables we incorporate will primarily be *global* properties, that is, indicators of labor markets, constructs that inherently are not reducible to the individual level.[2] Use of global variables avoids directly pitting an analytic variable against its individual-level counterpart, a strategy that produces upward bias in estimates of the analytic effects due to their reduced random measurement error as compared with their individual-level counterparts.

---

is almost exclusively based on models in which the contextual measures are mean levels of individual-level characteristics that also are included in the model (see Hauser, 1974; Alwin, 1976; Boyd and Iversen, 1979). These writers do admit to the possibility of other measures of the context that are not reducible to the individual level. Boyd and Iversen (1979) call these "integral" variables whereas Alwin refers to them as "organization" or "structural" characteristics. The mathematical and statistical discussion of the role of these other types of group level variables in contextual analysis is at best incomplete. Boyd and Iversen, for example, offer but one statement: "Generally speaking, in all the cases described above, the integral group variables would not replace the group mean variable $\bar{X}$, but would be added to the basic model" (1979:57). As will be described, almost all of the group-level variables in our analysis are not reducible to the individual level-characteristics. Nevertheless, we address the issues raised regarding the traditional contextual analysis since many of the arguments are applicable to our analysis as well.

[2] A dilemma arises since it can be difficult to classify an indicator as either global or analytical. In the sense that Lazarsfeld and Menzel (1969) defined analytic variables, we have none, since in no case do we derive an aggregate variable by performing any calculations on data from the respective survey subfiles. However, we do incorporate variables produced from governmental sources that are analytic in nature. For example, the percentage of workers who are unionized, an indicator representing one of the labor force consequences specified by dual labor market theory, is an analytic variable calculated on U. S. population data. The percentage of blacks in a local labor market is similarly constructed, but in this case there is no possibility of including that indicator with its individual-level counterpart since race is physically, not statistically, controlled in this analysis. This issue will continue to be discussed as it arises in analysis.

In addition, our models will be specified so as to provide a conservative test of the effect of the contextual variables by incorporating additional individual-level variables and attending to their measurement (see Hauser, 1974, for additional discussion of these and related issues). It is important to recognize that our theory argues that characteristics of labor markets are important to earnings attainment and that differential returns to these characteristics by ascribed status constitute structural sources of discrimination. Hence inclusion of these variables is justified by theory; to omit them would render the model misspecified, potentially biasing the effects of the individual-level variables (Farkas, 1974; Alwin, 1976).[3] Following Griffin (1976) we emphasize that such concern is not motivated by mere devotion to methodological precision. Policy recommendations urging the adoption of programs designed to upgrade the education and training of workers are based upon analyses of returns to individual investments in human capital. If it can be demonstrated that upward biases in returns to these investments occur when structural factors are omitted from the analyses, the wisdom of policy devoted to upgrading workers' skills without attention to the structure of the labor markets they face can be called into question. Production of such information provides additional justification for use of the contextual models proposed.[4]

Data Set and Samples

Since the individual-level characteristics utilized are derived from survey data previously produced, only those surveys in which the quality of measurement was high and survey procedures well-handled were considered. Several criteria were utilized in the selection process. First, given our interest in regional labor markets as determinants of economic status, only

---

[3]Positive bias will occur if both of the following occur: (a) positive intercorrelations are found between labor market and human capital characteristics and (b) the association between the labor market variables and the dependent variable is at least moderate (Rao and Miller, 1971; Hanushek and Jackson, 1977). Although we would expect positive bias due to the "matching" of individuals with high potential for productivity with the most favorable labor market positions, the direction of bias is of secondary interest to its existence.

[4]In this analysis we avoid usage of an analysis of covariance (ANCOVA) strategy to assess contextual effects (see Hauser, 1974, and Firebaugh, 1979). Although this strategy can be useful in preliminary analysis, usage of dummy variables to represent affiliation with a context can mask offsetting tendencies in the operation of characteristics associated with affiliation (see Alexander and Eckland, 1975). In addition, the ANCOVA strategy is impractical when a large number of dummies is required to represent all contexts. Alwin (1976) and Boyd and Iversen (1979) show the statistical comparability of the traditional contextual model and the ANCOVA model.

those data sets that provided regional identification information were considered. Although a variety of sources provide data on occupational and industrial affiliation, those that also included detailed locational data were rare. This criterion eliminated U. S. Census-produced sets that, due to confidentiality constraints, omit these data and the National Longitudinal Surveys (NLS), which are a generally popular source for researchers interested in employment issues.[5] Also, only data sets were considered that sampled respondents from a wide variety of areas to ensure variation in local labor market variables. Second, given our interest in studying racial discrimination, data sets were sought that provided an adequate number of black cases for subgroup analysis. Third, because of sensitivity to the need to provide a conservative test of the labor market theories discussed earlier, data sets were considered that provided as many well-measured variables suggested by *other* explanations as possible. Data sets were sought that contained well-measured indicators of investments in human capital (education, training, health, etc.) as well as some indicators of socialization experiences. In addition, data were sought that provided a detailed breakdown of areal, industrial, and occupational affiliations so that labor market characteristics corresponding to these dimensions could be attached at as detailed a level as possible and so that we could report the interrelations among characteristics of these several types of labor markets. Following are descriptions of the survey utilized and of the samples generated from it.

MICHIGAN PANEL STUDY OF INCOME DYNAMICS

The data sets are derived from the Michigan Survey Research Center's (SRC) Panel Study of Income Dynamics (PSOID). The PSOID was begun in 1968 and was designed as a panel study of short-term changes in family economic welfare. The original sample was partly derived from the Survey of Economic Opportunity (SEO) conducted by the Office of Economic Opportunity; those selected from the SEO sample all had 1966 incomes equal to or below twice the established poverty line [$2000 + $N(1000)$, where N = number of family members]. Household heads over 60 and those who refused to release their interview data for use by the Census were excluded. To accommodate the more limited geographical spread of the SRC interviews, only SEO sample families who resided in SMSAs were included in the sample, except in the South. So as to have all economic levels represented, an additional crosssection of families was interviewed from the SRC's multi-

[5]More recently produced files of younger workers included in the NLS do contain detailed locational data, but these files are restricted in age and were not available when our analysis was performed.

stage area probability sample of dwellings and their occupants. Thus, in 1968 a total of 4802 families were interviewed; the data were weighted to take account of these sampling characteristics and nonresponse. In each subsequent year, these families were reinterviewed, and households that had split off from those originally interviewed (e.g., children moving away from home) were followed up and interviewed also. Data were reweighted in 1972 to take account of response loss since 1968 and the incorporation of newly formed households into the sample. The Survey Research Center has endeavored to make careful adjustments in weighting factors to account for nonresponse, sample attrition, etc., as well as to adopt field procedures to minimize these losses, thus insuring a representative sample in years after the original survey (Institute for Social Research, 1972). In this analysis data from the 1975 and 1976 panels of the study were used.[6]

The PSOID data set meets the selection criteria outlined above. It contains detailed information on occupation and area of employment and an adequate breakdown of industrial affiliation, thus permitting the assignment of labor market characteristics based upon as detailed a classification as possible. It contains a good measure of labor earnings, the dependent variable of central interest. It also includes an oversampling of blacks and adequate numbers of women classified by marital status, thus permitting us to obtain reliable estimates of status variations in attainment processes. Finally, the data set contains a wealth of individual-level variables to be discussed later.[7]

From the 1975 panel of the survey, earnings attainment models will be

[6]As indicated later, several selected variables from previous years also are used. See Chapter 6 for a discussion of these variables.

[7]One potential problem with the Panel Study should be noted. Jencks and his colleagues (Jencks, Bartlett, Corcoran, Crouse, Eaglesfield, Jackson, McClelland, Mueser, Olneck, Schwartz, Ward, and Williams, 1979) compare the 1971–1972 Michigan Panel Study to several other sample surveys used in their study of inequality. They conclude that respondents surveyed by the Survey Research Center tend to be better off in terms of income and occupational status than respondents surveyed by the U. S. Census Bureau. Since the Census Bureau believes that their own surveys tend to underenumerate lower status respondents, the Panel Study may indeed overestimate average socioeconomic status. Jencks and his colleagues also document a small degree of upward bias in education, which, of course, is associated with socioeconomic status (Jencks *et al.*, 1979:260).

It is important to acknowledge what implications this bias, although it is small, could have for our analysis. If the socioeconomic status of all of our subgroups were equally underestimated, comparisons across subgroups would remain valid. However, low status respondents are *not* equally distributed across groups that vary by race and sex. Although we have no evidence concerning the magnitude of this problem, we must recognize that the findings we produce here may be generalizable to populations higher in status than the populations to which we wish to generalize. This may be particularly true for groups with black respondents that contain more lower status members in the population and therefore may be more likely to be underenumerated here as compared with the white males subgroup.

reported for white male, black male, white female, and black female house-hold heads.[8] Included were all heads who reported earnings in 1974, resided in a United States labor market, were not at that time serving in the armed forces, and were aged 25–64.[9] This age range was selected in order to eliminate students and retirees, whose attachment to the labor force is more tenuous than adults in the prime of their work lives, even though the excluded individuals may report some earnings. Workers reporting no earnings were excluded to eliminate missing data problems with the dependent variable (see Beck, Horan, and Tolbert, 1978, 1980; and Hauser, 1980, for a discussion concerning this issue).[10] In addition, from the 1976 panel we obtained samples of black and white wives who reported earnings for 1975, and who also met the additional criteria already discussed for the heads. The 1976 panel was chosen because that was the year the SRC interviewed wives in detail, independent of heads' data, thus permitting this type of analysis.[11] The numbers of cases to be included in the analysis are: white male heads, 1870; white female heads, 297; black male heads, 768; black female heads, 349; white wives, 817; black wives, 356.

The decision to utilize these subgroups is based on several considerations. Following the literature we have reviewed, we have taken as given that

[8]We wished to avoid problems of having respondents report earnings for 1 year but occupation for another (thus increasing the chances that earnings were not produced in the job reported). Although in most of the panels occupation is measured in a relatively crude 11-category classification scheme, in 1974 occupation was measured using detailed 1970 Census codes. To take advantage of this we chose to use 1975 panel data on household heads and to code their occupations as described in 1974 to correspond with their 1974 earnings reported in the 1975 panel. In making this selection we note that in the 1972 sample reweighting was done to achieve representativeness. Thus, although subsequent panels such as 1975 are slightly less representative than 1972, we believe the magnitudes of the differences across years are very slight. Thus we view the choice of 1975 panel data as one where the gains outweigh the costs.

[9]The PSOID follows the U. S. Census Bureau custom of designating the male as the head of the household. Two respondents were excluded from the sample since we were not able to attach local labor market characteristics to them. To maintain the representativeness of the sample, however, the very few additional respondents for whom occupation and/or industry were not ascertained were retained in the sample.

[10]We investigated using an interarea deflator to control for cost of living differences across areas and decided against it. Although the argument for use of such a deflator is strongest for viewing the impact of local labor market characteristics on earnings, the rationale for its usage when industrial and occupational characteristics are included is less clear. In addition, it has been argued that such deflators overcorrect. Whether this is true is difficult to evaluate, but if true it would be difficult to untangle from the effects we wish to interpret. In addition, the major focus on this analysis is to compare labor market effects across status groups. Since there is no reason to believe that such corrections are more important for some groups than others, it does not appear that failure to deflate earnings will hinder the major goal of our analysis.

[11]Although we could have obtained data for all respondents from the 1976 panel, this would have entailed a lack of correspondence between the years of measurement for occupation and earnings. Earnings were measured in 1974 dollars for all status groups.

there are race and sex differences in the earnings attainment process. One of our objectives is to specify in more detail what these differences are.[12] Differentiation between employed female heads of households and employed wives has received little attention, however. As the preliminary basis for separating these two categories throughout the analysis, we conducted a number of tests for interactions. In particular, we created a dummy variable for the distinction between wife and female head and created multiplicative terms of this variable with the human capital and labor market variables in our study. Numerous significant interactions were found that involved both personal and labor market characteristics.[13] The analysis that follows will allow for a thorough examination and discussion of these differences by presenting separate equations and tabulations by marital status for each race.[14]

Following our discussion in Chapter 1 concerning the importance of

[12]A series of Chow tests (Chow, 1960; Fisher, 1970) were conducted to make an overall assessment of the presence of status group interactions with the labor market variables. The Chow test was chosen because of the high degree of multicollinearity among interaction terms typically encountered when hierarchical procedures are used as suggested by J. Cohen and Cohen (1975) and Hanushek and Jackson (1977). The tests were conducted for four pairwise comparisons: white male heads versus black male heads; white male heads versus white female heads; white male heads versus black female heads; and black male heads versus black female heads. For each comparison the test consisted of checking for whether the coefficients for the labor market characteristics differ significantly net of human capital variables (i.e., after allowing the human capital variables to interact with the status group). The model used is presented in Table 5.7. For all four comparisons the tests indicated significant interactions at the .05 level or better: WMH versus BMH, $F = 4.42$ with 12 and 2571 degrees of freedom; WMH versus WFH, $F = 8.41$ with 12 and 2099 degrees of freedom; WMH versus BFH, $F = 1.78$ with 12 and 2151 degrees of freedom; BMH versus BFH, $F = 5.04$ with 12 and 1049 degrees of freedom. These are overall tests and thus do not indicate for which of the labor market variables there are interactions. The detailed analysis in the subsequent chapters will allow explication of these differences.

[13]Among white females interactions were found for weeks worked, tertiary sector growth, tertiary sector complexity, and class/authority. Among black females the significant interactions with tertiary sector growth and complexity, industrial concentration and investment, and class/authority all indicated advantages to household heads over wives. Black wives' earnings, however, were influenced more by education, labor force experience, and urban crowding. These variables are discussed later in this chapter.

[14]Comparisons of status attainment processes of men and women have been criticized recently because of what is referred to as the censoring problem (Fligstein and Wolf, 1978; Featherman and Hauser, 1976a; Heckman, 1974). If women who can afford to remain out of the labor force and/or who cannot find a job consistent with their background and training chose not to take a job, then the sample of employed women will overrepresent women whose training and background are more closely related to their occupational achievements. In short, the parameters estimated for women may well be biased relative to those estimated for males. Fligstein and Wolf, although limiting their analysis to occupational achievement as the dependent variable, find the censoring problem to be minimal. Thus, we acknowledge that although censoring may be a problem in this analysis, since earnings is the dependent variable, we do not expect it to be severe. Assessing the magnitude of any such bias is not within the scope of this research.

human capital and status attainment explanations of earnings, individual-level variables included in the models represent investments in earnings potential as well as socialization experiences. Although additional measures are added in later chapters, in the basic models presented throughout this book we incorporate years of schooling, weeks worked, occupational status, and job experience. Specific operationalizations are consistent across the subsamples and are summarized in Table 2.1.

Education is measured with dummy variables in order to allow for a nonlinear relationship with earnings. This decision reflects arguments by "credentialists" to the effect that it is the diploma or credential of years of schooling completed that produces earnings and not the actual number of years attended (Berg, 1970; Collins, 1979; Faia, 1981). Hence, we would expect a substantial difference in the effect of 12 versus 11 years of schooling. Categories similar to these have also proved useful in previous earnings research (Weiss and Williamson, 1972; Parcel, 1979). The omitted category is 0–7 years, with additional dummies representing 8 years, 9–11 years, 12 years, 13–15 years, and 16 or more years of schooling. A similar strategy is adopted for weeks worked. Here, 0–26 weeks serves as the omitted category with additional dummies representing 27–39 weeks, 40–47 weeks, 48–49 weeks, and 50–52 weeks worked.

Note: In addition to these decisions being justified on the basis of theory, we have empirical evidence that suggests that use of the sets of dummies results in greater explained variance than would interval scale measures of

Table 2.1

Measurement of Individual-Level Variables--Basic Set

Construct	PSOID heads of household and PSOID wives
Years of schooling	0–7 years (omitted category)
	8 years
	9–11 years
	12 years
	13–15 years
	≥16 years
Weeks worked	0–26 weeks (omitted category)
	27–39 weeks
	40–47 weeks
	48–49 weeks
	50–52 weeks
Work experience	Number of years worked since respondent was 18 years old
Occupational status	Duncan SEI
Earnings	Total labor income, in dollars

years of schooling and weeks worked. To compare measurement strategies, we estimated earnings functions using education, weeks worked, job status, and experience for each PSOID status group. In one specification education and weeks worked were measured with the dummies discussed in the text, but in the other specification, interval measures of these constructs were used. In every case, explained variance was lower when the interval measures were used. Although in most cases the differences were small (e.g., for black male heads $\bar{R}^2 = .235$ with dummies, .222 with interval measures), among black wives the difference was larger ($\bar{R}^2 = .520$ with dummies, .483 with interval measures), and among black female heads the difference was large ($\bar{R}^2 = .427$ with dummies, .285 with interval measures). In this latter case, the visibly nonmonotonic relationships between education and earnings and between weeks worked and earnings account for this finding (see Table 3.6 for the presentation with dummy variables). A second consideration is also relevant. We observed changes in the returns to experience and occupation across the two types of specifications. Since we recognize that poor measurement of given variables can bias slope estimates of remaining variables, it is also possible that use of interval measures in this case would bias returns to the labor market variables discussed later, as well as to the personal characteristics discussed here. For a technical discussion of this procedure see J. Cohen and Cohen (1975) on nominalization.

Experience is measured as the number of years respondents have worked since they were 18. We did *not* use a cruder estimate such as subtracting years of schooling plus six years from age (Mincer, 1974). Throughout the analysis, occupation was scored using the Duncan Socioeconomic Index (Hauser and Featherman, 1977).[15]

---

[15]The other occupation measure we considered using is the Siegel Prestige Scale (Siegel, 1971, see Hauser and Featherman, 1977, for actual scores). Our decision to use the Duncan SEI was based on: (a) the work of Featherman and Hauser (1977), who argue that prestige is a fallible index of occupational status with reference to occupational mobility; and (b) the work of Parnes, Shea, Spitz, and Zeller (1970), who find that the Duncan SEI (which is derived from male data) may be used for both males and females. We recognize, however, the existence of other evidence and opinions. Bose (1973) provides data that suggest that the Siegel prestige scores are basically invariant with respect to the sex of the occupational incumbent, and Treiman and Terrell (1975) argue that a prestige scale may be preferable when cross-sex comparisons in earnings attainment are made. In preliminary analysis we compared specifications of earnings functions with Siegel prestige scores and the Duncan SEI used to operationalize occupational status. We found that there were virtually no differences in the empirical results of the two specifications for either the male or the female status groups. Certainly the substantive interpretations they suggested were identical by status group. Since the purpose of our analysis is to study labor market effects upon earnings and not to settle any debate concerning the relative merits of the two measures, we adopt the Duncan SEI without further investigation.

Sources of Ecological Data

The ecological data attached to the survey respondents were produced from a variety of sources. Concerning areal or local labor market data, recall that theory suggested that both economic and social labor market organization could influence workers' earnings. Thompson's (1965) arguments drew attention to features of respective industries (manufacturing, service, retail, etc.) as defining labor market economic status. To capture these forces for manufacturing activity, variables were incorporated from the 1972 Census of Manufacturing, Area Series, which includes measures such as payroll size, number of production workers, capital expenditures, and number of establishments. Data concerning retail, wholesale, and service activity were produced from the 1977 City and County Data book on a county or SMSA basis as appropriate (see the following section, Matching Ecological and Survey Data); this source obtained these data from the 1972 Economic Censuses covering retail and wholesale trade and selected services. Variables for these industries included payroll, number of establishments, and number of paid employees in wholesale, retail, and services, as well as the change in wholesale and retail sales and change in service receipts between 1967 and 1972.[16] We also included data concerning the occupational distribution of the local labor market. State volumes of the 1970 Census provided data concerning the distribution of workers by race and sex that will be used selectively and discussed more fully later.

Concerning local labor market social organization, the City and County Data Book provided a number of indicators of interest. We incorporated median house value, per capita government expenditures, the rate of serious crimes, and an index of crowding in housing, the percentage of housing with an occupancy rate of greater than 1.01 persons per room. From U. S. Census sources we also included indexes of employment and basic population data from which indicators such as the percentage of blacks were calculated. A residential segregation measure was taken from Sorensen, Taeuber, and Hollingsworth (1975). The theoretical constructs, computed variables and data sources for areal labor markets are summarized in Table 2.2.

Similar summaries of the industrial and occupational labor market variables and data sources are presented in Tables 2.3 and 2.4 respectively. In

---

[16]There is often a gap of several years between the points of measurement for the ecological and individual data. Given the 5-year intervals between which the Economic Censuses produce data and given our interest in using 1975 and 1976 panel data, such slippage is inevitable. There is no reason to believe that introduction of this type of measurement error will differentially bias findings by status group, although it might weaken the impact of the ecological variables generally.

Table 2.2

Measurement of Ecological Constructs: Local Labor Markets

Construct	Computed variables	Sources[a]
Economic organization		
Manufacturing sector activity	Wages per man-hour[b]	1, Tables 2 and 4
	Value added per production worker[c]	1, Tables 2 and 4
	Capital expenditure per production worker[c]	1, Tables 2 and 4
	Number of workers per establishment	1, Tables 2 and 4
	Percentage employed in manufacturing	1, Tables 2 and 4; 2, Tables 91 and 125
Retail sector activity	Sales per retail establishment[c]	3
	Payroll per employee[c]	3
	Percentage establishments with payroll	3
	Percentage change in retail sales, 1967-1972	3
Wholesale sector activity	Sales per wholesale establishment[d]	3
	Payroll per employee[c]	3
Service sector activity	Service receipts per employee[c]	3
	Payroll per employee[c]	3
	Percentage establishments with payroll	3
	Percentage change in service receipts, 1967-1972	3

Unemployment rates	Percentage unemployed	2, Tables 85 and 121
	Percentage black males unemployed	2, Tables 85 and 121
	Percentage black females unemployed	2, Tables 92 and 126
Distribution of work force, not elsewhere classified	Percentage agriculture	2, Tables 87 and 123
	Percentage construction	2, Tables 87 and 123
Social organization		
Housing quality	Percentage owner-occupied housing	3
	Percentage housing with >1.01 persons per room	3
	Median house value (owner-occupied)^c	3
	Median rent (renter occupied)^e	3
Quality of urban life	Percentage below poverty level, 1969	3
	Per capita government expenditure^e	3
	Rate of serious crimes	3
Racial competition and segregation	Percentage blacks	2, U.S., Summary Table 67; States, Table 34
	Percentage blacks in professional jobs	2, Tables 93 and 127
	Residential segregation	17

^{a}Sources are identified in Table 2.5.
^{b}Measured in dollars.
^{c}Measured in thousands.
^{d}Measured in millions.
^{e}Measured in hundreds.

Table 2.3

Measurement of Ecological Constructs: Industrial Labor Markets (Economic Sectors)[a]

Construct	Computed variables	Sources[b]
Concentration	Percentage of firms with > $100 million assets	5, Table 6
	Concentration of four largest firms	7
	Percentage of receipts for firms with > $100 million assets	5, Table 6
Profitability	Average undistributed profit	10, July 1977, Table 6.23
	Average net profit[c]	5, Table 6
	Average profit[c]	4, Tables 1.1 and 2.1; 5, Table 6
	Value added per employee	10, Tables 1 and 6.8
Size	Average assets[c]	5, Table 6
	Average size of businesses (number of employees)	12, Table 6.8; 5, Table 6
State	Percentage of goods and services purchased by state	10, Feb. 1974, Table 1
	Government regulated (1 = yes; 0 = no)	6, Table 22.1

44

Industrial integration	Extent of intraindustry dependence on inputs	10, Table 1
Investment and growth potential	Percentage of increase in new firms, 1970-1974	5, Tables 6 and 7
	Depreciable assets per full-time employee	5, Table 2; 10, Table 6.8
	Investment credit per employee	5, Table 2; 10, Table 6.8
Work duration	Average job tenure--males	9, Table 5
	Average job tenure--females	9, Table 5
	Average weekly hours	8, Table C2
Wages and benefits	Average hourly earnings	8, Table C2
	Pension, profit sharing per full-time employee	4, Tables 1.2 and 2.2; 5, Table 5; 10, Table 6.8
	Other benefits programs per full-time employee	5, Table 5; 10, Table 6.8
Labor force distribution	Percentage of females	13, Vol. 1, Table 1
	Percentage of blacks	13, Vol. 1, Table 1
	Percentage of union members	11, Table 134

---

^{a}We credit Wallace and Kalleberg (1981) for suggesting many of the sources used here.

^{b}Sources are identified in Table 2.5.

^{c}Measured in thousands.

Table 2.4

Measurement of Ecological Constructs: Occupational Labor Markets

Construct	Computed variables	Sources[a]
Involvement	Involvement with data	15
	Involvement with people	15
	Involvement with things	15
Aptitudes	Intelligence	15
	Verbal ability	15
	Numerical ability	15
	Spatial perception	15
	Form perception	15
	Clerical perception	15
	Motor coordination	15
	Finger dexterity	15
	Manual dexterity	15
	Eye-hand-foot coordination	15
	Color discrimination	15
Educational preparation	General educational development (GED)	15
	Specific vocational preparation (SVP)	15
Temperaments	Variety of duties	15
	Repetitive operations	15
	No independent action	15
	Directing and planning others' activities	15
	Dealing with people	15
	Working alone	15
	Influencing people	15
	Stress	15
	Evaluation against judgmental criteria	15
	Evaluation against verifiable criteria	15
	Interpretation using personal viewpoint	15
	Precise attainment of limits	15
Physical demands	Strength (lift, carry, push, pull)	15
	Climbing and/or balancing	15
	Stooping (kneeling, crouching, crawling)	15
	Handling (reaching, fingering, feeling)	15
	Talking and/or hearing	15
	Seeing	15
Working conditions	Extreme cold	15
	Extreme heat	15
	Wetness and humidity	15
	Noise and vibration	15
	Hazards	15
	Fumes (odor, toxicity, dust, ventilation)	15

Table 2.4 *(continued)*

Construct	Computed variables	Sources[a]
Self-direction	Overall self-direction	15
Work force characteristics and distribution	Percentage of males	16
	Percentage of white males	16
	Percentage of white females	16
	Median earnings--males	16
	Median earnings--females	16
	Median years of schooling--males	16
	Median years of schooling--females	16
	Median age--females	14
	Median age--males	14

[a]Sources are identified in Table 2.5.

Table 2.3, the first group of constructs taps the dimensions specified by dual economy theory; the unit of analysis is the *industry*, and many of the specific items were derived from sources suggested by Wallace and Kalleberg (1981).

Economic concentration is measured by two financial indicators, the percentage of firms in an industry with greater than $100 million in assets and the percentage of the industry's receipts accounted for by these same firms. An additional indicator taps the percentage of sales that the largest firms in an industry account for in nine cities.[17] Profitability, a second key construct in dual economy theory, is tapped by three profit indicators and value added per employee. Value added refers to the increment in product value that is provided by labor, over and above capital and raw materials. The higher the value added, the greater the potential for profit. Size is operationalized both in terms of financial assets as well as by number of employees, and relationship to the state is tapped both by whether the industry is subject to government regulation and whether the industry is heavily dependent upon state purchase of its products. Industrial integration is tapped by a single indicator, the degree to which the industry depends upon inputs from other industries. Although the standard conceptualization of vertical integration is firm-specific, we advance an analogous hypothesis at the industry level: The greater the degree of industry integration, the greater the potential for industry profits. Finally, industry investment and growth potential is tapped

[17]The fact that development of this indicator is based on data from only nine cities is a severe weakness, but no better measures of concentration exist across the spectrum of industries. Scherer (1970) provides details concerning the development of this measure.

by two financial investment measures, depreciable assets per full-time employee and investment credit per full-time employee, plus the percentage of increase in new firms between 1970 and 1974, a growth in firms indicator.

From our theoretical argument, recall that economic organization at the industrial level influences work organization and outcomes at the occupational level. The next three sets of variables tap these constructs, although the measures remain aggregated by industry. Recall that workers in "good" jobs were less prone to turnover and layoffs. This work duration dimension is tapped by three measures: average job tenure for males, average job tenure for females, and average weekly hours. "Good" jobs are better rewarded financially, a notion that is tapped by average hourly earnings and two indicators of job benefits. Finally, we indicated that "good" jobs were often reserved for white males and were also often protected by a union. The indicators percentage females, percentage black, and percentage unionized are used to measure these concepts.

Two major sources supplied the data to define occupational labor markets (see Table 2.4). Data that describe the nature of tasks performed by respective occupational incumbents were provided by Spenner, Otto, and Call (1980). They took a variety of occupational characteristics derived from the third edition of the Dictionary of Occupational Titles (DOT) (U. S. Department of Labor, 1965) and aggregated and weighted the data to match the standard U. S. Census 3-digit occupational codes. This data file includes information on 42 job characteristics for 584 1970 Census occupational–industry categories. Because our analysis strategy involves measuring industry characteristics and including these as separate independent variables, we chose not to use the data that differentiate occupation by industry.[18] This resulted in 419 cases (occupations) to be used in the factor analysis discussed later.

The variables we used from the Spenner, Otto, and Call (1980) file are listed in Table 2.4. Most of the variables had already been grouped under a number of DOT subheadings:

1. Level of involvement: the degree to which the worker in an occupation is involved with data, people, and things (scored 0–8, with 0 indicating the most complex form of involvement and 8 indicating no involvement)

[18]The exception to this decision concerns occupation 280, salesmen and sales clerks, not elsewhere classified (n.e.c.). Because of the relatively large proportion of workers in this category and the large variation in occupation characteristics by industry, we used as separate cases the five occupation-by-industry categories. For the other nine occupations for which data were provided only for occupation by industry categories, we obtained a weighted average across the industries using the number of cases in each of the industries as the weight.

2. Aptitudes: specific capacities and abilities required of an individual to learn or adequately perform a task or job duty (scored 1–5 with a low score indicating high aptitude)

3. Temperaments: different types of occupation situations to which workers must adjust (scored 1 if present and 0 if absent)

4. Physical demands: the physical requirements of the job and the specific traits a worker must have to meet the requirements (most of these are scored as 1 if present and 0 if absent)

5. Working conditions: the physical surroundings of a worker in a specific job (scored 1 if present and 0 if absent[19]

Also included were measures of the general educational and specific training demands of occupations, as well as a measure of whether the occupation involves primarily self-direction or entails supervision by others. Spenner and his colleagues derived the level of involvement, aptitude, temperament, physical demands, and working conditions variables from the DOT (U. S. Department of Labor 1965). The general educational development (GED) and specific vocational preparation (SVP) measures were derived from both the DOT and Temme (1975). The self-direction measure was derived from Temme from data reported by Kohn (1969). Additional details concerning these data are provided by Spenner (1980).

From an earlier file of occupational characteristics produced by Spenner and Temme (1977), we also included variables such as the percentage male, the percentage white male, the percentage white female, and median earnings, and education, and age by sex, that were originally produced from 1970 Census sources. The race and sex distribution variables are useful in the analysis of occupational segregation and competition effects and will be discussed in Chapter 5.

A complete list of sources of ecological data is presented in Table 2.5.

Matching Ecological and Survey Data

To evaluate the effects of ecological variables upon individual-level outcomes, the ecological data must be matched to the survey respondents according to the contexts in which they live and work. The goal, for example, is to see that the accountant employed by EXXON in Houston is matched up

---

[19]We excluded one of the variables included in the data file. The variable measuring whether the worker had to work inside, outside, or both was not an ordinal-level variable and could not be used in the analysis with the other variables, all of which had ordinal or interval characteristics.

Table 2.5

Sources of Ecological Data

Source number	Source
1	*1972 Census of Manufacturing, Area Series* (U.S. Bureau of Census, 1975)
2	*1970 U.S. Census of Population,* State Volumes, and U.S. Summary Tables (U.S. Bureau of Census, 1970)
3	*1977 City and County Data Book* (U.S. Bureau of Census, 1978)
4	*1974 IRS Statistics of Income, Business Income Tax Returns* (Internal Revenue Service, 1974a)
5	*1974 IRS Statistics of Income, Corporation Income Tax Returns* (Internal Revenue Service, 1974b)
6	Scherer, 1970
7	Shepherd, 1969
8	*Employment and Earnings Bulletin,* Jan. 1977 (U.S. Bureau of Labor Statistics, 1977)
9	*Monthly Labor Review,* Dec. 1974 (U.S. Bureau of Labor Statistics, 1974)
10	*Survey of Current Business,* 1974 and 1977 (U.S. Department of Commerce—Bureau of Economic Analysis, 1974, 1977)
11	*1977 Handbook of Labor Statistics* (U.S. Bureau of Labor Statistics, 1978)
12	*National Income and Product Accounts for the U.S., 1929-1974* (U.S. Department of Commerce—Bureau of Economic Analysis, 1977)
13	*Equal Employment Opportunity Report,* 1975 (U.S. Equal Employment Opportunity Commission, 1975)
14	*1970 Census of Population,* Occupation Reports (U.S. Bureau of Census, 1970)
15	Spenner, Otto, and Call, 1980
16	Spenner and Temme, 1977
17	Sorensen, Taeuber, and Hollingsworth, 1975

to data describing the local labor market of Houston, the industrial labor market of chemical and allied products (which includes petroleum), and the occupational labor market corresponding to accountants, one of the many professional occupations for which there are occupational data. Decisions involving the level of detail at which to produce the areal, industrial, and occupational data were therefore influenced by the level of detail at which these contexts were coded in the survey data. In addition, for the areal data, we produced the relevant variables for 509 different counties and SMSAs; a listing of these local markets is available from the first coauthor.[20]

In order to locate the PSOID respondents' appropriate local labor markets, the following criteria were adopted. If the respondent reported residence in a county that was part of an SMSA according to the 1972 Census of Manufacturing, he or she was counted as residing in that SMSA and data were prepared on that basis. If the respondent reported residence in a county that was not part of an SMSA at that time, he or she was counted as residing in that county and data were prepared on that basis. It was assumed that a worker was employed in the county or SMSA where he lived; although this may be an inappropriate assumption in some cases, data limitations did not permit any investigation of this issue.

Data concerning respondents' industries of employment were available for a total of 31 categories as outlined in Appendix A. Since some of these categories were residual in nature (e.g., manufacturing, not ascertained whether durable or nondurable), we attached ecological data from more general categories to reduce the problem of missing data among these key constructs. For example, workers who were listed "employed in manufacturing, not ascertained whether durable or nondurable," had data from a more general category: manufacturing, both durable and nondurable.

The level of detail available on occupation varied among the PSOID respondents. For the sample of PSOID wives from the 1976 panel, a 2-digit occupational coding scheme was used (see Appendix A). Therefore, occupational data originally produced at the 3-digit level were aggregated so as to correspond to the cruder 2-digit scheme. The vast majority of the household heads from the PSOID had 3-digit occupational codes corresponding to the U. S. Census 3-digit scheme. To obtain this degree of detail we used respondents' 1974 occupations, which were at the 3-digit level in the analysis, along with remaining data, including earnings reported in 1975 for 1974. In a

---

[20]The 509 counties and SMSAs are those for which we have respondents included in the analysis plus additional areas represented in samples of black and white ever married, employed women who were included in the 1970 National Fertility Survey. This latter data set was used in preliminary analysis in our study of labor market effects on earnings. We retained the more general factor analytic solution on the advice that the broader the scope of input data, the more stable and general the factor solution.

few cases, however, this 1974 occupational listing was inappropriate due to changes in household composition.[21] In these cases, all of the occupational data were aggregated to the 1-digit level (see Appendix A) and attached as appropriate. One-digit occupational listings were provided for every household head from the 1975 panel. Computer programs specifically designed to handle the matching of data were used to produce the files, and checks were made to ensure that the matching was accurate.

Missing Data

Care was taken to minimize missing data problems by making reasonable assumptions concerning the assignment of individuals to areas, industries, and occupations. Table B.1 in Appendix B lists the frequency for which each variable is actually measured for each subsample. Inspection of the table suggests that the missing data problem has not been uniformly eliminated. Missing data is not a problem for the human capital variables except in the case of weeks worked, where we see that between .24% and 12.89% of the cases are missing due to nonresponse to survey items. Whereas variables tapping the economic organization of the local labor market are measured for most cases, there is some variation in the proportion of missing cases for several of the variables across status groups. This is due to the unavailability of some ecological data used to construct these measures for some of the less populated areas. In addition, there is a severe missing data problem for the segregation index, since that measure is only computed for 77 SMSAs (Sorensen *et al.*, 1975). For this reason, extreme care is taken in using that variable in analysis (see Chapter 3). Concerning the occupational labor market variables, missing data occurs in less than 1% of the cases, except for the job authority measure where nonresponse to survey items introduces between 1.22% and 14.33% missing cases. For the occupational and local labor market variables used throughout the volume, as well as the human capital variables, we regard the missing data pattern as essentially random and therefore view the problem as not particularly serious (Kim and Curry, 1977).

With reference to the indicators tapping industrial differentiation, the magnitude of the missing data problem is more severe and implications for analysis more serious. The problem is due to the nonapplicability of certain indicators to given industrial categories. For example, it makes no sense to

---

[21]The percentages of each sample for which we measured the occupational data on a 1-digit basis are: white male heads, 3.3%; black male heads, 3.7%; white female heads, 9.2%; black female heads, 6.1%.

ask how concentrated professional services in education and health are, which contributes to a substantial missing data problem for the concentration and investment variable. Uncertainty concerning the implications of a systematic missing data pattern suggests we use particular caution in interpreting relevant findings. For this reason, as discussed in Chapter 4, some of the analysis involving these variables is performed only for those cases for which these variables are measured. In general, however, we judge that the pattern of findings involving the industrial differentiation indicators is strong enough to conclude that the pattern of missing data has not contributed to erroneous inferences.

Factor Analysis of Ecological Data

As indicated earlier, we have produced numerous measures of characteristics of occupations, areas, and industries. We believe, however, that the actual underlying constructs for each of these three labor market contexts are considerably smaller in number than the measured variables. Past research is useful as a guide concerning what the underlying constructs are and which variables should be used to measure them. For example, work by O. Duncan and Reiss (1956) informs our discussion of local labor market economic and social organization. Analyses of industrial differentiation by Wallace and Kalleberg (1981) and Hodson and Kaufman (1981) aid in our analysis of industrial structure. Work by Miller, Treiman, Cain, and Roos (1980) and P. Cain and Treiman (1981) concerning dimensions of occupational differentiation is particularly useful. We will discuss our results as they relate to these previous studies. However, since we require measures that can be matched to the values of area, occupation, and industry included on the surveys we use, we conduct our own factor analyses. In each case we have used factor analysis as a data reduction technique (Kim and Mueller, 1978) to indicate the number of constructs (factors) underlying the measured variables and to identify which variables should be used to measure each of these constructs.

These factor analyses serve two important functions. First, the findings present a view of the respective labor markets as structures, a topic of theoretical interest in itself. The zero-order correlations among the factors we derive allow us to learn more about the internal workings of the respective macrolevel markets. Second, results of the factor analysis allow us to form composite measures to be used in subsequent analysis. Variables selected to represent each construct (factor) are (a) transformed to Z-scores in order to avoid problems posed by combining variables with different scales; (b) reverse coded when necessary so that all variables run in the same direction; and (c) summed to form a composite.[22] Use of composites avoids having to separately incorporate many interrelated variables into multivariate analysis, a procedure that would be statistically infeasible (R. Gordon, 1968).[23]

In each of the factor analyses we present, the unit of analysis is not the individual, as will be the case when we analyze earnings as the dependent variable, but instead is either the occupation, area, or industry. The factor analysis for local labor market differentiation is based on 509 cases (local markets); the analysis for industrial market differentiation is based on 31 cases; the analysis for occupational differentiation is based on 419 cases. These numbers of cases correspond precisely to available differentiation on the surveys used in analysis. Because the number of cases for each is different and because we view the three labor market contexts as conceptually distinct, each factor analysis of the occupational, areal, and industrial variables is conducted separately. The Rao maximum likelihood extraction method is used and both orthogonal (varimax) and oblique rotations are produced. Although the orthogonal and oblique rotations produced similar results, we have relied on the oblique solution, since it would be difficult to argue that the constructs that emerge are not interrelated. The Kaiser criterion (eigenvalue greater than 1.00) is used for determining the number of factors to be extracted. This is strictly a statistical criterion, however, and as will be seen, does not guarantee that all of the extracted factors can be meaningfully interpreted. A variable must have loaded $|\pm.4|$ or higher on a factor to be included in a composite.

As experienced users of exploratory factor analysis will recognize, ambiguities regarding which items belong to which factors almost always emerge, especially when a large number of items is analyzed. A few instances of this type of ambiguity were faced in these analyses. Although this does not mean

---

[22]Summing only those variables that correlate highly with the factors often is referred to as creating a factor-based scale (Kim and Mueller, 1978). As will be documented later, there is no reason to believe that using a more complicated weighting procedure would alter the results (Alwin, 1973).

[23]As with any multivariate procedure, there are some limitations inherent in the use of factor analysis. First, all factor analytic solutions are markedly determined by characteristics of input data. The greater the number of input variables and the more variety in "type" of input variables, the more likely the solution will contain more than one factor. Therefore, although extraction of multiple factors is consistent with our expectations concerning labor market structure, such patterns would also be consistent with the nature of our input data. In addition, it is important to remember that we use factor analysis here as an exploratory procedure. That is, in contrast to confirmatory factor analysis, we do not have hypotheses concerning how many factors will be extracted in each solution, nor precisely which items will load on which factors. We do have general expectations concerning the types of factors that will emerge, and these will be discussed in conjunction with each set of results.

that the involved factors do not represent unique dimensions, it does raise questions concerning how such items should be treated in the formation of composites. Including the same item in more than one composite artificially produces multicollinearity among the composites and therefore should be avoided. In addition, deciding that such an item should be included in one composite and not another also leads to inflated correlations among the composites due to that item's strong relationships with the other variables that are included in the composite it is deleted from. For these reasons we adopted the strategy of not using such items as part of any of the composites. Not only does this allow us to present a "cleaner" picture of structural differentiation, but it also facilitates our multivariate analysis using the composites later in the analysis. The implications of this decision are discussed more fully in conjunction with the factor analyses of industrial and occupational labor market variables (see *Note*, pp. 68–69 and footnote 31).

FACTOR ANALYSIS OF THE AREAL DATA

Areal characteristics were categorized a priori as representing either the economic organization or the social organization of the area (see Table 2.2).[24] For example, variables such as the percentage of retail establishments with payroll, wages per man hour, and percentage employed in manufacturing are indicators of the economic organization, whereas the percentage below the 1969 poverty line, median house value, and rate of serious crimes are indicators of the social organization of the area. Factor analyses were performed separately for the economic and social characteristics; those included are listed in Table 2.2.

Although detailed hypotheses are not specified concerning the patterns of findings anticipated from these factor analyses, we do have general expectations concerning the nature of the results. We expect the economic variables to load on factors that reflect the dimensions of economic differentiation indicated by Thompson (1965) and others discussed in Chapter 1. These dimensions should reflect Thompson's distinction between export and nonexport industrial activities. Similarly, we would expect that factors reflecting

---

[24]Hadden and Borgatta (1965) presented a factor analytic solution of city characteristics in which both economic and social characteristics loaded on the same factors. Hence the notion that social and economic variables may be the result of some common factor has some support. However, in this analysis we find it more useful to conduct separate analyses so as to assess whether the dimensions correspond to those suggested by the distinct theories of urban economic and social organization discussed earlier. Such a strategy will also allow us to look at the relationships between dimensions of economic and social organization, an analysis precluded by Hadden and Borgatta's strategy.

urban social organization be interpretable in terms of the concepts of crowding, residential segregation, and other aspects of the urban social system.

Economic Organization

Table 2.6 displays the oblique rotation factor pattern for the seven factors extracted that met the stated eigenvalue criterion. With a few exceptions the loadings allow for straightforward decisions about the dimensions being mea-

Table 2.6

Factor Pattern Matrix from Oblique Rotation of Local Labor Market Economic Organization Characteristics

Characteristic[a]	Factor						
	1	2	3	4	5	6	7
Percentage unemployed	-.02	.85	.35	-.12	-.05	-.06	.00
Percentage of black males unemployed	.16	.68	-.11	-.08	-.01	.01	-.07
Percentage of black females unemployed	-.21	.84	-.19	.19	.05	.08	.07
Percentage agriculture	-.32	.13	-.65	-.25	.09	-.11	.03
Percentage construction	-.24	-.08	.29	-.24	.09	-.04	.43
Percentage retail estab. with payroll	-.03	.07	-.12	-.14	-.18	.75	-.11
Percentage retail sales change	-.01	-.07	.61	.02	.06	.16	.46
Percentage service estab. with payroll	.06	-.03	.16	.05	.20	.67	.03
Percentage service receipts change	.12	.01	-.07	.07	-.07	-.05	.75
Wholesale sales receipts	.72	-.10	-.15	.03	.05	.04	-.01
Wholesale payroll per employee	.84	.02	.04	-.01	-.13	.06	.01
Retail sales receipts	.50	-.09	.18	.10	-.14	.38	.09
Retail payroll per employee	.24	.09	.17	-.02	.04	.02	.00
Service receipts per employee	-.01	.00	.04	.03	-.06	.00	-.02
Service payroll per employee	.58	-.02	.09	.01	-.18	.08	.23
Wages per man-hour	.36	.14	.03	.15	-.69	.03	-.05
Value added	.20	.01	-.12	.02	-.68	.20	.03
Capital expenditures per worker	-.05	-.02	-.03	-.08	-.41	-.04	.06
Percentage manufacturing	.12	-.02	.16	.76	.14	-.21	-.07
Number of workers per establishment	-.10	.00	-.08	.87	-.05	.06	.08

(continued)

Table 2.6 *(continued)*

Characteristic[a]	Factor						
	1	2	3	4	5	6	7
Factor correlations							
Factor 1	1.00						
Factor 2	.01	1.00					
Factor 3	.19	-.04	1.00				
Factor 4	.21	-.07	.13	1.00			
Factor 5	-.24	-.02	-.01	-.10	1.00		
Factor 6	.37	.05	.07	-.03	-.12	1.00	
Factor 7	.03	-.18	.18	-.18	.04	.07	1.00

[a]Characteristics are more fully described in Table 2.2.

sured and the variables to be used in measuring them. Factor 1 represents a dimension we call the *economic health of the tertiary sector*. The variables combined to form the composite are sales per wholesale establishment, wholesale pay per employee, sales per retail establishment, and service pay per employee. An area with a high score on this composite would have an economically productive tertiary sector, with high levels of sales and employee payrolls.

Level of unemployment is the dimension represented by Factor 2. The three variables with high loadings on this factor are the percentage unemployed, the percentage of black males unemployed, and the percentage of black females unemployed. A high score on this composite indicates high unemployment in the area.

Factor 4 represents a *manufacturing dominance* dimension. The composite measuring it combines the percentage of total workers employed in manufacturing and the number of workers per manufacturing establishment. A high score indicates that the proportion of workers the area has employed in manufacturing establishments is high and that the average establishment size is large.

We have called Factor 5 *health of the manufacturing sector*. The three variables with high loadings all refer to the manufacturing industry and are wages per man-hour, value added per production worker, and capital expenditures per production worker. An area with a high score would be characterized by an economically strong and productive manufacturing industry.

Complexity of the tertiary sector is the dimension captured by Factor 6. The variables used to create the composite are the percentage of retail establishments with payrolls and the percentage of service establishments with payrolls. A high score for an area would indicate that the retail and service establishments in the area are complex enough and sizeable enough to use formal payroll procedures, as opposed to informal pay arrangements.

The three variables with high loadings on Factor 7 are the percentage in construction, the percentage of change in retail sales from 1967–1972, and the percentage of change in service receipts from 1967–1972. We have called this dimension *economic growth of the tertiary sector*. The positive signs for all loadings indicate that the areas with the greatest change in retail sales and service receipts also have the highest proportion of all employees in the construction industry. Such a finding may reflect the need for construction of new retail and service establishments where these latter industries are growing. We also notice that the percentage of change in retail sales variable loads on Factor 3 as well as on Factor 7. It is incorporated here, however, since the substantive interpretation of Factor 7 is clearer than that for Factor 3 where it loads with percentage agriculture. It seems only minimally useful to suggest that agricultural areas experience little change in retail sales. The percentage of workers employed in agriculture is omitted from all of the composites, as are service receipts and retail payrolls, which loaded distinctly on none of the factors.

The configuration of factors that emerged from the analysis of the economic organization characteristics provides evidence consistent with Thompson's (1965) thesis. Manufacturing activity and activity in the sales–service sector are separate dimensions. In no case do the tertiary sector and manufacturing variables load together, which is consistent with Thompson's ideas regarding the roles of these respective industries in local labor market functioning. Concerning the internal organization of each sector, manufacturing sector organization is distinct from its economic productivity. Similarly, within the tertiary sector, economic productivity is distinct from sector growth and from its organizational characteristics. Unemployment rates for the local area form a distinct factor. We may describe the economic organization of a local labor market, then, in terms of the economic health and size of its manufacturing activities plus the economic health, growth, and complexity of its tertiary sector; local levels of unemployment contribute to this picture as well.

Social Organization

Table 2.7 displays the factor pattern for the two factors extracted from the nine social organization variables. Because two variables, the percentage of workers below the 1969 poverty line and the percentage of owner-occupied housing, had high loadings on both factors, they are not used in construction of the composites. Factor 1 represents an *urbanization* dimension. The four variables used in creating this composite are median house value, median

Table 2.7

Factor Pattern Matrix from Oblique Rotation of
Local Labor Market Social Organization Characteristics

	Factor	
Characteristic[a]	1	2
Percentage below poverty	−.59	.57
Housing		
Percentage owner-occupied	−.46	−.58
Percentage > 1.01 persons		
per room	−.15	.65
Median house value	.93	.07
Median rent	.89	−.17
Per capita government expenditure	.53	−.11
Rate of serious crimes	.74	.10
Percentage black population	−.12	.73
Percentage black professionals	.36	−.02
Factor correlations		
Factor 1	1.00	
Factor 2	−.15	1.00

[a]Characteristics are more fully described in
Table 2.2.

rent, per capita government expenditure, and the rate of serious crimes. The
signs of the loadings indicate that an area with a high score on any one of
these variables will be high on the others.

The second factor represents a *crowding* dimension and includes housing
with more than 1.01 persons per room and the percentage of blacks in the
population. A high score means the area is characterized by residential
crowding (i.e., within dwellings) and/or a racial distribution of the general
population conducive to the "crowding" of minorities into a few occupations
(Bergmann, 1971) and racial discrimination generally (Blalock, 1967).

Reliability

Since the composites derived are multiple-item measures, this feature of
their construction can be used to assess their reliability. Cronbach's alphas
for each of the measures are as follows: manufacturing sector health, .68;
manufacturing dominance, .78; tertiary sector health, .85; tertiary sector
growth, .64; tertiary sector complexity, .62; urbanization, .85; crowding, .65; unemployment, .82. We see that reliability varies by measure but
that all are at least at acceptable levels. We do not use these alphas to

"correct" for unreliability since these procedures can overcorrect for random measurement error. Rather, these data are presented to aid our interpretation of subsequent findings.[25]

Intercorrelations among the Composites

Table 2.8 portrays the intercorrelations among the local labor market constructs.[26] Looking first at the economic correlations within industrial sectors, there is essentially a zero correlation between productivity in the manufacturing sector and its dominance or relative market share. Thus across the local labor markets included in our analysis, productive markets may be large or small, and large markets may be more or less productive than given smaller ones. Although this finding is not necessarily contrary to previous theory, it is worthy of note since the effects of these two variables are predicted to be in the same direction. Thompson (1965) and others have argued that both size and productivity of the manufacturing sector should positively affect workers' earnings. These findings suggest, however, that these two features of economic organization do not often coincide. Relationships among the tertiary sector variables are modest to low, except for the relationship between tertiary sector productivity and complexity, which is positive and substantial. Since these are ecological correlations, we cannot conclude that the businesses that are complex are also the most productive. Theory cited by Spaeth (1979), however, supports the notion that division of labor and attendant organizational complexity increase the efficiency of organizations.

Concerning relationships of characteristics across these industrial groupings, the .48 correlation between manufacturing sector and tertiary sector health is consistent with the notion of wage roll-out effects between manufacturing and tertiary sectors. Even assuming that we question the direc-

---

[25]These reported reliabilities are based on computations where the SMSA/county is the unit of analysis. We also computed reliabilities for each of these indicators for each status group and found in some cases that the reliabilities of the measured variable varied by status. For example, although our reported reliability of tertiary sector complexity is .62, for the respective status groups reliabilities were higher and ranged from .66 to .79. Similarly, urban crowding has a reported reliability of .65. However, among blacks the reliabilities are over .70 whereas for white female heads the reliability is .36. Similar analyses were conducted for the industrial and occupational labor market characteristics, and similar findings were obtained. In many cases the status-specific reliabilities were higher than those based on occupations or industries as the unit of analysis, although this was not uniformly true. A table containing these data is available upon request from the first coauthor.

[26]We note that the correlations among these composites are similar but not identical to the correlations among the oblique factors upon which they are based. This generally is true for factor scores and composites, regardless of how they are constructed (Kim and Mueller, 1978).

Table 2.8

Correlation Matrix: Local Labor Market Variables, Aggregate Level

	Manufacturing sector health	Manufacturing dominance	Tertiary sector health	Tertiary sector growth	Tertiary sector complexity	Urbanization	Crowding
Manufacturing dominance	.049						
Tertiary sector health	.476	.108					
Tertiary sector growth	-.062	-.169	.128				
Tertiary sector complexity	.219	-.182	.391	.038			
Urbanization	.529	-.128	.723	.089	.408		
Crowding	-.196	.056	-.093	.127	.088	-.328	
Unemployment	.076	-.091	-.105	-.286	.105	.123	.039

tion of causality between manufacturing and tertiary sector wages, the magnitude of the relationship suggests that wage levels and productivity are compatible across industrial groups. Manufacturing productivity is also positively associated with tertiary sector complexity, though the magnitude of the association is reduced as compared with the productivity measures previously discussed. Manufacturing dominance and tertiary sector growth are inversely related. Such a finding is consistent with ideas concerning economic specialization as outlined by O. Duncan and Reiss (1956). It is intuitively clear that the areas that have dominant manufacturing sectors have less room and fewer resources for expansion of service and sales industries. In local markets with dominant export sectors, tertiary industries are likely to play a supporting role by supplying workers and manufacturing industries with modest services and retail goods, but the exporting of services is not well-developed, whereas areas with smaller manufacturing sectors may have more fully developed tertiary industries. The negative relationship between manufacturing dominance and tertiary complexity also supports theory concerning local labor market specialization. Those markets with dominant export sectors and supporting tertiary sectors are likely to have industries in those tertiary sectors that do not demonstrate a highly developed degree of organizational complexity. Such complexity is likely to be characteristic of those tertiary sectors engaged in export activity.

One final point concerning economic organization is useful. There is a negative relationship between tertiary sector growth and local unemployment. Although we may not conclude that it is the growth in the service and sales establishments themselves that reduces unemployment, such a hypothesis is quite plausible. This is particularly true since the relationship between manufacturing dominance and unemployment is weak. Hence we are unlikely to conclude that a dominant manufacturing sector reduces unemployment. This finding also supports Thompson's ideas concerning greater cyclicality in labor markets dominated by manufacturing industries as compared with those that specialize in services and sales.

In considering the social organization variables, a noticeable negative correlation exists between urban crowding and urbanization. Thus urban crowding, both at the ecological and household levels, is associated with characteristics of economically depressed areas. The more important finding, however, is that despite the relationship between these two dimensions of social organization, they evidence very different relationships with the economic variables discussed earlier. Crowding is weakly associated with these factors, although there is a modest negative relationship with manufacturing productivity. Urbanization, however, is strongly positively associated with manufacturing and tertiary sector productivity, as well as tertiary sector complexity. Thus there is congruence between local labor market economic organization and social dimensions related to housing and quality of life. Those markets with productive and highly organized industrial bases are also those with high housing values, high rents, high governmental expenditures, and high crime rates. It appears that economic prosperity comes at the price of higher costs of living and increased incidence of crime.

FACTOR ANALYSIS OF INDUSTRIAL CHARACTERISTICS

Two sets of industrial characteristics are also subjected to factor analysis. The first set consists of variables designed to tap characteristics of the economic sectors discussed by Averitt and others (the dual economy). These measures are global in nature and measure characteristics of emergent structures such as industrial concentration and firm profitability. Those variables listed under the concentration, profitability, size, state, industrial integration, and investment and growth headings in Table 2.3 were included in this analysis. In addition, socioeconomic consequences, some of which are discussed by dual labor market theory, may be viewed as being causally subsequent to these economic sectoral characteristics. Therefore, we have factor analyzed these variables, some of which are analytic-type, separately. The included measures are listed under the work duration, wages and benefits, and labor force distribution headings in Table 2.3.

Our expectations concerning results from these factor analyses are based on the discussion of dual economy and dual labor market theories in Chapter 1. The first set of results is expected to reflect such dimensions as size, profits, economic concentration, type of product market (local versus national/international), vertical integration, and product diversification. In addition, since our data were in many cases derived from sources similar to those used by Wallace and Kalleberg (1981), the findings are expected to be similar to theirs. We also expect worker outcomes such as benefits and wage levels to guide interpretations of factors derived in the second analysis.

Economic Structure

Table 2.9 displays the factor pattern from the oblique rotation of 15 variables measuring various aspects of the economic structure of industries. Using the eigenvalue criterion, four factors were extracted. The first factor has 6 variables with very high loadings: the percentage of firms with more than $100 million in assets; the average firm net profit; the average firm profit; the average firm assets; the average firm size; and the value added per employee. This rather clearly represents an *economic profitability* dimension. However, not much would be gained by including all of these indica-

Table 2.9

Factor Pattern Matrix from Oblique Rotation of Industry Economic
Organization Characteristics

Characteristic[a]	Factor			
	1	2	3	4
$100 million assets	.96	.02	.10	-.01
Concentration	.11	.81	-.16	-.40
Percentage of receipts	.01	.67	.58	-.22
Average undistributed profit	-.02	.04	.00	.24
Net profit	1.00	-.05	.06	.02
Profit	1.01	-.08	.05	.02
Average assets	.98	.00	.08	.00
Average size	.97	-.05	.13	-.02
State purchases	-.11	-.20	.06	.08
Government regulated	-.21	.68	.07	-.04
Percentage of increase in new firms	-.12	.13	-.88	-.34
Industrial integration	.16	.13	.51	-.23
Assets per employee	.02	.85	-.03	.26
Investment credit per employee	.27	.88	.07	.28
Value added per employee	.72	.16	-.29	-.09
Factor correlations				
Factor 1	1.00			
Factor 2	.24	1.00		
Factor 3	.18	.09	1.00	
Factor 4	-.23	-.15	.09	1.00

[a] Characteristics are more fully described in Table 2.3.

tors in a composite; the zero-order correlations among the first 5 variables
are all larger than .98 (data not shown). Because of this extreme multicollinearity we have selected average net profit to represent this subset and
have combined it with value added per employee to form the composite
measuring economic profitability. A high score on this composite is indicative of an industry in which the profits are high.

Factor 2 we have identified as a *concentration and investment* dimension.
Variables that have high loadings are: the concentration ratio of the four
largest firms; the percentage of total receipts for firms with greater than $100
million in assets; the degree to which the firms are government-regulated;
assets per employee; and the investment credit per employee. The percent-

age of total receipts variable is not used as a component, however, because it also loads highly on the third factor. An industry with a high score on this composite would be characterized as having a few firms that both control a high proportion of production and can invest in capital for use in production. These industries are also likely to be subject to some government regulation.

Factor 3 represents a *firm growth* dimension. The percentage increase in new firms from 1970–1974 loads in a direction opposite that of the integration measure. This indicates that in industries that depend least on inputs from other industries, there has been the least expansion with respect to new firms. It suggests that the industries which evidence room for new firms are those in which there is economic dependency on other industries. Industries such as steel or automobiles, where firms control several facets of the production, sales, or transportation processes, are therefore so large that the introduction of new firms becomes impossible. Industries composed of smaller firms requiring fewer assets in order to produce are also likely to be more dependent upon other industries for materials or transportation and sale of finished goods. It is in these industries that expansion is possible. However, industries high in industrial integration are the least susceptible to economic fluctuations in other industries, whereas the firms undergoing expansion are economically dependent upon other industries and are likely to be economically more unstable.

As in the previous factor analyses, several measures were not used in any composites. As discussed earlier, the percentage of total receipts for firms with greater than $100 million in assets variable is not used in any of the composites because it loads about the same on both the second and the third factors. In addition, we are unwilling to attempt a substantive interpretation of Factor 4 since none of the factor loadings is greater than .40.

Socioeconomic Consequences

The factor analysis of socioeconomic consequences (work duration, wages and benefits, and labor force distribution) included nine variables that produced three oblique factors as shown in Table 2.10. Factor 1 includes average job tenure of males and females and average weekly hours. This factor rather clearly represents a *work duration* dimension. It is consistent with dual labor market theory, which describes jobs in terms of their duration and stability over time (rate of turnover). A high score for an industry would indicate that, compared with other industries, the workers enjoy job security and full-time employment.

Factor 2 has been identified as the *employee benefits* dimension. The two variables describing job benefits load on this factor, which is also a dimension discussed by the dualists. They argue that jobs are differentiated with

Table 2.10

Factor Pattern Matrix from Oblique Rotation of Industry
Consequence Characteristics

Characteristic[a]	Factor		
	1	2	3
Average male job tenure	.99	.01	.05
Average female job tenure	1.02	−.07	.12
Percentage females	−.13	−.06	.90
Percentage blacks	−.05	.25	.27
Average earnings	−.16	.10	−.74
Average weekly hours	.63	.29	−.31
Percentage union members	.19	.28	−.33
Pensions per full-time employee	.07	.93	−.03
Benefit programs per full-time employee	.05	.86	−.15
Factor correlations			
Factor 1	1.00		
Factor 2	.21	1.00	
Factor 3	−.29	−.14	1.00

[a]Characteristics are more fully described in
Table 2.3.

reference to the socioeconomic rewards they command; fringe benefits are
an important part of these rewards for most workers.

Factor 3 we have chosen to label *sex discrimination*. The signs of the
loadings for the two variables associated with this factor indicate that in
industries where the percentage of females is high, the average hourly earnings are low. Although the sign of the percentage of employees unionized
variable is consistent with this dimension—the more highly unionized industries pay more and have fewer women—the magnitude of the loading, relative to its loading on the other factors, does not allow us to include it in the
composite. Again, these findings are consistent with dualist theory, which
suggests that women are less likely to have access to high-paying jobs, many
of which are protected by established unions.

It is useful to compare the results we present here with those discussed in
Wallace and Kalleberg (1981). As indicated, we expect similarity in the factor
analysis of the economic sector characteristics since we used similar sources
of data, and this expectation is confirmed. Both solutions suggest that economic concentration and profitability are distinct dimensions of economic
organization, although our profitability dimension included their "scale and
size indicators." In addition, our government regulation variable loads on

the capital intensity dimension, whereas in their solution, state variables load on a third factor. Our firm growth dimension does not appear directly represented in their solution. It is less useful to compare our solutions for worker outcome (their labor force consequence) variables due to dissimilarities in data input. We concur, however, with their argument concerning the multidimensionality of concepts derived from dual economy and dual labor market theories. As expected, and consistent with their findings, there is correspondence between dimensions underlying economic sectors and those describing worker consequences. We recognize, however, that there may be differences in the nature or degree of these relationships when they are considered from the viewponts of the respective status groups. This issue is evaluated in Chapter 4.

Reliability

As in the case of the areal composites, reliability estimates are provided for the industrial composites. Cronbach's alphas for these measures are: economic profitability, .82; concentration and investment, .87; firm growth, .60; work duration, .90; employee benefits, .90; sex discrimination, .81. With the exception of firm growth, the reliabilities are all high. This evidence provides some reassurance that the findings we present later involving the industrial variables will not be substantially influenced by unreliability.

Intercorrelations among the Composites

Table 2.11 displays the matrix of intercorrelations among these six composites. We are particularly interested in these sets of correlations since the dualist theories would lead us to expect interrelationships among the dimensions within each set—economic structure and labor force consequences—as well as across sets due to the causal relationship between them.

The correlations among the characteristics of economic sectors are all positive, but, with the exception of the relationship between profitability and concentration and investment, the magnitudes of the relationships are not large. If it were the case that industries were dichotomously distributed along these dimensions as the dual economy perspective would suggest, then these correlations would be much stronger. As it stands, industries in which there is growth in firms, for example, are not particularly concentrated nor highly profitable. These findings constitute another piece of evidence that fails to support the notion of an economic system that is segmented into a few internally homogeneous clusters.

There are somewhat stronger relationships among the characteristics representing worker outcomes. We have argued that these factors represent

Table 2.11

Correlation Matrix: Industry Data
Composites, Aggregate Level

	Profitability
Concentration and investment	.314
Firm growth	.137
Work duration	.160
Benefits	.646
Sex discrimination	-.078

characteristics of jobs described by advocates of dual labor market theory. In particular, the benefits and work duration variables are strongly and positively associated, and the higher the degree of sex discrimination, the lower the work duration and job benefits. These relationships among worker outcomes are all as predicted. There also appears to be substantial overlap between the two types of dualist constructs. Labor market positions in concentrated industries and in those that experience growth in firms are likely to be characterized by stable employment and job benefits. Labor market positions in concentrated industries also evidence less sex discrimination than those in less concentrated industries. Profitable industries also find it easy to provide high benefits for workers, again a finding predicted on the basis of theory. The notion that the economic organization influences characteristics of the labor market positions that individual workers hold is clearly supported in this analysis.

Note: To assess the possibility that factor-based scores produce results different from those obtained when factor scores are used, factor scores were obtained for the six industrial labor market characteristics identified by the factor analysis. This was accomplished with the SPSS Factor program, which uses the regression procedure for estimating factor score coefficients. All variables in the factor analysis of the *economic organization* characteristics were used in the construction of the factor scores for each of the three constructs. In constructing the three composites from the *industry consequence* characteristics, it was necessary to delete average male job tenure from the estimation procedure. This variable was so highly correlated with average female job tenure that the factor scores were declared indeterminant. All other variables were included in the construction of these factor score variables. In all instances the factor score coefficients based on the oblique solution were used.

Two types of information were examined to assess potential differences.

Concentration and investment	Firm growth	Work duration	Benefits
.094			
.464	.430		
.723	.320	.580	
-.396	-.081	-.301	-.270

First, the intercorrelations among the factor score variables were compared with those obtained when factor-based scales were used. Second, the factor score variables were substituted for factor-based scales in the regression equations used in Chapter 4, where the industrial characteristics are examined as determinants of earnings.

When the intercorrelations among the six factor-score composites were compared with the corresponding intercorrelations among the factor-based composites, small differences were observed, but no differences in interpretations resulted. Using greater than $|\pm.05|$ as the criterion for a meaningful difference, three correlations were unchanged, six factor-score correlations were larger than the factor-based correlations, and six factor-score correlations were smaller than the factor-based correlations. Substituting the factor-score composites for the industry characteristics in the Table 4.6, 4.8, 4.9, and 4.10 regression equations resulted, with a few exceptions, in no changes in substantive conclusions. Among black female heads the effect (standardized coefficient) of concentration and investment was increased by about one-third and the R^2 was increased by about 14% (Table 4.6). For the same status group the effect of sex discrimination was doubled (Table 4.9). Finally, for black male household heads firm growth became significant (beta went from .033 to .096) in Table 4.8. None of these differences, however, would lead us to alter substantive interpretations. Thus, these findings, along with recommendations by Alwin (1973) and Kim and Mueller (1978), lead us to conclude that the factor-based composites we use are appropriate.

FACTOR ANALYSIS OF OCCUPATIONAL CHARACTERISTICS

The final factor analysis reported here includes the occupational characteristics from the file created by Spenner et al. (1980). The variables used are listed under the headings of involvement, aptitudes, educational preparation, temperaments, physical demands, working conditions, and self-direction in Table 2.4; they define the nature of the occupational task performed. All of these variables were factor analyzed together for two reasons. First, just because the variables have been categorized as aptitudes, temperaments, etc., does not mean there is a unique aptitude factor, temperament factor, and so on. In fact, even a cursory examination of the variables suggests that some variables in one category will be highly correlated with certain variables from another category. For example, the temperament "influencing people" would be expected to be related to verbal aptitude. Second, several occupational characteristics have been measured that were not a priori placed in one of the general DOT categories but that undoubtedly measure some the of the same constructs as the other characteristics.

Both theoretical and empirical–descriptive materials provide guidance in deriving dimensions of occupational differentiation. As discussed in Chapter 1, Stolzenberg's (1975) theoretical arguments concerning occupational labor markets suggest that differences in the types of skills workers bring to the market and differences in the levels of demand for these skills promote segmentation along occupational lines. Thus, physical abilities such as strength, climbing, and manual dexterity, which are important in construction and building trades positions, contribute to differentiation of those positions from others, whereas the intellectual abilities such as verbal competency and numerical aptitude contribute to differentiation of various white-collar positions from each other and from manual positions generally. Spenner's (1979) analysis also emphasizes occupational differentiation on the basis of skill.

Economists and sociologists interested in dual labor market theory (Doeringer and Piore, 1971; Harrison, 1972; Wachter, 1974) provide additional theoretical impetus for our analysis when they describe jobs as varying along a good–bad continuum. As discussed in Chapter 1, jobs vary according to pay, desirability of working conditions, existence of job ladders, degree of variety in work, stability of positions across economic cycles, and enforcement of work rules, with good jobs having favorable values on these dimensions and bad jobs having unfavorable values. These characteristics suggest additional dimensions along which occupations may be differentiated. Finally, recall that recent work by Spaeth (1979), Kohn (1969), Kohn and Schooler (1978), and Temme (1975) emphasizes the importance of complexity in work tasks as a nonprestige dimension of occupational differentiation and/or work organization.

Empirical–descriptive work by Miller et al. (1980) of fourth edition DOT data (U. S. Department of Labor, 1977) also provides guidance for our analysis. They factor analyze DOT characteristics for 591 occupation categories used by the 1970 U. S. Bureau of Census (see their Appendix F). Using varimax rotation, they identify four dimensions of occupational differentiation: substantive complexity, motor skills, physical demands, and undesirable working conditions. We expect similarities between their analysis and the findings to be reported later. More generally, the factor analytic solution presented here is expected to reflect the dimensions implied by the previous theoretical discussion in this chapter and in Chapter 1. Occupational skill dimensions such as physical and manual dexterity, job variables such as pleasantness of working conditions, and occupational characteristics such as work complexity, are several of the dimensions featured most prominently in the perspectives we discuss.

Table 2.12 shows the factor pattern for the oblique rotation when all variables are included. Nine factors met the eigenvalue criterion; the first factor accounts for 50% of the explained variance, whereas the ninth factor accounts for only about 2%. Since only six of the nine factors could be given substantive interpretations, only these will be used as the basis for constructing composites to represent occupational dimensions.

We have labeled Factor 1 the *complexity* of work dimension. The variables with the large loadings that we combine to form the composite are: involvement with data; the intelligence, verbal, and numerical aptitudes required; general educational development and specific vocational preparation; absence of independent action, directing and planning, influencing people, and evaluation against judgmental criteria temperaments; and overall self-direction. Forming a composite from these items results in an occupational dimension for which a high score is indicative of occupations requiring general intelligence, verbal and numerical aptitudes, complex educational development, lengthy vocational preparation, the ability to plan and direct the activities of others, the ability to influence others, the ability to evaluate against judgmental criteria, and high involvement with data. In addition, high-score occupations are characterized by high overall self-direction and considerable independent judgment and action. Spaeth's discussion of occupational complexity nicely characterizes the dimension underlying this factor:

As the division of labor becomes more elaborate, occupations become increasingly specialized. On the one hand, the range of tasks allocated to certain occupations becomes narrower until workers spend their time repetitively carrying out simple operations that are small components of larger processes. Cases in point are the manufacture of pins and a modern assembly line (A. Smith, 1789; Stinchcombe, 1974). On the other hand, other occupations develop through the narrowing of areas of expertise rather than through the narrowing of tasks. Incumbents of these occupations are specialists who do a variety of tasks, all of which are directed to a narrow substantive area, such as a technical or professional specialty. Such "specialists can perform tasks that would not be possible without the expertise available in a narrower field (Blau, 1977:189)." Specialization therefore increases the variation in occupational complexity, from routine jobs consisting of a few simple, repetitive motions to professional and scientific occupations characterized by highly complex work applied to a narrowly defined field (1977:748).

Table 2.12

Factor Pattern Matrix from Oblique Rotation of Occupation
Characteristics

Characteristic[a]	Factor								
	1	2	3	4	5	6	7	8	9
Data	.53	.02	.07	.03	-.27	-.29	.19	-.13	-.17
People	.61	-.66	.04	.07	.14	.09	.10	.04	-.01
Things	.06	.50	-.18	.27	-.11	.30	-.06	-.22	-.07
Intelligence	.78	.03	.07	.02	-.04	-.29	.08	.06	.00
Verbal ability	.72	-.04	.14	.02	-.05	-.31	.10	.12	.02
Numerical ability	.65	.20	.11	.03	-.07	-.39	.04	.04	.24
Spatial perception	.61	.45	-.03	.33	-.17	.11	.06	.08	.04
Form perception	.39	.29	.11	.56	-.09	-.11	.04	-.02	-.03
Clerical perception	.21	.02	.20	.16	-.05	-.68	.06	-.03	.16
Motor coordination	-.08	-.09	-.07	.91	.07	-.04	-.03	.00	-.06
Finger dexterity	-.02	-.07	-.03	.89	.07	-.15	.12	-.09	-.06
Manual dexterity	-.07	.00	-.07	.79	.00	.30	.01	.04	.17
Eye-hand-foot	-.07	-.06	-.57	.08	-.19	.20	.07	.22	.04
Color discrimination	-.03	.09	.21	.41	-.27	.08	-.15	.08	-.17
GED	-.80	-.05	-.10	-.01	.08	.20	-.07	-.06	-.03
SVP	-.78	-.04	.18	-.09	.14	.10	-.08	.28	.13
Variety of duties	.05	-.05	.08	.02	.59	.01	-.05	-.03	.03
Repetition	.48	-.07	.01	-.07	-.60	.07	.09	-.14	-.09
No independence	.48	-.09	-.08	.05	-.33	-.07	.12	-.38	-.05
Directing	-.71	.06	-.09	.17	-.05	.01	-.02	-.10	-.03
Dealing with people	-.19	.73	-.19	.04	.21	-.06	-.15	-.11	-.05
Working alone	-.05	.00	.05	.00	.02	.00	-.01	-.10	.02
Influencing	-.57	.30	-.04	.23	-.19	-.12	-.03	-.01	.00
Stress	.10	.16	.13	-.05	.26	.07	.14	-.08	-.06
Judgmental eval.	-.61	.02	-.07	.14	.06	.03	.06	-.11	.27
Verifiable eval.	-.24	-.46	.09	-.04	.28	.02	-.04	.30	-.16
Personal interpret.	.02	.05	.00	.00	.10	.03	-.07	-.03	.50
Precise attain. of lim.	-.01	-.46	.20	-.27	-.02	-.01	.03	.40	-.07
Strength	.03	-.05	.36	-.08	-.01	-.44	.28	-.05	-.12
Climbing	-.03	-.06	.91	-.01	.01	.07	-.09	-.06	.04
Stooping	.11	-.10	.58	.04	.02	-.21	.07	-.04	.03
Handling	.57	-.19	.05	-.39	.11	-.07	.08	-.01	-.07
Talking/hearing	-.28	.53	-.16	.13	.29	.14	.00	.02	-.01
Seeing	.04	-.33	.03	-.47	.08	.16	.04	.11	.09
Extreme cold	-.01	-.04	.01	-.04	-.07	-.05	.07	.01	.19
Extreme heat	-.06	.05	-.04	.05	.02	.05	.79	.08	.02
Wetness and humidity	.00	-.07	.13	.06	-.09	.08	.56	-.15	.10
Noise and vibration	.04	-.09	.27	.00	.04	-.17	.19	.18	-.07

Table 2.12   *(continued)*

Characteristic[a]	Factor								
	1	2	3	4	5	6	7	8	9
Hazards	−.05	−.01	.69	−.04	.02	.01	.28	.09	−.08
Fumes	.00	.00	−.05	−.05	.05	−.18	.48	.07	−.08
Self-direction	−.63	.33	−.08	.01	.09	.24	−.17	.04	.06

Factor correlations

Factor 1	1.00								
Factor 2	−.11	1.00							
Factor 3	.20	−.20	1.00						
Factor 4	−.09	.44	−.13	1.00					
Factor 5	−.25	−.04	.18	−.25	1.00				
Factor 6	−.33	.09	−.33	.05	.14	1.00			
Factor 7	.31	−.13	.28	−.08	−.05	−.32	1.00		
Factor 8	−.06	−.26	−.09	−.17	.03	.00	−.01	1.00	
Factor 9	−.12	.00	−.07	−.06	.03	.00	.01	−.15	1.00

[a]Characteristics are more fully described in Table 2.4.

Factor 2 is best interpreted as an interpersonal relations dimension that we will call the *people–things* continuum.[27] The variables that unambiguously load on this factor are involvement with things, situations dealing with people, situations where one must evaluate against verifiable criteria, situations where precise limits must be attained, and talking and/or hearing as a physical demand. The signs of the loadings indicate that occupations requiring interpersonal skills are the ones in which people must be dealt with and talking and/or hearing is important. Also, they are jobs in which there is little involvement with things, little evaluation against verifiable phenomena, and little emphasis on the attainment of precise limits. A high score on the people–things composite represents an occupation requiring extensive skills in interpersonal relations.

Physical activities required is the dimension underlying Factor 3. Five variables are summed to form the composite for this construct: climbing, strength, and stooping as physical demands; eye-hand-foot coordination aptitude; and hazardous work conditions. A high score on this composite is indicative of an occupation requiring extensive physical activities.

[27]Due to the manner in which the raw data were coded, the "people" items load negatively, and the "things" items load positively on this factor. In constructing the composite we reversed the signs of the people-related variables so that a high score would represent an occupation requiring interpersonal relations skills.

Physical dexterity and perceptual abilities required is the construct represented by Factor 4. The six variables having high loadings and used in the composite for this factor are motor coordination, finger dexterity, manual dexterity, color discrimination and form perception aptitudes, and seeing as a physical demand. A high score on the physical dexterity composite indicates the occupation requires a high level of physical dexterity and general perceptual ability.

Uncertainty is the dimension underlying Factor 5. Job situations involving a variety of duties and frequent change, as well as situations involving repetitious operations, both load on this factor.[28] Our interpretation is based on Scott's identification of uncertainty or unpredictability as a dimension of technology characterized by the "variability of . . . items or elements upon which work is performed or . . . the extent to which it is possible to predict their behavior in advance (1981:211)." Scott identifies measures of uncertainty that include uniformity or variability of inputs, the number of exceptions encountered in the work process, and the number of major product changes experienced. Thus the item "situations involving a variety of duties often characterized by frequent change" would appear to be an indicator of uncertainty. A high score on the variable (measure) indicates occupations characterized by uncertainty, variety, and change.

Unpleasantness of the work activities is the dimension represented by Factor 7. Three of the working conditions characteristics load on this factor: extremes of heat plus temperature changes; wetness and humidity; and fumes, odors, toxic conditions, dust, and poor ventilation. A high score indicates that the occupation involves highly unpleasant working conditions. Whereas this dimension represents the environmental conditions typically associated with an occupation, the other six dimensions refer to incumbent characteristics and/or role performances associated with an occupation.

Factors 8 and 9 generally had very low factor loadings. In addition, the factors could be given no clear substantive interpretation. For these reasons, these last two factors are excluded from further discussion and analysis.

---

[28]In other factor analyses (Miller *et al.*, 1980; Baron and Bielby, 1982), items measuring repetitiveness of job duties (usually called routinization) have been included within the job complexity dimension—the higher the complexity, the lower the routinization. Indeed, the "repetitions" item has a high loading on Factor 1 and Factor 5 in our factor solution. In preliminary analyses we found that when this variable is used in combination with the variety variable, the correlation between this composite and the one for Factor 1 increased substantially (with the item included, the r is $-.48$; with it excluded, it is $-.13$). Although we wanted to avoid using single-item indicators, we decided not to use the repetition variable in any of the composites. Thus we delineated uncertainty as a separate dimension of occupational differentiation, although we acknowledge the relationship with complexity that is evidenced in our own analysis as well as in previous work.

Factor 6 was also excluded from further analysis since after using the strength aptitude variable for Factor 3, only the clerical aptitude variable remains as loading on this factor. Since we wished to avoid single-item measures, we decided not to include this factor in future analysis.

As noted, several indicators were omitted from all of the composites due to their high loadings on more than one factor. Thus, involvement with people, which loads highly on Factors 1 and 2, and the physical demand of handling, which loads highly on both Factors 1 and 4, were not included in any of the composites. Spatial perception, which loads highly on Factors 1, 2, and 4, was similarly omitted. Preliminary analysis indicated that including involvement with people in people–things increased its correlation with complexity from .32 to .41. In no case did we believe that omission of a variable from a composite would hinder our ability to interpret the findings.

Reliability

Again we are able to assess the reliability of these composites. Cronbach's alphas for these measures are as follows: unpleasantness of work activities, .60; physical dexterity, .86; physical activities, .86; complexity, .95; and people–things, .86. With the exception of the unpleasantness of work variable, which is only composed of three items, the other multiple-item composites have high reliability. Thus we concur with Miller *et al.* (1980:170) who argue that although individual items from the DOT vary greatly in their interrater reliability, building scales based on factor analytic procedures such as ours can produce composite measures of high reliability.

Discussion of Factor Analysis Results

There is a clear relationship between the dimensions derived from the factor analysis and those suggested by our discussion of previous literature. The importance of the aptitude and ability dimensions—clerical aptitude, physical activity, and physical dexterity—is suggested by Stolzenberg's (1975) discussion of the relationship between work skills and labor market segmentation. The second factor, people–things, emphasizes occupational variability according to a social skills continuum, a point suggested by Spenner's (1979) analysis. The unpleasantness of work dimension is compatible with dual labor market theory, which argues that good jobs involve work in pleasant surroundings whereas bad jobs are likely to entail work under unpleasant and/or dangerous conditions. The emphasis that Spaeth (1979), Kohn (1969), and others have placed on complexity is born out in the analysis, since the first factor we derive clearly taps the dimension of work complexity. Work complexity may differentiate good and bad jobs described by dual labor market theorists, particularly in the sense of distinguishing nonroutine from routine jobs. The theory also suggests that good jobs entail variety and change in work while bad jobs do not, a notion tapped by our uncertainty dimension.[29] In short, theoretical and empirical work that argues for the importance of nonprestige or nonsocioeconomic dimensions of occupational differentiation finds support from this analysis.

Viewed empirically, the findings here are quite consistent with those reported in Miller *et al.* (1980:Appendix F). Four of our factors are similar to theirs, including complexity, undesirable working conditions, motor skills (our physical dexterity variable), and physical demands (our physical activities variable). However, the item content of the factors across the two studies is exactly the same only for the physical demands and activities factor, and we derive two additional factors—people–things and uncertainty.[30] We attribute these differences to changes in the ratings from the third to the fourth edition of the DOT, and to the somewhat smaller number of occupations used in our analysis. Further comparisons of the two studies are hampered by Miller *et al.*'s omission of the full factor matrix and by their failure to present data showing the relationships among the factors (or factor scales). Overall, however, the similarities appear greater than the differences, suggesting considerable stability in the major dimensions of occupational differentiation represented by DOT data between 1965 and 1977.

Intercorrelations among the Composites

Although we had expected these six dimensions to be interrelated, high intercorrelations among them would pose multicollinearity problems, since these are meant to be explanatory variables used in the same analysis. Table

---

[29]Additional dimensions specified by dual labor market theory are not represented in this solution owing to lack of input data. It is true that one variable, "directing and planning others activities" is representative of one aspect of work authority that is also part of the dualist's good job–bad job distinction. However, other dimensions such as say over pay and promotion and span of control are not represented. The item "influencing others" may be relevant but may also reflect one aspect of many sales' jobs. Although Spaeth (1979) used a DOT measure of complexity of work with people as an indicator of job authority, this measure is not as closely related to the several dimensions outlined earlier as are the measures used by other researchers in this area (see Wright and Perrone, 1977; Robinson and Kelley, 1979; Kalleberg and Griffin, 1980). Miller *et al.* (1980:225) criticize the DOT data for omission of authority-related variables. For these reasons we prefer not to interpret these results as providing evidence on work authority as a dimension. Chapter 5 provides more direct findings concerning the authority–earnings relationship.

[30]P. Cain and Treiman (1981) summarize many of the points made in Miller *et al.* (1980) and also present their factor analysis of a 10% random sample of the fourth edition DOT occupations. In this factor analysis, their management factor is quite similar to our people–things. They also report complexity, motor skills, physical demands, and undesirable working conditions factors as we do, plus an interpersonal skills dimension not directly represented in our solution.

2.13 presents a correlation matrix for the composites created on the basis of the factor analysis. Only one of the correlations is greater than .5 and only two others are larger than .4. Occupations requiring considerable physical dexterity and perceptual abilities generally are the same ones that require only minimal interpersonal skills. Also, occupations involving considerable physical activity are not the ones high in work complexity or those that require interpersonal skills. Jobs with complex tasks are likely to involve some working with people in relatively pleasant working conditions. Those jobs requiring physical activity are likely to involve some unpleasantness in working conditions. The total pattern of correlations suggests occupational differentiation along the dimensions of job complexity, working conditions, and physical activity and social skills requirements. These relationships form the basis for our analysis of occupational differentiation and occupational characteristics' effects presented in Chapter 5. Overall, we may conclude that occupations may be differentiated in terms of six constructs that, although not orthogonal, represent fairly distinct dimensions. With the exception of the unpleasant working conditions dimension, these dimensions are based on characteristics of incumbents of an occupation and/or the occupational role performances per se.[31]

One final note is necessary. We had access to the Siegel Prestige Score, Temme Prestige Score, and the Duncan SEI score for each occupation. In one of the preliminary factor analysis runs the Temme score was included and found to load highly on the complexity factor, with the other factors remaining essentially unchanged. However, to be consistent with the bulk of the research we decided to omit Temme and retain the Duncan SEI as a single indicator, recognizing that its potential multicollinearity problems with the complexity factor will have to be confronted in the analysis. This issue is addressed theoretically and empirically in Chapter 5 and in Parcel and Mueller (1983).

Table 2.14 summarizes the local, industrial, and occupational labor market composites derived from the factor analyses and indicates the variables included in each. We now indicate the data analytic techniques used to evalu-

---

[31]To investigate whether factor-based scores produce results different from those that factor scores would suggest, we computed a matrix of occupational composites constructed using factor scores to represent the several occupational composites. In only a few cases were the correlations noticeably different from those reported in Table 2.13. Several correlations involving uncertainty were strengthened. It is likely that the decision to measure uncertainty with one variable did depress its intercorrelation with several other variables. The instances in which the correlations were weakened all involved complexity and/or people–things. In these cases it is possible that the additional variables, even though their weights were relatively small, introduced extraneous variation into the measures, thus weakening the correlations involved. Overall, however, these data do not suggest that decisions regarding exclusion of multiple-loading items resulted in severe and systematic changes in the intercorrelations.

Table 2.13

Correlation Matrix: Occupation Data
Composites, Aggregate Level

	Complexity	People-things
People-things	.319	
Physical dexterity	−.055	−.581
Physical activities	−.427	−.420
Unpleasantness of work	−.352	−.208
Uncertainty	.127	−.082

ate the impact of these composites and individual-level variables as determinants of workers' earnings.

Data Analysis

Presentation of the data will begin with the descriptive findings including means and standard deviations of variables used in analysis. In the case of ecological variables, however, the means are weighted by respondents' affiliations with contexts. So, for example, if whites have a higher mean than blacks on the industrial variable representing profits, this is a function of whites being more likely than blacks to be hired into profitable industries. Thus, there are racial differences in access to industrial profitability. A similar argument is applicable concerning zero-order correlations. In this analysis, the correlations among the aggregate indicators of local, industrial, and occupational labor market differentiation are *weighted ecological correlations*. Although this type of measure has been less frequently used than unweighted ecological correlations (i.e., correlations on ecological data where every case receives equal weight), in this analysis ecological data are attached to each respondent and the distribution of respondents across the contexts varies by status group. Thus, we expect there to be stronger relationships among local labor market variables among blacks than whites since blacks are more concentrated in a fewer number of local markets than are whites. In other words, the ecological data are weighted by the respective distributions of respondents across contexts, thus potentially producing different ecological relationships for each group. These data are useful in describing the economic and social organization of labor markets.

Our multivariate techniques are based on the general linear model. The bulk of our analysis will focus upon ANCOVA (analysis of covariance) models

Table 2.13 *(continued)*

Physical dexterity	Physical activities	Unpleasantness of work
.148		
.053	.360	
.166	.169	−.018

predicting earnings as a function of individual and labor market characteristics. Sets of labor market variables will be added to the basic investment variables in an effort to understand how these macrostructures affect earnings. Unstandardized regression coefficients will be compared across status groups. Additional analysis techniques including analysis of bias in regression coefficients will be discussed when relevant.

A second analytic technique used allows us to explore the implications of the models we estimate using regression analyses. This technique, regression standardization or regression decomposition, allows us to explore what might happen to the earnings levels of economic minorities if these groups had access to the levels of resources that white males enjoy and/or if these groups could convert these resources into earnings at the same rates as white males. Since the calculations are based on algebraic manipulations, we do not claim that they represent changes that would necessarily occur given implementation of various policies. Rather, the findings suggest what changes in earnings levels might occur given changes in access to or efficacy of income-producing resources. In particular, the findings are useful in suggesting whether a given earnings difference is substantially due to differences in access to resources or to differences in returns to resources. These and related issues are discussed more extensively in Chapter 3.

We have already noted how use of the contextual strategy we specify allows for inferences not possible when dummy variables are used to represent labor market affiliation (see the discussion of Harrison, 1972 and Wachtel and Betsey, 1972, in Chapter 1). G. Cain (1976), however, criticizes the strategies used in Harrison's and Wachtel and Betsey's studies on two additional grounds. First, he argues that analyses of wage attainment models on samples where values of the dependent variable are truncated, such as those analyses confined to low wage earners (Wachtel and Betsey, 1972), blue-collar workers (Bibb and Form, 1977), or to residents of poverty neigh-

Table 2.14

Labor Market Composites and Constituent Variables

Composite	Variables

Local labor market
  Economic organization
    Tertiary sector health
	Sales per wholesale establishment
	Wholesale pay per employee
	Sales per retail establishment
	Service pay per employee

Unemployment	Percentage unemployed Percentage of black males unemployed Percentage of black females unemployed

Manufacturing
  dominance
	Percentage of total employed in
	  manufacturing
	Number of workers per manufacturing
	  establishment

Manufacturing sector
  health
	Wages per man hour
	Value added per production worker
	Capital expenditures per production
	  worker

Tertiary sector
  complexity
	Percentage of retail establishments
	  with payrolls
	Percentage of service establishments
	  with payrolls

Tertiary sector
  growth
	Percentage of workers in construction
	Percentage of change in retail sales,
	  1967–1972
	Percentage of change in service
	  receipts, 1967–1972

Social organization Urbanization	Median house value Median rent Per capita government expenditures Rate of serious crimes
Crowding	Percentage of housing with greater than 1.01 persons per room Percentage of black population
Industrial labor market Economic profitability	Average net profit Value added per employee

Concentration and
  investment
	Concentration ratio of four largest
	  firms
	Government regulation
	Capital intensity (assets per
	  employee)
	Investment credit per employee

Table 2.14 *(continued)*

Composite	Variables
Firm growth	Percentage of increase in new firms, 1970–1974 Industrial integration
Work duration	Average job tenure--males Average job tenure--females Average weekly hours
Employee benefits	Pension benefits Other benefits
Sex discrimination	Percentage of females Average hourly earnings
Occupational labor market Work complexity	Involvement with data Intelligence, verbal and numerical aptitudes GED and SVP No independent action; direction and planning; influencing people; evaluation against judgmental criteria temperaments Overall self-direction
People-things	Involvement with things Situations dealing with people Situations where one must evaluate against verifiable criteria Situations where precise limits must be attained Talking and/or hearing as a physical demand
Physical activities required	Climbing, strength, and stooping as physical demands Eye-hand-foot coordination aptitude Hazardous work conditions
Physical dexterity	Motor coordination Finger dexterity, manual dexterity Color discrimination aptitude Form perception aptitude Seeing (physical demand)
Uncertainty	Variety of duties and frequent change in job situations
Unpleasantness of work activities	Extreme heat plus temperature changes Wet and humid conditions Fumes (odors, toxicity, dust, poor ventilation)

borhoods (Harrison, 1972), will produce estimates of returns to schooling
that are downwardly biased. Thus, truncation of the sample automatically
"stacks the deck" in favor of the structural perspectives and against that of
human capital.[32] Second, although the consistently found association between industry affiliation and earnings may be compatible with the segmentation perspectives, those industry variables may function as proxies for
other demand variables not related to dualist theories or for human capital
variables omitted from or poorly measured in the analysis.

Our analysis avoids both of these problems. We estimate the earnings
functions on all workers aged 25–64 who report earnings. Thus the samples
are not truncated or confined to those workers for whom the labor market
variables should be most important. Second, we strive to include as many
well-measured personal characteristics as possible so as to avoid erroneously
attributing variance to the labor market factors.[33] The material we discuss on
social selection in Chapter 6 is particularly important in this regard.

Our analysis also avoids the earlier emphasis upon assigning jobs and
industries to markets or sectors. Thus, although Wallace and Kalleberg's
(1981) and Kaufman et al.'s (1981) more recent works have suggested that the
economic and occupational structures are more complex than the dichotomously oriented theories would imply, earlier efforts did not acknowledge this. Instead, the emphasis appeared to be upon use of the perspectives
as opposed to evaluating their validity. Instead of asking whether the economy and the occupational structure were dichotomously distributed as the
theories suggested, priority was placed upon categorizing industries and
occupations into slots suggested by the perspectives. For example, in their

[32]It has been argued that this criticism assumes a priori that the only population relevant to
evaluating wage attainment theories is the general, U. S. population, although in fact, to test
particular ideas, analyses of certain subsamples (e.g., steelworkers, computer programmers, or
selected urban residents) may be more appropriate. Our position on this issue is that although
disaggregated analyses may indeed be useful in testing theory, it is often unclear how the
subsamples articulate with a larger population. Certainly researchers must caution readers
concerning potential threats to external validity, which thus may imply only partial confirmation
of a theory. A second issue that becomes troublesome in disaggregated analyses of this type is
that of social selection. If workers with minimal job skills are disproportionately found in
industries in the periphery of the economy, one explanation is that they are at a competitive
disadvantage compared with other workers, and thus have difficulty finding better jobs. To
suggest that these workers obtain minimal returns to schooling ignores this issue. This problem
will be discussed more fully in subsequent chapters.

[33]This statement should not be interpreted to suggest that previous analyses of earnings
attainment performed from the structural perspectives have totally ignored human capital
variables or that these researchers have claimed that the effects of human capital variables are
totally explained by structural factors. Rather, their emphasis has been on the impact of structural variables on earnings, which due to research priorities, data limitations or both, may result
in *relative* underemphasis concerning the role of personal characteristics.

analysis of economic sector-specific earnings functions, Beck *et al.* (1980) assign industries to sectors on the basis of inspection. Bibb and Form (1977) and Hodson (1978) have also used inspection-based strategies where the assignments were made in part on the basis of knowledge concerning where respective industries stood on the dimensions of concentration, size, etc. A recent effort by Tolbert, Horan, and Beck (1980) illustrates a more statistically sophisticated way of dichotomizing industries. These authors use factor analysis of relevant economic characteristics to derive a distribution of factor scores for the industries. They then argue that the core–periphery boundary falls at one of the gaps in the scores in the middle of the distribution.[34] These efforts to define boundaries for economic sectors parallel those of earlier researchers interested in defining good versus bad jobs in analyses of the dual labor market. Osterman (1975), for example, classifies occupations into the primary or secondary labor market according to his own personal judgment concerning their autonomy and stability. Andrisani (1973) defines secondary workers as those employed in occupations and industries in which the median earnings are below the thirty-third percentile.

Interestingly, a recent analysis of several of the industrial sectoral schemes reveals differences in assignment of workers to contexts and varying results from regression analyses depending upon which of several sectoral schemes is used (Zucker and Rosenstein, 1981). Although these authors suggest that additional theoretical development may be needed before these difficulties can be overcome, the contextual strategy offers one currently available solution. There is certainly much stronger agreement on theoretically relevant dimensions of differentiation and even on measures of these dimensions than there is on (*a*) the number of sectors that are relevant (see Kaufman *et al.*, 1981), and (*b*) which industries belong in which sectors. Our use of the contextual strategy rejects the a priori assumption that the economy or labor market is necessarily divided into two, three, or even a larger number of distinct segments. We do not assume that firms exhibit all of the characteristics associated with either the core or the periphery. Rather, we argue that the *characteristics* specified by the dual economy and dual labor market theories may to varying degrees affect workers who vary by ascribed statuses. We use these theories and the recent empirical investigations of them to specify contextual models of earnings attainment containing both individual-level characteristics and characteristics outlined by dualists' perspectives.

Of course, there are limitations to the contextual strategy. Although it is useful for the additive analyses we propose, if one wishes to test for sector by

[34]This latter paper has been criticized on this and related methodological grounds (see Hodson and Kaufman, 1981).

human capital interactions, some decision regarding assignment of workers to sectors must be made (see Chapter 7). In addition, the measurement of several theoretically meaningful dimensions of market differentiation does not guarantee that all will be equally useful in analysis. We find in Chapters 3, 4, and 5 that with respect to individual workers, multicollinearity among indicators of market differentiation dictates the omission of several variables of theoretical interest from the analysis. As with any methodological choice, it is the relative balance of advantages and disadvantages that is important.

Summary

This chapter has been devoted to two tasks. First, the data and methods to be used in the analysis were described. We indicated how contextual analysis will be used to evaluate the effects of labor market characteristics on workers' earnings. Our use of this method was compared with the contextual strategies of others, and we indicated how our analysis addresses problems that have been apparent in previous analyses. The survey from which our samples of workers was drawn was described, and the criteria for selection of cases were identified. The sources of ecological data were described as well as the variables computed to measure the respective dimensions of labor markets' organizations. In addition, the matching of the ecological and survey data was discussed, as was the problem of missing data.

The second task has been to present the findings from exploratory factor analyses aimed at portraying the structures of local, industrial, and occupational labor markets. In each case we were interested in understanding the nature of labor market differentiation. Theory suggested by Thompson (1965) and O. Duncan and Reiss (1956) that indicated local market differentiation on the basis of industrial characteristics was reflected in the solution that showed manufacturing and tertiary (sales–service) sector characteristics loading on separate dimensions. An additional factor solution suggested the relevance of urbanization and urban crowding as dimensions of local labor market social organization. The correlations among these factors suggest that there is a substantial relationship between the economic productivity of the manufacturing and tertiary sectors; that growth of the tertiary sector is more likely to occur when the manufacturing sector is small than when it is large (in terms of the relative share of the work force and mean establishment size); and that tertiary sector growth is negatively related to local levels of unemployment. There is also congruence between urbanization and the economic organization variables, but urban crowding is only weakly associated with the local labor market economic dimensions.

A second set of factor analyses were devoted to exploring industrial market differentiation. Our findings bring evidence to bear on the question concerning dimensionality of economic sectors and support research by Wallace and Kalleberg (1981) and others to suggest that economic sector differentiation is not unidimensional but multidimensional. Thus the notion that the United States economy is divided into two sectors—core and periphery—does not receive support here. The correlations among the composites measuring industrial economic organization and worker outcomes also reveal lack of support for the notion that the economic system is segmented into a few internally homogeneous clusters. They suggest, however, that worker outcomes such as levels of benefits and work duration are closely associated with each other and that there is substantial overlap between the economic organization and worker outcome characteristics. That is, positions in the core of the economy are likely to have secondary labor market characteristics.

A final factor analysis was conducted to derive dimensions of occupational labor market differentiation. Theoretical analyses by Spaeth (1979), the dual labor market theorists, Stolzenberg (1975), and others suggested the importance of work complexity and social, perceptual, and physical skills as dimensions of differentiation. Findings supported these expectations; several occupational composites covering task characteristics (e.g., task complexity or physical activities required) and working conditions (e.g., unpleasantness of work activities) were derived from the factor analysis of a variety of job characteristics. The correlations among the composites derived from the factor analysis suggested differentiation between jobs requiring interpersonal skills and those requiring perceptual abilities and physical dexterity. Similarly, jobs with complex tasks or those requiring interpersonal skills are not likely to be those that also require a great deal of physical activity. Taken together, these factor analyses provide summary pictures of the market structures we have discussed in theory.

In addition to these market structures being of interest in their own right, the factor solutions suggest composite variables that we use in subsequent analysis. That is, now that we understand something of the market structures themselves, we are interested in knowing what effects these dimensions have on workers' earnings. It is to this task that we now turn, beginning with analysis of the effects of local labor market characteristics on earnings for workers who vary by race and sex.

CHAPTER 3

Local Labor Market Characteristics' Effects on Earnings

Review of Theory and Hypotheses

It is useful to review the theory outlined in Chapters 1 and 2 concerning local labor market economic and social organization, as well as the hypotheses suggested concerning the effects of local labor market characteristics on earnings. Following work by Thompson (1965) and O. Duncan and Reiss (1956), we argued that it was meaningful to view local markets according to their economic specialization, that is, the nature of their export base. Urban areas specializing in manufacturing were expected to have higher mean levels of income, reduced income inequality, and greater temporal instability in income compared with areas specializing in retail trade or services. These latter areas were expected to have lower mean income levels, greater income inequality, but also greater income stability over time compared with manufacturing centers (Thompson, 1965). Arguments were also presented concerning local labor market social organization that focused on the importance of urban crowding and residential segregation (Blalock, 1967; Kain and Persky, 1969).

Our central focus, however, is on analysis of the relationships between dimensions of local market differentiation and earnings of workers who vary by race and sex. Of interest is whether findings produced by Parcel (1979) concerning the effects of local labor market characteristics on black and white males' earnings are replicated among female workers; that is, whether those previously produced findings have external validity. Also of interest are the effects of the local market composites (discussed in Chapter 2) on workers' earnings. These dimensions include measures of manufacturing sector productivity (or manufacturing sector health) and dominance; tertiary sector productivity, growth, and complexity; local market unemployment levels; urbanization, and urban crowding. Of particular interest is how the effects of these characteristics vary by race and sex.

Using theory and research derived from a variety of sources as discussed in Chapter 1, we expect that although manufacturing sector productivity should positively affect local wage levels generally, males would benefit from this resource more than females, since females are more likely to be employed in service and sales positions. We also suggested that blacks would especially benefit from residence in a local market with a strong manufacturing export sector since manufacturing industries provide job opportunities for blacks that other industries do not. We indicated that women would be less likely to benefit from manufacturing sector dominance since their job opportunities were stronger in other industries. This suggests that females and blacks could display stronger returns to the tertiary sector characteristics than white males. Concerning local labor market social organization, we suggested that blacks of both sexes would suffer economically in residentially segregated local markets and in those characterized by racial competition. Whites would benefit economically from residence in markets marked by racial competition; we advanced no hypothesis concerning the relationship between earnings and residential segregation among whites. In addition, there is insufficient theoretical guidance to suggest specific hypotheses concerning how the effects of urbanization could vary by race and sex.

Our central interest is in examination of unstandardized regression coefficients across status groups to assess the effects of labor market characteristics on earnings, independent of human capital and socialization variables. Several types of analysis complement this focus. We examine the structure of local labor organization that each status group faces by inspection of zero-order correlations among the labor market composites. Means and standard deviations for the variables in the analysis also are inspected, and a basic equation of earnings attainment is presented in which the labor market variables are excluded in order to assess the impact of the addition of these variables. Finally, a regression standardization (decomposition) procedure is used to evaluate the possible impact of changes in the distribution and/or efficacy of resources on earnings attainment for several subgroups of workers.

Local Labor Market Characteristics

STATUS-SPECIFIC CORRELATION MATRICES

The first question addressed concerns description of the local labor markets with which each status group is faced. Tables 3.1, 3.2, and 3.3 present the intercorrelations among the eight areal composites descriptive of market

Table 3.1

Correlations Among Areal Ecological Variables for Black and
White Male Heads[a]

	Manufacturing sector health	Manufacturing dominance	Tertiary sector health
Manufacturing sector health		.048	.718
Manufacturing dominance	.098		.006
Tertiary sector health	.514	-.076	
Tertiary sector growth	-.192	-.201	-.165
Tertiary sector complexity	.270	-.233	.412
Unemployment	.117	.079	-.166
Urbanization	.620	-.180	.815
Crowding	-.173	-.131	.228

[a]Whites below the diagonal; blacks above the diagonal.

Table 3.2

Correlations Among Areal Ecological Variables for Black and
White Female Heads[a]

	Manufacturing sector health	Manufacturing dominance	Tertiary sector health
Manufacturing sector health		.146	.558
Manufacturing dominance	.132		-.263
Tertiary sector health	.516	-.090	
Tertiary sector growth	-.151	-.219	-.231
Tertiary sector complexity	.116	-.090	.266
Unemployment	.124	-.016	-.009
Urbanization	.611	-.282	.754
Crowding	-.087	-.053	.293

[a]Whites below the diagonal; blacks above the diagonal.

Table 3.1 *(continued)*

Tertiary sector growth	Tertiary sector complexity	Unemployment	Urbanization	Crowding
-.094	-.055	-.075	.720	-.465
-.378	-.228	.208	-.063	.012
-.379	.108	-.203	.901	-.623
	-.018	-.340	-.303	.170
.062		-.116	.065	-.051
-.226	-.069		-.203	.279
-.015	.340	.048		-.726
.132	.274	-.093	-.127	

Table 3.2 *(continued)*

Tertiary sector growth	Tertiary sector complexity	Unemployment	Urbanization	Crowding
-.074	-.046	.167	.717	-.442
-.100	-.257	.277	-.296	-.034
-.497	.200	-.099	.847	-.461
	-.207	-.251	-.255	.199
.128		-.029	.185	.080
-.302	-.017		.096	.079
-.071	.288	.384		-.646
.051	.238	-.260	-.024	

Table 3.3

Correlations Among Areal Ecological Variables for Black and
White Wives (PSOID)^a

	Manufacturing sector health	Manufacturing dominance	Tertiary sector health
Manufacturing sector health		.156	.745
Manufacturing dominance	.065		.062
Tertiary sector health	.524	-.090	
Tertiary sector growth	-.199	-.178	-.152
Tertiary sector complexity	.230	-.199	.375
Unemployment	.049	.027	-.186
Urbanization	.634	-.177	.814
Crowding	-.146	-.104	.260

^{a}Whites below the diagonal; blacks above the diagonal.

economic and social organization for each status group. Although correlations have been presented in Chapter 2 that describe the structure of local markets in our sample, the matrices presented here are composed of weighted ecological correlations. In this case the correlations are weighted according to the distributions of respondents across local labor markets.[1] We know that blacks are proportionately more likely than whites to be concentrated in large urban labor markets. Since our samples reflect these distributional differences, we expect that the correlation matrices will exhibit racial differences in associations among variables. Since there are essentially no differences in the distribution of the sexes across local markets, we do not expect there to be noticeable differences in associations among variables by sex.

Looking first at the relationships within the manufacturing variables and within the tertiary sector variables we see that the slight relationship between manufacturing productivity and manufacturing dominance discussed earlier is duplicated for all status groups. However, the essentially zero

[1]The reader may question the validity of comparing correlation matrices across subgroups since differences may appear solely due to subgroup differences in the standard deviations of the variables (Kim and Mueller, 1976). In an additional analysis not presented here, we made analogous comparisons using covariance matrices and found that the conclusions reported here remained valid.

Table 3.3   *(continued)*

Tertiary sector growth	Tertiary sector complexity	Unemployment	Urbanization	Crowding
−.114	.063	−.200	.799	−.533
−.199	−.213	−.035	.030	−.208
−.350	.232	−.289	.910	−.555
	−.099	−.398	−.223	−.014
.111		−.140	.109	.017
−.228	−.106		−.307	.385
.007	.293	.119		−.673
.073	.273	−.121	−.092	

relationship between tertiary sector growth and tertiary sector productivity indicated at the aggregate level in Chapter 2 is not replicated here. Instead there are negative relationships between these variables that are large for blacks. These findings suggest that the respondents, especially the blacks, live in labor markets where there tends to be growth of the tertiary sector at the expense of its productivity. Those markets with the highest productivity are growing less than those areas that, on the average, pay lower wages and earn lower net profits. Since these are weighted ecological correlations, we cannot conclude that it is the expanding businesses themselves that are less productive. However, it may be that expansion has come at the expense of wages for workers.

Also apparent are positive relationships between tertiary sector productivity and tertiary sector complexity, particularly for whites. This positive relationship was present in Table 2.8 as well. The wage roll-out effects to which each status group is exposed, as evidenced by the correlations between manufacturing and tertiary sector health, are present and stronger than would be implied by the .476 correlation in Table 2.8, but the effects appear to be stronger for blacks than for whites. Thus blacks live in markets with stronger degrees of correspondence between manufacturing and tertiary sector profits and wages than do whites, although the relationships are strong for both races. The negative relationships between manufacturing dominance and tertiary sector growth and between manufacturing dominance and tertiary sector complexity are comparable to those shown in Table 2.8 and, in addition, do not show systematic racial differences. The negative correlation between tertiary sector growth and areal unemployment discussed in Chapter 2 is also reproduced for each status group.

Turning to the variables tapping social organization, there are strong negative relationships between urban crowding and urbanization among blacks, whereas there are weak negative relationships between these two variables among whites. Recall that the correlation of these two variables in Table 2.8 was −.328, intermediate between the values reported here. For blacks, urban crowding is associated with low housing values, low rents, low governmental expenditures, and lower crime rates. Relative lack of urban crowding is associated with higher housing values, higher rents, higher governmental expenditures, and higher rates of crime. Finding such striking racial differences in the magnitude of these relationships reflects, of course, the very different distribution of the races across local labor markets. This issue is considered again later.

Also of interest is the relationship between the social and economic dimensions of local labor market organization. The urbanization index is strongly associated with the economic organization variables for all status groups. For example, urbanization and manufacturing health are positively associated for all status groups with correlations ranging from .611 to .799. Urbanization and tertiary health are also positively associated with correlations ranging from .754 to .910 across the groups. Hence we conclude that all status groups live in markets where manufacturing and tertiary sector productivity are associated with higher housing values and rents, increased governmental expenditures and crime rates. These findings clearly support the notion that local market economic and social characteristics are interrelated.[2] The relationships between urban crowding and local market economic organization, however, do not fall into this pattern; these relationships are race-specific. For blacks the higher the urban crowding, the less productive the manufacturing sector. Although this relationship is still negative among whites, it is very modest in size. There is even greater racial disparity in the relationships between urban crowding and tertiary sector productivity. Among whites there are modest positive relationships that suggest that whites live in markets where tertiary sector productivity and urban crowding covary positively. Among blacks, however, the relationships are strongly negative. Thus for blacks urban crowding is associated with a nonproductive tertiary sector, as well as a nonproductive manufacturing sector as noted earlier.

---

[2]The reader should not infer that there is necessarily any causal relationship between the economic and social dimensions of local labor market organization. We infer neither directionality nor nonspuriousness, only that these characteristics covary as described.

In summary, as expected, we see that the major differences in local labor market social and economic organization that the status groups face break down along race- but not sex-based lines. This finding reflects, of course, the differential distribution of the races across local labor markets. Since blacks are proportionally more likely to be residents of a few large local labor markets than are whites, we observe stronger correlations among the local labor market variables for blacks than for whites. Blacks, then, generally live in local markets where there are strong positive relationships between manufacturing and tertiary sector productivity, but where tertiary sector productivity is inversely related to growth in that sector. Such growth is also inversely related to manufacturing dominance and to local labor market unemployment. Urban crowding is negatively associated with such urbanization measures as housing values and governmental expenditures and with manufacturing and tertiary sector productivity. Whites live in local labor markets that are similar to these economically but very different socially. For whites there is only a very weak relationship between urban crowding and the urbanization variable. If whites live in crowded markets, these areas are likely to have more productive tertiary sectors than was true for blacks. Such crowding is also accompanied by some weakness in manufacturing productivity, but this relationship is much more pronounced among blacks.

MEANS AND STANDARD DEVIATIONS

The means and standard deviations of the variables included in the analysis are presented in Table 3.4. An examination of race differences within each status group indicates that in all groups whites earn more than blacks. The magnitude of this racial earnings difference is not the same across status groups. Black males earn 66% of what white males earn; black female heads earn 74% of what white female heads earn; black wives earn 94% of what white wives earn. Concerning differences in other individual-level variables, male heads have more experience than do female heads, who have more experience than wives. We expect that necessity has forced female heads to acquire more labor force experience than wives and that differences in the nature of family responsibilities allow men to accumulate more work experience than women. Occupational status differentials vary by race, with whites clearly favored over blacks, regardless of household status. Education operates similarly in that whites attain more years of schooling than do blacks. Interestingly, in terms of absolute levels of schooling, the wives attain more than the female heads, who attain more than the male heads. Thus on the average there is over a 2-year difference between white wives and black

Table 3.4

Means and Standard Deviations for Variables Included in Analysis

	Male heads			
	Whites		Blacks	
	$\overline{X}$	S	$\overline{X}$	S
Earnings (dollars)	14,404	9415	9481	4791
Experience (years)	22.68	10.99	21.74	11.48
Occupational status	45.10	23.66	28.16	20.61
Education (interval)	12.59	3.06	10.40	3.50
Education (years)				
0–7	.0467	.2110	.2138	.4103
8	.0690	.2535	.0775	.2675
9–11	.1369	.3438	.2044	.4035
12	.3358	.4724	.3100	.4628
13–15	.1557	.3627	.1172	.3218
≥16	.2559	.4365	.0772	.2670
Weeks worked (interval)	47.43	5.33	47.37	5.66
Weeks worked				
0–13	.0031	.0553	.0020	.0442
14–26	.0169	.1289	.0057	.0754
27–39	.0485	.2148	.0998	.3000
40–47	.2413	.4280	.1693	.3753
48–49	.2912	.4544	.2564	.4370
50–52	.3990	.4898	.4668	.4993
Segregation	85.06	6.41	87.61	5.18
Percentage black population	9.57	9.25	21.88	11.61
Unemployment	4.44	1.61	4.21	1.40
Wage per man–hour	3.97	0.78	3.91	0.84
Manufacturing sector health	0.91	1.90	1.07	2.01
Manufacturing dominance	0.29	1.35	0.25	1.14
Tertiary sector complexity	0.29	1.39	.56	1.31
Tertiary sector health	3.31	4.00	4.19	3.73
Tertiary sector growth	−0.44	1.68	−0.11	1.58
Crowding	−0.27	1.08	0.97	1.60
Urbanization	1.99	3.74	2.09	3.90

Table 3.4 *(continued)*

	Female heads			
	Whites		Blacks	
	$\overline{X}$	S	$\overline{X}$	S
Earnings (dollars)	7416	4050	5502	3217
Experience (years)	18.53	11.17	18.28	10.35
Occupational status	44.65	21.01	31.91	21.56
Education (interval)	12.64	2.60	11.11	2.48
Education (years)				
0–7	.0205	.1419	.0962	.2953
8	.0459	.2096	.0569	.2319
9–11	.1683	.3748	.3139	.4647
12	.3980	.4903	.3624	.4814
13–15	.1656	.3723	.1124	.3163
$\geq$16	.2017	.4019	.0583	.2346
Weeks worked (interval)	45.15	8.36	45.37	6.78
Weeks worked				
0–13	.0222	.1476	.0085	.0917
14–26	.0160	.1255	.0258	.1587
27–39	.1205	.3262	.1368	.3442
40–47	.2321	.4229	.2527	.4353
48–49	.3209	.4677	.2789	.4492
50–52	.2884	.4538	.2974	.4579
Segregation	86.18	6.10	86.13	5.67
Percentage black population	9.81	7.80	17.98	8.78
Unemployment	4.50	1.58	4.01	1.12
Wage per man-hour	4.07	0.71	4.00	0.73
Manufacturing sector health	1.12	1.69	1.19	1.78
Manufacturing dominance	0.24	1.40	0.30	1.16
Tertiary sector complexity	0.37	1.15	0.50	1.12
Tertiary sector health	4.01	3.66	5.13	3.42
Tertiary sector growth	-0.40	1.66	-0.37	1.63
Crowding	-0.25	0.83	0.52	1.15
Urbanization	3.02	3.80	2.79	3.75

(continued)

Table 3.4 *(continued)*

	Wives			
	Whites		Blacks	
	$\overline{X}$	S	$\overline{X}$	S
Earnings (dollars)	5579	3904	5235	3306
Experience (years)	13.68	8.79	16.53	10.64
Occupational status	44.25	20.52	32.06	21.95
Education (interval)	12.74	2.44	11.61	2.58
Education (years)				
0-7	.0225	.1483	.0648	.2465
8	.0249	.1560	.0460	.2097
9-11	.1281	.3344	.2586	.4385
12	.4627	.4989	.4113	.4928
13-15	.1506	.3579	.1293	.3360
$\geq$16	.2112	.4084	.0901	.2867
Weeks worked (interval)	41.33	11.44	43.11	9.98
Weeks worked				
0-13	.0529	.2239	.0360	.1865
14-26	.0673	.2507	.0462	.2102
27-39	.2243	.4174	.1898	.3927
40-47	.1884	.3912	.2087	.4070
48-49	.2375	.4258	.2909	.4548
50-52	.2296	.4209	.2283	.4203
Segregation	85.28	6.55	88.28	4.89
Percentage black population	9.52	9.12	23.09	12.75
Unemployment	4.41	1.64	4.23	1.65
Wage per man-hour	3.94	0.75	3.77	0.81
Manufacturing sector health	0.82	1.83	0.78	1.93
Manufacturing dominance	0.21	1.33	0.05	1.09
Tertiary sector complexity	0.32	1.32	0.63	1.45
Tertiary sector health	3.33	3.97	3.80	3.69
Tertiary sector growth	-0.43	1.73	0.01	1.73
Crowding	-0.30	1.04	1.14	1.67
Urbanization	2.01	3.71	1.26	3.72

male heads in years of schooling, although their earnings ratio is .588 favoring the males.

Turning now to the variables representing characteristics of local labor markets, we observe major racial differences in the mean percentage of blacks who reside in the local labor market. Since blacks are more likely to live in areas that are concentrated with other blacks than are whites, such a finding is not surprising. It merely reflects the disproportionate distribution of the races across local markets. On the other labor market variables, race and sex variation in access to resources is minimal. Black wives live in markets where wages in manufacturing (wage per man-hour) lag 30¢ on the average behind white female heads, but the remaining status groups evidence much less variation. Residential segregation appears generally high, and unemployment is approximately 4% for each group. Concerning the composites, again we see that wives, particularly black wives, have reduced access to manufacturing resources (manufacturing sector health and dominance) compared with heads, but the differences in tertiary sector resources (health, growth, and complexity) appear to be associated with race. In each case, regardless of status group and regardless of resource, blacks have greater access (i.e., a higher positive composite or negative composite closer to zero) to tertiary sector characteristics than do whites. There are also observable differences in crowding. As was observed for the percentage black, blacks are more likely to be located in crowded labor markets than are whites.

HUMAN CAPITAL CORRELATIONS WITH EARNINGS

Table 3.5 presents the zero-order correlations between the basic human capital and socialization variables and earnings for each status group. For years of schooling, the interval scale is used as a summary measure, and as expected, positive relationships are observed for each status group. For weeks worked two measures are presented. The first uses an interval scale that indicates a positive relationship between earnings and weeks worked, although within status groups these relationships are generally weaker than those we observed for years of schooling. The second measure consists of the zero-order relationships between earnings and the two highest dummy variable categories used to capture weeks worked in our multivariate analysis: 48–49 weeks and 50–52 weeks. Within each status group, the zero-order correlation between earnings and 50–52 weeks is weaker than the relationship between 48–49 weeks and earnings. Thus, overall, the weeks worked–earnings relationship is nonlinear. Since the questions used to construct the weeks worked measure have the respondent exclude time not

Table 3.5

Zero-Order Correlations Between Earnings and Human Capital
and Socialization Variables

Variables	White male heads	Black male heads	White female heads	Black female heads	White wives	Black wives
Years of schooling						
Interval measure	.344	.285	.404	.403	.367	.523
Weeks worked						
Interval measure	.104	.183	.264	.124	.395	.291
48–49 weeks	.123	.066	.101	.347	.232	.110
50–52 weeks	−.079	.034	−.051	−.228	−.009	−.035
Experience	.050	.107	.211	−.073	.217	.047
Duncan SEI	.411	.383	.404	.461	.370	.556

spent working, including time off for vacations as well as unemployment, it is likely that the people who actually worked 50–52 weeks per year did so because they lacked jobs with paid vacations, a regulation number of sick days, etc. These are likely to be poorer-paying jobs in the secondary labor market. In contrast, workers who are employed in jobs that do entail these benefits actually earn more for less time on the job, since the jobs are likely to be in the primary labor market and thus differently constructed as we have previously discussed.

The remaining correlations between experience and earnings and job status and earnings are generally positive, with the job status relationship exceeding the experience relationship in strength within each status group. In the case of black female heads a negative relationship between experience and earnings is observed. This undoubtedly represents a cohort effect within this status group. Older black women are likely to have found more limited employment opportunities due to discrimination and their inferior levels of educational achievement relative to their younger counterparts, thus producing this negative relationship.

Multivariate Analysis

THE BASIC EQUATION: CROSS-STATUS COMPARISONS

The first equation is what we will call the basic equation (see Table 3.6). It estimates earnings in dollars as a function of education, weeks worked, job experience, and the Duncan SEI. To this equation will be added the several labor market composites discussed earlier. In the absence of these composites, however, an estimate can be obtained of the effectiveness of individual investment resources across the several status groups.

As shown in Table 3.6 there are clear racial differences in the education–earnings relationship. Among whites the relationship is positive and monotonically increasing such that each additional step of schooling is associated with greater earnings. However, among blacks the relationship is non-monotonic and more consistent with the "credentialist" notion that returns to education actually represent returns to degree attainment. For example, among black male heads there are distinct peaks at 12 and at 16 or more years of schooling. Such findings mean that, controlling for other human capital variables, black males with some college actually obtain lower returns

Table 3.6

Human Capital and Status Attainment Determinants of Earnings (the Basic Equation)[a]

Independent variables	Male heads			
	Whites		Blacks	
	Dev.	$b*$	Dev.	$b*$
Education (years)				
0–7	−4220.2	--	−1258.9	--
8	−2547.3	.045	−1052.2	.012
9–11	−1673.8	.093	−677.5	.049
12	−614.6	.181	1291.7	.246
13–15	92.6***	.166	−398.0***	.058
≥16	3102.6	.340	1752.2	.168
Weeks worked				
0–26	−4904.8	--	−5799.9	--
27–39	−2992.0	.044	−1934.4	.242
40–47	840.9	.261	467.0	.491
48–49	1043.5***	.287	550.8***	.579
50–52	−660.6	.221	37.3	.608
	b	$b*$	b	$b*$
Experience	108.9***	.127	81.1***	.194
Occupation	109.7***	.276	74.5***	.320
Constant	−2137		−1439	
$R^2/\bar{R}^2$	.220/.216		.246/.235	
	N = 1870		N = 768	

(continued)

Table 3.6 *(continued)*

	Female heads			
	Whites		Blacks	
Independent variables	Dev.	$b*$	Dev.	$b*$
Education (years)				
0–7	−2669.6	−−	−1529.6	−−
8	−2393.7	.014	−1147.0	.028
9–11	−1422.5	.115	181.2	.247
12	−244.9	.294	132.3	.249
13–15	440.8***	.286	−727.2***	.079
≥16	2124.4	.476	3244.7	.348
Weeks worked				
0–26	−5417.9	−−	−830.7	−−
27–39	−586.0	.389	−1698.6	−.093
40–47	593.3	.628	−446.1	.052
48–49	655.7***	.701	1966.3***	.391
50–52	−246.4	.579	−588.1	.035
	b	$b*$	b	$b*$
Experience	97.1***	.268	61.0***	.196
Occupation	39.4**	.205	68.3***	.457
Constant	−4231		−151	
$R^2/\bar{R}^2$	.366/.341		.445/.427	
	$N = 297$		$N = 349$	

to their educational investment than do high school graduates. Among black female heads the peaks are at 9–12 and at 16 years of schooling. Again, when other variables are controlled, those with some college obtain lower returns to their investment than do those with some high school or those who are high school graduates. The findings for wives are quite similar to those found for male heads, since the relationship is monotonically increasing among whites, but nonmonotic with peaks of returns at 12 and 16 or more years of schooling for blacks.

There are some clear similarities in the relationships between weeks worked and earnings across status groups. Regardless of race or sex, the relationship increases monotonically until the 50–52 weeks level, when there is a decline. This finding is compatible with our earlier discussion of zero-order correlations. Workers who work 50–52 weeks per year are likely to have secondary labor market jobs that pay less and thus are more weakly

Table 3.6 (continued)

Independent variables	Wives			
	Whites		Blacks	
	Dev.	$b*$	Dev.	$b*$
Education (years)				
0-7	-1722.2	--	-1537.9	--
8	-1416.9	.012	-996.9	.034
9-11	-1031.7	.059	-501.5	.137
12	-825.3	.115	304.9	.275
13-15	660.9***	.218	-731.4***	.082
≥16	2313.1	.422	2710.4	.368
Weeks worked				
0-26	-3711.2	--	-2952.5	--
27-39	-781.6	.313	-1505.5	.172
40-47	1061.7	.478	564.6	.433
48-49	1580.8***	.577	992.8***	.543
50-52	200.1	.422	534.8	.443
	b	$b*$	b	$b*$
Experience	83.1***	.187	15.3***	.049
Occupation	35.1***	.185	68.1***	.452
Constant	-2546		-1691	
$R^2/\bar{R}^2$	.413/.405		.535/.520	
	$N = 817$		$N = 356$	

^{a}All standardized coefficients for dummy variables in this table and in subsequent tables represent standardized deviations from the omitted category. Dev. denotes deviation from mean (in dollars); $b*$ denotes standardized coefficients; b denotes unstandardized coefficients.

$*p < .05,$ $**p < .01,$ $***p < .001.$

associated with earnings than jobs where the workers actually work fewer weeks per year. There also is an extreme decline in the earnings of black female heads at the 50–52 weeks worked level. This finding may suggest that these workers are particularly prone to employment in secondary labor market jobs, a notion evaluated in Chapters 4 and 5.

In regard to job experience, the first variation in patterns of statistical significance is observed. Although education and weeks worked were statistically significant across all status groups, job experience is significant for all groups except black wives. Such a finding may reflect the tendency for black wives to be segregated into entry-level positions in which there is minimal chance for advancement based on the accumulation of job-relevant skills. It may be that black female heads (and all male heads) are more likely to occupy positions where experience is directly rewarded in terms of promotions accompanied by pay increments. This explanation assumes that the authority dimension of occupational differentiation is not well-captured by the occupational status measure used, the Duncan SEI. There may also be industrial differences in access to positions for which experience is rewarded. Both of these possibilities will be evaluated in later chapters. The data in the table also suggest that among the status groups for whom experience is associated with earnings beyond the level of chance, the magnitude of the returns varies substantially. White returns exceed those of blacks, with each additional year of experience bringing white males $109 but a comparable investment brings black males only $81. Among female heads returns are $97 and $61 for whites and blacks respectively.

For occupational status, which is significant for every status group, the white returns do not always exceed those of blacks. Among male heads the whites are favored over blacks with returns of $110 and $74 respectively for every point on the Duncan SEI scale. Among the female heads, however, blacks obtain $64 for every point on the Duncan SEI scale, and whites obtain only $39. This reversal of the direction of the racial differences also is apparent among the wives. As will be seen, however, the strength of these black slopes may be partly artificial. In this case the artificial strength is caused not by multicollinearity but by a different artifact of the regression analysis. Given the nature of the least squares fitting procedures, the low level of job status black females evidence is compensated for by an inflated estimate of returns to job status, since earnings levels are not as low as the job status levels (controlling for other variables) would suggest. Therefore, the estimate of returns to job status is not independent of access to job status. This issue of the interrelation between access and returns to resources is discussed further in the section on regression standardization in terms of "interaction" between the means and slopes components of a decomposition of earnings differences.

In terms of the overall predictive success of the model, the explained variance differs substantially across status groups. Although much of the research that involves investment and socialization variables has been conducted on males, in our data the explanatory power is weakest for this status group. We also observe that, within household status groups, the models work better for blacks than for whites. The magnitude of this difference is greatest among wives where the included variables explain 52% of the · ▸ riance among blacks but 40.5% of the variance among whites. This racial difference in explanatory power has been observed in previous research (Blum, 1972; Treiman and Terrell, 1975; Harrison, 1972; Featherman and Hauser, 1976a, in the more complete specifications; Parcel, 1979), though it has received little comment. The differences in explanatory power reflect, in part, the magnitudes of the partial slopes for each specification. This issue will be discussed throughout the analysis.

EFFECTS OF LOCAL LABOR MARKET CHARACTERISTICS
ON EARNINGS

Replication of Previous Analysis

The second equation (Table 3.7) adds four ecological variables—an index of residential segregation, local unemployment rate, percentage black, and wage per man-hour—to the basic equation just discussed. These four variables were used by Parcel (1979) to tap local labor market social organization. Here they are used to evaluate whether the findings reported there for men aged 35–54 are replicated for men aged 25–64 and women workers.[3] For the first two status groups the basic findings are replicated for the wider age range of males. Among white male wage per man-hour is positively associated with earnings, as is the percentage black. Thus, white males' incomes benefit from their residence in a local labor market with a productive export sector (wage per man-hour) and also from the presence of large numbers of blacks who are likely to occupy the less desirable jobs. Whites also suffer from residence in residentially segregated local markets but are unaffected by the local level of unemployment.

Note: It is reasonable to question whether these findings concerning segregation are influenced by the pattern of missing data involving this variable. Recall that since segregation indexes are only available for 77 of the largest

---

[3]We do not strictly evaluate this replicability notion since the basic equation used in this research differs slightly. In particular, two dummy variables representing health limitations (1 means yes, health limits work; 0, otherwise) and interstate migration (1 means yes, respondent has migrated from the state in which he lived at age 16; 0, otherwise) have been excluded. Neither of these variables was significant for either race in the previous analysis. Because migration is of importance theoretically, however, several of the earnings models were reestimated to include an interstate migration variable. It was not statistically significant across the several status groups, and its inclusion did not substantially modify the effects of the remaining variables. Thus, there is no basis for arguing that omission of a migration variable disturbs the conclusions we draw concerning the roles of the local labor market characteristics.

Table 3.7

Replication of Previous Analysis (Parcel, 1979)^a

| | Male heads | | | |
| | Whites | | Blacks | |
Independent variables	Dev.	$b*$	Dev.	$b*$
Education (years)				
0–7	−3646.3	−−	−143.3	−−
8	−2095.3	.042	−563.5	−.023
9–11	−1735.4	.070	−509.9	−.031
12	−609.0	.152	756.8	.087
13–15	131.6***	.146	−1313.7***	−.079
≥16	2877.8	.302	1267.7	.079
Weeks worked				
0–26	−4837.9	−−	−5973.3	−−
27–39	−2798.5	.047	−2061.3	.245
40–47	625.3	.248	283.0	.490
48–49	1040.9***	.284	169.6***	.560
50–52	−555.1	.223	343.5	.658
	b	$b*$	b	$b*$
Experience	98.8***	.115	54.3***	.130
Occupation	100.6***	.253	77.7	.334
Segregation	−193.3	−.132	46.6	.050
Percentage black population	111.3***	.109	−62.4***	−.151
Unemployment	−33.1***	−.006	−67.8***	−.020
Wage per man-hour	1316.3	.109	1768.1	.310
Constant	9433		−9353	
$R^2/\bar{R}^2$	.249/.243		.390/.377	
	N = 1870		N = 768	

urban areas, there exists a high proportion of missing data for blacks and an even higher proportion for whites. To address this, for the four heads of household status groups, the equation in Table 3.7 was reestimated to include only those cases for which segregation was measured. In most cases, returns to experience and occupation were approximately equal to those reported in the table, although among white male heads, returns to experience doubled in this analysis. For both groups of whites returns to years of schooling were increased in this specification whereas for black male heads they were decreased. Returns to weeks worked were similar to those re-

Table 3.7 *(continued)*

Independent variables	Female heads			
	Whites		Blacks	
	Dev.	$b*$	Dev.	$b*$
Education (years)				
0-7	-2190.8	—	-1437.7	--
8	-2249.4	-.003	-1017.6	.030
9-11	-1485.3	.065	77.7	.219
12	-218.9	.239	32.6	.220
13-15	387.3_{***}	.237	-554.8_{***}	.087
$\geq$16	2087.9	.425	3812.0	.383
Weeks worked				
0-26	-5153.3	--	-1210.1	--
27-39	-633.3	.364	-1616.2	-.043
40-47	540.7	.595	-451.4	.103
48-49	547.1_{***}	.658	1893.5_{***}	.433
50-52	-98.5	.566	-509.6	.100
	b	$b*$	b	$b*$
Experience	95.9^{***}_{***}	.264	64.7^{***}_{***}	.208
Occupation	43.2	.224	61.3_{**}	.411
Segregation	-52.9	-.080	-72.2	-.127
Percentage black population	27.4_{*}	.053	-27.9_{*}	-.076
Unemployment	-269.2	-.105	-302.9	-.105
Wage per man-hour	460.9	.081	-199.5	-.045
Constant	-6		8448	
$R^2/\bar{R}^2$	.392/.360		.469/.445	
	$N = 297$		$N = 349$	

(continued)

ported in Table 3.7 except among black males, for whom they appeared strengthened. Concerning the segregation variable itself, findings suggest that the effects reported in Table 3.7 are not substantially affected by missing data. The effect remains statistically significant, of similar magnitude, and negative among white male heads. It remains negative but is not statistically significant for black female heads, with no major changes for the remaining groups. Changes in the remaining labor market coefficients appear to be due more to reductions in the numbers of cases than changes in the process of earnings attainment, although the magnitudes of several coefficients are

Table 3.7 *(continued)*

	Wives			
	Whites		Blacks	
Independent variables	Dev.	$b*$	Dev.	$b*$
Education (years)				
0–7	−1885.2	--	−1376.3	--
8	−1334.6	.022	−1069.5	.019
9–11	−953.0	.080	−451.7	.123
12	−865.3	.130	123.0	.223
13–15	715.8***	.238	−576.6***	.081
$\geq$16	2321.4	.440	3097.0	.388
Weeks worked				
0–26	−3674.1	--	−2919.9	--
27–39	−814.8	.306	−1504.0	.168
40–47	1051.2	.474	261.8	.392
48–49	1608.0***	.576	962.0***	.534
50–52	193.5	.417	837.8	.478
	b	$b*$	b	$b*$
Experience	84.4***	.190	24.5***	.079
Occupation	33.5***	.176	64.7***	.430
Segregation	−35.1*	−.059	−93.7**	−.139
Percentage black population	12.5	.029	−10.4	−.040
Unemployment	−108.3	−.046	69.5	.035
Wage per man-hour	209.0	.040	334.9	.082
Constant	−91		5417	
$R^2/\bar{R}^2$	.419/.408		.569/.550	
	$N = 817$		$N = 356$	

[a]For definitions of Dev., b and $b*$, see footnote a to Table 3.6.

*$p < .05$, **$p < .01$, ***$p < .001$.

noticeably smaller in these models. With reference to segregation, our findings suggest that whites should have little economic incentive to favor existing patterns of residential segregation. In fact, the negative effect segregation has on white male earnings suggests that these workers may even have an earnings incentive to see reductions in residential segregation.

Among black males there is also a positive effect of manufacturing wage levels that suggests that blacks too benefit from residence in a productive export sector. In fact, blacks obtain greater returns to manufacturing productivity (wage per man-hour) than do whites, a finding that will be explored in more detail in Table 3.8. In addition, the percentage black exerts a negative effect among black males, a finding that may reflect the "crowding" into certain jobs and consequent lowering of marginal productivity and reduction of wage levels that Bergmann (1971) discusses. Again, unemployment level is not statistically significant, but neither is residential segregation. Since segregation was negative and significant for this group in the Parcel analysis, it may be that the segregation effect is cohort-specific among males.

The patterns of findings are markedly different among the PSOID female heads and wives as compared with the males, thus suggesting sex differences in local labor market effects on earnings. First, for none of these female race and status groups is earnings significantly influenced by the level of manufacturing sector productivity (wage per man-hour). It is the case, however, that female heads' earnings are negatively affected by local unemployment levels and that blacks suffer somewhat more than whites. Although neither of the effects is large, their statistical significance suggests that even among female heads with some earnings, high areal unemployment rates hurt their personal earnings even with weeks worked controlled. It may be that among these workers, reductions in the number of hours worked per week contribute to this relationship. We note, however, that wives' earnings are not similarly handicapped. Black female heads and wives of both races are negatively affected by residential segregation. For blacks the effects are of modest size, and among white wives the effects are small—much smaller than the effect for white male heads. In addition, in no case does the percentage black exercise any influence on female earnings. It may be that the processes of competition and segregation hypothesized as operative for males at the local labor market level are operative for women workers at the occupational and/ or industrial levels.

To summarize, the findings from this second equation suggest major race and sex differences in the operation of the local labor market factors. By comparing R^2 values for Tables 3.6 and 3.7 we see that the magnitude of the local labor market effects is especially large for black male heads, and in general the effects are larger for black than white employees. Such findings suggest that the characteristics of local markets are likely to be especially important to understanding earnings attainment among black males, whereas earnings levels of other status groups may be more importantly affected by other structural factors. Turning to the specific nature of the findings, male earnings are observed to be more sensitive than female earnings to the level of manufacturing productivity, and blacks generally are more affected by this factor as well. Racial competition (the percentage black) at the local labor market level affects males but not females, with white males benefiting and black males being hindered, as predicted. Residential segregation effects are more difficult to explain, however. Black females, regardless of marital status, are hindered by residence in residentially segregated local markets, although black males are not. In addition, white male heads and their wives are also hindered in these markets, although why this should occur is not clarified by theory.

Local Labor Market Economic and Social Organization Characteristics' Effects on Earnings

Table 3.8 includes the variables from Table 3.6, the five composites representing economic activity in the local labor market (manufacturing sector health and dominance; tertiary sector health, growth, and complexity) and the crowding index that represents one dimension of local labor market social organization.

Note: Preliminary analysis revealed that we could not incorporate both the urban crowding index and the urbanization index into the same analysis because of the high correlation between these two variables that resulted in tipping. Since more meaningful theoretical interpretation was possible for urban crowding, urbanization was dropped from the regression analysis. Since preliminary analysis suggested that local labor market unemployment was not important for any status group, it is not included in this specification. In addition, two other equations not presented here were estimated in which the economic organization composites and urban crowding were each added to the basic equation presented in Table 3.6. The interpretations of these models are generally compatible with those suggested in Table 3.8. However, the simultaneous inclusion of the crowding variable and the economic organization composites causes the former variable to be reduced in size. Among white males urban crowding is not significant in the model shown in Table 3.8, although in the specification that excludes the economic variables, it is positive as predicted and significant at the .001 level. Among black males, although it is significant in both specifications, it is reduced in magnitude by 43% in Table 3.8 compared with the model omitting the economic variables. These findings are compatible with those we presented in Table 3.1 indicating some degree of relationship between social and economic organization variables for whites but stronger relationships for blacks. This pattern is not replicated for women workers, since the crowding variable does not affect their earnings levels.

Concerning the magnitude of the local labor market effects, the corre-

Table 3.8

Basic Equation Plus Local Labor Market Composites[a]

Independent variables	Male heads			
	Whites		Blacks	
	Dev.	$b*$	Dev.	$b*$
Education (years)				
0–7	−3721.8	--	−295.1	--
8	−2165.3	.042	−522.6	−.013
9–11	−1609.5	.077	−590.7	−.025
12	−562.2	.159	776.6	.104
13–15	−69.6***	.141	−1130.1***	−.056
≥16	2904.2	.307	1501.4	.100
Weeks worked				
0–26	−5044.9	--	−5991.3	--
27–39	−2932.4	.048	−1987.3	.251
40–47	735.9	.263	217.5	.486
48–49	991.6***	.291	221.0***	.567
50–52	−559.4	.233	323.2	.658
	b	$b*$	b	$b*$
Experience	104.5***	.122	60.0***	.141
Occupation	101.8***	.258	72.3***	.311
Crowding	353.3	.040	−520.3***	−.173
Manufacturing dominance	−97.9	−.014	438.5**	.105
Manufacturing sector health	108.7	.022	712.1***	.299
Tertiary sector health	216.2***	.092	−16.5	−.013
Tertiary sector growth	−269.1*	−.048	−.5	.000
Tertiary sector complexity	357.2*	.053	224.7*	.061
Constant	−2234		−548	
$R^2/\bar{R}^2$	.245/.238		.402/.389	
	$N = 1870$		$N = 768$	

(continued)

Table 3.8 *(continued)*

Independent variables	Female heads			
	Whites		Blacks	
	Dev.	$b*$	Dev.	$b*$
Education (years)				
0–7	−1713.7	--	−1351.4	--
8	−1993.6	−.014	−1357.4	−.000
9–11	−1183.6	.049	167.4	.219
12	−248.9	.177	73.4	.213
13–15	356.8**	.190	−718.5***	.062
≥16	1813.6	.350	3579.8	.360
Weeks worked				
0–26	−5601.3	--	−1270.3	--
27–39	−505.0	.410	−1933.9	−.071
40–47	425.2	.629	−214.1	.143
48–49	595.7***	.716	1912.3***	.444
50–52	−54.1	.622	−575.8	.099
	b	$b*$	b	$b*$
Experience	85.6***	.236	61.3***	.197
Occupation	40.3***	.209	62.6***	.419
Crowding	−204.3	−.042	−416.1**	−.149
Manufacturing dominance	39.8	.014	−104.8	−.038
Manufacturing sector health	88.9	.037	−222.8*	−.123
Tertiary sector health	173.0*	.156	−3.7	−.004
Tertiary sector growth	324.0*	.132	67.1	.034
Tertiary sector complexity	264.5	.075	386.0**	.134
Constant	−4107		126	
$R^2/\bar{R}^2$	.410/.374		.481/.454	
	$N = 297$		$N = 349$	

Table 3.8 *(continued)*

| Independent variables | Wives | | | |
| | Whites | | Blacks | |
	Dev.	$b*$	Dev.	$b*$
Education (years)				
0–7	−1718.6	--	−997.5	--
8	−1354.2	.015	−777.5	.014
9–11	−945.2	.066	−482.2	.068
12	−816.5	.115	−48.4	.142
13–15	592.4***	.212	−682.1***	.032
≥16	2282.5	.418	3697.3	.407
Weeks worked				
0–26	−3680.6	--	−3110.3	--
27–39	−789.2	.309	−1393.4	.204
40–47	1077.6	.477	205.6	.408
48–49	1560.0***	.572	918.8***	.554
50–52	200.0	.418	921.0	.513
	b	$b*$	b	$b*$
Experience	82.7***	.186	18.4***	.059
Occupation	34.2***	.180	58.5	.388
Crowding	−2.9	−.001	−93.4	−.047
Manufacturing dominance	61.0	.021	135.3	.045
Manufacturing sector health	−32.1	−.015	−106.1	−.062
Tertiary sector health	93.1**	.095	150.4*	.168
Tertiary sector growth	−12.3	−.006	−348.2***	−.182
Tertiary sector complexity	−16.4	−.006	−337.8***	−.148
Constant	−2762		−1224	
$R^2/\bar{R}^2$	.420/.408		.606/.586	
	$N = 817$		$N = 356$	

[a] See footnote a on Table 3.6.

* $p < .05$, ** $p < .01$, *** $p < .001$.

sponding R^2 values for Tables 3.6 and 3.8 are consistent with what was found using local labor market variables as measured in Table 3.7: Local labor market conditions are somewhat more important in affecting black earnings, particularly the earnings of black male heads.

An examination of the respective coefficients shows that there is substantial race and sex variation in whether workers' earnings levels are influenced by specific local market economic factors and the magnitudes of these effects. It appears that only earnings of black male heads of households are influenced by manufacturing economic activity once tertiary economic variables and crowding are controlled. In particular, it is black male heads' earnings that are strongly responsive to the economic productivity of the manufacturing sector, with additional financial benefits accruing to these workers who live in local markets where manufacturing activity is proportionally dominant.[4] It is the tertiary sector variables that influence earnings for the remaining status groups. For white male heads there are positive returns to economic productivity of the tertiary sector, as well as to the complexity of this sector. Such findings may reflect the opportunities for high-paying jobs that white males find in the retail, wholesale, and service sectors, whereas high-earnings jobs for black males may be more plentiful in manufacturing. Black males, however, obtain small positive returns to tertiary sector complexity as well as strong returns to manufacturing variables.

The economic productivity of the tertiary sector also contributes positively to the earnings attainment for women workers. White female heads and wives of both races demonstrate statistically significant positive effects, with white female heads evidencing the strongest effects. Growth of the tertiary sector also appears to help white female heads, possibly in increasing the sheer number of job opportunities, but it does not *positively* influence the earnings levels of anyone else. In contrast, among white male heads and black wives the net effect of tertiary growth is negative. Among black wives this finding may reflect the fact that the types of jobs within the tertiary sector that are created by growth and that are open to black women may be low-paying. Thus, net of the general economic productivity of the sector, this growth may hinder earnings attainment for this group. The same factor is also negative for white males. Here again, once tertiary sector productivity and complexity are controlled, it may be that growth of the sector negatively influences earnings, possibly through the type of jobs that some white males obtain due to this growth.

---

[4]We also see that the manufacturing productivity factor is statistically significant and negative for black female heads. It is likely that the relationship $(-.442)$ between manufacturing productivity and urban crowding has led to this outcome; manufacturing productivity was not significant in the equation that excludes urban crowding. This problem does not appear in the remaining files.

The effects of tertiary sector complexity also vary by status group. Black male and female heads obtain positive returns to this factor, but among black wives the effect is negative. Since the signs of these coefficients are consistent with the signs of the zero-order correlations, a substantive (as opposed to statistical "tipping") explanation is appropriate. Among black female heads the tertiary complexity variable is the only economic organization variable that is statistically significant. Black female heads may be able to obtain positions in tertiary firms that involve supervision of others and generally enough responsibility to warrant reasonable levels of pay. Black wives, in contrast, may be more likely to occupy menial positions involving little initiative and responsibility. Thus the process of occupational and authority differentiation that accompanies an increase in the complexity of this sector may influence black women very differently. For those women who can take advantage of this differentiation, benefits accrue. For others, such differentiation may actually result in their obtaining jobs inferior to those that would be obtained in a labor market with a less complex tertiary sector. White women are not affected by this complexity either positively or negatively. Again we suggest that there may be dimensions of occupational or industrial differentiation that the Duncan SEI does not capture. The tenability of this explanation is evaluated in Chapters 4 and 5.

Table 3.8 also shows that both male and female black heads are disadvantaged by urban crowding, although among wives, neither black nor white earnings is influenced by crowding. It is unclear why there should be a sex differential in the magnitudes of the effects of this factor, although a similar finding was observed in analysis of the percentage black in Table 3.7; the effect among black males is over four times that for their wives. It may be that the concentration of black males in urban areas, operating through a residential segregation mechanism, prevents them from obtaining "good jobs" that go to benefit whites and thus "crowds" blacks into "bad jobs," thus lowering their marginal productivity and hence their earnings (see Bergmann, 1971, and Snyder and Hudis, 1976, for discussions of the crowding hypothesis and for findings concerning its effects on earnings). Wives may be less affected by this since there is less racial variation in the types of jobs they obtain than in the types of jobs male heads obtain.

Finally, for all status groups the influence of the human capital variables is only slightly reduced when the local labor market characteristics are included (compare Table 3.6 with Tables 3.7 and 3.8). From this and the examination of the R^2 values across status groups for the three equations we conclude that: (a) the human capital and local labor market characteristics essentially operate independently of each other in their influence on earnings; and (b) with the exception of black males, the human capital variables are substantially more important in explaining labor earnings than are the local labor market characteristics. We have not investigated the notion that the human capital variables interact with the labor market characteristics in their influence on earnings, but this possibility will be assessed in Chapter 7.

To summarize, among whites, males' tertiary sector characteristics predict earnings, whereas among black males manufacturing variables and urban crowding are more important. Female heads and wives also evidence effects due to tertiary sector variables, although among women workers only black female heads evidence additional (negative) effects of urban crowding. It appears, then, that local labor market economic organization has a greater effect upon workers' earnings than does social organization, although the nature and magnitude of these effects vary by race and sex.

Regression Standardization

Two types of issues have been raised in our discussion so far. First, when various local labor market variables have demonstrated statistically significant effects on labor earnings, we offered interpretations of these findings in terms of the theories reviewed in Chapter 1. At times these interpretations have involved labor market characteristics other than those referring to *local* labor markets. For example, we suggested that tertiary sector effects among female workers described in Table 3.8 could reflect the types of jobs women could obtain there. Such reasoning suggests that incorporation of these job characteristics could "explain" the local labor market effects, thus reducing the magnitude of their coefficients and changing patterns of statistical significance. This question will be addressed in Chapters 4 and 5 in which we introduce industrial (economic sector) and occupational determinants of labor earnings and simultaneously control for the local labor market factors discussed in this chapter. Such analysis will enable us to ascertain whether industrial sectors and occupational labor markets at least partially tap sources of variation largely independent of local markets.

The second issue raised concerns the magnitude of the regression coefficients presented in Tables 3.6 through 3.8. For earnings functions we are accustomed to interpreting regression coefficients in terms of a single unit change in the independent variable being associated with a specific dollar change in earnings. However, the validity of this interpretation must be questioned for several of the coefficients presented earlier. We have already suggested that some coefficients may be artificially inflated, not due to multicollinearity, but to interdependence of access and returns to resources; if this is the case, then it is inappropriate to conclude that if blacks' levels of access to resources increased their returns to these resources would be unchanged. These returns could decrease, thus potentially "balancing out" the increased access and resulting in no net gains in earnings.

To investigate this problem we use regression standardization to decompose the earnings differences between pairs of status groups. Use of standardization techniques for the study of race and sex outcome differences is not new (see O. Duncan, 1969; Coleman, Blum, Sorensen, and Rossi, 1972; Blum, 1971; Blinder, 1973; R. Hall and Kasten, 1973; Suter and Miller, 1973; Siegel, 1965; and see Althauser and Wigler, 1972, for a review). More recently, however, Iams and Thornton (1975) have indicated that under certain conditions, estimates derived from several of the previously utilized procedures may be misleading. Their arguments suggest that failure to separate out an interaction component from the remaining terms may lead to erroneous inferences. In this analysis we adopt their procedure and decompose the equation in Table 3.8 into several components as follows:

$$\bar{Y}_1 - \bar{Y}_2 = (b_{0_1} - b_{0_2}) + \Sigma \bar{X}_{i_2}(b_{i_1} - b_{i_2}) + \Sigma b_{i_2}(\bar{X}_{i_1} - \bar{X}_{i_2})$$
$$+ \Sigma(\bar{X}_{i_1} - \bar{X}_{i_2})(b_{i_1} - b_{i_2}).[5]$$

Such a decomposition will allow us to separate out changes in status group earnings differences due to (a) the difference in intercepts; (b) the difference in slopes; (c) the difference in levels of resources; and (d) an interaction term, interpreted as the effect of jointly changing both means and regression coefficients over the effects of changing them one at a time (Iams and Thornton, 1975:344).[6]

As has been discussed by Winsborough and Dickinson (1971), one must be especially cautious in interpreting the efficacy (slopes) and intercept components. In particular, if the independent variables do not have meaningful zero points, then it is inappropriate to separate these two components (see also Althauser and Wigler, 1972, for discussion regarding the interpretation of regression standardization results). Instead, the sum of the two may be viewed as that part of the earnings gap due to differences in how the two status groups translate the resources (independent variables) into earnings. This component also is often referred to as the "discrimination" component. For any particular resource variable, the magnitude of the efficacy component will not be meaningful, but the sign will be, assuming that the coefficients involved are statistically significant. Although this is not uniformly true, we do not anticipate that our inferences will be systematically biased for this reason. If the slopes component is positive, that indicates that the status group with the higher earnings receives the higher earnings, in part, because the slope for the resource is larger for the higher earnings group. A

[5]$\bar{Y}$ is mean earnings; 1 is the first group; 2 is the second group; b_0 is the Y-intercept; $\bar{X}_i$ is the mean of the ith resource; and b_i is the partial slope of the ith resource.

[6]The notion of "joint" or simultaneous change in means and regression coefficients can also be viewed as the additional amount of the $\bar{Y}$ gap that could be closed as the differences in average resources are eliminated once efficacy is equalized. Since it is generally problematic to infer changes over time from cross-sectional data, inferences of this type should be made cautiously.

negative efficacy component for a variable would signify that this variable actually operates to reduce the gap.[7] In this analysis we combine the slopes and intercepts components.

We argue that these data have policy implications because they identify the relevant variables and what it is about these variables that produce the earnings differences. Of particular interest are those indicators representing features of local labor market social and economic organization. It is appropriate to view them as ecological resources, analogous to personal resources, which may facilitate earnings attainment. However, given that there are negative signs associated with several of the indicators for certain status groups, these factors may be operating as mechanisms of race and/or sex discrimination, as opposed to resources to facilitate earnings attainment. It is important to recognize, however, that the data do not indicate the policy decisions that should be made. For example, findings that black males have lower education means (composition component) and that the returns to education (slope) are lower for black men than white men would allow numerous policy decisions. Some of these are (a) to increase the education level of blacks; (b) to decrease the education of whites; (c) to do both a and b; (d) to increase the efficacy of education for blacks; (e) to decrease the efficacy for whites; (f) to do both d and e; and (g) to implement various combinations of a–c with d–f. Not only are such decisions difficult to make from an ethical standpoint, but the practicality and the "costs" of each are not clearly understood. For these reasons, suggestions will not be offered concerning what specific policy actions should be taken.[8]

To investigate these issues three pairs of equations are decomposed that compare white male heads to black male heads, to white female heads, and to black female heads, respectively.[9] We wish to know how changes in the

---

[7]A number of the composites used to measure the labor market characteristics are sums of Z-scores and thus have ranges of values from negative to positive. These variables have been transformed by adding a constant to all scores so that all values are positive. This facilitates interpretation as just discussed but also serves to reiterate our point about the arbitrariness of the zero point for these variables.

[8]A lengthy discussion of these issues is found in the so-called Coleman Report (Coleman et al., 1966) and the reviews and rejoinders associated with it (Bowles and Levin, 1968a, 1968b; Coleman, 1968; G. Cain and Watts, 1968). Althauser, Spivak and Amsel (1975) also provide comments on these issues.

[9]Given the six subgroups in this analysis there are 15 possible comparisons that could be presented. We have chosen to compare three groups of economic minorities with workers in the economic majority (i.e., with white males). Inferences concerning how given changes in the allocation of resources would affect the several groups of workers are easier to make if each is compared with the same standard, and the choice of white males as that standard is a logical one. Inspection of summary percentages comparable to those reported in Table 3.9 for the remaining comparisons reveals general similarities across race and sex comparisons. Thus our choices of the three remaining heads of household groups do not appear misleading. We

Table 3.9

Summary of Regression Standardization Components

Pair and variables	Composition	Slopes and intercepts	Interaction
White male heads versus black male heads			
(1) Human capital	40.8%	27.4%	31.8%
	($2012)	($1346)	($1564)
(2) Human capital and	43.6%	46.6%	9.8%
local labor market	($2146)	($2296)	($481)
Initial gap: $14,404 - 9,481 = $4,923			
White male heads versus white female heads			
(1) Human capital	8.1%	88.6%	3.3%
	($564)	($6190)	($233)
(2) Human capital and	5.4%	91.6%	3.0%
local labor market	($375)	($6400)	($212)
Initial gap: $14,404 - 7,416 = $6,988			
White male heads versus black female heads			
(1) Human capital	21.7%	62.9%	15.4%
	($1931)	($5599)	($1371)
(2) Human capital and	18.6%	61.4%	20.0%
local labor market	($1657)	($5461)	($1783)
Initial gap: $14,404 - 5,502 = $8,902			

distribution of resources or in the efficacy of resources between the pairs of groups would influence their earnings differences. The findings presented in Table 3.9 summarize the results of the decomposition of these three sets of equations. For each equation the composition component refers to the difference in mean levels of resources; the slopes plus intercepts' components refers to the difference in slopes or in efficacy plus difference in constants; the interaction component refers to the effect of jointly changing both levels and efficacy over the effects of changing them one at a time. For each pair of equations, two decompositions are summarized. The first is based on Table 3.6 (what we have called the basic equation), and the second is based on Table 3.8, which includes the local labor market composites plus the human

recognize, however, that the similarities in the summary percentages may mask differences in the operation of specific variables across comparisons. Thus we will generalize very cautiously from the cross-race, cross-sex, and race-by-sex comparisons we present here to comparisons involving other status groups.

capital and status attainment variables. Use of this stepwise strategy allows the results of each decomposition to serve as a baseline for the next.

In comparing white and black male heads using the basic equation, differences in access to resources account for 40.8% of the original earnings gap ($2012), whereas only 27.4% of that gap ($1346) can be attributed to differences in returns to resources plus the intercept difference. This finding suggests that racial differences in access to human capital resources are more important for explaining earnings differences among males than are differential returns to these resources (plus the difference in constant terms). In addition, a sizeable positive interaction term (31.8%) suggests that jointly changing access to and efficacy of human capital resources would have associated with it an additional positive earnings boost ($1564) for blacks.

Interpretation of these findings changes, however, when the local labor market characteristics are introduced (see summary of second equation). In this case the changes in the black–white male earnings difference attributable to composition (43.6%) and to slopes and intercepts (46.6%) are approximately equal, and the interaction component is still positive but much smaller (9.8%) than in the first specification. In tracing the source of this change in findings, the contribution of each variable to the summary decomposition presented in the Table 3.9 second specification, was examined (data not presented). The data suggest that black males would benefit from equalization of returns to such resources as years of schooling, work experience, and job status, as well as tertiary sector productivity and urban crowding.[10] They would not benefit from equalization in the efficacy of resources such as weeks worked, manufacturing sector productivity, or manufacturing sector dominance.

Concerning access to resources, blacks would benefit substantially from access to higher-status jobs and could also derive a nontrivial positive bonus if changes in the slopes of and access to the job status resource occurred simultaneously. Although they would apparently benefit from equalization of resources captured by urban crowding, the sizeable negative interaction term associated with this variable suggests that if changes in efficacy and access were made simultaneously, the net impact of these changes, although still positive, would be relatively small. In addition, the full decomposition suggests a substantial positive bonus if efficacy of and access to educational resources were also changed simultaneously. Again, inferences derived from this full decomposition should be interpreted cautiously due to the slopes and intercepts issue previously noted.

---

[10]Throughout this analysis we should be cautious in interpreting a decomposition where the variable is significant for one status group but not for the other. Clearly, when the terms are significant for neither group, no interpretation is warranted.

Turning to the cross-sex comparison between white male and white female heads and the sex–race comparison between white male heads and black female heads, two key differences are observed in comparing these findings with those for the racial earnings difference just discussed. First, introduction of the local labor market characteristics produces smaller net changes in the summary percentages for these comparisons than for the race comparison. In both cases the changes are practically zero. The second major difference observed when the sex and sex–race comparisons are contrasted with the race comparison is the proportion of the earnings difference attributed to the composition and the slopes and intercepts components. For these women workers differences in returns to resources are far more important than differences in access to resources, whereas in the racial comparison we found these components to be approximately equally important. This is particularly true for the white male heads–white female heads comparison, where 91.6% of the earnings gap in the second specification is attributed to slopes and intercepts.

The race and sex comparison shows a pattern intermediate between the race and sex comparisons we have included. In the second specification, 61% of the earnings gap is attributed to slopes and intercept differences, whereas 18.6% is attributed to composition and 20.0% to the interaction component. Thus, when compared with white male heads, both white and black female heads would benefit substantially from equalization with these males in the translation of given resources into earnings, although the degree of benefit would favor whites. Blacks are more affected by their lack of access to resources, although the degree of difference (18.6%) does not approach that indicated in the white male–black male comparison (43.6%). Black female heads could also expect a more sizeable positive interaction effect from the simultaneous changes of composition and slopes and intercepts than is suggested for the other economic minorities.

The similarities in the summary percentages for the two sex difference comparisons mask differences in the operation of specific variables (data not presented). Although both black and white female heads would benefit from increased efficacy of occupational status, urban crowding, experience, and years of schooling, white female heads would benefit from increases in the efficacy of tertiary sector complexity, and black female heads would not. In contrast, black female heads would benefit from increased efficacy of weeks worked and manufacturing and tertiary sector productivity, and whites would not. Differences in access to years of schooling, experience, and job status contribute importantly to the compositional component difference present in the race and sex comparison, whereas these same variables plus tertiary sector growth contribute to the sizeable (20.0%) interaction term.

In general, these three decompositions reveal that the mechanisms through which the respective status groups attain earnings are race- and sex-specific. Black males would benefit approximately equally given equalization with white males in the efficacy (slopes) of and access to resources, whereas female heads, particularly whites, would benefit more from equalization in the efficacy (slopes) of resources than from equalization in access to these resources. Like O. Duncan's (1968), these findings suggest that compensatory programs designed to promote equalization of resources between black and white males could reduce their earnings gap by 44%, whereas comparable programs aimed at promoting equalization of resources between white males and white females or between white males and black female heads would have a much smaller impact. Sex differences in earnings, then, appear to be substantially a function of forms of discrimination not directly connected to lack of access to the resources studied here. Therefore, we infer that reduction of the earnings gaps by sex would require major changes in the operation of the social structures involved. Since women fail to obtain the returns to relevant resources that men obtain, policy must look to changing the mechanisms that prevent women from enjoying the benefits in earnings that men with comparable economic resources enjoy.

Although we have cautioned against viewing "supply" and "demand" explanations as a simple dichotomy, such a distinction is useful here. A central version of the supply arguments suggests that earnings differences are attributable to differing levels of personal resources—education, work experience, family background, weeks worked, and job status. Therefore, reduction or elimination of earnings differences markedly depends on reduction or elimination of gaps in access to resources. For this reason the supply arguments appear much more successful in explaining race differences in earnings than explaining sex differences. Even for the difference in black and white male earnings, the supply argument can only account for 44% of the gap. In contrast, a central version of the demand argument suggests that regardless of levels of resources, differential operation of these resources by ascribed status is evidence for differential demand for labor by ascribed status. This demand argument appears to explain sex differences in earnings much more successfully than the supply perspective. For women, unequal access to resources as compared with men is simply not an important explanation of sex-based earnings inequality.[11]

One must recognize, however, that these summary statements mask differences in how changes in the efficacy of and access to specific resources

[11]This usage of "supply" and "demand" is somewhat inconsistent with our usage of supply and demand to refer to "types" of variables. In this second usage supply variables are personal characteristics whereas local, industrial, and occupational labor market characteristics are demand variables. Still, it is useful to connect the results of the regression standardizations to these more general concepts.

would operate by status group (data not presented). Although all three status groups would benefit from equalization in returns to (or efficacy of) years of schooling with white male heads, only black female heads would benefit from equalized efficacy for weeks worked. Both black male heads and white female heads would lose economically should this occur. All groups would benefit from equalization with white males in efficacy of occupational status, but white female heads would not benefit from equalization of access to job status, and black female heads would so benefit. Black male heads would appear to benefit *more* from equalization in access to job status than from equalization in its effectiveness as an income producing resource. Both black groups would benefit from equalization in efficacy of tertiary sector productivity, but black females would gain from equalization in the efficacy of manufacturing sector productivity, and black males would lose. The women workers would lose from equalization of the efficacy of tertiary sector growth, whereas black males' earnings would be essentially unaffected. These findings underscore the fact that despite some similarities in the disadvantages experienced by these three economic minority groups, implementation of some policies would differentially benefit some workers depending on ascribed status. The degree of benefit from policies aimed at promoting racial equality would vary by sex, whereas the degree of benefit from policies aimed at promoting sex equality would vary by race.

Summary and Conclusions

This chapter has addressed questions concerning the impact of local labor market characteristics on workers' earnings. A general concern involved the issue of external validity: Were the findings produced by Parcel (1979) for black and white males replicable for female workers? Although we found a general replication of those findings for the wider age range of respondents studied here, we also found that several of the labor market effects were sex-specific. In particular, manufacturing sector productivity affected earnings for none of the female race–status groups we studied. We also observed that women workers' earnings were unaffected by local labor market racial crowding, whereas white males' earnings benefited and blacks' earnings suffered as predicted.

Inclusion of the local labor market composites representing manufacturing sector health and dominance, tertiary sector health, growth, and complexity, and urban crowding in the basic equation predicting earnings provided generally compatible evidence. Black males' earnings were importantly affected by manufacturing sector characteristics, a finding compatible with our hypothesis. Women workers' and white males' earnings were more substantially influenced by tertiary sector characteristics. Although these latter findings are compatible with our expectations for women workers, we did not predict that white males' earnings would also be noticeably affected by these characteristics. These findings suggest that the distribution of employment across industries materially affects the extent of influence of particular types of market characteristics, an idea noted by Bluestone *et al.* (1973).

The pattern of results suggests several major conclusions. In general, local labor market characteristics appear to be most important in the earnings attainment process of black males. This is particularly true for the manufacturing sector characteristics, which supports ideas by Franklin (1968) and others concerning the importance of the manufacturing sector in influencing blacks' wages. However, we see that the magnitude of this influence does not extend to black women. This discrepancy represents one major sex difference in the operation of local labor market effects on workers' earnings. These findings also help to place in perspective the role of intraarea wage roll-out effects as discussed by Thompson (1965) in that once other local labor market characteristics are controlled, these roll-out effects are important only for black male workers. We recognize that previous analysis has suggested that the economic productivity of the manufacturing sector has direct effects on tertiary sector productivity (Parcel, 1981), thus suggesting the importance of *indirect* effects on workers' earnings even when direct effects are absent or weak. However, evidence concerning direct effects of manufacturing sector characteristics points to much stronger relationships for black males than remaining workers.

In addition, we have found that racial crowding at the local labor market level affects earnings only for black males. Based on this finding, we conclude that theory suggested by Blalock (1967) and others concerning the importance of racial competition may be limited in its applicability, assuming market economic characteristics are controlled. We have also found that human capital and socialization variables are important predictors of earnings even when controls for local market characteristics are introduced. Thus we conclude that despite criticisms of these perspectives as inadequate to explaining individual earnings attainment, our findings thus far do not support the notion that these theories are of minor importance to understanding economic inequality. In fact, for several groups of women workers the personal variables are major predictors of earnings.

Each of these conclusions will be reevaluated as we continue to incorporate economic sector and occupational labor market characteristics into our models in succeeding chapters. Thus these conclusions must be viewed as tentative. In addition, conclusions regarding the findings from the regression standardization must also be viewed as tentative. It appears at this stage that race and sex discrimination differ in major ways. Race discrimination appears to be a function both of differential access and differential efficacy of resources, whereas sex discrimination appears to be more substantially affected by differential efficacy than by distribution of income-producing resources. We will continue to evaluate this conclusion as the analysis proceeds.

CHAPTER 4

Economic Sector and Dual Labor Market Characteristics' Effects on Earnings

Review of Theory and Hypotheses

It is useful to review the theories outlined in Chapter 1 concerning economic sectors and the dual labor market, since it is from these theories that hypotheses are derived concerning the effects of sector and market characteristics on workers' earnings. We have previously suggested that the economic sector perspective posits a U. S. economy divided into distinct sectors. One is the core, composed of a few firms that tend to be large, oligopolistic, profitable, capital-intensive, and vertically integrated. The other is the periphery, composed of many smaller firms that tend to be less profitable, more locally oriented, more labor-intensive, and not vertically integrated. In addition, dual labor market theory posits a dichotomized U. S. occupational structure. The primary labor market is characterized by jobs with at least moderately long job ladders, variety in work, good working conditions, and stable employment experience. They pay well, and workers who obtain such positions must possess educational credentials and/or specific work skills. The secondary labor market is characterized by jobs with no chances for advancement, routinized work, poor working conditions, and unstable work experience. Pay is poor, and those occupying such positions are likely to have fewer educational credentials and job skills than workers in the primary market.

Although our analytic strategy does not assume that the economy or the labor market is necessarily divided into a finite number of discrete segments, we hypothesize that the characteristics underlying the sector and market differentiation specified by the theory *are* relevant to the earnings attainment processes of individual workers. That is, characteristics associated with the core, such as profitability, oligopoly power, capital intensity, and large firm size, are expected to be positively associated with earnings. Similarly, characteristics associated with the primary labor market, such as good working conditions, stability in employment experience, and presence of job ladders and skilled work are also expected to be positively associated with earnings. Indicators of economic differentiation derived from a factor analysis include measures of industrial profits, concentration, and firm growth; a similar factor analysis produced indicators of worker outcome characteristics such as work duration, benefits, and sex discrimination. With the exception of the sex discrimination measure, relationships between these industrial characteristics and workers' earnings are expected to be positive.

Also of interest are potential race and sex differences in the magnitudes of these expected relationships. On the basis of dualist theory, which argues that blacks and women have reduced access to favorable positions in the primary labor market and are excluded from certain jobs in core industries, we expect that white males should obtain larger returns to these characteristics than would the other status groups. This idea also is evaluated in Chapter 5 when measures of additional characteristics differentiating primary from secondary labor market jobs are incorporated.

As in our analysis of local labor market effects on earnings, several types of data are presented. We begin by describing the distributions of workers to industries, the configurations of industrial labor market resources with which each status group is faced, and the levels of industrial resources to which each group has access. These descriptive data are useful for portraying patterns of industrial segregation by race and sex and for demonstrating what implications industrial segregation has for the distribution of industrial resources across status groups. Zero-order correlation matrices of the industrial characteristics by status group are of particular interest. Inspection of these data will suggest the extent to which there is overlap between characteristics associated with the core sector and primary labor market positions. Although theory has suggested there should be substantial overlap, past empirical evaluations have yielded equivocal results. Our analytic data are focused on portraying the impact of industrial resources on workers' earnings. After indicating how these relationships vary across the several status groups, we present a cumulative model that includes both industrial and local labor market variables in addition to the individual-level characteristics included in all our models. Finally, the issue of deriving policy implications from the analysis is pursued by indicating how changes in the distribution and efficacy of the industrial and/or local labor market resources would affect race–sex differences in earnings.

Industrial Labor Market Characteristics

RACE AND SEX INDUSTRIAL SEGREGATION

The first type of analysis undertaken is descriptive. Table 4.1 presents a frequency distribution of the respondents by industry across the six status groups. For each group where the percentage of workers in an industry is equal to or greater than 5.0, the percentage is italicized.[1] One major pattern is evident. Whereas there are some racial differences in the distribution of workers across industries, the more extreme differences in distribution are by sex. From this we infer that industrial segregation is more pronounced by sex than by race. Looking at the respective status groups, among white males there is a diversified distribution such that the highest proportion of white male workers is employed in construction. Even in this industry the percentage is not especially high, 10.2. An additional 8.9% are employed in retail trade, and 7.8%, 6.1%, and 5.9% are employed in machinery manufacturing, government, and educational services, respectively. The distribution of black male heads is also fairly diversified. For this group the highest concentration of workers is in government employment (9.3%), with the construction and transportation industries claiming 8.2% each. Motor vehicle manufacturing accounts for 7.4% of employment, and educational services account for 7.3%. In general, the males have access to employment in durable goods manufacturing industries (whites in machinery, blacks in motor vehicles and metals) but are not prominent in the nondurable manufacturing positions. They also have access to employment in construction and transportation.

The employment patterns among females are quite different from those among males. Over 50% of white female heads are employed in three industries: retail trade, medical and dental services, and educational services. White female heads are not strongly represented in any of the manufacturing industries, durable or nondurable. Modest percentages of these workers are concentrated in personal services (6.0); finance, insurance, and real estate (5.4); and government (5.3). Together these six industries account for 68.1% of the white female head work force. Thus among white female heads there is a less diversified industrial distribution than among male workers. White wives display a similar degree of concentration in a few industries. Over 46% of white wives are employed in retail trade, medical and dental services, and

---

[1]In some cells in Table 4.1 the frequency of cases is reported as zero whereas the percentage is reported as .1. This discrepancy arises because of rounding error and the SPSS weighting schemes used to provide representative samples of workers. Variation in the percentages associated with a single frequency within a status group is also caused by weighting and rounding requirements (see black male heads, mining versus tobacco workers).

Table 4.1

Frequency and Percentage of Respondents Across Industry Groups by Status Group[a]

| | Male heads | | | |
| | Whites | | Blacks | |
Industry group[b]	N	%	N	%
Agriculture, forestry, & fishing	105	5.6	28	3.7
Mining & extraction	16	.9	1	.2
Metal industries	74	3.9	47	6.2
Machinery	145	7.8	34	4.4
Motor vehicles	88	4.7	57	7.4
Other durables	85	4.5	38	4.9
Durables, NA	--	--	--	--
Food & kindred	48	2.6	15	2.0
Tobacco	3	.2	1	.1
Textile & apparel	27	1.4	17	2.3
Paper & allied	9	.5	3	.4
Chemical, rubber products	58	3.1	18	2.4
Other nondurables	3	.1	1	.1
Nondurables, NA	3	.2	--	--
Manufacturing NA durable or nondurable	5	.3	7	.9
Construction	190	10.2	63	8.2
Transportation	93	5.0	63	8.2
Communication	25	1.3	9	1.2
Other public utilities	43	2.3	19	2.4
Retail trade	166	8.9	52	6.7
Wholesale trade	69	3.7	18	2.3
Trade, NA retail or wholesale	21	1.1	5	.6
Finance, insurance & real estate	85	4.5	20	2.6
Repair service	60	3.2	25	3.3
Business services	27	1.4	17	2.3
Personal services	18	1.0	27	3.6
Amusement & recreation	13	.7	2	.2
Printing & publishing	38	2.0	8	1.0
Medical & dental services	41	2.2	13	1.8
Educational services	110	5.9	56	7.3
Other professional services	54	2.9	10	1.3
Armed services	8	.4	2	.2
Government	115	6.1	72	9.3
NA, DK	25	1.3	19	2.5
Total	1870	100.0	769	100.0

(continued)

Table 4.1 *(continued)*

| Industry group[b] | Female heads | | | |
| | Whites | | Blacks | |
	N	%	N	%
Agriculture, forestry, & fishing	--	--	2	.5
Mining & extraction	--	--	--	--
Metal industries	8	2.8	1	.3
Machinery	13	4.5	19	*5.4*
Motor vehicles	6	2.0	5	1.3
Other durables	5	1.8	1	.2
Durables, NA	--	--	0	.1
Food & kindred	1	.4	7	2.1
Tobacco	--	--	7	2.1
Textile & apparel	5	1.7	18	*5.3*
Paper & allied	2	.7	--	--
Chemical, rubber products	6	2.1	3	.9
Other nondurables	--	--	1	.2
Nondurables, NA	--	--	--	--
Manufacturing NA durable or nondurable	1	.4	--	--
Construction	2	.7	--	--
Transportation	0	.1	0	.1
Communication	8	2.8	9	2.5
Other public utilities	--	--	--	--
Retail trade	52	*17.4*	31	*8.9*
Wholesale trade	4	1.5	0	.1
Trade, NA retail or wholesale	2	.8	--	--
Finance, insurance & real estate	16	*5.4*	19	*5.4*
Repair service	--	--	0	.1
Business services	6	2.1	3	.7
Personal services	18	*6.0*	51	*14.6*
Amusement & recreation	3	1.0	0	.1
Printing & publishing	6	2.0	1	.3
Medical & dental services	48	*16.0*	63	*18.0*
Educational services	53	*18.0*	62	*17.9*
Other professional services	13	4.3	14	4.0
Armed services	--	--	--	--
Government	16	*5.3*	30	*8.5*
NA, DK	1	.4	2	.5
Total	297	100.0	349	100.0

Table 4.1 *(continued)*

Industry group[b]	Wives			
	Whites		Blacks	
	N	%	N	%
Agriculture, forestry & fishing	4	.5	--	--
Mining & extraction	1	.1	--	--
Metal industries	4	.4	0	.1
Machinery	36	4.4	1	.2
Motor vehicles	8	1.0	7	2.1
Other durables	10	1.2	4	1.0
Durables, NA	--	--	--	--
Food & kindred	9	1.1	6	1.8
Tobacco	1	.2	1	.2
Textile & apparel	40	4.9	32	*9.0*
Paper & allied	3	.4	2	.4
Chemical, rubber products	12	1.5	7	1.9
Other nondurables	1	.1	--	--
Nondurables, NA	--	--	1	.3
Manufacturing NA durable or nondurable	2	.2	1	.2
Construction	14	1.7	--	--
Transportation	9	1.1	--	--
Communication	19	2.3	6	1.8
Other public utilities	4	.4	1	.2
Retail trade	117	*14.3*	19	*5.2*
Wholesale trade	15	1.8	7	2.0
Trade, NA retail or wholesale	3	.4	0	.1
Finance, insurance & real estate	51	*6.3*	39	*10.9*
Repair service	3	.3	0	.1
Business services	20	2.5	0	.1
Personal services	56	*6.9*	57	*15.9*
Amusement & recreation	5	.6	--	--
Printing & publishing	14	1.7	6	1.8
Medical & dental services	106	*13.0*	66	*18.5*
Educational services	160	*19.5*	64	*18.0*
Other professional services	40	4.9	14	3.9
Armed services	--	--	1	.2
Government	43	*5.3*	14	3.8
NA, DK	7	.9	2	.6
Total	817	100.0	356	100.0

[a]The percentage is italicized when the number of workers in an industry is equal to or greater than 5.0% of the total.

[b]NA means not ascertained; DK means don't know.

educational services. Again, modest percentages of these workers are located in personal services (6.9); finance, insurance, and real estate (6.3), and government (5.3). Taken together, 65.3% of white wives are employed in these six industries.

Black female workers evidence similar patterns. Over 50% of black female heads are employed in three industry groups: medical and dental services, educational services, and personal services. Additional concentrations of workers are found in retail trade (8.9%); government (8.5%); finance, insurance, and real estate (5.4%); machinery manufacturing (5.4%); and textiles and apparel (5.3%). Together these industries employ 84% of the black female heads in our sample. Among black wives we see 10.9% in finance, insurance, and real estate; 9.0% in textiles and apparels; 5.2% in retail trade; with over 50% in medical and dental services, educational services, and personal services. Together these six industries account for 77.5% of black wives' employment.

In sum, black female workers are even more severely grouped into a few industrial groupings than are white female workers, who are more segregated than male workers. The racial differences in the distributions are somewhat more noticeable among women than among men. Although both black and white women are heavily concentrated in medical and dental services and educational services, black women are more concentrated in personal services than whites, and whites are more concentrated in retail trade than blacks. Concerning sex differences, women are less concentrated in durable goods manufacturing than are men, and black women in particular are proportionately more likely to be found in the nondurable textile and apparel industries than are male workers.[2]

[2]To check on the representativeness of our sample, the distributions listed in Table 4.1 were compared with the breakdowns by race and sex provided in the 1970 Census. Although the interviews used to provide the PSOID data we use were conducted in 1975 and 1976 and the Census distributions were from 1969, the sampling frame used for the PSOID was constructed in 1968 and reweighted in 1972. Hence there are only a few years of difference between the two. Among the white males our sample shows more workers in metals, machinery, other durables, and chemicals than the Census reports, and fewer workers in retail trade. Among black males machinery, motor vehicles, and educational services are overrepresented, and retail trade is underrepresented. White female heads appear overrepresented in machinery, medical and dental and educational services; white wives show similar tendencies concerning machinery and education and are also overrepresented in textiles and underrepresented in retail trade. Black female heads appear overrepresented in machinery, textiles, medical and dental and educational services, and underrepresented in personal services. Black wives also appear overrepresented in textiles, medical and dental and educational services, and finance and underrepresented in retail trade. It appears that for many of the status groups, including both groups of males, there is overrepresentation in durable goods industries and underrepresentation in retail trade. In addition, among women there appears to be overrepresentation in medical and dental and educational services as compared with the Census distribution. It may

It is useful to interpret these findings in terms of what may be called industrial segregation. Although the notions of residential and occupational segregation have received more theoretical and empirical attention, it is apparent that there are clear sex differences in access to industrial groups. These patterns undoubtedly arise both by employer discrimination and by the aggregated "choices" of workers to seek jobs with particular firms. Knowledge of these distributions is useful in interpreting the patterns we will observe among the economic sector and dual labor market characteristics discussed later. Given the greater degree of industrial segregation among women than men, we expect the relationships among the industrial labor market characteristics (zero-order correlations) to be stronger for women than men and particularly strong for black female workers, since they are the most industrially segregated subgroup in the analysis. We now turn to analysis of how these patterns of segregation are manifested in status group differences in access to resources.

STATUS-SPECIFIC LABOR MARKET CONFIGURATIONS

The correlations among the variables representing economic sector (profitability, concentration and investment, and firm growth) and dual labor market (work duration, benefits, and sex discrimination) characteristics for each status group are presented in Tables 4.2, 4.3, and 4.4. Of interest are both status group differences in these patterns and a comparison of the patterns observed here with those discussed in Chapter 2 (Table 2.11). In the previous discussion we reported that characteristics representing economic sectors were not strongly interrelated, although there were somewhat stronger relationships among the characteristics representing worker outcomes, and relationships between sector and outcome characteristics were of the appropriate signs and often strong. In these tables we recognize that the distributions of workers across industries as shown in Table 4.1 will affect the correlations among these indicators. Looking first at the indicators representing economic sectors, two major findings are evident. First, although in Chapter 2 positive though not particularly strong relationships among these

---

be that the PSOID sampling frame did not allow representation of trends other sources (including the U. S. Census) have documented concerning the shift away from durable goods manufacturing to retail and to some services. On the other hand, it appears that medical and dental and/ or educational services are overrepresented in many of the status groups, a finding for which we have no ready explanation. In most cases, however, these differences are not very large, which suggests that we retain confidence in the representativeness of our sample. Of course, we also acknowledge the argument that due to systematic biases in underenumeration in the Census, sample results may actually be more accurate than those from the Census.

Table 4.2

Correlations Among Dual Economy and Dual Labor Market Variables for Black and White Male Heads[a]

	Profitability	Concentration and investment	Firm growth
Profitability		.387	-.381
Concentration and investment	.380		.236
Firm growth	-.298	.244	.577
Work duration	.112	.543	.577
Benefits	.178	.716	.407
Sex discrimination	-.038	-.301	-.081
Earnings	.032	.024	-.098

[a]Whites below the diagonal; blacks above the diagonal.

characteristics were observed, in Tables 4.2, 4.3, and 4.4 there are negative relationships between the firm growth and profitability measures, thus suggesting that workers are employed in firms in which profits may accrue at some point after growth is realized. Second, in this chapter the data indicate that there are major differences in the relationships by sex. The positive relationships between the concentration and investment and the profits indicators, and between indicators of firm growth and concentration, which are observed for all status groups, are noticeably stronger for women than for men. Both of these findings are due to the differential distribution of workers across industries as shown in Table 4.1.

Table 4.3

Correlations Among Dual Economy and Dual Labor Market Variables for Black and White Female Heads[a]

	Profitability	Concentration and investment	Firm growth
Profitability		.459	-.011
Concentration and investment	.590		.029
Firm growth	-.419	.014	
Work duration	.310	.619	.422
Benefits	.041	.885	.290
Sex discrimination	-.231	-.329	-.630
Earnings	.179	.316	-.225

[a]Whites below the diagonal; blacks above the diagonal.

Table 4.2   *(continued)*

Work duration	Benefits	Sex discrimination	Earnings
.166	.145	−.075	.236
.567	.699	−.358	.160
.618	.422	−.127	−.068
	.738	−.367	.206
.775		−.257	.133
−.366	−.219		−.210
−.034	.055	.069	

When the relationships among the worker consequence variables are examined, an analogous pattern is found. Although the signs of the relationships are the same in these tables as in Table 2.11, the magnitudes of the correlations are often stronger in the status-specific matrices, particularly the relationship between the indicators of benefits and work duration. Also, among white females the negative relationships of the sex discrimination measure with both of the remaining worker outcome variables are noticeably stronger than those we observed in Chapter 2. Finally, in looking at the relationships between the economic sector and the worker consequence variables, we again see some basic similarities with Table 2.11 but also a few

Table 4.3   *(continued)*

Work duration	Benefits	Sex discrimination	Earnings
.333	.579	−.094	.098
.551	.836	−.101	.674
.547	.325	−.529	−.094
	.676	−.389	.280
.806		−.254	.348
−.645	−.505		.103
.153	.124	−.093	

Table 4.4

Correlations Among Dual Economy and Dual Labor Market Variables
for Black and White Wives^a

	Profitability	Concentration and investment	Firm growth
Profitability		.639	-.322
Concentration and investment	.504		-.053
Firm growth	-.428	-.005	
Work duration	.205	.550	.471
Benefits	.139	.860	.225
Sex discrimination	-.168	-.316	-.397
Earnings	.176	.311	-.152

^{a}Whites below the diagonal; blacks above the diagonal.

differences. In particular, the relationship between the worker benefits and profitability measures is usually much weaker in the status-specific matrices than in Table 2.11. Sex differences in this case include the stronger negative relationships for females between the sex discrimination and firm growth variables shown in Tables 4.3 and 4.4 than was shown in Table 2.11.[3]

To summarize, there are clear similarities between the relationships among industrial characteristics presented in Chapter 2 and those obtained when viewing industrial structures from the points of view of the six status groups. In each case there are relationships of the appropriate signs among most of the indicators, suggesting covariation among characteristics describing economic sectors, covariation among characteristics describing worker outcomes, and covariation between these two types of indicators. However, differences that have been observed in the findings across chapters are due

[3]We are also interested in the patterns of zero-order relationships between these industrial labor market characteristics and the local labor market variables used in Table 3.8. To investigate this and analogous questions, correlation matrices are presented between types of labor market characteristics for each of the six status groups in Appendix C. Inspection of the relevant correlations reveals no systematic patterns for any of the six status groups. Among white male heads 33 of 36 correlations are between ±.10. Comparable figures for the remaining groups are: black male heads, 29 of 36; white female heads, 30 of 36; black female heads, 23 of 36; white wives, 30 of 36; black wives, 21 of 36. We see that the relationships tend to be somewhat stronger among blacks than among whites, and this is particularly true for black women. There also tend to be positive relationships between manufacturing dominance and both the firm growth and work duration measures, suggesting that areas with a high proportion of manufacturing firms are also those areas where workers tend to remain with firms over time and where there is also economic growth, as defined by increase in new firms. Other relationships are much more variable across status groups and thus will not be discussed further.

Table 4.4 *(continued)*

Work duration	Benefits	Sex discrimination	Earnings
.186	.285	−.100	.320
.422	.886	−.007	.570
.578	.154	−.417	−.218
	.592	−.210	.119
.695		−.192	.242
−.467	−.389		.275
.201	.189	−.026	

to the differential weighting of characteristics that the distributions of workers to industries generates. Not only does this phenomenon produce the sex differences in the magnitudes of the correlations discussed earlier, but it also accounts for the general lack of marital status or racial differences in these same patterns.

That there are often stronger correlations among the variables for women workers than for men suggests that the dual economy and dual labor market model may "fit better" for female than for male workers. That the correlations are generally stronger in Tables 4.2, 4.3, and 4.4 than in Table 2.11 suggests that industrial labor market positions occupied by the several groups of workers correspond more closely to the tenets of dual economy and dual labor market theory than our intial analysis might have indicated. Workers do indeed participate in industries that show close positive relationships between concentration and profitability, between work duration and benefits, and clear inverse relationships between benefits and sex discrimination. These data may help to explain the conflicting findings that we have observed in this area. The fact that individuals' employment patterns approximate the model implied by dualist theory whereas the ecological analysis reported in Chapter 2 produces weaker findings points to the importance of weighting the values of the industrial variables by the distribution of employment.[4]

[4]It is important to recall that dual economy theory is formulated not in terms of individual workers but in terms of firms and their characteristics. Thus our reference to individuals' employment patterns following the dualist model is derived from the connection that is expected between the dual economy and dual labor market characteristics since the latter theory is constructed in terms of individuals and their jobs.

ACCESS TO RESOURCES

It is useful to examine briefly the means of the industrial resource indicators across the several status groups (see Table 4.5). Since each variable is
composed of two or more Z-scores, the means will be close to zero if the
distribution of workers across industries is relatively even across industries.
Generally speaking, the means will be positive if workers are disproportionately employed in industries that have high values for the variables forming
the composites and negative if workers are disproportionately employed in
industries that have low values for the variables forming the composites.
Since the scale values and scale zero points have no inherent meaning,
although the means are useful for comparing the relative access to labor
market resources across status groups, we should not make inferences concerning absolute levels of access from these data.

Among male workers the racial differences in average access to industrial
resources are relatively slight. Blacks do have slightly greater access to
positions in industries that are concentrated and in which there is investment and to positions where there is longer work duration, and they have
less access to positions where there is sex discrimination. In general among
male workers the average access to each industrial resource is, although
usually negative, still close to zero. This is consistent with what is known
concerning the distribution of male workers across industrial categories. In
contrast, among female heads the means are often more strongly negative.
Although access to positions with industrial profits is essentially zero for
whites and somewhat variable for blacks, female heads of both races lack
access to positions characterized by concentration and investment, firm
growth, worker job stability, and work benefits. They have access to positions in industries that pay well and from which women are, proportionately to men, excluded. These findings are essentially duplicated for black
and white wives.

It appears, then, that in terms of *access* to industrial resources conducive
to earnings attainment, males of both races are better off than females of
both races. This is consistent with what dual labor market theory would lead
us to expect concerning sex differences in the occupation of labor market
positions. The findings are also consistent with the notion that there is
overlap between dual economy and dual labor market resources since the
economic sector variables are also differentially distributed by sex. However, the lack of systematic and strong *racial* differences in access to any of
these resources is inconsistent with the perspectives. If blacks were disproportionately employed in secondary labor market positions and/or on the
periphery of the economy, then they would be expected to have reduced
access to the earnings-producing industrial resources discussed earlier.

Table 4.5

Means and Standard Deviations for Variables Included in the Analysis

| | Male heads | | | | Female heads | | | | Wives | | | |
| | Whites | | Blacks | | Whites | | Blacks | | Whites | | Blacks | |
	$\bar{X}$	S	$\bar{X}$	S	$\bar{X}$	S	$\bar{X}$	S	$\bar{X}$	S	$\bar{X}$	S
Profitability	-.01	.85	-.14	.87	-.00	1.08	.15	1.78	.08	1.17	.02	1.21
Concentration and investment	.08	3.09	.23	3.25	-.89	2.87	-1.02	3.01	-.86	2.99	-.90	2.90
Firm growth	-.47	1.63	-.30	1.72	-1.56	1.95	-1.52	2.15	-1.51	2.00	-1.39	2.19
Work duration	-.66	2.45	-.30	2.37	-2.02	2.34	-1.85	2.15	-1.92	2.27	-1.86	1.97
Benefits	-.34	1.27	-.34	1.29	-.68	1.17	-.71	1.43	-.76	1.09	-.85	1.06
Sex discrimination	-.56	1.98	-.78	1.90	1.18	1.78	1.24	1.66	1.15	1.80	1.29	1.66

Since this is not the case, we must assume that racial discrimination is not manifested in terms of differential access to these industrial labor market characteristics. It is still possible that racial discrimination may be evident in the *efficacy* with which these resources produce earnings for blacks, a notion to be evaluated shortly.

Multivariate Analysis

DUAL ECONOMY EFFECTS

Preliminary analysis (not presented here) suggested that it would not be useful to include the indicator of economic sector profitability along with those for concentration and investment and firm growth in multivariate analysis. For several status groups, the close relationship between the profits and concentration variables resulted in tipping of coefficients when both variables were included in earnings equations. In other cases it appeared as though the close relationships between measures of profitability and education were producing comparable effects, even when the concentration indicator was excluded. Although this latter finding provides additional evidence for the social selection effects to be discussed in Chapter 6, at this point the variables will be omitted from the analysis.

Two regression analyses presented in Table 4.6 allow us to evaluate the impact of economic sector organization on workers' earnings. The model at the top includes measures of concentration and investment and firm growth along with the human capital and socialization variables discussed in Chapter 3, and the model at the bottom regresses earnings on these two economic indicators without including any of the human capital and socialization variables. Despite the fact that the firm growth measure is negative and significant for all subgroups in the bottom panel, when the personal characteristic variables are introduced it is significant for only one status group, black male heads.[5] The indicator of concentration and investment behaves differently. It is significant and positive for all groups in the smaller specification and for all groups except white male heads when the personal characteristic variables are included. For all groups except black male heads, inclu-

[5] It appears that for five out of six status groups, the zero-order relationships between human capital variables and earnings are greater than those between the firm growth variable and earnings, thus eliminating the effects of this variable when human capital variables are controlled. Among black males the effect turns positive, although it is weak. It is possible that the .236 correlation between measures of firm growth and concentration and investment and the −.226 correlation between measures of firm growth and education (the interval measure was used here; data not presented) contribute to this minor instance of tipping.

Table 4.6

Human Capital and Dual Economy Determinants of Earnings[a]

	Male heads			
	Whites		Blacks	
Independent variables	Dev.	$b*$	Dev.	$b*$
Education (years)				
0-7	-4248	--	-1395	--
8	-2570	.045	-725	.037
9-11	-1693	.093	-755	.054
12	-631	.182	1188	.250
13-15	62***	.166	-239***	.078
$\geq$16	3164	.344	2178	.199
Weeks worked				
0-26	-4832	--	-5658	--
27-39	-2924	.044	-2250	.213
40-47	818	.257	369	.472
48-49	1020***	.282	402***	.553
50-52	-641	.218	220	.613
	b	$b*$	b	$b*$
Experience	108.5*** ***	.127	91.2*** ***	.218
Occupation	110.6	.278	80.9	.348
Concentration and investment	12.2	.004	274.2*** *	.186
Firm growth	88.3	.015	245.8	.088
Constant	-2087		-1822	
$R^2/\bar{R}^2$	.220/.215		.291/.279	

Dual Economy Determinants of Earnings[b]

Concentration and investment	155* ***	.051	275*** **	.187
Firm growth	-640	-.111	-312	.112
Constant	14,094		9325	
$R^2/\bar{R}^2$	.012/.011		.037/.035	
	N = 1870		N = 768	

(continued)

Table 4.6   *(continued)*

Independent variables	Female heads			
	Whites		Blacks	
	Dev.	b^*	Dev.	b^*
Education (years)				
0–7	−2379	−−	−177	−−
8	−2214	.008	−427	−.018
9–11	−1249	.105	212	.056
12	−296	.252	−399	−.033
13–15	338 **	.250	−147 ***	.003
≥16	2094	.444	2327	.183
Weeks worked				
0–26	−5035	−−	−1439	−−
27–39	−395	.374	−793	.069
40–47	363	.564	−35	.190
48–49	547 ***	.645	708 **	.300
50–52	−71	.556	−104	.190
	b	b^*	b	b^*
Experience	94.3 ***	.260	12.0 ***	.038
Occupation	32.4	.168	33.4	.224
Concentration and investment	231.3 **	.164	544.5 ***	.509
Firm growth	−46.3	−.022	−60.1	−.040
Constant	−3055		3068	
$R^2/\bar{R}^2$	.388/.360		.549/.532	

Dual Economy Determinants of Earnings[b]

	Whites		Blacks	
Concentration and investment	451 ***	.320	725 ***	.678
Firm growth	−475 ***	−.229	−171 **	−.114
Constant	7079		5985	
$R^2/\bar{R}^2$	.153/.147		.468/.465	
	$N = 297$		$N = 349$	

Table 4.6 *(continued)*

Independent variables	Wives			
	Whites		Blacks	
	Dev.	b^*	Dev.	b^*
Education (years)				
0–7	−757	——	−1240	——
8	−1097	−.014	−1195	.003
9–11	−792	−.003	−819	.056
12	−811	−.007	−135	.165
13–15	550***	.120	−736***	.051
≥16	2074	.296	5522	.586
Weeks worked				
0–26	−3553	——	−1976	——
27–39	−728	.302	−1823	.018
40–47	909	.447	913	.356
48–49	1464***	.547	488***	.339
50–52	311	.417	772	.349
	b	b^*	b	b^*
Experience	81.3***	.183	43.0***	.138
Occupation	32.0***	.168	−15.5	−.103
Concentration and investment	231.5***	.177	723.3***	.635
Firm growth	−66.8	−.034	−40.7	−.027
Constant	−1162		2401	
$R^2/\bar{R}^2$	.441/.432		.678/.666	

Dual Economy Determinants of Earnings[b]

Concentration and investment	405***	.310	638***	.560
Firm growth	−295***	−.151	−284***	−.188
Constant	5483		5416	
$R^2/\bar{R}^2$	.119/.117		.361/.357	
	$N = 817$		$N = 356$	

[a] For definitions of Dev., b and b^*, see footnote a to Table 3.6.

[b] Human capital and socialization variables excluded.

$^*p < .05$, $^{**}p < .01$, $^{***}p < .001$.

sion of the human capital and socialization variables reduces the magnitudes of the concentration and investment coefficients. Among white male heads it appears that the relationships between the human capital variables and concentration and investment are strong enough to render the latter measure nonsignificant when both are included in the same equation. This finding, along with the differences in the magnitudes of the concentration and investment effects across these two models for other status groups also provides evidence for social selection on the basis of industry.

A comparison across the status groups of the unstandardized coefficients associated with the concentration indicator shows that the benefits that accrue to employment in the core of the economy vary by race, sex, and marital status. Black male heads, white female heads, and white wives all receive modest amounts of yearly earnings ($274, $231, and $232, respectively) for each "point" on the concentration and investment scale. However, returns for black female heads ($544) and for black wives ($723) are considerably stronger. A comparison of the coefficients associated with the human capital variables in Table 4.6 with those in Table 3.6 suggests that there are greater changes in these variables across the two specifications for black female heads and black wives than for the remaining status groups. This is caused by stronger relationships between human capital variables and the concentration measure among black female workers than among the other status groups. For example, the zero-order correlation between education and the concentration and investment variable is .321 for black female heads and .403 for black wives, whereas it varies between −.006 and .165 for the remaining status groups. Similarly, the zero-order correlation between job status (Duncan SEI) and the concentration and investment variable is .360 for black female heads and .636 for black wives, whereas it varies between −.012 and .355 for the other status groups.

Other changes are introduced when the concentration and investment and firm growth variables are controlled. Among black female heads the weeks worked–earnings relationship is flatter, and the education effect is also reduced. Work experience, which was positive and significant in Table 3.6, is no longer significant in this specification, and returns to occupational status are reduced substantially. Among black wives introduction of the industrial characteristics also causes noticeable changes. The weeks worked–earnings relationship is reduced, and the experience and education effects are heightened. It is likely that the close relationships between education and experience and the industrial characteristics result in this "incipient tipping," which heightens these human capital effects.[6] Returns to occupational status

---

[6]In extreme cases multicollinearity (R. Gordon, 1968) can either severely reduce or inflate affected coefficients. The most familiar situation occurs when one or more variables is "tipped" in the direction opposite from that predicted by theory. However, it can also happen that the

are reduced from the moderately high level observed in Table 3.6 to no statistical significance for this relationship in Table 4.6. Again, the close relationship between the industrial characteristics and occupational status accounts for this finding.

MISSING DATA

The pattern of findings presented in Table 4.6 may also be influenced by the high proportion of cases for which data on concentration and investment are missing. Since this variable is unmeasured for workers in medical, dental, and health services, educational services, and for those working in government, the concept is disproportionately unmeasured for many professional and white-collar workers who are located in the service and government industries. The problem is especially severe for black female workers since they are heavily segregated within a fewer number of industries, including those for which the indicator is missing. Two types of analyses are relevant here. At a descriptive level, we investigate whether those respondents for whom concentration and investment are measured differ from those for whom it is missing. This analysis is confined to black female heads and black wives since the missing data problem is most severe here. As Table 4.7 indicates, there are large differences between the workers for whom concentration and investment is present versus missing, especially among black wives. Those for whom it is missing earn more, have more schooling, work *fewer* weeks per year, have higher status jobs that involve more complex work, and work in more profitable industries. They also live in areas with more productive manufacturing sectors generally. These data are consistent with our inference that workers for whom the variable is missing are disproportionately in professional and generally white-collar jobs.

Also of interest is whether the earnings attainment processes we have described differ depending on whether the measure is present for all workers, (i.e., whether we use listwise deletion or whether we use pairwise deletion, as we have done throughout this analysis). It is therefore relevant to compare the findings produced in Table 4.6 with those produced for workers from whom the variable is measured (data not presented). Again, analysis is confined to black female workers. Our central interest is in comparing the magnitudes of concentration and investment effects between the general samples and subsamples. Although this indicator remains statis-

---

magnitude of an effect is increased (artificially) in the predicted direction, and the magnitude of this increase may vary considerably. We believe that the increases here are due to such multicollinearity; we label this phenomenon "incipient tipping."

Table 4.7

Descriptive Characteristics for Black Female Workers, Concentration and Investment Missing and Present

Concentration and investment	Earnings	Years of schooling	Weeks worked	Duncan SEI
Black female heads				
Missing	$5859	11.6	43.7	33.7
Present	$5206	10.7	47.0	30.4
Black wives				
Missing	$6528	12.6	42.9	41.2
Present	$4334	10.9	43.3	25.7

a Among wives the data refer to the number of months with their present employer.

tically significant at the .001 level and large in magnitude in the subgroup analysis, there are reductions in the sizes of its effects. Among black female heads the unstandardized coefficient drops from $544 in Table 4.6 to $463 for the subsample, and among black wives the coefficient drops from $723 to $370. Among wives the firm growth measure is positive and significant in the subgroup analysis.

Clearly it is difficult to know with certainty how our findings would differ if the variable were measured for all respondents. In the case of measures of concentration and investment, it is obviously impossible to conceptualize this variable for industries such as education and health, in which services, by definition, must be provided by a variety of establishments. In the case of government, the concept of concentration and investment is also meaningless. It is clearly the case, however, that concentration and investment, where relevant, is still an important predictor of earnings. Thus our general inferences concerning its role remain undisturbed, although we should view with caution the magnitude of its coefficient, given missing data for a high proportion of cases.

A CUMULATIVE MODEL

Table 4.8 allows us to pursue the strategy of presenting a cumulative explanation of earnings attainment by adding the indicators of economic sectors to the equation in Table 3.8 that contained both the human capital and local labor market variables. Hence we are interested in evaluating whether workers' employment in positions in the core of the economy facili-

Table 4.7 *(continued)*

Complexity	Experience	Manufacturing sector health	Years on job	Profitability
−4.5	19.5	1.42	6.8	.543
−5.4	17.2	1.00	6.7	−.111
−.44	18.0	1.27	91.0^{a}	.543
−7.27	15.5	.43	80.1	−.297

tates earnings attainment after characteristics of the local labor market have been controlled. It is not intuitively obvious that the effects of these two structures should be independent. In fact, one could argue that the areal effects discussed in the previous chapter that captured local labor market industrial organization (manufacturing and tertiary sector activity) could be explained by characteristics representing the industries in which the respective workers are employed. If this were true, the variables representing economic sectors would explain variance previously attributed to the local labor market factors and would add little to the overall explanatory power of the model.

The data in Table 4.8 suggest that the addition of concentration and investment and firm growth variables do contribute to the overall explanatory power of the model for all groups except white male heads ($p < .001$ for the remaining groups). In each case this effect is due to the role of concentration and investment since in no specification is firm growth statistically significant. The pattern and statistical significance of the local labor market effects in this specification is very similar to that shown in Table 3.8. Black male heads' earnings are still strongly affected by manufacturing sector activity, although no other status group is similarly affected. Other groups, in contrast, are affected to varying degrees by tertiary sector activity, with stronger effects among the female heads and black wives than among white male heads or white wives. Also, as in Table 3.8, there are negative effects of urban crowding on black male and female heads, although the effects are not significant for any of the remaining groups. Thus there is no support for the notion that introducing controls for characteristics of workers' personal industrial affiliations will explain the areal effects discussed in Chapter 3.

Table 4.8

Human Capital, Areal and Industrial Labor Market
Determinants of Earnings[a]

Independent variables	Male heads			
	Whites		Blacks	
	Dev.	$b*$	Dev.	$b*$
Education (years)				
0–7	−3742	—	−371	—
8	−2180	.042	−275	.005
9–11	−1620	.078	−644	−.023
12	−572	.159	707	.104
13–15	−95***	.140	−991***	−.042
≥16	2946	.310	1671	.114
Weeks worked				
0–26	−4988	—	−5802	—
27–39	−2881	.048	−2289	.220
40–47	718	.259	147	.466
48–49	972***	.288	66***	.535
50–52	−543	.231	496	.656
	b	$b*$	b	$b*$
Experience	104.3***	.122	68.3***	.164
Occupation	102.5***	.258	76.9***	.331
Crowding	353.5	.040	−458.6***	−.153
Manufacturing dominance	−107.3	−.015	362.1**	.086
Manufacturing sector health	109.2	.022	713.8***	.300
Tertiary sector health	214.3***	.091	−19.9	−.016
Tertiary sector growth	−270.2*	−.048	−98.0	−.032
Tertiary sector complexity	358.4*	.053	167.0	.046
Concentration and investment	15.2	.005	263.8***	.179
Firm growth	62.9	.011	92.1	.033
Constant	−2191		−805	
$R^2/\bar{R}^2$	.245/.238		.434/.420	
	N = 1870		N = 768	

Table 4.8 *(continued)*

Independent variables	Female heads			
	Whites		Blacks	
	Dev.	$b*$	Dev.	$b*$
Education (years)				
0–7	−1166	—	112	—
8	−1645	−.025	−395	−.037
9–11	−922	.023	146	.005
12	−312	.104	−504	−.092
13–15	225*	.128	−31***	−.014
≥16	1693	.284	2611	.182
Weeks worked				
0–26	−5165	—	−1992	—
27–39	−258	.395	−1158	.089
40–47	98	.550	371	.320
48–49	435***	.647	538***	.353
50–52	227	.604	−58	.275
	b	$b*$	b	$b*$
Experience	80.7***	.222	8.7**	.028
Occupation	31.5**	.163	23.7***	.159
Crowding	−187.3	−.039	−487.2	−.175
Manufacturing dominance	104.9	.036	48.1	.017
Manufacturing sector health	62.7	.026	−183.4	−.102
Tertiary sector health	212.5**	.192	38.6	.041
Tertiary sector growth	412.3**	.169	328.3**	.167
Tertiary sector complexity	286.4	.081	546.0***	.190
Concentration and investment	303.8***	.215	614.9***	.574
Firm growth	−75.3	−.036	−73.0	−.049
Constant	−2599		3332	
$R^2/\bar{R}^2$	.446/.408		.600/.577	
	$N = 297$		$N = 349$	

(continued)

Table 4.8 (continued)

Independent variables	Wives			
	Whites		Blacks	
	Dev.	b*	Dev.	b*
Education (years)				
0–7	−730	−−	−778	−−
8	−1009	−.011	−1045	−.017
9–11	−721	.001	−770	.001
12	−800	−.009	−334	.066
13–15	492***	.112	−707***	.007
≥16	2035	.289	5843	.574
Weeks worked				
0–26	−3541	−−	−2196	−−
27–39	−736	.300	−1705	.058
40–47	927	.448	626	.347
48–49	1449***	.544	510***	.372
50–52	314	.416	988	.405
	b	b*	b	b*
Experience	81.0***	.182	46.8***	.150
Occupation	31.2***	.164	−13.3	−.088
Crowding	−9.8	−.003	45.4	.023
Manufacturing dominance	8.6	.003	115.8	.038
Manufacturing sector health	−38.0	−.018	−6.6	−.004
Tertiary sector health	79.7*	.081	128.4*	.143
Tertiary sector growth	−37.2	−.016	−159.5*	−.083
Tertiary sector complexity	−18.3	−.006	−366.3***	−.160
Concentration and investment	224.7***	.172	668.1***	.586
Firm growth	−70.3	−.036	19.2	.013
Constant	−1344		2238	
$R^2/\bar{R}^2$	.446/.433		.717/.700	
	N = 817		N = 356	

[a]See footnote a on Table 3.6.

*$p < .05$, **$p < .01$, ***$p < .001$.

The data also suggest that the magnitudes of the concentration and investment effects are very similar in this specification to those shown in Table 4.6.
Although there are slight reductions in returns to this indicator for black
male heads and for wives of both races, the effects among female heads of
both races are heightened when controls for local labor market variables are
introduced. Therefore the magnitude of the concentration and investment
effect is not reduced by the introduction of controls for local labor market
economic and social organization. There also remain large variations by
status group in the magnitude of this effect.

As in Table 4.6, we recognize that the findings may be influenced by the
pattern of missing data on concentration and investment. Again we compare
the data in Table 4.8 with the same specifications for black female subsamples for which concentration and investment is measured for all workers
(data not presented). The findings are similar to those described above for
Table 4.6. Among black female heads returns to concentration and investment drop from $615 to $484, and among black wives they drop from $668 to
$332. Again, the firm growth variable is statistically significant and positive
among the black wives subgroup. As might be expected, there are also some
changes in the human capital and socialization variables when Table 4.8 is
compared with the same specification of the subsamples. For example,
weeks worked effects appear stronger in the subsamples whereas years of
schooling appear weaker. These changes are understandable in light of the
descriptive data discussed earlier that indicated major economic differences
between workers for whom these data were measured and unmeasured.
Certainly we would expect that a sample including a high proportion of
professional workers would evidence strong returns to years of schooling
whereas a sample excluding many of these workers would evidence strong
returns to weeks worked.

DUAL LABOR MARKET EFFECTS

We are also interested in evaluating the impact of indicators of the *dual
labor market* on workers' earnings, independent of the human capital variables in the basic equation. Table 4.9 presents an equation estimating earnings as a function of the human capital variables plus two indicators of the
dual labor market, work duration and sex discrimination. Again, as in the
previous section, it was necessary to omit one of the dualist indicators,
worker benefits, because of high correlations with remaining variables, in
order to provide interpretable results across the status groups.

The effects of work duration are similar to concentration and investment in
that this indicator contributes positively to earnings attainment indepen-

Table 4.9

Human Capital and Dual Labor Market Determinants of Earnings[a]

Independent variables	Male heads			
	Whites		Blacks	
	Dev.	$b*$	Dev.	$b*$
Education (years)				
0–7	−4355	−−	−1338	−−
8	−2614	.047	−1091	.014
9–11	−1770	.094	−458	.074
12	−641	.186	1278	.253
13–15	173***	.174	−301***	.070
≥16	3182	.350	1334	.149
Weeks worked				
0–26	−5094	−−	−7047	−−
27–39	−3123	.045	−3106	.247
40–47	812	.269	19	.554
48–49	1041***	.296	628***	.700
50–52	−616	.233	429	.779
	b	$b*$	b	$b*$
Experience	111.6***	.130	73.8***	.177
Occupation	111.9***	.281	96.2***	.414
Work duration	−41.8*	−.011	437.4***	.217
Sex discrimination	−238.5	−.050	−677.6***	−.269
Constant	−2783		−3614	
$R^2/\bar{R}^2$	.222/.217		.389/.378	
	$N = 1870$		$N = 768$	

dently of the human capital variables for every group except for white males. Thus the earnings levels of workers are facilitated by employment in work environments in which there is relatively high employee stability, that is, relatively low worker turnover. That white male earnings levels are indifferent to this factor is again not predicted by theory but may reflect the differential efficacy that structural factors at this level have on the earnings of various types of workers. The possibility cannot be ignored, however, that structural factors are generally differentially important by status group, regardless of the level at which they are conceptualized or measured. This issue will be investigated as we proceed with the analysis. Concerning the magnitudes of the work duration effects, the sizes of the unstandardized regression coefficients are very similar across the groups (excluding white

Table 4.9 *(continued)*

Independent variables	Female heads			
	Whites		Blacks	
	Dev.	$b*$	Dev.	$b*$
Education (years)				
0-7	-4817	--	-716	--
8	-2263	.132	-688	.002
9-11	-1594	.298	269	.142
12	-259	.552	47	.114
13-15	455***	.485	-1461***	-.073
≥16	2473	.723	2927	.266
Weeks worked				
0-26	-5958	--	-112	--
27-39	-611	.431	-2015	-.204
40-47	414	.665	-387	-.037
48-49	559***	.753	1556***	.233
50-52	87	.677	-191	-.011
	b	$b*$	b	$b*$
Experience	101.7***	.280	66.5***	.214
Occupation	31.4**	.163	76.7***	.514
Work duration	433.1***	.250	422.4***	.282
Sex discrimination	51.9	.023	221.4*	.114
Constant	-5829		1518	
$R^2/\bar{R}^2$	.411/.384		.489/.469	
	$N = 297$		$N = 349$	

(continued)

male heads) with the exception of black wives, for whom the effects are somewhat smaller. It appears, then, that the work duration dimension positively contributes to the earnings levels of all but white male workers.[7]

The effects of the sex discrimination measure are more variable. Both

[7]The effects on the human capital variables that resulted from introduction of the dual labor market variables are not as strong or as consistent as those shown in the comparison of Table 3.6 and 4.6. As we would expect, the human capital variables for white male heads are not affected across the two specifications. Black male heads and white women workers, regardless of marital status, show heightened effects of education, whereas occupational effects are also heightened for black male heads and white wives. Although the weeks worked and experience effects do change across the specifications, the changes are generally not large, nor are they consistent in direction.

Table 4.9 *(continued)*

| Independent variables | Wives | | | |
| | Whites | | Blacks | |
	Dev.	$b*$	Dev.	$b*$
Education (years)				
0–7	−2595	—	−1018	—
8	−1491	.044	−663	.023
9–11	−1092	.129	−447	.076
12	−725	.239	223	.185
13–15	706***	.303	−882***	.014
≥16	2200	.502	2599	.314
Weeks worked				
0–26	−3542	—	−2780	—
27–39	−850	.288	−1580	.143
40–47	720	.427	559	.411
48–49	1627***	.564	1034***	.525
50–52	411	.426	487	.415
	b	$b*$	b	$b*$
Experience	70.6***	.159	41.3**	.133
Occupation	44.6***	.235	66.0***	.438
Work duration	453.2***	.264	341.2***	.203
Sex discrimination	108.7	.050	374.9***	.189
Constant	−2753		−1212	
$R^2/\bar{R}^2$	.465/.456		.583/.567	
	$N = 817$		$N = 356$	

[a]See footnote a on Table 3.6.
* $p < .05$, ** $p < .01$, *** $p < .001$.

black and white male heads are negatively affected by employment in industrial markets in which there is a high proportion of female workers and wages are low. This effect is clearly more damaging for blacks than for whites, however. Concerning the other status groups, white women workers' earnings are not significantly affected by this variable. However, black women workers, regardless of marital status, evidence positive returns to this indicator, although the magnitude of the effect for black female heads is small. These positive signs are consistent with the zero-order correlations between earnings and this variable and reflect industrial segregation of black women workers into a few major industrial groups. These industries (educational services, medical and dental services, finance, and personal services) may actually provide these workers with reasonable levels of earnings, although among males there are clearly better opportunities for "good" jobs in durable and continuous process manufacturing and construction. Thus for males, employment in these same industries is undoubtedly a hindrance to earnings attainment whereas for black women, it provides a reasonable boost.[8]

In addition to assessing whether the dual labor market indicators predict earnings independent of the human capital variables, we are also interested in assessing the effects of dual economy and dual labor market variables when they are simultaneously controlled. Such analysis is useful in the study of the degree to which there is overlap between the dual economy and the dual labor market. Recall that our analysis of the correlations among these indicators suggested some overlap; multivariate analysis allows another type of evaluation of this issue. Accordingly, Table 4.10 presents an earnings function for male heads in which independent variables include indicators of human capital as well as the composites representing the dual economy and the dual labor market presented in Tables 4.6 and 4.9.

Among white males the simultaneous inclusion of both types of dualist indicators does little to change the findings discussed in the previous tables. The dual economy indicators remain nonsignificant as does the work duration measure, whereas the indicator of sex discrimination remains significant and negative. Among blacks, however, there is a different pattern. For these workers simultaneous inclusion of both types of dualist indicators results in the dual labor market variables rendering nonsignificant the dual economy indicators. Thus variance, which in Table 4.6 we attributed to characteristics of the dual economy in this model, must be attributed to characteristics of the dual labor market. In addition, the dual labor market variables have greater explanatory power than the dual economy variables for black male heads since the level of explained variance is higher in Table 4.10 than 4.6 ($p < .001$), as well as in Table 4.9 compared to 4.6 ($p < .001$). For the remaining status groups (not presented), the zero-order correlations between the dual labor market and dual economy variables were so high that the resulting regression coefficients were uninterpretable. In these models not only is there tipping involving the two sets of dualist variables but tipping involving the human capital variables as well. Again, patterns of social selection that maximize the relationships between personal and structural characteristics contribute to these findings. This general issue will be discussed later. For these reasons, the dual labor market variables were not included in the cumulative model presented in Table 4.9.

[8]We hypothesized that some of this effect would disappear if occupational labor market characteristics were controlled. Empirical investigation of the hypothesis (data not included) indicates that it is supported for black female heads. Among black wives multicollinearity between these industrial and occupational characteristics prevents our evaluating the issue.

Table 4.10

Human Capital, Dual Economy, and Dual Labor Market Determinants of Earnings for Male Heads[a]

Independent variables	Whites		Blacks	
	Dev.	$b*$	Dev.	$b*$
Education (years)				
0–7	−4397	—	−1271	—
8	−2665	.047	−1087	.010
9–11	−1834	.094	−422	.071
12	−685	.186	1325	.251
13–15	96 ***	.173	−321 ***	.064
≥16	3343	.359	895	.121
Weeks worked				
0–26	−5018	—	−6949	—
27–39	−3008	.046	−3096	.241
40–47	830	.266	61	.549
48–49	1041 ***	.293	579 ***	.687
50–52	−644	.228	436	.770
	b	$b*$	b	$b*$
Experience	111.6 ***	.130	70.1 ***	.168
Occupation	112.8 ***	.284	95.0 ***	.409
Concentration and investment	−1.8	−.001	−45.9	−.031
Firm growth	205.3	.036	−212.0 ***	−.076
Work duration	−126.6 *	−.033	570.1 ***	.282
Sex discrimination	−271.7	−.057	−661.1 ***	−.262
Constant	−2771		−3332	
$R^2/\bar{R}^2$	.223/.217		.392/.379	
	$N = 1870$		$N = 768$	

[a]See footnote a on Table 3.6.
* $p < .05$, ** $p < .01$, *** $p < .001$.

Regression Standardization

Table 4.11 presents the results of the regression standardization used to decompose earnings differences between white male heads and three other status groups: black male heads, white female heads, and black female heads. Two equations for each set of status groups were estimated and decomposed in a stepwise fashion in order to assess the contribution of industrial labor market characteristics net of human capital and areal variables. Hence, the data in the first line serve as a baseline for the comparison. The model used here is that reported in Table 3.8 and also decomposed in Table 3.9. The second equation is that reported in Table 4.8. As in Chapter 3, we do not interpret the slopes and intercepts components separately since such an interpretation requires that zero points of the variables be meaningful, a condition that many of our variables do not meet. Recall also that joint variation for two sets of variables, in this case industrial and human capital and areal variables, will be attributed to the human capital and areal labor market component.

The comparison of white and black male heads suggests that introduction of industrial labor market variables changes the relative "balance" between the composition and the slopes and intercepts components. Although in the first equation essentially equal amounts of improvement for blacks would be

Table 4.11

Summary of Regression Standardization Components

Pair and variables	Composition	Slopes and intercepts	Interaction
White male heads versus black male heads			
(1) Human capital and areal labor market	43.6% ($2146)	46.6% ($2296)	9.8% ($481)
(2) Human capital, areal and industrial labor markets	47.5% ($2337)	39.5% ($1945)	13.0% ($640)
Initial gap: $14,404 - 9,481 = $4,923			
White male heads versus white female heads			
(1) Human capital and areal labor market	5.4% ($375)	91.6% ($6400)	3.0% ($212)
(2) Human capital, areal industrial labor markets	8.0% ($558)	90.4% ($6316)	1.6% ($113)
Initial gap: $14,404 - 7,416 = $6,988			
White male heads versus black female heads			
(1) Human capital and areal labor market	18.6% ($1656)	61.4% ($5465)	20.0% ($1780)
(2) Human capital, areal and industrial labor market	4.5% ($405)	60.2% ($5355)	35.3% ($3141)
Initial gap: $14,404 - 5,502 = $8,902			

realized given equalization of access to resources or efficacy of resources, introduction of the industrial labor market variables tips the balance in favor of composition. If only one type of factor could be changed, blacks would benefit by an average of $2337 given equalization of access to resources, whereas they would benefit by $1945 given equalization of the efficacy of these resources. A relatively minor amount ($640) of additional gain would accrue to blacks given simultaneous equalization of both of these components. We must interpret these findings with caution, however, since, as the data presented in Table 4.8 indicate, the industrial labor market variables are not statistically significant among whites. Therefore, although the direction of the difference is probably valid, the magnitude of the change should not be viewed too literally.

The decompositions of the earnings differences between white male and female heads and between white male and black female heads present a contrasting picture. For the white male and female heads comparison the introduction of the industrial labor market resources results in virtually no change in the importance of the three components in explaining sex inequality; 90% of the male–female earnings gap among whites is still due to differential slopes and intercepts. This pattern is analogous to that shown in Table 3.9, in which the introduction of the local labor market characteristics resulted in essentially no changes in the importance of the three components in explaining sex inequality in earnings. The race–sex comparison, white male heads versus black female heads, shows somewhat different results. Although the percentage of earnings difference allocated to slopes and intercepts is still high (60.2), the distribution of percentages has changed across the remaining two components. Although in the first specification shown there is little difference in the amount of improvement in earnings black female heads would realize due to composition or interaction, introduction of the industrial labor market variables shifts the bulk of the explanatory power (excepting that for slopes and intercepts) to interaction. Thus the findings suggest that 35.3% of the earnings gap between white male heads and black female heads could be eliminated only given the simultaneous equalization of access to resources and effectiveness of these resources (including intercepts). Changes in access to resources alone would have relatively little impact.

Inspection of the behavior of specific variables included in the model (data not included) suggests some similarities and some differences across status groups. Both female heads groups would benefit from equalized access to industrial concentration and investment, although among males the composition component is small. Finally, both female groups evidence a negative interaction term associated with the concentration and investment measure, although for the comparison between black and white males the interaction term is small. These findings suggest that for female heads, there may be some overestimation of the magnitudes of returns to concentration and investment, which again cautions us against too literal an interpretation of these regression coefficients. Changes in the magnitudes of the remaining coefficients for the several comparisons are small and thus do not warrant interpretation.

Summary and Conclusions

The focus of this chapter has been on industrial labor market determinants of workers' earnings. Dual economy theory and dual labor market theory were used to suggest relevant hypotheses. Both descriptive and analytic issues were empirically evaluated.

Descriptive analysis revealed substantial industrial segregation by sex but not by race. That is, findings indicated that a high proportion of women were concentrated in a few industries and that this pattern was more pronounced for black females than for white. In contrast, male workers of both races were much more evenly distributed across the industrial categories used in analyses. These differential distributions have major implications for respondents' access to industrial resources. Findings indicated that women workers lack access to industrial positions characterized by concentration and investment, firm growth, worker job stability and employee benefits, whereas males of both races have higher mean levels of access to these resources. Thus, not only are women workers segregated into fewer industries than are men, but this pattern of segregation results in women obtaining reduced access, relative to men, to the income producing resources available in the industrial context. The findings for women are consistent with dual labor market theory and with the implications of dual economy theory that can be read to suggest that women will obtain inferior labor market positions to those men obtain. However, these perspectives also suggest that blacks will obtain inferior positions to those occupied by whites. On this latter point, we cannot conclude that the dualist expectations are supported. The findings do not suggest that in terms of access to industrial resources, blacks are disadvantaged relative to whites. These findings call into question, then, a major precept of dual labor market theory that posits racial differentials in access to industrial market positions.

A second descriptive focus concerned the configurations of industrial labor market resources with which the respective status groups are faced. These configurations bring evidence to bear on the issue of the industrial market structures each status group encounters. Although on the basis of dual economy and dual labor market theory, it is expected that relationships among relevant composites should be strong, recall that in Chapter 2, although the relationships were generally positive, they were not as strong as expected. In this analysis findings suggested that when these relationships are viewed from the points of view of the individual workers, they are stronger and thus more consistent with hypotheses based on dualist theories. This finding is particularly true for women workers who, due to the patterns of industrial segregation discussed previously, evidence particularly strong correlations.

The multivariate analysis also brings evidence to bear on dualist hypotheses. In particular, an important question concerned the relative importance of characteristics suggested by dualist theories compared with human capital and status attainment variables in the prediction of workers' earnings. As discussed in Chapter 1 (e.g., Bibb and Form, 1977; Wachtel and Betsey, 1972; Harrison, 1972), this issue has aroused considerable controversy. The findings suggest that industrial concentration and investment *is* a statistically significant predictor of earnings net of human capital and areal labor market characteristics for all groups except white male heads. Among white males correspondence between these industrial resources and human capital resources results in the latter retaining statistical significance when both types of variables are simultaneously controlled. Although analysis suggested possible overestimation of the magnitudes of concentration and investment effects for women workers, the differential pattern of statistical significance and general magnitudes of the concentration and investment coefficients suggests changes in the emphases implied by the dualist perspectives. In particular, women workers obtain strong returns to industrial resources whereas white male returns appear much weaker. This pattern is directly opposite from those implied by dualist arguments—that due to discrimination white male returns to industrial characteristics should exceed those for other groups, including female workers. At the very least, these findings dictate caution in the acceptance of dualist notions concerning the distribution of the advantages and disadvantages of industrial resources across race and sex groups. These resources appear to be of far less importance to white males than expected, but of greater importance to white females than is generally believed.

The final analysis presented continued the use of regression standardization begun in Chapter 3 in order to better understand what implications various changes in the distribution and/or efficacy of resources would have for race and sex discrimination. The findings produced in Chapter 3 were reinforced since the data continue to suggest that the process of racial discrimination is substantially different from the process of sex discrimination; thus we retain the inference that policies for reducing and eliminating each type of discrimination would likely be distinct. This issue will continue to be addressed in the next chapter, in which we develop our model of earnings attainment further by incorporating occupational labor market characteristics and indicators of class/authority position.

CHAPTER 5

Occupational Labor Market Characteristics' and Class/Authority Effects on Earnings

Review of Theory and Hypotheses

Theory discussed in Chapters 1 and 2 concerning occupational labor markets and class/authority relations guides analysis in this chapter. Recall that theoretical analyses by Stolzenberg (1975) on occupational labor market segmentation and work by Spaeth (1979), Miller *et al.* (1980), Kohn (1969), and others suggested several nonprestige dimensions of occupational differentiation relevant to earnings attainment. The factor analysis of numerous occupational characteristics indicated underlying dimensions including work complexity, people–things, physical activities, physical dexterity, uncertainty, and unpleasantness of working conditions. Following the literature just cited, we expect earnings to be higher when the skill and task requirements are complex, when the job requires a high level of social relations skills, and when physical dexterity–perceptual skills are required. We also expect earnings to be lower when the job involves unpleasant working conditions and greater physical activity.

These hypotheses are also consistent with the dual labor market perspective. In Chapter 2 we indicated that the dimensions of occupational differentiation used in this analysis were relevant to the "good" job–"bad" job distinction. Thus, good jobs involve complex work and demand physical dexterity and perceptual skills, whereas bad jobs involve unpleasant working conditions and demand greater physical activity. Following the dualist notion that black and women workers are more likely to be employed in the secondary labor market (i.e., in "bad" jobs) than are white males who obtain good jobs in the primary labor market, we expect white males to have greater access to income producing resources (e.g., complexity, physical dexterity) than other workers. Similarly, we also expect them to obtain stronger returns to these characteristics than workers in the remaining status groups.

Literature describing the social organization of occupational labor markets suggests that concentration of an economic minority in an occupation is negatively related to earnings of minority workers (Bergmann, 1971; Blaxall and Reagan, 1976; England, 1981). Thus we expect that the higher the economic minority percentage in an occupation, the lower the wages for economic minority workers employed in those occupations. In addition, literature concerning the relationship between class/authority and earnings suggests additional hypotheses. Given that individuals are differentially distributed in the class/authority structure by race and especially sex, we expect race and sex differences in earnings to be partly due to this differential access to authority levels. Given previous research (Wright and Perrone, 1977; Robinson and Kelley, 1979; Kalleberg and Griffin, 1980), we also expect that class/authority will have a substantial effect on earnings net of the occupational labor market dimensions already mentioned.

As in Chapters 3 and 4, the primary focus is on examination of unstandardized regression coefficients across status groups to assess the effects of occupational labor market characteristics and class/authority indicators on earnings, net of investment and socialization variables and measures of local and industrial labor market resources. Additional analysis complements this emphasis. We present descriptive data on sex and race differences in access to occupations, occupational labor market resources, and class/authority positions. We also inspect status-specific correlation matrices of the occupational resources to describe the occupational labor market configurations faced by the respective status groups. Finally, we continue to use regression standardization to arrive at policy implications concerning race–sex differences in earnings. In particular we continue to expand the examination of the influence of labor markets on race and sex earnings inequality by incorporating both occupational labor market reousrces and indicators of class/authority position.

Occupational Labor Market Characteristics

RACE AND SEX OCCUPATION SEGREGATION

If the occupational labor market is important, as hypothesized, then differential access to occupational labor market resources by sex and race would, in part, account for earnings differences among these status groups. This differential access by sex is hidden by measures of central tendency for describing the occupational achievement differences of men and women

(Wolf and Rosenfeld, 1978). For example, for our data mean Duncan SEI for white men is 45.1 and for black men is 28.2, whereas the respective means for white and black female heads are 44.7 and 31.9 and for white and black wives, 44.2 and 32.1. That this apparent similarity in achievements for men and women misrepresents the real patterns of achievement can be seen when the occupational distributions of men and women are examined.

Table 5.1 displays, for each of the six status groups, the distribution of cases across the 10 major U. S. Census occupation categories. Both race and sex differences are apparent. Blacks, regardless of sex, are less likely to be employed in professional occupations and are less likely to be managers and proprietors. Blacks are more likely, however, to be employed in service positions and as operatives. Considering sex differences, women are over-represented in both clerical and service occupations but are underrepresented in craft, farm, manager and proprietor, and laborer occupations. Thus, to the extent that occupations represent labor markets that influence labor earnings, we can expect there to be race–sex differences in earnings merely because of the differential race–sex distributions.

Two additional types of data are needed to show the link between race–sex occupational segregation and race–sex differences on the dimensions we use to measure occupational labor market differences. Table 5.2 displays the means for each occupational characteristic, as well as the mean Duncan SEI score, for each of the 10 occupational categories and for each of the six status groups. In brief, the upper part of Table 5.2 shows how the major occupational categories are differentiated with regard to the occupational characteristics measured whereas the lower part shows how men and women and blacks and whites differ in the types of skills and tasks they perform when they work. These data show differentiation along both race and sex lines.

Looking first at race differences, we find that blacks are low on complexity primarily because they are underrepresented in the professional and mana-gerial occupations, which are especially high on complexity. In addition, the service and operative occupations, where blacks are overrepresented, are especially low on complexity. Similarly, the distribution of the two races in the occupational structure is consistent with blacks' overall high means on unpleasant work conditions and work involving physical activities. In short, when compared with whites, blacks frequently are engaged in occupations requiring work in an unpleasant environment, requiring less complexity, and involving more physical activities.

Women, when compared with men, receive low means for physical ac-tivity primarily because of their underrepresentation in craft, farm, and laborer categories. In addition, the higher mean for social relations skills for women can be explained by their overrepresentation in the clerical and service occupations, where interpersonal skills are important, and as just

Table 5.1

Occupational Distribution of Status Groups

	Male heads				Female heads				Wives			
	Whites		Blacks		Whites		Blacks		Whites		Blacks	
Occupation	N	%	N	%	N	%	N	%	N	%	N	%
Professional	359	19.2	57	7.5	70	23.7	38	10.9	183	22.7	50	14.0
Managers	376	20.1	44	5.8	22	7.5	6	1.7	44	5.5	8	2.3
Sales	109	5.8	11	1.4	8	2.7	9	2.6	54	6.7	2	.6
Clerical	100	5.4	92	12.1	96	32.5	83	23.8	267	33.1	82	23.0
Craft	446	23.9	147	19.3	4	1.4	26	7.4	9	1.1	3	.8
Operatives	245	13.1	216	28.3	25	8.5	37	10.6	102	12.7	63	17.7
Laborers	56	3.0	84	11.0	1	.3	1	.3	4	.5	1	.3
Farm	78	4.2	2	.3	0	0	0	0	1	.1	0	0
Farm labor	15	.8	21	2.8	0	0	2	.6	1	.1	0	0
Service	84	4.5	88	11.5	69	23.4	147	42.1	141	17.5	147	41.3
Total	1868	100.0	762	100.0	295	100.0	349	100.0	806	100.0	356	100.0

Table 5.2

Means for Occupational Characteristics and Duncan SEI Score by Occupation and Status Group

	Complexity	Unpleasantness of work	Physical dexterity	Physical activities	Uncertainty	People-things	Duncan SEI
Occupation							
Professional	10.2	-.8	.3	-2.2	.05	1.4	72.0
Managers	8.1	-.8	-3.7	-2.5	.04	3.6	62.8
Sales	2.4	-1.0	-6.0	-2.7	-.76	4.8	48.6
Clerical	-3.2	-1.0	-.6	-2.9	-.09	1.8	47.6
Craft	-2.5	.4	3.1	3.3	.33	-4.5	31.4
Operatives	-9.6	1.2	.2	1.2	-.73	-2.0	19.7
Laborers	-13.0	1.8	-3.1	5.5	-.46	-.2	12.1
Farm	3.8	-.4	.0	1.4	1.54	1.4	25.0
Farm laborer	-7.5	1.1	-1.4	3.9	1.09	.3	16.3
Service	-7.3	1.0	-2.1	.6	.46	3.2	20.6
Status group							
White male heads	1.5	-.2	-.6	.4	.2	.1	45.1
Black male heads	-5.3	.4	-.9	1.6	-.2	-.5	28.2
White female heads	-.0	-.2	1.1	-1.7	-.3	2.8	44.6
Black female heads	-5.0	.5	-1.9	-.4	.4	1.8	31.9
White wives	-1.0	-.2	-.0	-1.5	.1	2.4	44.2
Black wives	-4.5	.5	-1.3	-.6	.3	2.1	32.1

discussed, their underrepresentation in craft and labor occupations, where social relations are less important.

There also appears to be a race by sex interaction with physical dexterity. White women, when compared to black women, are more often in jobs requiring physical dexterity and perceptual abilities (see lower part). This race difference is not found for men, however. Finally, there are no large or readily interpretable race or sex differences for uncertainty even though we have already documented that uncertainty varies by occupation and that there are race and sex differences in the distribution of workers across occupations.

In sum, the data presented thus far clearly show differential access by race and sex to the occupational structure and thus to occupational labor market resources. Whereas the occupations of men and women are differentiated primarily in terms of physical activity and interpersonal relations dimensions, the occupations of blacks and whites are differentiated more in terms of complexity, pleasantness of work conditions, and physical activity.

STATUS-SPECIFIC CORRELATION MATRICES

An examination of the intercorrelations among the occupational characteristics for the various status groups adds to the already apparent pattern of sex-based occupational differentiation, although some race differences also

Table 5.3

Correlations Among Occupational Characteristic Variables for Black and White Male Heads[a]

	Uncertainty	Unpleasantness of work	Physical dexterity	Physical activities
Uncertainty		.159	.232	.162
Unpleasantness of work	.017		-.017	.444
Physical dexterity	.307	.143		.237
Physical activities	.269	.424	.440	
People–things	-.225	-.210	-.737	-.567
Complexity	.289	-.365	-.219	-.544
Clerical aptitude	-.050	.392	.182	.667
Duncan SEI	.040	-.368	-.258	-.665
Percentage male	.339	.115	.294	.372
Earnings	.021	-.110	-.008	-.259

[a]Whites below the diagonal; blacks above the diagonal.

are observed. Tables 5.3, 5.4, and 5.5 present these correlation matrices.

With only a few exceptions, the signs of the intercorrelations at the occupational level (Table 2.13, Chapter 2) are retained at the individual level of analysis reported here. In the few instances where the signs in this chapter are reversed, the ecological correlations were either nonsignificant or small in magnitude. So, as we concluded in Chapter 2, in general, persons occupy positions that, if requiring considerable physical dexterity and perceptual ability, do not require interpersonal skills, and vice versa. However, differentiation by sex is immediately apparent; this relationship is stronger for men than women and is especially weak for white women. From this it appears that women, and especially white women, are more often segregated into occupations where the normative pattern does not hold; that is, they are in occupations in which the physical dexterity required is only minimally related to social relations skills.

The relationship between physical dexterity and physical activities also clearly differentiates men from women. The jobs men have generally require similar levels of physical dexterity and physical activity. However, for the jobs women occupy, there is a negative relationship between these two characteristics. Thus, women are segregated into jobs in which, if physical activity is required, physical dexterity and perceptual ability are not and vice versa. This finding certainly is consistent with our earlier findings that women are overrepresented in the clerical and service occupations.

Table 5.3 (continued)

People-things	Complexity	Clerical aptitude	Duncan SEI	Percentage male	Earnings
.084	.248	−.003	.064	.033	−.056
−.089	−.232	.319	−.309	.033	−.049
−.632	−.066	−.001	−.171	.148	−.105
−.437	−.500	.640	−.651	.488	−.274
	.354	−.359	.453	−.377	.121
.422		−.664	.874	−.062	.308
−.382	−.729		−.772	.259	−.250
−.424	.867	−.776		−.244	.383
−.432	−.003	.099	−.115		−.020
.143	.350	−.317	.411	.028	

Table 5.4

Correlations Among Occupational Characteristic Variables for Black and White Female Heads[a]

	Uncertainty	Unpleasantness of work	Physical dexterity	Physical activities
Uncertainty		.069	-.003	.068
Unpleasantness of work	.117		.017	.376
Physical dexterity	.238	-.089		-.198
Physical activities	-.214	.464	-.239	
People-things	.209	-.246	-.056	-.065
Complexity	.155	-.336	.068	-.570
Clerical aptitude	-.175	.337	-.381	.719
Duncan SEI	.118	-.421	.037	-.693
Percentage male	-.246	.075	-.441	.043
Earnings	.010	-.132	.117	-.261

[a]Whites below the diagonal; blacks above the diagonal.

Table 5.5

Correlations Among Occupational Characteristic Variables for Black and White Wives[a]

	Uncertainty	Unpleasantness of work	Physical dexterity	Physical activities
Uncertainty		-.179	-.215	.071
Unpleasantness of work	-.041		.155	.833
Physical dexterity	.344	-.084		-.139
Physical activities	-.169	.817	-.198	
People-things	.477	-.413	-.142	-.426
Complexity	.220	-.661	-.010	-.581
Clerical aptitude	-.246	.827	-.416	.824
Duncan SEI	.215	-.828	.078	-.780
Percentage male	-.576	.123	-.547	.277
Earnings	.030	-.293	.120	-.263

[a]Whites below the diagonal; blacks above the diagonal.

Table 5.4 *(continued)*

People-things	Complexity	Clerical aptitude	Duncan SEI	Percentage male	Earnings
.329	.185	-.060	.079	-.304	-.238
-.215	-.234	.234	-.393	-.075	-.160
-.457	.131	-.313	.104	.323	.127
-.230	-.640	.758	-.747	.054	-.401
	.272	-.204	.392	-.603	.078
.343		-.674	.858	.203	.371
-.160	-.564		-.790	-.046	-.478
.308	.849	-.735		.091	.461
-.340	.248	.097	.217		.180
.089	.451	-.348	.404	.190	

Table 5.5 *(continued)*

People-things	Complexity	Clerical aptitude	Duncan SEI	Percentage male	Earnings
.687	-.048	.176	-.128	-.795	-.209
-.407	-.532	.650	-.675	.256	-.281
-.349	-.038	-.376	.114	.028	.030
-.325	-.647	.835	-.810	.071	-.375
	.550	-.275	.453	-.564	.191
.592		-.695	.952	.191	.533
-.372	-.644		-.863	.024	-.526
.574	.938	-.812		.133	.556
-.412	.018	.393	-.103		.190
.069	.357	-.314	.370	-.008	

Sex differences also are found for the relationship between uncertainty and social relations skills. Women occupy positions for which social relations skills increase as the level of uncertainty increases, whereas men are in occupations for which decreased uncertainty has associated with it more interpersonal skills. In addition, we found that, whereas the jobs men have exhibit a positive correlation between uncertainty and physical activities, women hold jobs for which this relationship is negative or very weak.

Probably the most interesting findings to emerge from this analysis are the differences between the two wives' status groups and the other four status groups. There are five correlations for which black and white wives are different from the other four status groups. In all five instances the signs of the coefficients are consistent with those for the other female status groups (and usually the male status groups), but the magnitudes are substantially larger. To summarize these differences, black and white working wives hold occupations for which there are the following strong relationships:

1. As uncertainty increases, social relations skills increase.
2. As physical activity increases, the degree of work unpleasantness increases.
3. As the need for interpersonal skills increases, unpleasant working conditions decrease.
4. As job complexity increases, unpleasant working conditions decrease.
5. As job complexity increases, the need for interpersonal relations skills increases.

Thus, working wives of both races appear to be segregated into occupations in which unpleasant work conditions accompany noncomplex work tasks, limited interpersonal skills, and considerable physical activity.

Even with all of these differences among status groups, there is one correlation that is consistent for all groups: There is a fairly large negative relationship between complexity and physical activities. So, even with the considerable segregation by sex and more limited segregation by race, persons who have jobs high in complexity will not be involved in many physical activities and vice versa.

Multivariate Analysis

EFFECTS OF OCCUPATIONAL LABOR MARKET
CHARACTERISTICS ON EARNINGS

We now turn to the examination of the influence of the occupational labor market characteristics on earnings. Prior to examining the equations that simultaneously control for the variables presented in earlier chapters, it is informative to briefly discuss the zero-order correlations of earnings with each of the occupational labor market characteristics (see Tables 5.3 through 5.5).

Four of the six variables have correlations with earnings as hypothesized. The largest correlation is with complexity; across the six status groups complexity correlates .30 or higher with earnings. As hypothesized, social relations skills is positively, but very weakly, related to earnings for all status groups except for black female heads where there is no relationship. As expected, the degree of unpleasantness of the work setting is negatively, but not strongly, related to earnings. This relationship just misses being significant for white female heads and is noticeably stronger for black and white wives. Physical activities, as hypothesized, is negatively related to earnings, with this relationship being strongest for black women (black female heads and wives). A similar race–sex pattern is found for uncertainty. We had hypothesized a negative relationship, but for black women there is a positive relationship, and for the other status groups there is no relationship. Finally, although we had expected increased physical dexterity and perceptual abilities to result in higher earnings, this is found only for white wives and black female heads, where the relationship is positive but very weak. For black male heads there is a weak negative relationship, and for the other three status groups there is no significant relationship. Overall, however, there is no interpretable race–sex pattern here.

In general, these data indicate that we can expect some race–sex differences in how these variables influence earnings and that certain of these variables will be substantially more important than others. We now undertake the examination of the influence of these occupational characteristics within a multivariate framework.

The equation presented in Table 5.6 includes education, weeks worked, experience, task complexity, physical dexterity, uncertainty, and unpleasantness of work situation. In preliminary analyses we estimated regression equations that included the four human capital variables in our basic model (education, weeks worked, experience, and Duncan SEI) and the six occupational labor market variables. However, because of high multicollinearity among several of these variables, the coefficients of some variables were reduced to nonsignificance, changed from nonsignificance to significance, or even tipped in sign in some instances. This problem was especially exaggerated when using the Duncan SEI and complexity in the same equation. These two variables correlate .85 or higher for each of the status groups, indicating that the major dimension underlying the Duncan SEI is complexity. Because of this, the Duncan SEI variable is not controlled for in this

Table 5.6

Human Capital and Occupational Labor Market Determinants
of Earnings

Independent variables	Male heads			
	Whites		Blacks	
	Dev.	$b*$	Dev.	$b*$
Education (years)				
0-7	-4869	--	-1802	--
8	-3344	.041	-1105	.039
9-11	-2262	.095	-1007	.067
12	-849	.202	1492	.318
13-15	560***	.209	565***	.159
≥16	3774	.401	1913	.207
Weeks worked				
0-26	-4943	--	-6089	--
27-39	-3324	.037	-1892	.263
40-47	901	.266	510	.517
48-49	1093***	.291	589***	.609
50-52	-691	.221	-4	.634
	b	$b*$	b	$b*$
Experience	119***	.139	95***	.229
Complexity	312***	.263	149***	.240
Physical dexterity	275***	.119	-45***	-.028
Uncertainty	-943	-.091	-1003	-.178
Unpleasantness of work	162	.033	54	.028
Constant	1814		92	
$R^2/\bar{R}^2$	.213/.207		.232/.218	
	$N = 1870$		$N = 768$	

$R^2/\bar{R}^2$ data for additional specifications

3 Human capital vars.	.175/.171	.181/.170
6 Occupational vars.	.151/.148	.140/.134
4 Occupational vars.	.143/.142	.119/.114

Table 5.6 *(continued)*

| Independent variables | Female heads | | | |
| | Whites | | Blacks | |
	Dev.	$b*$	Dev.	$b*$
Education (years)				
0–7	-2049	--	-1851	--
8	-2291	-.013	-982	.063
9–11	-1244	.075	-283	.226
12	-154	.230	182	.304
13–15	524**	.237	238***	.205
≥16	1641	.366	3945	.423
Weeks worked				
0–26	-5206	--	-768	--
27–39	-735	.360	-1017	-.027
40–47	651	.612	-547	.030
48–49	714***	.684	1721***	.348
50–52	-323	.547	-593	.025
	b	$b*$	b	$b*$
Experience	95***	.263	48**	.155
Complexity	169***	.305	118***	.271
Physical dexterity	66*	.087	10***	.011
Uncertainty	-471	-.114	-888	-.242
Unpleasantness of work	98	.059	-40	-.039
Constant	-1523		2997	
$R^2/\bar{R}^2$	.397/.368		.424/.400	
	$N = 297$		$N = 349$	

$R^2/\bar{R}^2$ data for additional specifications

3 Human capital vars.	.342/.319	.349/.329
6 Occupational vars.	.221/.205	.267/.254
4 Occupational vars.	.220/.209	.242/.233

(continued)

Table 5.6 *(continued)*

Independent variables	Whites		Blacks	
	Dev.	$b*$	Dev.	$b*$
Education (years)				
0–7	−1715	−−	−1210	−−
8	−1529	.007	−986	.014
9–11	−1056	.057	−653	.074
12	−793	.118	270	.221
13–15	612***	.213	−584***	.064
≥16	2304	.421	2850	.352
Weeks worked				
0–26	−3719	−−	−2845	−−
27–39	−719	.321	−1609	.147
40–47	963	.469	587	.422
48–49	1541***	.574	1099***	.543
50–52	265	.430	426	.416
	b	$b*$	b	$b*$
Experience	85***	.190	25***	.080
Complexity	105***	.188	168	.370
Physical dexterity	106***	.115	89***	.075
Uncertainty	−617	−.101	−835	.174
Unpleasantness of work	−44	−.016	−140	−.067
Constant	−842		1917	
$R^2/\bar{R}^2$	.425/.415		.543/.524	
	$N = 817$		$N = 356$	

$R^2/\bar{R}^2$ data for additional specifications

3 Human capital vars.	.391/.384	.447/.431
6 Occupational vars.	.173/.167	.329/.318
4 Occupational vars.	.154/.150	.319/.312

[a]As discussed in the text the Duncan SEI variable is not controlled for in this chapter because of its high correlation with complexity.

*$p < .05$, **$p < .01$, ***$p < .001$.

chapter.[1] Physical activity correlates over .80 with unpleasant work conditions for two of the status groups and correlates over .50 with complexity for all status groups. Because including it substantially reduces the net influence of each of these three variables, it was not included in the equation presented. Finally, the specification also excludes the social relations composite for two reasons. First, its zero-order correlation with earnings is weak. Second, for certain status groups the social relations composite is highly correlated with uncertainty, physical dexterity, physical activity, and complexity. So, when this variable is included in the specification with the other composites, there is little increase in explained variance, yet the coefficients for these high correlated variables are reduced in magnitude.[2]

We first examine the variance explained by various sets of variables (see bottom panel of Table 5.6). The R^2 for just the human capital variables is of course less than that reported in Table 3.6, where the Duncan SEI also is included. We still find the major differences to be sex-linked; these human capital resources are substantially more important in explaining earnings for women. Although the R^2 for just the four occupational characteristics varies by status group (the range is from .12 to .32), there is no clear differentiation by race or sex.[3] It would appear, however, that black women are influenced more by these occupational characteristics than are the other status groups. As may be seen by comparing the explained variances for various specifications, there is considerable covariation between the human capital and occupational characteristics. Using unique explained variance as the criterion, the data clearly show that the human capital variables are more important than the occupational labor market variables measured (compare upper and lower panel R^2 values). Nevertheless, we may conclude that the characteristics of the worker's occupational labor market independently influence his or her earnings. In addition, the earlier observation that black females' status groups are most strongly influenced by occupational characteristics is supported; the R^2 increments for black female heads and black wives are 8

---

[1]When one equation is estimated that includes just Duncan SEI and the other variables and another equation is estimated that includes just complexity and the other variables, both Duncan SEI and complexity are highly significant. When both variables are included in the same equation, complexity goes to nonsignificance, and although the Duncan SEI remains significant, its magnitude is greatly reduced. For additional discussion concerning the relationship between the Duncan SEI and the several occupational labor market characteristics discussed here see Parcel and Mueller (1983).

[2]When the two excluded variables are added to the four that are retained, the increase in R^2 is less than or equal to .02 across the six status groups.

[3]The R^2 values for the combined influence of the six occupation characteristics are included to demonstrate that the decision to eliminate two of the variables does not seriously alter the inferences drawn.

percentage points or larger, whereas for the other status groups, they are less than 6 percentage points.

Turing to the importance of particular variables in the equation in Table 5.6, we note that across all status groups the human capital variables remain statistically significant, and since the patterns are as reported in previous chapters, they will not be discussed here. Using statistical significance as the criterion, complexity and uncertainty are significant for all status groups. Physical dexterity is significant only for white male heads and white wives. Thus, no patterns emerge suggesting sex or race differences in how the variables operate to influence earnings.

A comparison of the magnitudes of the same coefficient across status groups does reveal some status group differences, but still race–sex differences are minimal. The major difference is for complexity. Being in occupations characterized by more complexity, although advantaging all, benefits white males substantially more than it does blacks or women. This is especially significant given, as shown earlier, that women and blacks are underrepresented, when compared with white males, in the occupations characterized by high complexity.[4] Thus, the minority groups are doubly disadvantaged; they are excluded from high complexity occupations that are rewarded with high earnings, but even when they are in these occupations, the dollar return to the increased complexity is lower than it is for white males.

Although there is race differentiation regarding the zero-order correlation of unpleasantness of work conditions with earnings, its net influence is non-significant and thus does not aid us in explaining earnings or race–sex differences in earnings. So, although the races are differentially found in unpleasant jobs, our data indicate that it is not the influence of this variable that contributes to racial differences in earnings.

Recall that for uncertainty there were no zero-order correlations with earnings except for black women, for whom the relationship was negative. Table 5.6 suggests that there is a net negative influence of uncertainty on earnings for all status groups, with the only differences in magnitude appearing for white women, for whom the coefficients are smaller than for the other status groups. This change from a zero coefficient to a significant one after introducing controls, usually referred to as a suppressor effect, suggests that net of human capital variables and other occupational characteristics, the less uncertainty associated with the job activities, the higher the earnings. To determine why this is happening we estimated several other equations in which we observed the change in the coefficient for uncertainty as the other

---

[4]This is even more extreme for blacks, whose occupations are much lower in complexity than those in the white population (see Table 5.2).

occupation variables are added one at a time (data not included). Although there is some variation by status group, complexity is the variable that operates rather consistently to increase the negative influence of uncertainty. That is, the influence of uncertainty is suppressedd until the complexity of the job is controlled. This means that among individuals at the same level of complexity, earnings will be higher for those with jobs involving the least uncertainty. This finding is difficult to explain with conventional theories since they do not specify the relationship between earnings and the variety of duties and frequency of change associated with the occupation.

Table 5.7 presents regression data that allow us to determine the influence of the occupational characteristics net of human capital resources and the six areal and two industrial labor market characteristics examined in Chapters 3 and 4. Complexity continues to be the dominant variable across status groups, although it no longer is statistically significant for black wives. In addition, with other labor market conditions controlled, there actually is more evidence of sex and race differentiation by occupational labor market characteristics. Although white male heads remain the group to benefit most from being employed in more complex occupations, there now is a clearer distinction between men and women: Men consistently benefit more than women from access to occupational complexity. Race differences also are apparent: Black women and black men obtain lower returns to occupational complexity than their white counterparts. Of course, this lower rate of return is but part of the black disadvantage; as shown in Tables 5.1 and 5.2, blacks are in the less complex jobs to begin with.

With the exception of black wives, uncertainty continues to influence earnings. No easily recognizable race–sex differences are apparent, and since the discussion of the direction of this influence was presented earlier, it will not be repeated here. A substantive interpretation of the newly significant unpleasant work conditions variable for black males (positive influence) and physical dexterity for black wives (negative influence) does not appear warranted. The coefficients barely reach significance; the standardized coefficients are small, and one has been tipped from a positive to negative sign.

Finally, the pattern of race–sex differences in the total net influence of all occupation characteristics on earnings is somewhat changed. When we control only for human capital variables, the net explained variance of occupational variables for black female heads is .075 and for black wives it is .096, these being the largest for any of the status groups. When the other labor market variables are also controlled, these respective increments are .018 and .009, the smallest of all the status groups. From this we can infer that the various labor market characteristics do covary with each other, a topic discussed more fully in Appendix C. Even with the covariation of variables across the three labor market contexts, our earlier conclusions about local

Table 5.7

Human Capital and Areal, Industrial, and Occupational Labor
Market Determinants of Earnings

| | Male heads | | | |
| | Whites | | Blacks | |
Independent variables	Dev.	b^*	Dev.	b^*
Education (years)				
0–7	−4290	−−	−658	−−
8	−2866	.038	−365	.016
9–11	−2159	.078	−758	−.008
12	−798	.175	799	.141
13–15	297***	.177	−206***	.030
≥16	3576	.365	1300	.109
Weeks worked				
0–26	−4979	−−	−5844	−−
27–39	−3068	.044	−2168	.230
40–47	735	.260	372	.487
48–49	999***	.288	−37***	.530
50–52	−551	.230	445	.655

	b	b^*	b	b^*
Experience	113***	.132	77***	.184
Crowding	332	.038	−455***	−.152
Manufacturing dominance	−48	−.007	287*	.069
Manufacturing sector health	86***	.017	805***	.338
Tertiary sector health	257	.109	−88*	−.069
Tertiary sector growth	−212*	−.038	−269*	−.089
Tertiary sector complexity	346	.051	193	.053
Concentration and investment	21	.007	345***	.234
Firm growth	149***	.026	79***	.028
Complexity	298***	.252	211	.338
Physical dexterity	266***	.115	−93***	−.058
Uncertainty	−820	−.080	−676*	−.120
Unpleasantness of work	137	.028	127	.066
Constant	1539		1881	
$R^2/\bar{R}^2$	.241/.232		.433/.416	
	N = 1870		N = 768	

Table 5.7 *(continued)*

Independent variables	Female heads			
	Whites		Blacks	
	Dev.	$b*$	Dev.	$b*$
Education (years)				
0–7	−633	−−	145	−−
8	−1599	−.050	−220	−.026
9–11	−708	−.007	42	−.015
12	−229	.049	−512	−.098
13–15	324	.088	293***	.015
≥16	1205	.182	2369	.162
Weeks worked				
0–26	−4965	−−	−1833	−−
27–39	−366	.370	−936	.096
40–47	119	.531	251	.282
48–49	498***	.631	487**	.324
50–52	159	.574	−29	.257
	b	$b*$	b	$b*$
Experience	80***	.219	2***	.005
Crowding	−223	−.046	−495***	−.178
Manufacturing dominance	91	.032	−5	−.002
Manufacturing sector health	125*	.052	−193*	−.107
Tertiary sector health	175***	.158	10**	.011
Tertiary sector growth	430	.176	291***	.147
Tertiary sector complexity	293	.083	530	.185
Concentration and investment	302***	.214	633***	.592
Firm growth	−49***	−.023	−133*	−.089
Complexity	152	.274	63**	.144
Physical dexterity	64*	.085	−55	−.056
Uncertainty	−479	−.116	−393*	−.107
Unpleasantness of work	102	.062	−36	−.034
Constant	−234		4902	
$R^2/\bar{R}^2$	.476/.434		.609/.583	
	$N = 297$		$N = 349$	

(continued)

Table 5.7 *(continued)*

| Independent variables | Wives | | | |
| | Whites | | Blacks | |
	Dev.	b^*	Dev.	b^*
Education (years)				
0–7	-667	--	-533	--
8	-1136	-.019	-945	-.026
9–11	-771	-.009	-670	-.018
12	-716	-.006	-367	.025
13–15	473***	.104	-614***	-.008
≥16	1905	.269	5344	.510
Weeks worked				
0–26	-3550	--	-2256	--
27–39	-689	.306	-1727	.063
40–47	863	.442	610	.353
48–49	1420***	.542	584***	.391
50–52	355	.421	948	.407
	b	b^*	b	b^*
Experience	83***	.187	42***	.136
Crowding	-13	-.004	72	.036
Manufacturing dominance	-7	-.003	109	.036
Manufacturing sector health	-30*	-.014	-4**	-.002
Tertiary sector health	80	.081	146*	.163
Tertiary sector growth	-56	-.025	-159***	-.083
Tertiary sector complexity	1	.000	-368	-.161
Concentration and investment	240***	.184	621***	.545
Firm growth	-28***	-.015	41	.027
Complexity	133**	.239	7*	.016
Physical dexterity	75***	.081	-103	-.087
Uncertainty	-662	-.108	-307	-.064
Unpleasantness of work	130	.046	82	.039
Constant	349		1897	
$R^2/\bar{R}^2$	.459/.444		.724/.705	
	$N = 817$		$N = 356$	

*$p < .05$, **$p < .01$, ***$p < .001$.

and industrial labor markets are not altered much. The statistical significance of only four coefficients across all status groups was altered. The variables involved are teritary sector growth for white male heads and black male heads, and manufacturing sector health and firm growth for black female heads. In all cases either the coefficient had been small and barely significant and then became significant or vice versa. We believe these small changes do not merit discussion and interpretation.[5]

Table 5.8 presents a summary of increment in R^2 values obtained to assess the increase in explained variance due to addition of the respective sets of labor market variables net of human capital and previously discussed labor market variables. The impact of the respective sets is strongest among black male heads and weakest for white wives and white male heads. Increments in explained variance for the respective markets are consistent in magnitude for white female heads, whereas for black female workers, there are large increments due to the addition of the industrial labor market characteristics, modest increments due to local characteristics, and no significant increments due to the addition of occupational labor market characteristics. These findings serve to summarize the discussion in Chapters 3, 4, and 5 concerning the relative importance of the several types of labor market characteristics across status groups, and generally highlight our conclusion concerning ascriptive status differences in structural influences on earnings attainment.

We also are interested in the relationship between the concentration of economic minority workers in an occupation and earnings of majority and minority workers. To assess this relationship we used the percentage male as

---

[5]As in Chapter 4, we are interested in knowing whether the pattern of missing data on concentration and investment has affected our interpretation of the occupational labor market effects in a fundamental way. To address this we compared the model in Table 5.6 with the same specification for workers for whom concentration and investment is measured (data not presented). As in Chapter 4 this analysis is confined to black female heads and black wives, the two status groups for whom the missing data problem is most severe. For Black female heads there is general similarity in the magnitudes of the occupational labor market coefficients between the sample and subsample. There are no major changes in the magnitudes of the coefficients associated with complexity, physical dexterity, and unpleasant working conditions, although the coefficient associated with uncertainty increases from 888 in Table 5.6 to 1137 in the subsample. Among black wives, however, complexity drops from 168 to 86 (which is still statistically significant), and uncertainty drops from 835 to 751 (which retains significance at the .001 level). Unpleasant working conditions attains significance ($b = -326$, $p < .01$) as does physical dexterity ($b = 159$, $p < .05$). It appears that these changes are due to the economic characteristics of the subsample. When a high proportion of professional workers is excluded, the explanatory power of characteristics predictive of earnings attainment among professional workers is decreased, and the explanatory power of characteristics predictive of earnings in nonprofessional positions is increased. The more extreme degree of industrial segregation among black wives than among black female heads may account for the marital status difference in the degree of these changes.

Table 5.8

Net Contributions to Explained Variance of the Three Sets of
Labor Market Variables

Status group	R^2 increments[a] due to		
	Local labor markets	Industrial labor markets	Occupational labor markets
White male heads	2.73	.06	3.31
Black male heads	14.76	4.61	6.48
White female heads	5.54	3.61	4.43
Black female heads	5.02	13.00	1.81
White wives	.63	2.65	2.96
Black wives	4.02	10.53	.89

[a]The R^2 increments are increases associated with the indicated
labor market variables *after* education, weeks worked, experience,
and the previously discussed labor market variables have been
included in the equation.

the measure of concentration; we make no prediction concerning the relationship with males' earnings, although for females a positive effect is
expected.

Because of multicollinearity problems for several status groups, this test
was conducted only for white male and female heads (see Table 5.9). The
zero-order correlation of percentage male with earnings for males is .028 (not
significant), whereas for females it is .190 as predicted. Thus, without any
controls women would appear to benefit when they are employed in occupations with greater concentrations of men. However, once the other variables
we have been examining are included in the equation, we find male concentration to have a significant positive influence for both white men and
women. Inclusion of this variable does not alter the inferences already drawn
for white males and produces only a minor change for white female heads
(compare the equations in Tables 5.7 and 5.9).

These data suggest that the greater the concentration of the economic
minority group (women) in an occupation, the lower the earnings will be for
the minority and majority groups. Relevant theory states that this is due to
the increased competition among the minority group members, but the data
do not allow for a direct test of this argument. We also find that men can
expect their earnings to be negatively influenced if they are employed in
female-dominated occupations. By tradition those jobs dominated by women
such as nurse, teacher, and service occupations are low-paying occupations,
regardless of the sex of the incumbent. It is important to emphasize, how-

Table 5.9

Human Capital and Areal, Industrial, and Occupational
Determinants of Earnings with Control for Percentage
Male for White Male and Female Heads

Independent variables	Male heads		Female heads	
	Dev.	$b*$	Dev.	$b*$
Education (years)				
0–7	−4403	−−	−907	−−
8	−2967	.039	−1621	−.037
9–11	−2296	.077	−863	.004
12	−820	.180	−199	.086
13–15	355***	.183	412	.121
≥16	3692	.375	1235	.213
Weeks worked				
0–26	−5028	−−	−5169	−−
27–39	−2983	.047	−269	.395
40–47	746	.263	203	.561
48–49	1012***	.292	467***	.651
50–52	−576	.232	112	.592

	b	$b*$	b	$b*$
Experience	112*****	.131	79****	.219
Percentage male	26	.062	22	.152
Crowding	331	.038	−206	−.042
Manufacturing dominance	−41	−.006	105	.037
Manufacturing sector health	76***	.015	89**	.037
Tertiary sector health	262	.112	193***	.174
Tertiary sector growth	−214*	−.038	426	.174
Tertiary sector complexity	345	.051	249	.070
Concentration and investment	−4	−.001	262***	.185
Firm growth	104***	.018	−121**	−.059
Complexity	288***	.244	110**	.198
Physical dexterity	238***	.103	110	.146
Uncertainty	−973	−.094	−328	−.079
Unpleasantness of work	116	.024	44	.027
Constant	−741		−1668	
$R^2/\bar{R}^2$	.244/.235		.488/.445	
	$N = 1870$		$N = 297$	

*$p < .05$, **$p < .01$, ***$p < .001$.

ever, that relative to other variables in the equation, this is not a major determinant of earnings.

EFFECTS OF CLASS/AUTHORITY POSITION ON EARNINGS

In Chapter 1 we reviewed literature from dual labor market theory, stratification theory on class differentiation, and organizational theory on authority hierarchies, which leads us to expect earnings to vary by class/authority position even after human capital and labor market characteristics are taken into account. We expect workers to earn less than either supervisors or employers, and employers with large numbers of employees should earn more than supervisors. Among supervisors, pay should be higher for those with a larger span of responsibility (influence over pay and promotions) and those with a larger span of control (large number of subordinates). Among workers, earnings should be positively related to the vertical complexity of the firm. In addition, to the extent that the sexes and the races are differentially distributed in class/authority positions and there are differential returns to these positions, a portion of race and sex earnings differences should be explained by this construct.

Class/authority is operationalized as several sets of dummy variables that capture the various dimensions known or hypothesized to be related to earnings. First, we are able to differentiate among persons who own their own business (employers) and those who work for others (employees). For the employers it also is possible to differentiate by the number of employees in the business. Among the employees we are able to differentiate between those who do and do not supervise, and among these we can differentiate by whether the person's supervisor has a supervisor (our measure of vertical complexity).[6] For those who supervise, it is possible to differentiate by span of

---

[6]The convention in other research is to use "manager" rather than "supervisor" to refer to persons who supervise others. Both terms pose problems. Manager is probably more appropriate for white-collar jobs, whereas supervisor is more appropriate for blue-collar positions. We have chosen to use supervisor primarily because the questions in the survey ask specifically about supervising rather than managing. In addition, some researchers (Wright and Perrone, 1977; Kalleberg and Griffin, 1980) have argued that teachers should be viewed as workers even though most teachers indicate that they supervise others (assumed to be their students by these researchers). We concur with this argument for elementary and high school teachers but believe college and university teachers who say they supervise others most likely do so. Teaching assistants, research assistants, work–study personnel, and secretaries typically are within the span of control and responsibility of college and university teachers. For this reason only elementary and high school teachers have been placed in the worker category; college and university teachers are given a class/authority code based on their response to the questions identified in footnote 7.

responsibility (whether the supervisor does or does not have authority regarding the pay and promotion of subordinates) as well as by span of control (the number of people supervised). For these two dimensions defined just for supervisors, large span of responsibility is operationalized as having say about the pay and promotion of subordinates, whereas small span of responsibility refers to having no influence over this; large span of control is operationalized as supervising 10 or more employees, whereas small span of control refers to supervising 1–9 employees. For the dimension defined for both supervisors and workers: High vertical complexity is defined as the stiuation in which the employee's supervisor also has a superivsor, whereas low vertical complexity refers to the situation in which the employee's supervisor has no supervisor.

In some instances it is useful to compare employer with supervisor and with worker; large span of responsibility with small span of responsibility; large span of control with small span of control; and low vertical complexity with high vertical complexity. A more reliable estimate of the total influence of class/authority on earnings is possible, however, by using a set of dummy variables that represent 14 mutually exclusive and exhaustive categories:[7]

1. Employer, no employees
2. Employer, 1–2 employees
3. Employer, 3–19 employees
4. Employer, 20 or more employees
5. Supervisor with large span of control, large span of responsibility, and in a firm with low vertical complexity
6. Supervisor with small span of control, large span of responsibility, and in a firm with low vertical complexity
7. Supervisor with large span of control, small span of responsibility, and in a firm with low vertical complexity
8. Supervisor with small span of control, small span of responsibility, and in a firm with low vertical complexity
9. Supervisor with large span of control, large span of responsibility, and in a firm with high vertical complexity
10. Supervisor with small span of control, large span of responsibility, and in a firm with high vertical complexity

---

[7]The following survey questions are used in creating the dummy variables: Do you work for someone else, yourself, or what? The self-employed are then asked: When you work for yourself, do you employ other people? If they answer yes, they are asked to indicate the number of employees. Those who work for others (assumed to have at least one supervisor) are asked if they supervise the work of others and if they do, how many they supervise and whether they have say regarding their pay and promotions. Finally, everyone working for others is asked: Does your boss have a supervisor over him/her?

11. Supervisor with large span of control, small span of responsibility, and in a firm with high vertical complexity
12. Supervisor with small span of control, small span of responsibility, and in a firm with high vertical complexity
13. Worker in a firm with high vertical complexity
14. Worker in a firm with low vertical complexity.

All 14 categories are used for white male heads, but for the other status groups some of the categories had to be combined because of small cell sizes. For black male heads the following categories had to be combined: 3 and 4; 5 and 6; 7 and 8. For the four female status groups the combined categories are 1–4; 5–8; 9 and 10.[8]

Table 5.10 presents the distribution of cases for race and sex status groups by class/authority category. Considering the basic employer– supervisor–worker distinction, the major difference is between white males and the other status groups. White males, when compared with the other groups, are more likely to be employers and supervisors and less likely to be workers. Among women whites are more likely than blacks to be supervisors and less likely to be workers. Considering just supervisors, differentiation by race and sex clearly is present. Male supervisors, and especially white male supervisors, more often than females are in positions where the span of responsibility includes decisions about pay and promotion of subordinates. In addition, for each of the three race comparisons white supervisors more often than black supervisors are in the high responsibility positions. Considering the span of control of supervisors, a race by sex interaction is apparent.

---

[8]A qualifying statement about the interpretation of one of these class/authority dimensions is necessary. For workers (employees who do not supervise) the question about number of superiors clearly measures what is referred to as vertical complexity, the number of levels in the authority hierarchy of a firm. This also may be viewed as a proxy for firm size since vertical complexity is positively correlated with firm size. For supervisors, however, the question about number of superiors is not so easily interpreted. For example, a person may be next to the bottom in the hierarchy of a large firm and thus answer "two or more superiors," or a person may be next to the top in a large firm and answer "only one superior." In the first instance, we would be correct in saying the person belongs to a firm high in vertical complexity (coded as 1), but in the second instance, our coding as a firm with low complexity (coded as 0) would be incorrect. Thus, for supervisors, the person's relative position in the authority hierarchy is confounded with the degree of vertical complexity of the firm. And, unfortunately, the two influences operate in opposite directions. In our first example, the high vertical complexity (coded 1 because of 2 or more superiors) will have a high earnings mean; in the second example, the high position in the firm (coded as 0 because of only one superior) also will have a high earnings mean. As a result, the correlation between this variable and earnings is reduced substantially. For these reasons, we would hypothesize this variable to be related to earnings for workers but do not expect a very strong, if any, relationship for supervisors.

Table 5.10

Percentage Distribution of Cases by Class/Authority
Category for Each Status Group[a]

Class/authority	Males Whites	Males Blacks	Female heads Whites	Female heads Blacks	Wives Whites	Wives Blacks
Employer	19.0	7.0	4.6	4.9	7.2	4.2
20 or more employees	8.7	24.5	--	--	--	--
3–19 employees	31.4		--	--	--	--
1–2 employees	19.2	51.0	--	--	--	--
No employees	40.5	24.5	--	--	--	--
Supervisor	39.3	23.4	28.3	17.0	27.4	22.7
Responsibility(Resp.)						
Present	56.9	44.2	37.2	23.5	39.8	31.2
Absent	43.1	55.8	62.8	76.5	60.2	68.8
Span of control(SC)						
Large	43.2	27.9	25.6	31.4	12.7	27.5
Small	56.8	72.1	74.4	68.6	87.3	72.5
Vertical complexity(VC)						
High	75.9	89.0	62.8	82.4	70.1	86.2
Low	24.1	11.0	37.2	17.6	29.9	13.8
Worker	41.7	69.6	67.1	78.1	65.4	73.1
Vertical complexity						
High	86.6	83.7	74.6	81.6	77.8	75.5
Low	13.4	16.3	25.4	18.4	22.2	24.5
Joint categories						
Resp. present, low VC						
Large SC	7.1 }	6.1 }	37.2	15.7	29.9	12.7
Small SC	6.5 }					
Resp. absent, low VC						
Large SC	3.1 }	4.9 }				
Small SC	7.3 }					
Resp. present, high VC						
Large SC	25.0	18.4 }	24.4	21.6	23.5	26.6
Small SC	18.3	19.6 }				
Resp. absent, high VC						
Large SC	8.0	8.0	10.3	27.4	5.9	10.1
Small SC	24.7	42.9	28.2	35.3	40.7	50.6
N[b]	1752	697	276	299	807	351

[a] The percentages for employer, supervisor, and worker total 100 as do the independent breakdowns within each of these major categories.

[b] The number of cases for which class/authority information is available.

Although white male supervisors are more likely than black male supervisors to have a large span of control, black women are more likely than white women to have a large span of control. Also, regardless of sex, black supervisors are more often than white supervisors employed by firms in which there is high vertical complexity.

Examining only workers, we find small sex differences; male workers, more often than female workers, are in firms with high vertical complexity. This latter finding is consistent with dual labor market theory since it suggests that women are segregated into the secondary labor market, which is characterized by smaller firms (low vertical complexity). In sum, these data on the allocation of men and women and blacks and whites into class/authority positions are generally consistent with past theory and research; men and whites more often are in class/authority positions that are hypothesized or known to be rewarded with the highest earnings.

To assess whether class/authority is related to earnings for each status group we regressed earnings on the total set of dummy variables representing class/authority. The adjusted R^2 values are: white male heads, .18; black male heads, .20; white female heads, .06; black female heads, .21; white wives, .14; black wives, .15. So, with the exception of white female heads, the zero-order relationship of class/authority with earnings is fairly large. To determine the form of this relationship, Table 5.11 presents unadjusted earnings means (actually presented as deviations from the grand mean) for the various dimensions for each status group.

Supervisors across all status groups earn more than workers, but employers, with the exception of white male heads, actually earn less than workers. This is misleading, however, because most of the women employers are in the "no employees" category (data not shown in Table 5.10). Men also are well below their grand mean in the employer with no employees category. For white males the pattern reported by Aldrich and Weiss (1981) is found. There is a monotonic increase in the earnings of the employer as the number of employees increases.

Considering only supervisors, we generally find the hypotheses supported: Supervisors with the largest spans of control and the largest spans of responsibility earn the most. The exceptions to these generalizations are for black women. Black female heads are not rewarded for being in positions of greater responsibility, nor are black wives rewarded for supervising more subordinates. As expected, the differences between those with only one and those with two or more superiors are not significant for any of the status groups.

An examination of earnings for various combinations of levels of these dimensions clearly shows their importance in explaining earnings differences. White males, for example, differ by over $10,000 for one compari-

Table 5.11

Unadjusted Earnings Means for Status Groups by Class/
Authority Category[a]

Class/authority	Males Whites	Males Blacks	Female heads Whites	Female heads Blacks	Wives Whites	Wives Blacks
Employer	2140	778	--	--	--	--
20 or more employees	18107	1106	--	--	--	--
3-19 employees	6587		-505	-1942	-2704	-736
1-2 employees	375	2815	--	--	--	--
No employees	-3923	-3762	--	--	--	--
Supervisor	1908	1858	1589	2244	1848	960
Responsibility(Resp.)						
Present	4295	4326	3465	2030	3025	1898
Absent	-1253	-133	488	2312	1074	526
Span of control(SC)						
Large	4503	5082	4269	4860	2131	-150
Small	-66	691	654	1072	1806	1389
Vertical complexity(VC)						
High	2108	2002	1622	2175	1770	1041
Low	1276	688	1532	2599	2029	417
Worker	-2171	-118	-255	-220	-455	-200
Vertical complexity						
High	-1972	597	128	709	130	577
Low	-3450	-3777	-1379	-1936	-2101	-2586
Joint categories						
Resp. present, low VC						
Large SC	6704 } 2497		1532	2599	2029	417
Small SC	818 }					
Resp. absent, low VC						
Large SC	1144 } -1750					
Small SC	-3567 }					
Resp. present, high VC						
Large SC	5714 } 5627		3087	1843	2748	2139
Small SC	2667 } 3709					
Resp. absent, high VC						
Large SC	73	414	1791	4926	897	1415
Small SC	-1303	-713	314	181	1324	379
Grand mean	14,404	9481	7416	5502	5579	5235

[a] The unadjusted means (in dollars) are expressed as deviations from the grand mean.

son (supervisors with responsibility, large span of control, and only one superior versus supervisors with no responsibility, a small span of control, and only one superior). We also observe an interaction of vertical complexity with span of control for white males. For those who supervise 10 or more employees (Large SC), it is the Low VC (low vertical complexity) category that has the highest earnings, but for those who supervise fewer than 10 employees (Small SC), it is the High VC (high vertical complexity) category that earns the most. Among black males, however, the high vertical complexity supervisors consistently have higher earnings than those who are in low vertical complexity firms. As discussed previously, we are reluctant to attempt an interpretation because of the ambiguity in meaning of the number of superiors variable. The data for women show no clear advantage for either supervisory situation. Finally, the low earnings of workers is especially pronounced for workers who are in low vertical complexity firms; for all status groups except for white male heads, workers with two or more superiors (high vertical complexity) earn significantly more than those with just one superior.

It is possible, of course, that the influence of class/authority is partly or entirely spurious due to other variables influencing both class/authority and earnings. To assess this possibility, we have examined the influence of class/authority net of the human capital variables and the local, industrial, and occupational labor market characteristics. Comparing the explained variance for an equation with human capital variables and characteristics of the three labor markets (Table 5.7) with the R^2 for the equation with class/authority variables added gives the variance that is uniquely accounted for by the set of all class/authority dummy variables. All of the R^2 increments, except for white female heads, are statistically significant, and the improvement in variance explained for several of the status groups must be considered large given the number of variables already in the equation; however, the patterns in the R^2 increments do not vary systematically by race and sex.[9]

Table 5.12 displays adjusted earnings means based on controlling for the variables identified above. Comparing these values with the corresponding values in Table 5.11, we rather consistently observe reductions in magnitudes of the differences between various class/authority categories, but overall the patterns found for the unadjusted means remain.[10] Supervisors still earn more than workers, although the advantage is small for most status

[9]The R^2 increments are as follows: for white male heads, 10.42; for black male heads, 7.89; for white female heads, 1.30; for black female heads, 7.08; for white wives, 4.82; for black wives, 4.69.

[10]Because job tenure with the firm is known to be related to advancement in the authority hierarchy, we also estimated adjusted means from equations that included this variable. In no instances were the patterns we report changed.

Table 5.12

Adjusted Earnings Means for Status Groups by Class/
Authority Categories[a]

Class/authority	Males Whites	Males Blacks	Female heads Whites	Female heads Blacks[b]	Wives Whites	Wives Blacks
Employer	1954	-319	217	-1822	-2048	-110
20 or more employees	15,829	-1352	--	--	--	--
3-19 employees	5814		--	--	--	--
1-2 employees	782	1435	--	--	--	--
No employees	-3308	-3525	--	--	--	--
Supervisor	427	591	660	880	820	165
Responsibility(Resp.)						
Present	2057	2278	1627	608	1401	2444
Absent	-1537	-424	171	967	504	-626
Span of control(SC)						
Large	2481	3055	2241	3708	1141	-2090
Small	-1048	-253	116	-367	796	955
Vertical complexity(VC)						
High	272	596	639	883	645	72
Low	899	701	784	864	1306	574
Worker	-1293	-167	-293	-77	-117	-45
Vertical complexity						
High	-1577	295	-341	171	238	209
Low	-1103	-2688	-130	1110	-1288	-1654
Joint categories						
Resp. present, low VC						
Large SC	4909	836				
Small SC	1043		691	773	1131	1237
Resp. absent, low VC						
Large SC	1099	126				
Small SC	-2955					
Resp. present, high VC						
Large SC	3461	3730	1247	148	1197	2510
Small SC	100	1090				
Resp. absent, high VC						
Large SC	-609	2820	1109	3844	452	-2634
Small SC	-1818	-1068	-10	-625	421	230
Grand mean	14,404	9481	7416	5502	5579	5235

[a]The adjusted means (in dollars) are expressed as deviations
from the grand mean and are obtained by controlling for weeks
worked, education, experience, and the local, industrial, and
occupational labor market characteristics--the variables in
Table 5.7.
[b]The industrial labor market variables are not controlled.

groups. As before, with the exception of white male heads, employers earn about the same as or less than workers. In addition, the monotonic increase in earnings by firm size for white male heads also continues to hold after controls. The patterns found for various dimensions in the supervisory category also remain. For all status groups but black female heads, supervisors who must take responsiblity for pay and promotion decisions about subordinates earn more than those who do not have this responsibility. Also, for all but black wives, the greater the span of control, the higher the earnings. The adjusted means for comparing supervisors by vertical complexity continue to show no significant differences. Examination of just workers indicates that the earnings advantage enjoyed by those with two or more more superiors (firms with high vertical complexity) exists only for three status groups: black male heads and both black and white wives.

Considering the various *combinations* of supervisory dimensions (see "Joint categories," Table 5.12), we find reductions in the magnitudes of the influence of dimensions, but little change in the patterns. As with the unadjusted means, the highest earnings go to white male heads who, regardless of the vertical complexity, have positions with large spans of responsiblity and control. For white male heads, the status group for which the most complete examination of the joint influence of the three supervisory dimensions is possible, the data show distinct earnings advantages for those with responsibility versus those without it and advantages for those with a large span of control versus those with a small span of control. Also, as was observed for the unadjusted means, there is some evidence of an interaction between span of control and number of superiors, but this is not as strong for these adjusted means.

Among black male heads, having a large span of control is the dimension leading to the highest earnings. For the one comparison possible across all six status groups (no responsibility, low vertical complexity, but varying on span of control), there are race by sex interactions. Males who have a large span of control, regardless of race, earn more than those with a small span. Among women, however, this pattern is found for white but not black women. Black women either earn the same or less when they have a large span of control.

The findings concerning class/authority and earnings can be summarized as follows. First, the data on the distribution of cases by race and sex into various class/authority positions generally show that males as compared with females and blacks when compared with whites are more often in positions hypothesized or known to be rewarded with higher earnings. Second, with the exception of white female heads, the *total* set of class/authority dummy variables has a significant and meaningful net influence on earnings. Third, owning a buisness, as compared with being employed provides earnings advantages but only if the employer is a white male who employs others. Fourth, among supervisors, vertical complexity of the firm is unrelated to earnings, but earnings are higher if the span of control is large (except for black wives) and the span of responsibility is large (except for black female heads). Fifth, not having a supervisory position (i.e., being a worker) generally has a negative influence on earnings, but this is accentuated for blacks when they are employed in a firm with low vertical complexity.

Regression Standardization

Table 5.13 presents the results of the regression standardization used to decompose the earnings differences between white male heads and black male heads. Three equations for each status group were estimated and decomposed in a stepwise fashion, first, to assess the contribution of occupational labor market characteristics net of human capital and local and industrial labor market characteristics and, second, to assess the contribution of class/authority net of all of these variables. As in the earlier chapters we will not attempt a detailed interpretation of the slope and intercept components separately. Such an interpretation requires that zero points of the variables be meaningful—a condition not met for many of our variables.

The data from the first standardization serve primarily as a baseline, since the importance of these variables has been discussed in earlier chapters. It indicates that 33.6% ($1656) of the $4923 earnings advantage to white men would be removed if black men had the same distributions as white men on human capital, local labor market, and industrial labor market variables. If blacks are also placed in occupations with the same characteristics as those occupied by white men, the gap would be reduced another $453 (see Row 2). If these two male populations are also given the same class/authority distributions, the gap would actually be increased by about $100 (see Row 3). Caution is necessary in automatically assuming class/authority is less important than the occupational labor market characteristics, however. The stepwise procedure used attributes what is common to the two sets of variables to the occupational characteristics.

An examination of the effect of each occupational characteristic in the final step of the decomposition also aids in the interpretation (data not presented). Blacks would gain substantially only if they were employed in jobs with the same complexity levels as whites; moving blacks to jobs with white workers' levels of uncertainty, unpleasantness, and physical dexterity skills would have little effect or actually increase the earnings gap. Although the total

Table 5.13

Summary of Regression Standardization Components

Pair and variables	Composition	Slopes and intercepts	Interaction
White male heads versus black male heads			
(1) Human capital and areal and industrial labor markets[a]	33.6% ($1656)	65.9% ($3243)	.5% ($24)
(2) Human capital and areal, industrial, and occupational labor markets	42.8% ($2109)	41.7% ($2055)	15.4% ($759)
(3) Human capital and areal, industrial and occupational labor markets and class/authority	40.8% ($2007)	34.9% ($1717)	24.3% ($1198)
Initial gap: $14,404 - 9,481 = $4,923			
White male heads versus white female heads			
(1) Human capital and areal and industrial labor markets	8.6% ($602)	90.9% ($6347)	.5% ($38)
(2) Human capital and areal, industrial, and occupational labor markets	10.1% ($705)	88.1% ($6157)	1.8% ($125)
(3) Human capital and areal, industrial, and occupational labor markets and class/authority	13.0% ($905)	81.4% ($5688)	5.6% ($394)
Initial gap: $14,404 - 7,416 = $6,988			
White male heads versus black female heads			
(1) Human capital and areal and industrial labor markets	14.2% ($1266)	68.6% ($6106)	17.2% ($1530)
(2) Human capital and areal, industrial, and occupational labor markets	26.2% ($2332)	49.9% ($4443)	23.9% ($2126)
(3) Human capital and areal, industrial, and occupational labor markets and class/authority	22.7% ($2020)	45.0% ($4004)	32.3% ($2877)
Initial gap: $14,404 - 5,502 = $8,902			

[a]As discussed in the text the Duncan SEI variable is excluded. Therefore, the first equation figures do not match those in Equation 2 of Table 4.11.

compositional component is large (41%), the differences in how blacks and whites translate all of these resources into earnings is also a very important component; it accounts for 35% of the total gap. It means that if black males were to retain their current levels on the independent variables but could translate these into earnings using the same equation as white males, the gap would be reduced by 35% or $1717. The interaction component also is fairly large (24%), and what is especially interesting is the change in the component across the three steps: It becomes substantially larger as the occupation and class/authority variables are added. This finding suggests that not only will independently giving blacks and whites similar distributions and comparable rates of return aid in reducing the earnings gap, but doing both will also have the positive consequence of reducing the gap even more.

We also have used regression standardization to decompose the earnings differences between white male heads and white female heads. A comparison of the three steps indicates that only a small part of the large earnings gap left unaccounted for by compositional differences in human capital resources and local and industrial labor market characteristics is due to a more limited access of white women to the more highly rewarded occupations and class/authority positions occupied by men. In particular, the compositional component with all variables included is only 13% or $905 of the original $6988 gap. Most of the gap (81.4%) is due to sex differences in how these resources are translated into earnings. Altering the composition *and* also giving women the same rates of return as men does not result in interaction to any substantial degree, thus not altering the inference that it is the differences in regression equations that characterize white male and white female earnings differences.

As in the previous two chapters, the third regression standardization involves a comparison of white male heads and black female heads. When the two status groups are made equivalent on human capital and local and industrial labor market characteristics, 69% of the large $8902 gap is due to differences in how these resources are translated into earnings, as is shown in Step (1). Giving black women the same means on these variables as white men would account for only 14% ($1266) of the gap. The part of the gap due to the compositional component would be reduced another $1066 if these women were placed in occupations with the same characteristics as those occupied by white males. Providing the additional composition equalization on class/authority variables would actually increase the gap several hundred dollars. Successively giving black women the occupational and class/authority characteristics of the white males also alters the balance in the importance of the slopes and intercepts and interaction components; the slopes and intercepts component becomes smaller, and the interaction component becomes larger.

Summary and Discussion

The data presented suggest that there is differential access by race and sex to occupational labor market resources. The occupations of blacks and whites are differentiated primarily in terms of task complexity, pleasantness of work conditions, and physical activities; for men and women, the differentiating characteristics are physical activity and interpersonal relations. These findings are consistent with the research that shows women to be underrepresented in craft, farm, and laborer occupations and overrepresented in clerical and service occupations and also with the research that shows blacks to be underrepresented in professional and managerial positions but overrepresented in service and operative occupations. In addition, these data for blacks generally are consistent with dual labor market theory, which portrays minority members as segregated in the secondary labor market, in which there are unpleasant work conditions, considerable physical activity, and limited task complexity. These differences in the race and sex compositions of occupations also are reflected in the correlation matrices of occupational characteristics specific to each status group. As with the distributional data, the major differences here are by sex.

The regression analysis of the influence of complexity, uncertainty, unpleasantness, and physical dexterity net of human capital variables revealed that complexity and uncertainty are important for all status groups. The greater the task complexity, the greater the earnings, and the greater the uncertainty, the lower the earnings. Unpleasant work conditions was not significant for any status group, and physical dexterity had a positive net effect only for white males and white wives. When the effects for these four occupational characteristics were examined net of local and industrial labor market characteristics, these patterns were left essentially unchanged.

The effects involving complexity are of particular interest since that variable relates closely to our discussion of the dual labor market. As we recall, "good" jobs are high in task complexity, and "bad" jobs are low in complexity. That white males have both greater access to occupational complexity and evidence stronger returns to this characteristic is clearly consistent with dual labor market theory. The fact that white males and white wives obtain net positive returns to physical dexterity but the other groups do not does suggest a racial differential in the impact of this resource, an idea also consistent with dualist thinking. It is less clear, however, whether the remaining regression results involving the occupational labor market characteristics support that perspective. Being in a job that involves change and variety has negative earnings consequences regardless of status group and thus does not appear to be a characteristic that varies in impact as the theory might suggest. In addition, although jobs can vary in terms of uncertainty, there does not appear to be a systematic variation in access to this resource by status group. The nonsignificant findings regarding the net impact of unpleasant working conditions across groups is also inconsistent with our expectations concerning the differential effects of such characteristics by ascriptive status.

Our limited investigation of minority concentration effects on earnings suggested that both white male and white female heads suffer economically from being in female-dominated occupations. These findings suggest that the competition argument (i.e., the notion that crowding of an economic minority into an occupation lowers wages for all incumbents regardless of status) is supported at the expense of the segregation argument (i.e., that such competition raises earnings for majority group workers). Perhaps a more important finding, however, is that the magnitudes of these effects are relatively small. Thus compared to the influence of the human capital and remaining labor market characteristics, it does not appear that the net effect of miniority concentration is substantial. Such findings suggest that in terms of promoting sex equality in earnings, job characteristics such as complexity and investment variables such as years of schooling and experience may be more important than this feature of occupational social organization.

The findings on class/authority also are consistent with our conclusions thus far that white males manage the greatest earnings advantages from occupational labor market characteristics. Although class/authority position was found for all but white female heads to have a significant effect net of human capital variables and the three sets of labor market variables, white males benefit the most. This also is consistent with the dual labor market hypothesis that white males are more often in the primary labor market, in which authority hierarchies are integral components of firms and thus related to reward structures. Also consistent with dual labor market theory is, first, the positive relationship of firm size with employer earnings and, second, the generally higher earnings of minority workers the larger the firm (as measured by vertical complexity).

Finally, the regression standardization revealed differences in how occupational and class/authority variables operate to produce race and sex differences in earnings. Prior to considering these variables we found that over 90% of the earnings gap between white men and white women is due to differences in efficacy (translation of resources) that favor males, whereas this gap is 69% for the white male and black female comparison and 66% for the white male and black male comparison. For the sex comparisons for white status groups, taking occupational characteristics and class/authority variables into account resulted in a small increase in the importance of composition differences and in the interaction of the composition and slopes components, but still over 81% of the gap can be explained by slope and intercept differences. However, for the earnings gap between black women and white men, and especially between black and white men, the composition and interaction components due to occupational characteristics and class/authority variables are more important. The implications seem clear. White status group sex differences in earnings must be reduced by seeing that the resources women have access to are translated into earnings in the manner characterizing the male population. Reducing the gaps between black and white men and black women and white men, however, must rely on reducing the compositional differences and simultaneously equalizing rates of return to these resources.

CHAPTER 6

Social Psychological Effects on Earnings; Social Selection and Earnings Attainment

Introduction

In this chapter the objective is to evaluate the extent to which the various labor market and personal characteristic effects discussed in previous chapters remain unchanged under new conditions. Two major analyses are conducted. First, we investigate whether the findings are maintained when controls for family background and social psychological variables are introduced. The analysis thus far includes basic human capital variables such as education, weeks worked, and experience in the models previously estimated; there are, however, additional personal characteristics that can affect earnings, and that, if included, could modify the findings already discussed. Incorporation of these variables should provide a more stringent test of our thesis concerning the role of labor market factors in earnings attainment.

Second, we investigate the relationships between labor market characteristics and human capital variables by focusing on the issue of social selection. We argue that workers who embody high amounts of human capital also tend to be located in labor market and sector positions with high potential for productivity. It is important to study the dimensions along which this selectivity occurs, which personal characteristics are selected for, and whether the magnitude of such selection varies by race and sex. The analysis provides one way to critically evaluate the models presented thus far by investigation of the changes that occur in human capital variables when various types of structural characteristics are included or excluded as determinants of earnings.

Family Background Variables

Our first concern is with evaluating whether parental status and family background factors contribute to earnings attainment independent of the human capital variables featured in this analysis thus far. On the basis of previous research, we do not expect these background factors will importantly affect earnings attainment net of respondents' educational and occupational status. In particular, one major finding from the status attainment tradition is that educational attainment mediates the effects of background factors on attainment of adult socioeconomic status (Blau and Duncan, 1967; Featherman and Hauser, 1978), and this finding is expected to be replicated here. To assess this notion, several background variables have been used including father's years of schooling (interval scale), mother's years of schooling (interval scale), number of siblings (interval scale), and father's occupational status. The last concept was measured by assigning aggregated Duncan SEI scores to the eight major Census occupational categories used in the PSOID study. These variables were included singly and in several combinations in equations containing the basic variables—weeks worked, years of schooling, work experience, and occupational status.

No consistent patterns of statistical significance emerged to suggest that there are important direct relationships between background status and earnings net of the human capital variables already included. When each indicator was included separately, the only variable that was statistically significant for white male heads was the number of siblings ($p < .05$, $b^* = -.053$), although none of the four variables was statistically significant for black female heads. Among both black male and white female heads there were statistically significant effects of mother's education (black male heads, $p < .001$, $b^* = .249$; white female heads, $p < .05$, $b^* = .154$). Father's education was also significant for white female heads ($p < .05$, $b^* = .170$), but when both of these factors were controlled simultaneously, neither of the variables attained statistical significance. Due to the inconsistent operation of these variables across status groups and the small magnitudes of the few effects that are statistically significant, it appears that family background factors do not importantly contribute to our explanation of earnings attainment net of the basic human capital variables, nor do they contribute to our understanding of ascriptive status differences in earnings attainment.

Social Psychological Variables

PAST RESEARCH AND CURRENT EXPECTATIONS

A second major goal is to incorporate several measures of social psychological characteristics into the models to assess whether they and the labor market factors affect earnings independently of each other. Although previous studies have investigated the role of social psychological characteristics in status attainment, the focus has often been on studies of adolescents' and young adults' educational and occupational attainments.

In many cases, variables such as achievement values, influences of adult significant others (e.g., parental encouragement), and peer influences have been investigated as intervening between exogenous variables, such as mental ability and parental and background status, and causally subsequent dependent variables, such as educational, occupational, and earnings aspirations or actual educational, occupational, and earnings attainment. Examples of research in this tradition are provided by Rehberg, Schafer, and Sinclair (1970); Alwin and Mueller (1971); Sewell, Haller, and Ohlendorf (1970); Sewell and Shah (1967); and Alexander, Eckland, and Griffin (1975). Spenner and Featherman (1978) summarize findings from a variety of studies in this area. This investigation differs from many of these studies in several ways. First, we investigate the role of social psychological variables on earnings attainment, a dependent variable that has received less attention than aspirational constructs and educational and occupational attainment. Second, we are studying adults and thus will be making inferences concerning the effects of adult social psychological orientations on subsequent earnings. Many previous studies have focused on these attainment relationships among adolescents and young adults.[1] Finally, we systematically investigate these relationships for status groups that vary by race and sex. Although there is evidence to suggest that causal processes involving ambitions differ by race and sex (Spenner and Featherman, 1978), we provide more detailed information concerning how several social psychological constructs may differentially affect earnings attainment depending on ascribed status.

Theoretical guidance for this analysis is derived from Spenner and Featherman (1978), who organize variables from cognitive and affective domains under the umbrella of achievement orientation. These variables include locus of control, self-esteem, future orientation, delay of gratification, competence, intelligence, risk preference, intrinsic–extrinsic motivation, and values. They suggest that achievement motivation theory (Atkinson and Birch, 1970) interrelates many of these concepts by positing achievement behavior as a product of psychological determinants such as future orientation or competence and of situational determinants such as subjective estimation of success probability (Spenner and Featherman, 1978:385). They note, however, that the ability of the theory to account for achievement behavior outside the laboratory is limited and that there have been both conceptual and measurement criticisms of the perspective. They also indi-

[1]Investigations that have used adults as respondents include Featherman's (1972) study of work orientation effects on several socioeconomic outcomes and G. Duncan and Morgan's (1975) study based on Income Dynamic data. These findings are important in helping us formulate our expectations concerning the magnitudes of effects and are discussed later.

cate that, on the basis of research by O. Duncan, Featherman, and B. Duncan (1972), Featherman (1972), and G. Duncan and Morgan (1975), ambition among adult males is not a major determinant of socioeconomic success and that life-cycle contingencies such as migration, childbearing, and job loss play a much more substantial role. Thus, although they recognize the modest role that adolescent ambition plays in the attainment of years of schooling and jobs early in the career, they also urge recognition of the major impact that career contingencies can have upon attainment later in adult life independent of motivational constructs (Spenner and Featherman, 1978:408).

There does not appear to be consensus, however, concerning the effects of social psychological variables on the socioeconomic achievement of adults. Andrisani (1977) argues that internal–external locus of control *does* have a statistically significant and nontrivial impact on several measures of adult earnings and occupational attainment, independent of controls for education, experience, on-the-job training, marital status, and several locational variables. G. Duncan and Morgan's (1981) attempt to replicate these findings with different data suggests that the findings in question are either not statistically significant or weak, although Andrisani (1981) counters that measurement and methodological differences, as well as differences in scope of the analyses, limit the accuracy of the comparison. On the basis of exploratory analysis G. Duncan and Morgan (1981) hypothesize that the influence of such variables may be important to specific subgroups such as the young, the old, workers in areas of high unemployment, and younger workers with high scores on a mental ability measure, although these effects may be lost when a more general population is analyzed. It may be, then, that the subgroup analysis used here will reveal variations in the magnitude of effects of variables such as locus of control orientation.

Although mental ability and ambition are related, there are additional important arguments concerning the role of mental ability in status attainment. Jencks, Smith, Acland, Bane, Cohen, Gintis, Heyns, and Michelson (1972) indicate that mental ability has minimal impact on earnings attainment, and Sewell, Hauser, and Featherman (1976) demonstrate only a modest relationship between mental abilities and indicators of subsequent achievement. In contrast, Griffin (1976) and Griliches and Mason (1973) argue that omission of mental ability measures from earnings attainment models biases upwards returns to schooling, thus overestimating the importance of this variable in earnings attainment. Such biases are due (in this case) to positive intercorrelations between earnings, mental ability, and years of schooling. By analogy we argue that it is also advisable to include a mental ability measure to avoid upward biases in the estimation of labor market effects, the indicators of which are also positively related to earnings and mental ability. For example, occupational complexity is positively related to earnings, and it is reasonable to hypothesize some degree of positive relationship between mental ability and complexity, since performance of jobs with a high degree of complexity is likely to require higher than average mental ability. Thus inclusion of mental ability in the equation guards against upward biases in earnings returns to occupational complexity.

Although similar arguments for inclusion of other social psychological variables are more tenuous, we will include in the earnings equations measures of several of the ambition correlates noted by Spenner and Featherman (1978) to provide a more stringent test of the role of labor market variables. Although we do not expect that the effects would be especially strong, it would be inappropriate to completely ignore these variables in our analysis. Since the social psychological variables were measured in adulthood (but prior to measurement of earnings), we expect stronger relationships than others have obtained in the study of adolescent psychological construct effects on adult attainment. Second, given the variation observed in magnitudes of effects across status groups thus far in this analysis, it is unlikely that these effects will be uniformly small for all respondents. Finally, even if the magnitudes of the net effects are small, their inclusion may modify the magnitudes of variables already included, a topic worthy of investigation in its own right.

DATA AND METHOD

Ideally it would be desirable to introduce controls for several social psychological variables for all the respondents studied in the previous chapters; owing to data limitations, however, an alternative strategy will be followed. Although the 1975 panel of the Income Dynamics data set does not contain adequate data on the social psychological variables, the 1972 panel contains a large variety of questions asked of household heads that renders this type of analysis feasible. Therefore, in this section of the analysis we will study only household heads (thus omitting the samples of black and white wives) and will further confine the sample to those heads represented in the panels throughout the 1972–1975 period.[2] This results in slightly reduced numbers

[2]As in any panel study, there was attrition over time from the original PSOID sample due to death and to changes in household composition stemming from marriage, divorce, and remarriage. These household composition changes are recorded on each panel, and thus it is possible to eliminate those 1975 respondents who were not part of the panel in 1972 and would therefore not provide data on the key variables used in this portion of the analysis. Due to the manner in which the household composition changes were reported, we adopted the conservative strategy of eliminating any head who had not been continuously in that position between 1972 and 1975. It is therefore possible that we have omitted from our sample respondents who were heads in

of cases available for analysis in this section as compared with previous chapters. The number of cases available are as follows: white male heads, 1691; black male heads, 661; white female heads, 217; and black female heads, 283.

Several different social psychological dimensions are incorporated into analysis. They include measures of personal efficacy, achievement motivation, level of interpersonal trust, risk avoidance, and mental ability. Selection and construction of these measures followed one of two models. In the case of mental ability, we adopted the total score for a 13-item sentence completion test that was developed for the PSOID by Veroff, McClelland, and Marquis (1971) as a measure of intellectual functioning. This measure was taken directly from the 1972 Panel Study, as was a composite measure of risk avoidance. The latter included nine questions concerning whether all of the cars owned by the head were insured, whether the head's newest car was in good condition, to what extent the head used seat belts, whether the head had medical insurance or some provision to cover health care costs, whether the head smoked less than one pack of cigarettes a day, and to what extent the head had savings that could be used for unexpected expenses.

The remaining dimensions were derived from a variety of questions also included in the 1972 and 1975 Panels. The 1972 Survey included 16 questions designed to tap achievement orientation in which the items focused on the head's degree achievement orientation for his/her child, achievement orientation towards his/her job, the extent to which the head valued an achievement orientation at the expense of social approval, and the extent to which the head manifested an achievement orientation in a test-taking situation. Questions designed to tap personal efficacy were asked in both 1972 and 1975. The 1975 version included 5 questions that asked whether the respondent planned ahead, whether things usually turned out as expected, whether the respondent finished things, and whether the respondent felt that he/she had control over his/her life.[3] The trust–hostility dimension was measured by 5 questions that tapped the extent to which the respondent

---

1972 and in 1975 but who were not household heads for either one or both of the intervening years, 1973 and 1974. It seems unlikely, however, that very many people would fall into this category and there is no reason to expect that their omission would bias the analysis. On the other hand, it would be unacceptable to risk including a respondent who could not be positively identified as providing both the 1972 and the 1975 data, a possibility that could not have been eliminated if a less conservative strategy had been followed.

[3]The 1972 version of efficacy included 6 questions, 4 of which were similar to those used in 1975 but also 2 additional questions that tapped whether the respondent would rather save for the future or spend money to enjoy life today and whether the respondent spent much time thinking about things that might happen in the future. As indicated later, both sets of questions were included in preliminary analysis but only the 1975 questions were retained.

became angry easily, whether it mattered what others think, whether the respondent trusted most other people, believed that the life of the average person is improving, and thought that there are many people who have good things that they do not deserve.

In the case of these three constructs, we performed a preliminary analysis to determine whether the items designed to measure the three constructs did indeed relate consistently to each other. Using all of the cases to be included in this portion of the analysis combined into a single file (N = 2852), we performed a factor analysis using the Rao extraction procedure and oblique rotation. Three separate factor solutions were obtained: one for personal efficacy, one for trust–hostility, and one for achievement motivation. The factor solution for personal efficacy indicated that one factor was sufficient to represent the five variables included from the survey, and that all of the variables loaded on that factor at .29 or higher.[4] Therefore in this analysis a personal efficacy composite (efficacy) will be formed where all five variables are included in the composite, and a high score indicates a high degree of personal efficacy. The factor solution for trust–hostility also indicated that one factor was sufficient to represent the five variables included from the survey but that only three items—those dealing with whether the respondent trusted people, whether the life of the average person was improving, and whether there are many people who have good things they do not deserve—loaded strongly enough ($\geq$.30) to conclude that they represented the factor. In this case only these three items were included in the composite (trust), and again, a high score indicates a high degree of trust in other people.

In the case of achievement motivation, the factor analytic solution suggested that the 16 items that were input could be represented by five factors, on which 12 of the 16 items loaded at the ±.30 level or higher. Three of the five factors could be substantively interpreted in terms of: (a) achievement orientation in testing situations; (b) achievement orientation for heads' children; and (c) achievement orientation in a work situation; the remaining two factors appeared to represent achievement orientations in general social interaction. In preliminary analysis we created six composites: one for each of the five factors and one final composite that included all of the 12 variables that had loaded $\geq$+.30 on any of the factors (achievement). We found that when the individual achievement composites were selectively included in regression analyses along with the human capital and labor market variables, achievement served as a more effective control than did

---

[4]Generally in this work we have used a ±.30 loading as the cutoff point for inclusion of a variable in a composite, but an exception was made in this case because of the closeness of the loading to this cutoff and the desire to improve the reliability of the measure so that it could serve as a more effective control.

Table 6.1

Reliability of Social Psychological Variables
Across Status Groups: Household Heads

	Males		Females	
Variable	White	Black	White	Black
Achievement motivation	.59	.60	.57	.59
Interpersonal trust	.38	.46	.34	.36
Personal efficacy	.50	.45	.35	.54

any of the other achievement composites singly or in combination. Therefore, only achievement is included in subsequent analysis. As in the case of
the other composites, a high score on this variable indicates a high degree of
achievement orientation.[5]

Table 6.1 presents the reliability estimates for the three social psychological variables we constructed on the basis of factor analysis. The reliabilities
for the achievement variable are moderate, and those for the remaining
measures are weaker. As expected, reliabilities improve when a large as
opposed to a small number of items are included. These moderate to low
reliabilities may contribute to the underestimation of the true effects of these
factors on earnings, and this should be kept in mind in interpreting subsequent findings.

Our analytic strategy will be to estimate a series of equations in which the
social psychological, class/authority, and labor market variables are
cumulatively added to a basic model of earnings attainment. This strategy
reflects a conceptualization that differs from those used in much of the status
attainment literature in that it is not assumed that the social psychological
variables operate causally prior to years of schooling (i.e., as determinants of
educational attainment). Nor does the analysis reflect the assumption that
these constructs are determinants of the labor market positions respondents
occupy, although the findings may suggest this idea to be tenable. Rather,

[5]In an additional preliminary factor analysis, we explored the factor structure of one additional set of questions that one could argue represented a social psychological state potentially
related to earnings attainment. The state was aspiration–ambition and it was represented by
five survey questions covering such things as whether the head would move in order to find a
better job or whether he or she would quit a job that was not challenging. Analysis suggested
that there were two factors that were found to underlie the five items but that only two items
loaded on these factors $\geq |\pm.30|$, one item on each factor. Since it appeared that there was no
single dimension for which we could identify several items to form a composite and since there
was already developed a measure of achievement motivation that might be expected to be
related to aspiration–ambition, nothing further was done with the aspiration–ambition items in
this analysis.

the strategy places the variables "on equal footing" with the human capital, class/authority, and labor market variables, thus allowing a stringent test of the labor market effects mentioned earlier in the chapter.

FINDINGS AND DISCUSSION

Table 6.2 presents the means and standard deviations of the composites used in the analysis for each of the four status groups. White male heads score most highly on personal efficacy, and black female heads score the lowest, with the remaining groups intermediate, differences that are entirely consistent with general notions concerning which status groups have the most and least actual control over their lives' events. The means on achievement orientation suggest a sex difference with males scoring higher than females. Again white males obtain the highest score and black females obtain the lowest. Differences in the degree of interpresonal trust break down along racial lines with whites exhibiting a greater degree of interpersonal trust than blacks. Similar differences can be observed for the risk avoidance and mental ability measures, with whites exhibiting higher scores on these dimensions than blacks. There is also greater variance in the mental ability scores among blacks than among whites.

Note: Inspection of the means for earnings, human capital, and labor market variables for these subsamples (data not presented), as compared with descriptive data presented in Table 3.5 and relevant tables from Chapters 4 and 5, suggests that there are very minor differences between these subsamples and the samples analyzed in previous chapters. Earnings levels of white males ($\bar{X}$ = $14,567), black males ($\bar{X}$ = $9769), and white female heads ($\bar{X}$ = $7769) in the subsamples exceed earnings levels of these groups generally, but the earnings level for black female heads ($\bar{X}$ = $5382) is less than that reported in the larger sample. Levels of occupational status, years of schooling, and weeks worked are very similar within status groups across the two samples, and in the vast majority of cases there are only minor differences in access to ecological resources. There appears to be some tendency for those respondents who live in households that undergo one or more changes in household composition (through divorce, death, separation, etc.) to also be those who accumulate less work experience. Although we have no evidence that disruption of household organization forces disruption of work experience, if only for brief periods of time, the fact that earnings levels are higher in three out of four of the subsamples than in the comparable larger samples suggests that stability in household composition may be conducive to earnings attainment. Note that this argument does not work for

Table 6.2

Means and Standard Deviations for Social Psychological Variables Used in Analysis: Household Heads

| | Males | | | | | Females | | | | |
| Variable[a] | White | | Black | | | White | | Black | | |
	$\overline{X}$	S	$\overline{X}$	S		$\overline{X}$	S	$\overline{X}$	S	
Personal efficacy	20.32	4.56	18.03	5.06		18.13	4.64	15.71	5.54	
Achievement motivation	43.64	8.24	41.49	8.66		38.87	8.34	37.81	8.39	
Interpersonal trust	11.45	3.36	9.44	3.83		11.67	3.21	8.30	3.68	
Risk avoidance	5.30	1.57	4.62	1.55		5.27	1.53	4.16	1.18	
Mental ability	10.18	1.87	8.32	2.44		10.25	1.61	8.48	2.24	
	$N = 1691$		$N = 661$			$N = 217$		$N = 283$		

[a]Composite measures for personal efficacy, achievement motivation (orientation), and interpersonal trust were constructed on the basis of factor analysis results described in the previous section.

black female heads, and the tendency is a weak one in any case. Overall it is reassuring that the necessity to limit this portion of the analysis to subsamples has not resulted in major biases that are detectable through inspections of these means.

Table 6.3 presents the zero-order correlations between each of the composites and earnings for the four status groups.[6] In most cases the relationships are positive and modest in size, with many in the .20–.30 range. Achievement orientation, risk avoidance, personal efficacy, and mental ability all fall into this pattern. The correlations between level of interpersonal trust and earnings are more variable, with moderately positive relationships observed for white male and female heads and essentially zero relationships among black male and female heads.

Tables 6.4a–6.4d and 6.5a–6.5b summarize the results of multivariate analysis involving the social psychological variables as predictors of earnings controlling for the several sets of labor market variables discussed in earlier chapters.[7] Tables 6.4a–6.4d allow comparison of earnings functions for black and white male heads. Equation 1 estimates a basic equation describing earnings as a function of weeks worked, education, and work experience (Table 6.4a).[8] This equation serves as a baseline against which to compare

[6]There is probably a varying amount of "causal distance" between earnings and these variables. In the case of achievement orientation, it is likely that past experiences with success and failure in adult life are reflected in the items used in our measure. Thus, although one generally thinks of achievement orientation as formulated early in life, we cannot argue with certainty that what we have measured here was formulated at that time. The personal efficacy and interpersonal trust measures are similar. Since events in adult life can importantly affect feelings of competence and feelings of trust in others, we do not assume that our measures represent the internal states of the respondents prior to adulthood. Risk avoidance may be somewhat more stable over the life cycle than achievement orientation, personal efficacy, and interpersonal trust. Although there may be change in this construct due to events in adult life, we do accept the notion that the tendency to take or avoid risks is relatively stable over time. Finally, the mental ability measure used here is also seen as reflecting adult levels of mental ability, not those that may have been operative during the respondents' years in school. Mental abilities can improve or decay as a function of use. Hence, in contrast to some analyses, it is not assumed that the effect of mental ability (as measured) on earnings is importantly mediated by years of schooling.

[7]The findings from this multivariate analysis are partly dependent on the interrelationships among the several social psychological constructs we have included. For all of the status groups these relationships are low and positive with most falling between .10 and .25 (data not included). The one systematic exception to this is among black female heads where the relationships between mental ability and achievement, trust, and risk avoidance are all greater than +.35. Thus we expect that for this subgroup there will be some competition among these variables for predictive power in the earnings equation.

[8]This model differs from the basic equation presented in Chapter 3 in that an interval measure of education is used here instead of the set of dummies to avoid tipping when the measure of mental ability is included, and the Duncan SEI is omitted to avoid comparable effects when work complexity is included in the model.

Table 6.3

Zero-Order Correlations of Social Psychological Variables
with Earnings: Household Heads

	Males		Females	
Variable	White	Black	White	Black
Personal efficacy	.179	.245	.206	.281
Achievement motivation	.226	.295	.273	.250
Interpersonal trust	.187	.075	.235	.022
Risk avoidance	.286	.399	.241	.336
Mental ability	.238	.331	.198	.158

Table 6.4a

Human Capital Determinants of Earnings for Black and White Male
Heads: Equation 1

	Equation 1			
	Whites		Blacks	
Independent variables	Dev.	b^*	Dev.	b^*
Weeks worked				
0–26	−5098	--	−6652	--
27–39	−3289	.042	−1245	.310
40–47	445	.256	373	.559
48–49	1255***	.312	323**	.640
50–52	−557	.240	−2	.680
	b	b^*	b	b^*
Education	1206***	.399	540***	.395
Experience	120***	.138	88***	.197
Mental ability	--	--	--	--
Risk avoidance	--	--	--	--
Achievement motivation	--	--	--	--
Interpersonal trust	--	--	--	--
Personal efficacy	--	--	--	--
Constant	−8456		−4492	
$R^2/\bar{R}^2$	.175/.172		.157/.149	
	$N = 1691$		$N = 661$	

$**p < .01,$ $***p < .001.$

Table 6.4b

Human Capital and Social Psychological Determinants of Earnings
for Black and White Male Heads: Equation 2

| | Equation 2 | | | |
| | Whites | | Blacks | |
Independent variables	Dev.	$b*$	Dev.	$b*$
Weeks worked				
0-26	-4774	--	-5756	--
27-39	-2509	.052	-1099	.267
40-47	311	.235	85	.465
48-49	1034_{***}	.285	-40_{**}	.524
50-52	-420	.230	295	.619
	b	$b*$	b	$b*$
Education	838_{***}^{***}	.277	188_{*}^{**}	.138
Experience	86	.099	43_{***}	.097
Mental ability	263_{***}	.053	382_{***}	.191
Risk avoidance	644_{**}	.109	896_{**}	.286
Achievement motivation	82_{*}	.073	68_{*}	.120
Interpersonal trust	154_{*}	.056	-114_{**}	-.190
Personal efficacy	114	.056	100	.104
Constant	-16453		-9795	
$R^2/\bar{R}^2$	.206/.201		.300/.288	
	N = 1691		N = 661	

$*p < .05,$ $**p < .01,$ $***p < .001.$

the remaining equations. As in previous analysis, it appears that the shapes
of the weeks worked–earnings relationships vary by race. Although the
magnitudes of the deviations from the mean have shifted slightly from those
shown in Table 3.6, there is still the peak for whites occurring at the 48–49-
week level, whereas the peak for blacks is 40–47 weeks. Returns to experience still favor whites, and using the interval measure of education suggests
that whites obtain over *twice* the returns in dollars to an additional year of
schooling: For each additional year of schooling completed, blacks earn an
additional $540 and whites earn an additional $1206, controlling for experience and weeks worked.

In Equation 2 (Table 6.4b) five social psychological variables have been
added to the basic equation just discussed. For male heads all of the variables
are statistically significant for both races. Returns to the mental ability and
risk avoidance measures are greater for blacks than for whites, and returns to

Table 6.4c

Human Capital, Social Psychological and Class/Authority
Determinants of Earnings for Black and White Male Heads:
Equation 3

	Equation 3			
	Whites		Blacks	
Independent variables	Dev.	b^*	Dev.	b^*
Weeks worked				
0-26	-4190	--	-5549	--
27-39	-2018	.050	-1175	.251
40-47	537	.218	105	.405
48-49	811***	.246	-135**	.497
50-52	-481	.196	356	.604
	b	b^*	b	b^*
Education	763***	.253	212*	.156
Experience	67***	.077	41***	.092
Mental ability	110***	.022	386***	.193
Risk avoidance	581	.099	716*	.229
Achievement motivation	30	.027	45*	.080
Interpersonal trust	111	.040	-95*	-.075
Personal efficacy	87	.043	72*	.075
Employer^a				
0 Employees	-4285	-.092	-4983	-.062
1-2 Employees	109	.024	2660	.206
3-19 Employees	4420	.138	-2310	.012
20+ Employees	15410	.240		
Worker, Hi VC	-1325	-.013	175	.295
Worker, Lo VC	-1071		-2743	
Sup, Resp, S-Sp, Lo VC	1026	.035	1026	.100
Sup, Resp, L-Sp, Lo VC	6031	.124		
Sup, No Resp, S-Sp, Lo VC	-3247	-.038	-770	.045
Sup, No Resp, L-Sp, Lo VC	1807	.035		
Sup, Resp, S-Sp, Hi VC	590	.047	838	.157
Sup, Resp, L-Sp, Hi VC	3511	.152	3581	.282
Sup, No Resp, S-Sp, Hi VC	-1907***	-.027	-628***	.123
Sup, No Resp, L-Sp, Hi VC	-1063	.000	3014	.168
Constant	-10371		-10458	
$R^2/\bar{R}^2$	.322/.312		.400/.380	
	$N = 1691$		$N = 661$	

^{a}The coefficients for the class and authority variables
represent deviations from the omitted category: workers in
low vertical complexity firms.

* $p < .05$, ** $p < .01$, *** $p < .001$.

Table 6.4d

Human Capital, Social Psychological, Class/Authority and Labor Market Determinants of Earnings for Black and White Male Heads: Equation 4

	Equation 4			
	Whites		Blacks	
Independent variables	Dev.	b^*	Dev.	b^*
Weeks worked				
0-26	-3940	--	-5178	--
27-39	-1915	.046	-980	.241
40-47	430	.202	31	.415
48-49	550**	.221	-564***	.423
50-52	-247	.195	606	.591
	b	b^*	b	b^*
Education	551***,**	.182	-33	-.024
Experience	52	.060	29***	.064
Mental ability	110**	.022	287***	.144
Risk avoidance	423	.072	526	.168
Achievement motivation	-12*	-.010	26*	.047
Interpersonal trust	143	.052	-88*	-.069
Personal efficacy	84	.041	62	.065
Employer[a]				
0 Employees	-4051	-.097	-4642	-.075
1-2 Employees	623	.026	1086	.115
3-19 Employees	4489	.129⎫	-166	.051
20+ Employees	15206	.232⎭		
Worker, Hi VC	-1121	-.024	88	.205
Worker, Lo VC	-666		-1938	
Sup, Resp, S-Sp, Lo VC	780	.024⎫	746	.071
Sup, Resp, L-Sp, Lo VC	5324	.104⎭		
Sup, No Resp, S-Sp, Lo VC	-3279	-.046⎫	547	.057
Sup, No Resp, L-Sp, Lo VC	1653	.028⎭		
Sup, Resp, S-Sp, Hi VC	107	.022	391	.102
Sup, Resp, L-Sp, Hi VC	3078	.124	2872	.214
Sup, No Resp, S-Sp, Hi VC	-2234***	-.051	-344	.093
Sup, No Resp, L-Sp, Hi VC	-732	-.001	2649	.134

(continued)

Table 6.4d *(continued)*

Independent variables	Equation 4			
	Whites		Blacks	
	Dev.	b^*	Dev.	b^*
Concentration and investment	81	.027	363***	.249
Firm growth	77	.013	145***	.051
Manufacturing sector health	194	.039	608**	.243
Manufacturing dominance	−15***	−.002	435	.097
Tertiary sector health	281*	.122	−40	−.030
Tertiary sector growth	−283	−.052	−105	−.034
Tertiary sector complexity	94*	.014	123*	.033
Uncertainty	604	.060	443	.079
Unpleasantness of work	135***	.028	65	.035
Physical dexterity	273***	.120	−8***	−.005
Complexity	192	.164	204***	.323
Crowding	359	.042	−412***	−.128
Constant	−5432		−3198	
$R^2/\bar{R}^2$	.371/.357		.568/.545	
	$N = 1691$		$N = 661$	

aThe coefficients for the class and authority variables represent deviations from the omitted category: workers in low vertical complexity firms.

$^*p < .05, ^{**}p < .01, ^{***}p < .001.$

the achievement and efficacy variables favor whites. In the case of the trust measure, although whites obtain positive returns to this factor, the effect among blacks is negative. Recall from Table 6.3 that the zero-order correlation between earnings and trust was essentially zero; hence the observed negative partial in Equation 2 represents a suppressor effect. As would be expected, increment in R^2 tests reveal that for both races, the set of social psychological variables explains a statistically significant increment in explained variance.

Equations 3 and 4 allow us to address the central question posed in this analysis: Are labor market factors statistically significant predictors of earnings when additional controls for the social psychological variables have been introduced? Equation 3 (Table 6.4c) introduces the multiple-category version of the class/authority variable discussed in Chapter 5 in addition to the variables presented in Equation 2. For both races, the class/authority effects noted in the previous chapter are maintained when the social psychological controls are included; we continue to find that supervisors earn more than workers and that employers with a large number of employees earn the

Table 6.5a

Human Capital, Social Psychological and Labor Market
Determinants of Earnings for Black Female Heads:
Equations 1 and 2

Independent variables	Equation 1		Equation 2	
	Dev.	b^*	Dev.	b^*
Weeks worked				
0–26	-1838	--	-1436	--
27–39	-1185	.071	-979	.049
40–47	-408	.190	-404	.137
48–49	1746$_{***}$	.453	1896$_{***}$	.421
50–52	-336	.201	-593	.113
	b	b^*	b	b^*
Education	581***	.440	460***	.349
Experience	32	.101	15	.048
Mental ability	--	--	-110$_{***}$	-.072
Risk avoidance	--	--	599	.208
Achievement motivation	--	--	18	.044
Interpersonal trust	--	--	-52$_{***}$	-.056
Personal efficacy	--	--	147	.238
Constant	-3512		-5561	
$R^2/\bar{R}^2$	.254/.237		.363/.337	
			$N = 283$	

*** $p < .001$.

most. Among supervisors, those who have a large span of control (number of subordinates) and a large span of responsibility (decisions about pay of subordinates) earn the most. The independence of class/authority from other determinants of earnings is again highlighted by these findings.

In contrast, the effects of the social psychological variables have diminished in this specification. This is particularly true among whites, for whom the achievement, trust, and efficacy variables, as well as the risk avoidance measure, are now not statistically significant. Such findings suggest that these social psychological factors are partly manifest in the positions of class/authority that these heads occupy and that these factors may play an important causal role in such attainment. Among blacks the changes are less dramatic. Though the effects of the risk avoidance, achievement, and efficacy measures are reduced in this specification, these variables remain statistically significant. The relatively small changes here and the more minor variations in the remaining coefficients suggest that among blacks,

Table 6.5b

Human Capital, Social Psychological and Labor Market
Determinants of Earnings for Black Female Heads:
Equations 3 and 4

Independent variables	Equation 3		Equation 4	
	Dev.	b^*	Dev.	b^*
Weeks worked				
0–26	−1397	−−	−1668	−−
27–39	−867	.057	−1334	.036
40–47	−196	.160	−327	.179
48–49	972$_*$	.299	1163$_{***}$	.358
50–52	−89	.175	145	.243
	b	b^*	b	b^*
Education	343***	.259	154$_{**}$	.117
Experience	24$_*$	.076	40$_*$	.126
Mental ability	−195$_{***}$	−.128	−170$_{***}$	−.111
Risk avoidance	666	.231	566	.196
Achievement motivation	23	.057	27	.065
Interpersonal trust	−22$_{**}$	−.024	−28$_{**}$	−.031
Personal efficacy	99	.162	93	.152
Employer	−2235	−.045	−2786	−.097
Worker, Lo VC	−1624	−−	−1451	−−
Worker, Hi VC	437	.300	394	.268
Sup, Lo VC	587	.122	575	.112
Sup, Resp, Hi VC	1877	.143	843	.094
Sup, No Resp, S–Sp, Hi VC	−848$_{***}$	.055	−1432$_{***}$	.001
Sup, No Resp, L–Sp, Hi VC	2947	.324	4342	.411
Manufacturing sector health	−−	−−	−9	−.005
Manufacturing dominance	−−	−−	−162$_{***}$	−.056
Tertiary sector health	−−	−−	−263	−.280
Tertiary sector growth	−−	−−	−32	−.016
Tertiary sector complexity	−−	−−	262$_{***}$	.090
Crowding	−−	−−	−650$_{***}$	−.225
Uncertainty	−−	−−	681$_{***}$	.185
Unpleasantness of work	−−	−−	−217$_*$	−.209
Physical dexterity	−−	−−	−99$_{***}$	−.103
Complexity	−−	−−	134	.290
Constant	−5279		−852	
$R^2/\bar{R}^2$	.457/.423		.606/.565	

$^*\, p < .05,\quad ^{**}\, p < .01,\quad ^{***}\, p < .001.$

there is less mediation of social psychological factors by attainment of class/authority positions. Thus these social psychological factors are less useful to blacks than to whites in attainment of an important income producing resource, position in the class/authority structure of work organizations.

Equation 4 (Table 6.4d) includes all of the variables from Equation 3 plus the local, industrial, and occupational labor market variables discussed in previous chapters. To evaluate the impact of inclusion of the social psychological variables on the magnitudes of the labor market effects previously discussed, we estimated an equation (not presented here) containing all of those variables shown in Equation 4 except the social psychological variables so that the magnitudes of the labor market and remaining human capital variables could be compared across specifications. Among white male heads introduction of the social psychological variables produces only a very slight weakening in the class/authority effects, with no change in the pattern of the findings and essentially no changes in magnitudes or patterns of the areal, industrial, or occupational labor market effects. Thus among the subsample of white male heads, introduction of the social psychological variables does not disturb previous conclusions concerning labor market variables. Among blacks the changes in coefficients are somewhat more noticeable, although still not especially large. As among the whites, the patterns evidenced for the class/authority effects are similar across specifications, with minor reductions in the magnitudes of the coefficients that do not necessitate changes in interpretation. There is a 31% reduction in the magnitude of manufacturing dominance in the more complete model and a 21% reduction in returns to work uncertainty under these same conditions. In addition, the unpleasant work conditions variable is no longer statistically significant in the more complete specification. It appears, then, that most of the labor market effects remain when the additional controls are introduced, although there are greater changes for blacks than for whites across specifications.

It is also important to assess what changes have occurred in the estimation of weeks worked, experience, and education across the four specifications. Among whites returns of weeks worked weaken slightly as we add the several sets of variables, although the basic shape of the relationship remains the same. Among blacks there are changes in the relationship at the two highest levels of weeks worked (due to inclusion of the social psychological variables) and some overall strengthening of the weeks-worked effect in the final equation. The changes in education and work experience are more extreme. Among whites returns to years of schooling drop by over 54% between the first and fourth specifications ($1206 versus $551), with over 30% ($1206 versus $838) due to the inclusion of the social psychological variables. Among blacks we see that inclusion of these variables results in a reduction

of over 65% in returns to schooling (from $540 per additional year of school-
ing to $188 per additional year), and in the final specification, with the labor
market variables controlled, education is not a statistically significant predictor of earnings. For whites there is a 56% reduction in returns to experience
($120 per additional year of experience versus $52 per year of experience),
whereas among blacks a 50% reduction occurs when the social psychological
variables are introduced. Returns to experience become nonsignificant for
blacks in the final specification when the labor market variables are
included.

Additional analysis (not presented here) suggests that the large drops in
returns to years of schooling observed between Equations 1 and 2 are largely
due to inclusion of the mental ability variable, a finding consistent with other
investigations suggesting that omission of a mental ability measure biases
upwards returns to years of schooling (Griffin, 1976; Griliches and Mason,
1973). However, the race differential in this bias, which indicates that educational returns for blacks are more extremely overestimated with the omission
than are returns for whites, has not been featured prominently in these
discussions. Such a finding is important in that it cautions against blacks'
reliance on years of schooling to substantially increase earnings later in adult
life when in fact, for blacks mental ability is a more important determinant of
earnings than is education (see Equation 2). Similarly, the racial differential
in the degree of bias in returns to experience suggests that we should not
overestimate the extent to which blacks benefit from additional work experience without taking into account the role of social psychological factors such
as those included in this analysis.

Overall, then, the findings have suggested that there is greater "matching" between the social psychological variables and education and experience for blacks than for whites. Although there are also racial differentials in
the degree of relationship between the social psychological and labor market
characteristics, the magnitudes of these latter differentials are smaller.
Hence we find minimal direct selection into labor market positions on the
basis of the social psychological characteristics discussed here, particularly
among whites. However, we do find more substantial relationships between
these internal states and education and experience. Thus, to the extent that
education and experience are selected for, we also will find some degree of
indirect selection on the social psychological variables, particularly mental
ability. The degree of selection is greater for blacks than for whites.

The findings among female heads differ from those described for males.
Among white female heads in a number of specifications the social psychological variables were consistently not statistically significant net of the basic

human capital variables (education, weeks worked, and experience). Nor were they significant net of these factors plus the several sets of authority and labor market variables (data not presented).[9] It appears, then, that although the zero-order correlations between earnings and the social psycholgocial variables are similar for white female heads and male heads, the net effects differ substantially. Among white female heads the lack of direct effects of these factors on earnings suggests that their role in status attainment is largely indirect, perhaps operating through educational attainment, whereas among male heads direct effects of these variables do operate independently of the human capital variables included in the basic equation. These negative findings do assure us, however, that the labor market effects reported for white female heads in the previous chapters are not fundamentally altered due to the role of these internal states.

The findings among black female heads represent a pattern that contrasts with those described for white female heads and for male heads of either race (Tables 6.5a and 6.5b). Equation 2 indicates that risk avoidance and efficacy are positive and statistically significant. Equation 3, which includes the "short set" of class/authority variables discussed in Chapter 5, indicates that, when the sets of variables are simultaneously controlled, both the social psychological and class/authority variables retain the general patterns of statistical significance observed in Equation 2 and Chapter 5 respectively.[10] Equation 4 includes the occupational and areal labor market variables in addition to those included in Equation 3.[11] The same general patterns of statistical significance remain for the social psychological and class/authority variables that were observed in Equation 3. Comparing Equation 4 to a specification that omits the five social psychological variables (data not presented), we see that although the magnitudes of the authority earnings relationships are weakened slightly, the shapes of the relationships remain the same. The majority of the labor market effects are also maintained in terms of statistical significance and magnitude, although tertiary sector com-

[9]The only exception to this generalization concerns the trust variable, which is positive and significant when Equation 4 is estimated for this group of respondents. However, given that in several specifications it was not significant, it would not be appropriate to interpret this finding since to do so would be capitalizing on chance.

[10]Notice that the coefficient associated with mental ability is negative and statistically significant in Equations 3 and 4. It is probably inappropriate to conclude that there are negative returns to this factor for black female heads since theory predicts a positive sign and since it is likely that positive relationships between the mental ability and authority measures have contributed to tipping of the mental ability coefficient..

[11]The industrial labor market variables are excluded from this specification because including them results in tipping that would render the equation uninterpretable.

plexity is no longer significant in Equation 4, and there is a 17% reduction in the negative effect of urban crowding.[12]

Concerning changes in the human capital variables across specifications, the general shape of the weeks worked–earnings relationship is maintained. However, returns to schooling drop by 21% ($581 per additional year versus $460 per additonal year) between Equations 1 and 2, and in the final equation education is not statistically significant. In contrast, experience achieves statistical significance in the final specification.

In general, then, the labor market and class/authority effects discussed in previous chapters remain largely undisturbed by introduction of additional controls for social psycholgoical characteristics. In contrast, with the exception of white female heads for whom the social psychological variables were not statistically significant, there are substantial reductions in returns to years of schooling, to the point of not attaining statistical significance for black male and female heads of household. Returns to work experience are also reduced in magnitude in this specification for black female heads and white male heads and to the point of failing to attain statistical significance for black male heads.

These findings shed light on the long-term debates between proponents of the human capital tradition and those who argue for the importance of structural factors in status attainment. On the basis of the findings presented here it appears that the relative importance of each varies by status group. For example, for white males, education and work experience are worthwhile investments, but for black male heads these factors are not statistically significant once the remaining controls are introduced. On the other hand, the controls that represent the structural factors—characteristics of labor markets and class/authority positions in organizations—are statistically significant, and in some cases the returns for blacks exceed those for whites. It appears, then, that the human capital perspective is more powerful for white males than for black males and that the labor market perspectives are more powerful for black males than for white males. Black female heads are an intermediate case in which both perspectives are useful to some extent, although the close relationships among the several sets of variables for black female heads preclude a more definitive statement at this point. As dis-

---

[12]We also notice that there are some differences between the labor market effects reported here and those reported in Table 5.7. Tertiary sector growth is no longer statistically significant. The variables representing uncertainty, unpleasant working conditions, and physical dexterity are now significant, and returns to complexity have increased. Tertiary sector health is now negative and statistically significant, whereas it previously was not significant. It appears that the close relationships between the authority and labor market variables have contributed to the tipping of tertiary sector health and the heightening of the occupational labor market effects.

cussed earlier, the influence of class/authority remains largely unchanged, suggesting the independence of class/authority and the remaining labor market influences. Among whites it appers that the social psychological constructs are useful in attainment of class/authority positions that in turn influence earnings, whereas among blacks such resources are predictive of earnings directly but do not promote attainment of class/authority positions. This interpretation is based on the assumption that the social psychological variables come causally prior to attainment of class/authority positions, not a totally unwarranted assumption.

Social Selection and Earnings: Race and Sex Differences

PAST RESEARCH AND CURRENT EXPECTATIONS

Thus far the focus has been on analysis of the effects of local, industrial, and occupational labor market characteristics on earnings. Findings have indicated that returns to both these structural characteristics and the human capital and socialization variables vary by race and sex. Evidence suggests that the effects of the three types of markets operate largely independently of each other, that is, that the areal effects reported in Chapter 3 are not "explained by" the inclusion of industrial and/or occupational characteristics in more complete models. In the current chapter additional evidence for the stability of the labor market effects was provided by indicating that they are maintained when controls for social psychological variables are included.

In other cases, however, we have noted that addition of new sets of variables to models has resulted in either changes in the magnitudes of coefficients already included or uninterpretable findings due to multicollinearity between and among "new" and "old" variables. These two outcomes are, of course, merely different points on the same continuum. In the statistical literature the first phenomenon is discussed as specification error (Rao and Miller, 1971; Hanushek and Jackson, 1977), and researchers are cautioned that omission of theoretically relevant variables will bias estimates of those variables that are included. In the second case the relationships involving the relevant variables are so strong that affected coefficients may be tipped (R. Gordon, 1968) in the direction opposite from what theory predicted or exaggerated in strength in the predicted direction. If this happens, the researcher is advised to omit one or more of the culprit variables or to form an index with those that are highly related on the grounds that they must be measuring the same concept.

In this section we are explicitly interested in the patterns of findings resulting in bias and tipping that we have uncovered in this analysis and in the theoretical implications of these patterns. The relationships of particular interest are those between human capital and socialization variables and the structural variables representing characteristics of local, industrial, and labor market variables, because it is these relationships that are indicative of what we call social selection in socioeconomic attainment. Thus, if there are strong relationships between human capital and labor market resources, we infer that social selection has occurred. In this analysis social selection refers to the processes through which there is nonrandom allocation (sorting and selecting) of workers to contexts such that patterns of relationships between worker characteristics and characteristics of environments result. Concerning the direction of these relationships, it is expected that those workers with high investment in human capital are allocated to labor market positions with favorable combinations of market resources. For example, we expect to observe positive relationships between years of schooling and industrial concentration and investment since workers with schooling and/or training are in a better position to compete for jobs in profitable firms, and these firms need to hire trained workers in order to utilize advanced technology in production. By studying the race and sex differences in these patterns of relationships, we can obtain a better understanding of race and sex discrimination and of inequality generally.

Although interest in social selection is represented in several literatures within sociology, there have been relatively few theoretical statements concerning it and very little direct evidence presented to portray its dynamics. One exception in the theoretical area is Kerckhoff's (1976) juxtaposition of the socialization and allocation perspectives on status attainment. He shows how each perspective calls attention to differing mechanisms to explain attainment and indicates that contextual analysis can provide important evidence in studying allocation, a view that we share. Turning to empirical treatments, the issue of social selection has surfaced within the context of school and college attendance in the sociology of education and stratification literatures. However, researchers have not actually measured the extent of selection. Instead, they have made indirect inferences concerning its operation as a social process from various forms of causal analysis. For example, Heyns (1974) argues that there are patterns of social selection within schools that are manifest in differential placement into college preparatory curricula and that verbal ability mediates social class effects in predicting such placement. In turn, curriculum placement is an important determinant of access to counseling services that can facilitate future attainment.

Alexander and McDill (1976) provide evidence that although academic ability is an important determinant of curriculum placement, socioeconomic status of the family of origin is also important and, depending upon how it is measured, *may* be the most important determinant of curriculum assignment. Curriculum placement then affects objective outcomes, such as access to high-status and high-ability peers, math achievement, and class rank, as well as subjective outcomes, such as college plans, self-conceptions of academic competence, and degree of scholarly orientation toward academic affairs. Although they later indicate that inclusion of precurriculum controls reduces the effects of curriculum placement influences from 20% to 50% (Alexander, Cook, and McDill, 1978), they still argue that the consequences of curriculum placement are "pervasive and frequently substantial" (Alexander *et al.*, 1978:62). Within this literature, then, the existence of social selection is inferred due to correlations between ability and family socioeconomic status, on the one hand, with curriculum placement and attendant objective outcomes (e.g., access to high-status peers and class rank) on the other.

Alwin, Hauser, and Sewell (1975) address the educational selection issue at the college level by emphasizing the nonrandom allocation of students to colleges on the basis of mental ability, past academic performance, aspirations, socioeconomic background, religion, and ethnicity. They argue that once family background, ability, grades, and other related variables are statistically controlled, college categories (which presumably represent characteristics of the colleges themselves) add only 2.4 percentage points to the explained variance in earnings (Alwin *et al.*, 1975:131). They interpret these findings to suggest that the structural characteristics of college type contribute only minimally to explaining earnings once the personal background characteristics are controlled. However, their analysis strategy attributes joint variation between background characteristics and college types to the background variables; it is precisely this joint variation that we will view as evidence of social selection.

In another study, Davis (1965) discusses the processes through which students are recruited to various fields after they are enrolled in college. He indicates that student characteristics associated with a field among beginning students are those that tend to characterize new recruits as well as discriminate between leavers and stayers (Davis, 1965:44), thus increasing homogeneity within subfields and by implication increasing the correspondence between career demands and personal attributes. Althauser *et al.* (1975: 155–158) argue that for the elite black and white college graduates surveyed in their analysis, self-selection due to failure to graduate from high school, failure to gain college admission and/or failure to graduate from college, probably results in a narrowing of the success gap for blacks and whites who do survive all of these hurdles. Finally, in an analysis of the effects of schooling in our society, Collins (1979) argues that college attendance, once an "incidental accompaniment of high status," has become a requirement for many positions that had not previously required an advanced degree. Thus Collins's thesis is that educational credentials serve as screening (selection) devices for access to elite positions in society. Berg (1970) provides compatible arguments, and at the societal level Suleiman (1978) describes how the educational system in France functions to provide an elite for French society.

The occupational sociology and organizational literatures also make reference to selection, usually within the context of discussing both socilaization and selection for careers. Wanous (1980) provides a comprehensive discussion of organizational selection. He emphasizes the complementary nature of selection and socialization as mechanisms to facilitate workers' productivity within organizations. He analyzes organizations' recruitment procedures and individuals' choices of organizations and emphasizes the continuous nature of the matching process between organizational needs and individual needs and abilities. D. Hall (1971) views career choice as the matching of personal identity and role requirements, with career development described as a spiraling combination of career choice, subidentity growth, and commitment. Maccoby (1976) recognizes three types of social selection including: (a) "survival of the fittest" organizations; (b) selection of recruits into organizations, (the successful companies being those that over time most effectively match structures and people with market requirements); and (c) an internal selection process in which traits useful to the organization are reinforced and other traits not useful or detrimental are weakened or suppressed (Maccoby, 1976:173). Although the last form of selection he identifies is viewed as socialization by sociologists, Maccoby recognizes that some people are not the "right" types to advance above their current stations within organizations. These selection decisions are based on characteristics such as aggressiveness, decisiveness, and energy levels—traits that may not be easily modified in adult life. For Maccoby, then, social selection involves the matching of personal and organizational characteristics, which in turn, among profitable companies, are both matched to market characteristics.

The complementary relationship between socialization and selection is also recognized by Brim and Wheeler (1966), who argue that careful selection of recruits into an organization can screen out those who lack appropriate personal characteristics for expected roles and thus would present problems for the socialization program (1966:27). They suggest that differential outcomes across organizations may be due largely to differential input; so, for example, if certain universities graduate a large number of Ph.D.s, it may be because they admit a large number of people who are "Ph.D. material." They note that there may be interaction effects between environmental and personal characteristics such that distinct outcomes are produced (1966:103).

More recently sociologists have directly acknowledged the phenomenon of matching between persons and jobs. Granovetter (1981) focuses on the issue of why workers who embody given characteristics obtain jobs with given characteristics. He reviews literature from both economics and sociology that informs the matching process. For example, he argues that persistent differences in wages across local labor markets, occupations, and industries run counter to economists' notions of equilibrium but that such differences could be explained by studies of matching processes (1981:35). He also advocates more theoretical work using elements from both sociology and economics to promote understanding of worker allocation to jobs. Sorensen and Kalleberg (1981) identify two contrasting models of job matching as "vacancy competition" and "wage competition"; the former model emphasizes jobs being obtained due to vacancies being created by workers who leave, whereas the latter emphasizes matching through market mechanisms involving the correspondence of the wage rate with the value of the marginal product (i.e., the neoclassical model). Although both of these theoretical analyses provide support for our investigation of social selection, they provide no actual data concerning patterns of relevant relationships.

Finally, researchers have acknowledged the selective nature of geographical migration. Blau and Duncan (1967:259) argue that urban migration is selective of men with high potential for socioeconomic success, whereas farm migration is not selective of this group. These patterns result in migrants evidencing achievement superior to both those left behind and those they join in their new communities, except in the case of rural to urban migration where initial differences are extreme (1967:273). They draw analogies between such migration and the process of overcoming other obstacles, such as having immigrant parents or many siblings, to suggest that those who have mastered such disadvantages have better chances for future socioeconmic advancement than others (1967:412). Other researchers have commented on the obvious selectivity of migration of rural blacks to northern cities (Weiss and Williamson, 1972; Long and Heltman, 1975; Bacon, 1971; Masters, 1975; Cutright, 1974; see Greenwood, 1975, for a general discussion of migration issues).[13]

These arguments suggest several generalizations concering social selection and its relation to economic status attainment. First, social selection occurs at least several times during the socioeconomic life cycle. It occurs when students are assigned to tracks in school and when students and colleges make choices concerning entrance to particular institutions of higher

[13]Although geographical selection is not the focus of this analysis, the Panel Study data do permit study of geographical mobility, thus allowing inferences concerning this form of selection.

learning. It occurs in the selection of fields of study and potentially at numerous points throughout workers's careers.[14] It is interesting that at each of these points of passage, both the student or worker and the relevant institutions exercise some degree of choice concerning which direction will be taken, although the matching of preferences on each side is never perfect. Clearly, selections made later in life are at least partially dependent on selections made earlier. In terms of this analysis such a generalization suggests that we be alert for selection operating via several institutions relevant to earnings attainment. Although we do not adopt a life-cycle approach in this analysis, selectivity is expected to be operating between several personal characteristics and several structural characteristics. These are investigated in more detail later.

Second, there is a close and complementary relationship between socialization and selection since they both contribute to observed relationships between institutional characteristics and outcomes. For this reason it is often difficult to determine whether such outcomes are due to socialization or selection, or to some combination of both. In terms of empirical research, arguments in favor of one factor or another have often hinged on the adequacy of measurement of respective variables (Alexander *et al.*, 1978; Bowles and Levin, 1968a) or on which variables were or should be entered first into multivariate analyses (Bowles and Levin, 1968a, 1968b; Coleman, 1968; M. Smith, 1968; G. Cain and Watts, 1968). Although this latter decision makes no difference when one analyzes the relative magnitudes of the regression coefficients, when increment in R^2 criteria are used, joint variation between the two types of variables will be attributed to those variables entered first. Since researchers often enter what are viewed to be causally prior socioeconomic background factors before they enter characteristics of institutions, the latter characterstics may end up adding only minimally to explained variance (e.g., Alwin *et al.*, 1975). As we have indicated, such a strategy is conservative in terms of the importance it attributes to structural factors, and debates concerning which variables should be entered first have obfuscated the relationships between sets of variables (i.e., analysis of social selection).

Perhaps the clearest case of this is shown in the exchange between Coleman (1968) and Bowles and Levin (1968a, 1968b). Bowles and Levin argue that the Coleman Report mistakenly downgrades the importance of students' social class backgrounds and teacher and school characteristics and emphasizes the role of peer characteristics. Yet the social class background and achievement characteristics of students are highly related to those of their peers, thus making it difficult to statistically separate out their respective

---

[14]This argument is compatible with Spilerman's (1977) concept of career trajectories although the notion of selection is not prominently featured there.

influences. They argue that poor measurement of school resource variables biases downward their importance relative to the better-measured personal characteristics. Coleman (1968) replies that when school resource variables are entered first into analyses of student outcomes they still are not substantial predictors of student achievement, though M. Smith (1968) suggests that the magnitudes of the resource variables are increased when objectively measured parental status variables are included with the resource variables.

These arguments have also occurred elsewhere in the field in somewhat more general form. Debates between proponents of the human capital tradition and those who argue for the importance of structural variables in economic attainment are one example. In Chapter 1 we reviewed arguments concerning the biasing of results due to omission of key variables or poor measurement. Recall that Wachtel and Betsey (1972) acknowledged the correspondence between personal and structural characteristics and deliberately set up their statistical analysis so that this collinearity would be eliminated. Other proponents of structuralist perspectives have acknowledged the tendency for selection to occur as we have described but have emphasized the other side of the coin, that is, educational variations within job status (e.g., Berg, 1970). Researchers have also argued for the importance of a particular type of variable in the explanation of earnings or inequality. For example, Stolzenberg (1978) urges us to "bring the boss back in" as a predictor of earnings, and Baron and Bielby (1980) make analogous arguments concerning characteristics of the firm. Although these types of investigations are clearly important, at some point it becomes necessary to move beyond the study of respective types of variables to examine their interrelation and to do so in a way that brings evidence to bear on the social processes that produced these patterns as opposed to treating them as a statistical obstacle.

STRATEGY FOR ANALYSIS

The strategy in this investigation is as follows: First, we identify and review the findings presented thus far that might be argued to be the product of social selection. Second, we present more systematic and precise estimates of the nature of this phenomenon and its variation by status group than have been presented previously. Third, we discuss this evidence in terms of its implications for the study of inequality and discrimination.

In two previous chapters there were data to suggest correspondence between personal and structural characteristics. In Chapters 4 and 5 we found covariance between years of schooling and industrial concentration and investment and several occupational labor market characteristics respectively. In both chapters there were status group differences in the extent of this covariation. These findings suggest that our analysis of social selection be concentrated in this area. In contrast, in Chapter 3 there was no evidence to suggest systematic correspondence between personal and local labor market characteristics. Hence we do not pursue the possibility of selectivity effects here.[15]

We are now interested in providing more precise estimates of the degree of social selection evident between personal and labor market characteristics. To do this we will provide estimates of the degree of bias in regression coefficients representing human capital characteristics when various sets of structural characteristics are omitted.[16] The greater the degree of bias, the greater the selectivity involving the labor market. Following Rao and Miller (1971) and Griffin (1976) we estimate the percentage of bias using the following equation: bias $= 100\% - (b_{\text{true}}/b_{\text{biased}})$, where b_{true} represents the relevant partial slope from an equation assumed to be true (i.e., one that includes the labor market variables) and where b_{biased} represents the partial slope of the same variable from an equation assumed to be biased (i.e., one that excludes the labor market variables). In other words, when there are strong partial relationships between personal and structural characteristics, omission of structural characteristics from earnings equations will produce bias that is interpreted as evidence for social selection. When these partial relationships are weak, omission of structural characteristics produces minimal or no bias, thus suggesting weak or absent selection effects.

These estimates are entirely dependent upon the accuracy of the equations used to provide input. In particular, the equations we designate as

[15]These findings should not be interpreted as inconsistent with the selective migration phenomenon we documented previously, since we have not investigated whether or not migrants have greater potential than nonmigrants. Rather, the findings from Chapter 3 suggest that there do not appear to be systematic relationships between personal characteristics such as years of schooling and local labor market factors such as economic health of the manufacturing or tertiary sectors. If such relationships did exist, then we would expect to find noticeable reductions (assuming positive selection) in returns to these human capital variables once the local labor market variables were included. Failing to find such changes, we conclude that there does not appear to be a strong tendency for those workers with access to human capital resources to be disproportionately located in the local labor markets whose characteristics favor high earnings attainment.

[16]An alternative method would be to inspect zero-order correlations between relevant personal and structural characteristics. This method allows a clear view of nonrandom placement of individuals to positions in the social structure. To the extent that the issue of social selection is a descriptive one, this strategy is perfectly appropriate. However, visual inspection of numerous correlations can be tedious. In addition, given our interest in comparing these processes across status groups, it would be more appropriate to compare covariances than correlations. However, computation of degree of bias in unstandardized regression coefficients addresses both of these problems in that it provides a parsimonious indication of selection based on unstandardized measures. It is also a conservative strategy. It is possible that moderately high covariances would produce trivial degrees of bias once other variables were controlled. Certainly inspection of covariances or correlations and computations of bias in regression coefficients should be viewed as complementary strategies.

"true" are true only by assumption. However, we have developed clear theoretical arguments that indicate what variables the true and biased models should contain, and this is really all that can be expected. In addition the method does allow us to provide estimates concerning which personal characteristics and human capital investments are selected by which labor markets, and whether and to what extent such selection varies by status group. In general we expect to observe matching between favorable values of human capital variables and favorable values of labor market characteristics. In most cases this means positive bias; for example, returns to years of schooling are biased upward due to omission of occupational labor market characteristics. In some cases, there may be negative biases if the effect of the labor market characteristic on earnings is negative and the workers with high values have low access to that handicapping characteristic. In other cases, negative biases may actually reflect negative selectivity whereby workers with favorable distributions of human capital are disproportionately allocated to labor market positions with unfavorable characteristics. We expect there to be very few of these cases.

FINDINGS AND DISCUSSION

The first substantive question addressed concerns whether and to what extent there is selectivity between personal characteristics and variables representing dimensions of industrial labor markets or economic sectors. To evaluate the degree of bias, two equations were estimated. The biased equation included the indicators of years of schooling, weeks worked, experience, and the Duncan SEI plus the six local labor market characteristics included in Table 3.8 in Chapter 3. The true equation included these variables plus concentration and investment and firm growth. To facilitate comparisons, years of schooling and weeks worked were measured by interval-level measures instead of the sets of dummy variables; use of one variable allows us to report a single summary measure of bias instead of having to interpret several.[17] In this table and each of the others in this section, biases that are

---

[17]There are two problems with this strategy. First, it entails loss of information in that the degree of bias present may vary depending on the level of education attained or the number of weeks worked. Thus use of an interval measure masks these differences in presenting an overall summary. We judged, however, that the loss of information entailed in using the single-variable measures was a less severe problem than the interpretational issues that would result if the dummy variables were used. Second, if there is nonlinearity, use of interval measures represents a form of specification error that can affect the magnitudes of the remaining coefficients (i.e., experience and the Duncan SEI) and thus estimates of bias for these. In this case we will note when the interpretations would differ given two different measurement strategies for weeks worked and years of schooling.

less than 10% are neither reported nor discussed. Although this is an arbitrary criterion, it allows examination of the major instances of bias present without cluttering the discussion by reporting findings that could be attributed to measurement error (errors in variables) or chance.

Table 6.6 reports the percentage of bias in returns to the four human capital and socialization variables, net of areal effects, owing to omission of the dual economy indicators. Consistent with our previous discussion in Chapter 4, for black female heads there are strong upward biases in returns to years of schooling, weeks worked, experience, and job status. Such findings suggest that for this status group, omission of these industrial indicators biases upward estimates of returns to all of the human capital and socialization variables. Inspection of the relevant zero-order correlations suggests that selectivity between each of these characteristics and concentration and investment is particularly strong; that is, among black female heads, there is a clear tendency for workers with higher than average years of schooling to locate in firms that are in oligopoly positions and have high degrees of investment, where they also tend to work more weeks per year and have higher-status jobs.[18]

These workers also tend to have somewhat *less* job experience than their counterparts in less concentrated industries. The positive bias in this case is due to the negative relationship between experience and earnings for this status group (see Table 3.5) and the weak but negative relationship between concentration and investment and experience.[19] Thus, there is no tendency for the more concentrated firms to recruit more experienced workers. In this case the experience measure is probably serving as a proxy for age/cohort. Featherman and Hauser (1976b) have documented cohort differences in the process of status attainment among males, so it is reasonable to expect analogous differences among females. In this case, younger women are more likely to obtain jobs in firms with primary sector characteristics than are older women, who are relegated to service and sales positions (i.e., those

---

[18]It is inappropriate to conclude that the relationship between weeks worked and concentration and investment is strictly linear. The zero-order correlation between concentration and investment and the dummy representing 48–49 weeks worked is .494, whereas the correlation between this variable and the dummy representing 50–52 weeks worked is −.318. Thus the workers in the most concentrated and investment-oriented industries are not working the most weeks per year but rather have some amount of vacation time off from work as part of their benefits package. Additional analysis using dummy variables to measure weeks worked thus reveals negative biases for the 50–52 weeks worked dummy for this status group.

[19]The sign of the bias is the product of two terms: (*a*) the true effect of the omitted variable on the dependent variable; and (*b*) the regression coefficient of the omitted on the included variable with no other independent variables present. A formal discussion of these issues is presented by Rao and Miller (1971).

Table 6.6

Percentage of Bias in Returns to Human Capital Variables Owing to Omission of Dual Economy Indicators, Net of Areal Effects[a]

Status group	Years of schooling (%)	Weeks worked (%)	Experience (%)	Duncan SEI (%)
White male heads	--	--	--	--
Black male heads	--	-12	-15	--
White female heads	--	--	--	36
Black female heads	41	32	70	60
White wives	12	--	--	14
Black wives	-16	10	-65	60

[a]Only biases with an absolute value of 10% and larger are reported in this and subsequent tables. The dual economy indicators are (1) concentration and investment and (2) firm growth.

with secondary sector characteristics). The degree of bias represented here is one of the strongest observed in this analysis.

Note: Given our discussion in Chapter 4 concerning the missing data problem with the concentration variable, it is possible that these estimates of bias are inflated due to the pattern of missing data. To evaluate this notion, we recomputed the biases reported in Table 6.6 for the black female heads (BFH) and black wives (BW) for whom concentration and investment was measured. The following shows the percentage of bias on returns to human capital variables owing to omission of dual economy indicators, net of areal effects, for workers for whom concentration and investment is measured.

	Years of schooling (%)	Weeks worked (%)	Experience (%)	Duncan SEI (%)
BFH	68	—	56	49
BW	43	—	52	80

Among black female heads, although there are some changes in the magnitudes of the reported biases, the pattern of findings is quite similar. Biases in returns to experience and job status have dropped by over 10% each, but the biases remain positive and substantial. Biases in years of schooling are actually increased to 68%. Reported biases in weeks worked have dropped to below 10%. Among black wives, however, the changes in the pattern of findings are more noticeable. Biases in returns to job status increase from 60% to 80%, and bias in returns to experience is still strong. However, in the subgroup analysis the bias in returns to experience is positive as predicted, and this finding is replicated for biases in returns to schooling. Biases in weeks worked drop to below 10% in the subgroup analysis. It appears that the general prediction made concerning the predominance of positive biases is confirmed for the subsample. The substantial negative bias in returns to experience observed in the analysis of the larger sample is a function of the composition of the sample, which, in terms of this dimension, contains subsamples with differing characteristics.

The other major pattern of positive bias found in this analysis involves returns to the Duncan SEI. It appears that for all the female status groups, there are upward biases in estimates of returns to socioeconomic status when the industrial labor market characteristics are omitted. Such findings suggest that for women there is a positive relationship between industrial sector characteristics and the status of jobs they occupy once they are employed by the firms. This relationship is stronger for black than for white women, thus indicating a racial differential in this form of selectivity. All groups of female workers, however, contrast with male workers, who evidence no appreciable degree of selectivity between industrial labor market characteristics and occupational status.

White male workers show no degree of selectivity involving industrial labor market characteristics since these variables do not affect their earnings attainment net of human capital characteristics. Viewed in another way, however, there is selectivity because the industrial characteristics are significant when human capital variables are omitted. Among black male heads, however, there appear to be some negative selection effects. However, the negative zero-order correlation between weeks worked and concentration and investment ($r = -.098$) is apparently due to those who work 50–52 weeks per year ($r = -.179$) being in less concentrated industries than those who work 48–49 weeks per year ($r = .114$), thus producing an overall negative effect. We also expect that the negative bias involving experience is due to a cohort effect similar to that discussed for black female heads. Younger black males are more likely to obtain jobs in the core of the economy than are their older counterparts. Such a pattern also accounts for the negative degree of bias on experience evidenced among black wives.[20] We also observe small degrees of positive bias for years of schooling among white wives and for weeks worked among black wives.

[20]The other instance of negative bias among black wives appears to be due to incipient tipping between years of schooling and concentration and investment (zero-order $r = .403$). Thus years of schooling is artificially inflated when the concentration variable is included, which leads to an apparent negative bias if it is omitted.

In summary, the patterns of social selection between industrial and personal characteristics are pervasive but vary by race and sex. Blacks are more likely to be differentially selected than are whites on experience, where younger blacks are more likely to be in primary industrial sector positions than are older blacks. Women evidence a greater degree of positive selectivity between job status and core characteristics than do men, and with the exception of white female heads, the same is true, although to a lesser degree, for years of schooling. Selectivity is greatest for black female heads when the status groups are compared in terms of the magnitudes and pervasiveness of effects.

The next question addressed concerns biases in human capital characteristics due to omission of occupational labor market characteristics. Table 6.7 summarizes the relevant findings where the true equation contains human capital variables plus areal, industrial, and occupational labor market variables, whereas the biased equation contains all of these except the occupational labor market characteristics. Again interval-level measures of years of schooling and weeks worked are used in place of the sets of dummies.

The most striking effect is consistent upward biases in returns to years of schooling across all of the status groups. The degree of bias ranges from 25% for black female heads to 53% for black male heads. We also note, however, that the Duncan SEI is omitted from both of these specifications, as we discussed in Chapter 5. The introduction of the complexity variable in the true equation is essentially what accounts for these observed biases. That there is selectivity between years of schooling and complexity is not surprising. Jobs that are high on complexity attract more highly educated workers and pay well enough to discriminate on schooling (and other characteristics) in the hiring process. It is useful to be reminded, however, that earnings are not produced merely as a function of years of schooling but rather from jobs that vary in the degree to which work activities are complex.

Table 6.7

Percentage of Bias in Returns to Human Capital Variables Owing to Omission of Occupational Labor Market Indicators, Net of Areal and Industrial Effects

Status group	Years of schooling (%)	Weeks worked (%)	Experience (%)
White male heads	32	14	15
Black male heads	53	--	--
White female heads	39	--	--
Black female heads	25	--	--
White wives	27	--	--
Black wives	27	--	23

Notice that for white male heads, returns to weeks worked and experience are also biased upward due to omission of the occupational labor market characteristics. Thus for this status group, omission of occupational labor market characteristics has more pervasive effects on the personal investment variables included in the model than for the other categories of workers. This is also true to some extent for black wives, for whom we observe biases in returns to experience when the occupational indicators are omitted. Thus, for both of these groups, such findings again remind us that earnings are generated within the context of the job and not automatically as a function of work experience.

Table 6.8 allows evaluation of whether omission of the class/authority variables from earnings attainment equations biases upward returns to the personal investment characteristics that have been discussed. These biases are additive with those presented in Table 6.7. In this case the true equation is one that includes investment variables, areal, industrial, and occupational labor market characteristics plus the most complete versions of the class/ authority variables appropriate for each status group. The biased equation contains all of these variables except the class/authority indicators. This provides a very conservative test of the selectivity notion, asking whether omission of class/authority introduces biases *after* occupational, industrial, and areal effects have been controlled.[21] Thus biases reported here can be added to those reported in Table 6.7 in order to estimate the sum of biases introduced by the omission of both types of variables.

The findings indicate that omission of authority does introduce bias net of variation explained by all of the remaining labor market characteristics. For male workers and white female heads, returns to work experience are overestimated if the authority variables are omitted. Thus for these groups, more experienced workers are selected into positions of authority that then yield dividends in earnings. Although black female heads do not appear to be able to translate work experience into promotions on the authority ladder, there is evidence of selectivity for such advancement on the basis of years of schooling. For both white male heads and black female heads, it appears that returns to weeks worked are inflated owing to omission of the authority indicators. Thus for these groups, having a steady job that is not prone to layoffs or periods of seasonal inactivity contributes to earnings partly because being in these jobs means being promoted to authority positions. Viewing Tables 6.7 and 6.8 together, we observe the strong degree of upward bias (64%) in returns to schooling for black female heads if occupational labor market and authority variables are omitted. Under these same conditions,

[21]It is not possible to make exactly this argument for the biases reported in Tables 6.6 and 6.7 since the Duncan SEI is included in the equations reported in Table 6.6 but not those in Table 6.7. Thus it is likely that variation "explained by" omission of occupational labor market variables in Table 6.7 was already controlled for by inclusion of SEI in Table 6.6.

Table 6.8

Percentage of Bias in Returns to Human Capital Variables
Owing to Omission of Authority Variables, Net of Areal,
Industrial, and Occupational Labor Market Effects

Status group	Years of schooling (%)	Weeks worked (%)	Experience (%)
White male heads	--	22	15
Black male heads	--	--	17
White female heads	--	--	10
Black female heads	39	28	--
White wives	--	--	--
Black wives	--	--	--

white male heads have returns to experience overestimated by 30% and returns to weeks worked overestimated by 36%. Thus there is strong evidence to suggest that there are patterns of social selection involving labor market and personal characteristics.

The final issue addressed concerns the relationship between the basic human capital variables we have discussed and the social psychological variables introduced earlier in the chapter. Although the argument involving selection is less relevant, it is still of interest to know whether and to what extent returns to the investment variables are biased due to omission of social psychological characteristics. To evaluate this notion, we used the samples of male heads and black female heads discussed earlier in the chapter and estimated two additional equations. The biased equation included only the investment variables, whereas the true equation included investment and social psychological variables. Inspection of Table 6.9 indicates that omission of these variables biases upward returns to most or all of the investment variables for each status group. Biases are most extreme in returns to schooling (66%) and experience (49%) for black male heads, although white male heads experience considerable biases in returns to schooling (32%) and experience (30%). Black female heads evidence upward biases in returns to all three factors, with the strongest degree of bias shown by returns to experience.

Summary and Conclusions

In this chapter we have subjected our previously discussed findings to two additional tests. In the first case, we found that the labor market effects reported earlier were not diminished by controlling for family background

Table 6.9

Percentage of Bias in Returns to Human Capital Variables
Owing to Omission of Social Psychological Variables

Status group	Years of schooling (%)	Weeks worked (%)	Experience (%)
White male heads	32	15	30
Black male heads	66	--	49
Black female heads	18	26	34

and social psychological factors, although for some status groups the magnitudes of the originally included human capital and status attainment variables were reduced when the social psychological variables were included. The findings concerning family background variables were not surprising. Given that education mediates family background effects on socioeconomic attainment (as has been discussed by numerous authors in the status attainment tradition), it is not unanticipated that inclusion of labor market effects would further diminish their predictive power. With reference to the minimal effects of the social psychological variables on earnings net of the remaining predictors, the findings are more compatible with those presented by G. Duncan and Morgan (1981) and with arguments summarized by Spenner and Featherman (1978) than with ideas advanced by Andrisani (1977, 1981). These findings serve to reassure us that the labor market effects presented and discussed in previous chapters do hold up when additional personal controls are introduced. As such they reinforce our general belief that structural determinants of earnings attainment are important and worthy of further investigation.

In the second case we have found varying amounts of correspondence between personal and structural characteristics in the earnings determination process. In contrast to many previous analyses that have mentioned selection but inferred its operation indirectly, we have measured the degrees of correspondence by assessing the amount of bias in relevant regression coefficients. These findings highlight the limited utility of viewing personal and structural factors as representing "competing" explanations of earnings attainment. Although the juxtaposition of theories that stress the importance of different types of variables has been useful in previous studies as well as in our own, we seriously question whether future study will find this strategy to be of great utility. Instead, from our findings it appears that we ought to pay more attention to the processes through which workers are allocated to positions, thus producing congruence between personal and structural resources. The variations we have described in the degree of such congruence suggest that there are ascriptive status differences in these selection processes. These differences are evident in the magnitudes of the nonrandom allocations as well as in the variation in which personal characteristics are selected for by status groups. Although these findings provide more precise and concrete evidence concerning selection than have the studies we initially discussed in this section, we regard these findings as instructive rather than definitive. It is our hope that this discussion will provide the basis for more detailed investigation of these selection processes.

CHAPTER 7

Nonadditive Models of Earnings Attainment

Introduction

By examining the effects of labor market variables separately by race and sex status groups, we have allowed for and found interactions of these variables with race and sex. Except for this, however, the analyses in the preceding chapters are based on the assumption that any effects the various labor market characteristics have on earnings are additive in nature. The objective of this chapter is to relax this assumption and explore the possibility that the labor market variables interact among themselves and with human capital and other personal characteristic variables. This could result, then, in alterations in some of the previous conclusions.[1] Practical considerations require limitation of the number of types of tests made. Therefore, we do not test for all possible interactions, but rather for those for which there is at least some guidance on the basis of theory or research. In some instances, however, the literature has only been suggestive, and the tests must be viewed as exploratory. In examining the possible interactions, we decided to limit the analysis to the four heads of household status groups. Although this is difficult to

[1]Although at the outset of this project we seriously considered testing for these interactions prior to estimating the additive effect models as presented in the previous chapters, this strategy was not followed for three reasons. First, it is our premise that the effects hypothesized in the literature are primarily additive, and any interactions that exist will not substantially mask these effects. Second, examining additive effects before considering interactions is consistent with an incremental strategy of model building. Finally, because the literature generally does not systematically and explicitly discuss hypotheses about interactions, the testing and discussing of these would have resulted in a disjointed presentation.

justify on theoretical grounds, the sheer volume of tests and subsequent subgroup analysis that would have been required for the six status groups has forced us to restrict the analysis.

Initially, we will test for farm/nonfarm interactions with labor markets and age/cohort interactions with labor markets. The remaining types of interactions examined are more substantively based. These include education interactions with labor markets and class/authority, occupational labor market interactions with local and industrial labor markets, and class/authority interactions with local, industrial, and occupational labor markets. Unless indicated otherwise, hierarchical testing procedures and the .05 level of significance are used.

Farm/Nonfarm Differences

We were concerned with the possibility that including cases with farm occupations might in some way influence our findings. The potential problem involves the difficulties in assessing income in kind for agricultural positions. In short, there is a potential source of bias in the dependent variable when earnings are measured for farm occupations. Some researchers (e.g., Wright and Perrone, 1977; Kluegel, 1978; Stolzenberg, 1978) choose to avoid this problem by excluding farmers from their analysis. Because of the small proportion of cases categorized as farm, however, we retained these cases, assuming any biasing effect would be small. To empirically assess this assumption we estimated all of the basic equations presented thus far for the nonfarm samples of white and black male heads (data not presented). The differences between these coefficients and those reported previously are very small, and in no instance would we find it necessary to alter our conclusions. The proportion of those in farm occupations in the four female status groups is so small (less than 1%) that no attempt was made to assess the effect of excluding the farm occupation cases.

Interactions of Age/Cohort with Labor Market Characteristics

Although age has been used by researchers in the human capital and status attainment tradition as a proxy for labor force experience, this research has incorporated a measure of actual labor force experience as well as numerous other controls. Therefore, we expect that the additive effects of whatever additional variables age captures will not be large.[2] Any age differences that exist could of course be cohort effects rather than effects of variables associated with growing older. That is, because different birth cohorts uniquely experience, at different points in the life cycle, events in history, such as wars, recessions, and baby booms, the socioeconomic outcomes they experience are often affected. Our data, as is true for all cross-sectional data, will not allow for disentangling these age effects from cohort effects. We will, however, be able to determine if the generalizations we have drawn in the preceding chapters portray the influence of labor market characteristics across major age/cohort categories.

Because the issue of whether age/cohort interacts with labor market characteristics has received little theoretical or empirical attention, testing for significant interactions is undertaken without specific hypotheses. Nevertheless, we have several general expectations. Given the documented advances of blacks, and especially young blacks, during the late 1960s and the 1970s, more age/cohort interactions are expected for blacks than whites. However, given the absence of socioeconomic improvements for women over the same period of time, comparable interactions by sex are not expected.

To determine if the influences of labor market variables on earnings vary by age/cohort, multiplicative terms of age (a dummy variable representing 25–44 years versus 45–64 years) with each of the labor market variables and class/authority have been created and examined within a conventional regression hierarchical testing strategy. The age/cohort breakdown chosen essentially dichotomizes cases by whether persons were born pre- or post-1930, thus providing a meaningful categorization in terms of predepression and postdepression cohort effects. Each set of age/cohort by labor market interaction terms was added to an equation with education, weeks worked, work experience, the dummy variable for age/cohort, and the six local, two industrial, and four occupational labor market variables. This allows for an estimate of the net explained variance of each set of these interactions as well as significance tests of particular age/cohort by labor market characteristic interactions. Data have been included only on the interactions reaching statistical significance; the results of all tests conducted are summarized in the discussion.

---

[2]There are minimal age/cohort differences in earnings. In fact, there are significant age/ cohort differences in earnings for only black male heads and white female heads. With the means adjusted for human capital and labor market variables, younger black male heads earn $1127 less than their older counterparts. Among white female heads, however, it is the younger women who earn $1396 more than the older women.

AGE/COHORT BY LOCAL LABOR MARKET
CHARACTERISTICS

The interaction tests clearly indicate that age/cohort generally does not interact with labor market variables. Only for black male heads are statistically significant interactions found.[3] As reported in Chapter 3, manufacturing dominance has a net positive influence on earnings, but as shown in Table 7.1, it is only older black males who benefit from residence in areas with greater manufacturing dominance; younger black males are not influenced by this variable. This is consistent with the findings of Featherman and Hauser (1978), who show that it is the younger blacks who are more similar to whites. Overall, however, from one locale or region to another, local labor market characteristics operate similarly for the two birth cohorts.

AGE/COHORT BY INDUSTRIAL LABOR MARKET
CHARACTERISTICS

Differentiation by race is apparent in the age/cohort interactions with industrial labor market characteristics. Interactions are found only for black men and women; concentration and investment has no net effect for the younger cohort but has a significant positive influence on the earnings of the older cohort.[4] Although initially concentration and investment was found to have a positive influence for both black men and women (see Chapter 4), we learn from these data that it is only the older blacks who benefit from employment in industries with high concentration and investment ratios.

AGE/COHORT BY OCCUPATIONAL LABOR MARKET
CHARACTERISTICS

The pattern of finding only a few age/cohort by labor market interactions is continued in the analysis of the interactions with occupational labor market characteristics. Across the four status groups only two interactions are statistically significant: task complexity for white male heads and physical dex-

[3]Because of multicollinearity of certain interaction terms with a number of the occupational and industrial labor market variables for black female heads, the test for local labor market interactions was made net of the human capital variables and the additive effects of local labor market variables.

[4]Multicollinearity of interaction terms with other labor market characteristics for black men and women required that the significance tests be conducted net of only the human capital variables.

Table 7.1

Age/Cohort by Labor Market Characteristic Interactions

Status group	Interacting variable	Regression coefficients by age[a] 25–44	45–66
White male heads	Complexity	238[*]	313[*]
Black male heads	Manufacturing dominance[b]	-36	863[*]
	Concentration and investment[c]	95	1057[*]
	Physical dexterity[b]	-3	-340[*]
White female heads	(None significant)	--	--
Black female heads	Concentration and investment[c]	347	914[*]

[a]With the exceptions indicated, the following variables are controlled: education, weeks worked, experience, the six local, two industrial, and four occupational labor market variables.

[b]Concentration and investment is not controlled.

[c]These variables are controlled: education, weeks worked, experience, occupation, and firm growth.

[*]$p < .05$.

terity for black male heads. Table 7.1 shows that although task complexity is positively related to earnings for both younger and older white men, the influence is stronger within the older cohort. Among black males we had found earlier (Chapter 5) that physical dexterity requirements are not related to earnings, but here the data suggest that this is true only for younger black males; older black male heads actually receive lower earnings the greater the physical dexterity the job requires.

AGE/COHORT BY CLASS/AUTHORITY INTERACTIONS

Again, differences are observed by race. Testing for age/cohort interactions with the employer–supervisor–worker class/authority breakdown net of the three human capital, six local, two industrial, and four occupational labor market characteristics, we found significant interactions only for black male and female heads. To show the pattern of these interactions, we have obtained adjusted earnings means for class/authority categories for young and older black men and women (see Table 7.2). Because there are few similarities by sex, the interaction patterns are discussed separately for black men and women.

For black men members of the older cohort earn about $1400 more than those in the younger cohort, and as mentioned earlier, the advantage remains after controls for other variables are introduced. Among black males, however, the most striking difference is in the relative position of older and younger employers. Whereas the adjusted mean ($6719) for employers in the older cohort is well below the grand mean, younger cohort employers have an adjusted mean ($12,860) well above the cohort's grand mean. On the other hand, supervisors and workers in the older cohort earn more than their counterparts in the younger cohort ($11,436 versus $9094 and $10,729 versus $8755, respectively). Considering the two dimensions of supervisory position, regardless of cohort, those with greater spans of responsibility (e.g., determination of pay and promotions) and control (number of subordinates) earn substantially more than those with small spans. The earnings increment associated with a large span of control, and especially a large span of responsibility, is greater for members of the older cohort, however. (See the differences between means for small span and large span across the two cohorts.)

Among black female heads employers in both cohorts have earnings well below the earnings of supervisors and workers, although it is the youngest employers who are disadvantaged the most. As with the black males, the older supervisors earn more than the younger supervisors. Older workers, however, earn slightly less than the younger workers. Considering supervisory dimensions, there are several interesting patterns. The distinction

Table 7.2

Age/Cohort by Class/Authority Interactions[a]

Class/authority	Black male heads			Black female heads		
category	25–44	45–64	Total	25–44	45–64	Total
Employer	3879	−3637	−319	−3653	−2271	−1822
Supervisor	113	1080	591	225	1959	880
Large span of control	2941	3543	3055	−664	8023	3708
Small span of control	−428	−868	−253	567	−894	−367
Responsibility	1488	2801	2278	958	936	608
No responsibility	−552	−252	−424	−234	2076	967
Worker	−226	373	−167	124	−382	−77
Grand mean	8981	10,356	9481	5546	5434	5502

[a]Data expressed as adjusted earnings means deviated from the grand mean. The adjusted means are obtained by controlling for education, weeks worked, experience, and the six local, two industrial and four occupational labor market variables.

between large and small span of control is more important among members of the older cohort. In fact, this is the only difference among the four possible comparisons for supervisory dimensions that is statistically significant. Recall that although the largest effect for black male heads also was for span of control and for the older cohort, the expected patterns for supervisory dimensions were also found for the other three comparisons.

To summarize this section, the major finding is that the age/cohort interactions that are found exist primarily for the black but not the white population. Considering the labor market characteristics, we found that in the instances where age/cohort interactions exist, it is only the older blacks whose earnings are significantly affected by the interacting labor market characteristics (manufacturing dominance, concentration and investment, and physical dexterity). For the only interaction for the white population, we found that older white males receive greater earnings returns to task complexity than do the younger white males. The class/authority interaction with age/cohort also was found only for blacks. Among males it is the older blacks who receive the greatest benefits from supervisory and large span of control and responsibility positions; older employers, however, are severely disadvantaged when compared with younger employers. Among black females the older employers earn more than the younger, and span of control is important only for the older black females. Thus, these data are only partly consistent with those of other researchers who find that it is the younger rather than older blacks who are more like the white population. As is found for the white male population, areal manufacturing dominance and firm concentration and investment were not important for young black males. In addition, it is the young black male employers who are above their group grand mean; white male employers also are above their group grand mean.

Interactions of Education with Labor Market Characteristics

Theoretical and empirical literature concerning labor market effects on earnings has pointed to the existence of interactions between human capital resources and labor market or sector characteristics. Because of its theoretical prominence in the human capital and status attainment perspectives and its empirically demonstrated relationship to earnings, the role of education has received the most attention. Consistent with this emphasis, we undertake an investigation of education interactions with labor market characteristics and class/authority.

We first consider the possibility that the effects of years of schooling vary by areal characteristics. Review of existing empirical literature suggests disagreement concerning whether these interactions exist. Mueller's (1974) analysis of occupational and earnings attainment in the 15 largest U. S. SMSAs indicated homogeneity in the influence of education across these SMSAs. In addition, categorizing by city size, Mueller (1977) found no differences in the education effect for black and white males. Gross regional differences in the effect of education have been found, however. Featherman and Hauser (1978:Chapter 7) report differences in returns to education by North and South regions but also find that this varies by whether the person is a native or migrant to the region. In addition, Hanushek (1973) reports variation in returns to education as a function of local labor market residence.

Although theoretical analyses provide no explicit guidance, conceptualizations of city types by Thompson (1965) and O. Duncan and Reiss (1956) make inferences concerning areal differences in returns to schooling at least plausible. These authors argue that local labor markets vary according to the development of their export base or the nature of their functional specialization. Local markets with strong export activity or those that specialize in high-level manufacturing or services demand a skilled work force and are thus more likely to reward more educated workers whereas other areas need a more modestly skilled work force and are unlikely to provide above average rewards for additional schooling. We will evaluate these notions in our analysis, although we can provide no predictions concerning race and sex differences in the magnitudes of these potential effects.

Turning to the literature concerning education by industry interactions, conflicting hypotheses also are found. The major theoretical guidance for the existence of such interactions comes from dual economy theory. To recast the discussion from Chapter 1 in slightly different terms, relevant arguments suggest that returns to schooling will be greater in the core than in the periphery. Oligopoly position and large firm size are associated with an elaborate division of labor in which educational credentials are important to gaining promotions and thus higher earnings. The capital intensiveness of these firms also demands the hiring of highly skilled, educated workers, which suggests that these characteristics are differentially rewarded. In the periphery, however, division of labor is less elaborate and capital not as crucial to production; hence there is no reason to pay for highly skilled labor. Evidence in support of the basic prediction is provided by Beck et al. (1978). However, Hauser's (1980) reanalysis of the same data places the findings of interaction between education and industrial sector in some doubt. Hodson's (1978:Table 7) findings imply that there are differential returns to education by sector affiliation since according to his estimates, the earnings gap across sectors increases with level of schooling completed. There are conflicting arguments as to how this hypothesized interaction varies by race and sex. According to Daymont (1980), however, blacks may be at a greater disadvantage in the competitive sector than in the core, though Beck *et al.* (1978, 1980) argue the reverse.

The arguments concerning occupational labor market by education interactions are somewhat more consistent. Indeed, two strands of literature suggest that such an interaction exists. Stolzenberg (1975:650) in his discussion of occupational labor markets indicates that formal schooling can be expected to vary in its influence on earnings across occupations. He argues that skill differentials across occupations produce segmentation by occupation and that the more highly skilled occupations will be more highly rewarded. Snyder, Hayward, and Hudis (1978) and Spilerman (1977) provide compatible arguments, and supporting evidence is provided by Thurow (1969) and Rees and Schultz (1970). In addition, dual labor market theory suggests that "good" jobs requiring varying degrees of education and skill will reward these characteristics whereas "bad" jobs requiring little skill and minimal schooling will not reward these characteristics. Hence, education by job characteristic interactions would be expected if those characteristics differentiate between "good" jobs (those in the primary labor market) and "bad" jobs (those in the secondary labor market). Based on the notion that blacks and women are supposedly differentially allocated to the secondary labor market, we might, for example, expect that among these status groups, returns to schooling would be lower in low complexity jobs.

In order to empirically evaluate these ideas, the interval-level measure of education was used in obtaining multiplicative interaction terms of education with the six local, two industrial, and four occupational labor market variables. The interactions with each of these three sets of labor market variables were tested net of the additive effects of weeks worked, experience, education, and the six local, two industrial, and four occupational labor market characteristics. A total of 16 interactions were found to be significant, 11 for blacks and 5 for whites. Table 7.3 displays unstandardized regression coefficients for the influence of education for three equation specifications: when no variables are controlled, when weeks worked and experience are controlled, and when the six local, two industrial, and four occupational labor market variables also are controlled.[5]

Considering first *local* labor market characteristics, we find, with one exception, that education interactions are evident only for blacks. Both black male heads and white female heads (the one exception) obtain greater returns to schooling in those areas where manufacturing activity plays a promi-

---

[5]The variable found to interact with education, and thus used as the basis for the subsample creation, is not controlled when the education coefficients are estimated (see Table 7.3).

Table 7.3

Education by Labor Market Characteristic Interactions

Status group	Interacting variable[a]	Unstandardized education coefficients after control for		
		No controls	Human capital[b]	Human capital and labor market[c]
White male heads	Complexity			
	Low	338*	340*	235*
	Medium	622*	698*	465*
	High	1103	1342	1225
	Physical dexterity			
	Low	1015*	1180*	995*
	Medium	531*	647*	373*
	High	1529	1621	695
White female heads	Manufacturing dominance			
	Low	529*	570*	-115*
	High	729	858	584
	Firm growth			
	Low	566*	741*	442*
	High	346	451	160
	Concentration and investment			
	Low	333*	431*	207
	High	407	511	-101
Black male heads	Manufacturing sector health			
	Low	410*	547*	362*
	Medium	182*	187*	-131
	High	275	458	95
	Manufacturing dominance			
	Low	337*	383*	133*
	High	397	652	248
	Tertiary sector health			
	Low	413*	576*	374*
	High	142	275	-45
	Tertiary sector growth			
	Low	8*	75*	32*
	Medium	646	1035*	453
	High	405	430	135

(continued)

Table 7.3 *(continued)*

Status group	Interacting variable[a]	No controls	Human capital[b]	Human capital and labor market[c]
	Firm growth			
	Low	738*	780*	232
	Medium	123*	249*	83*
	High	300	563	222
	Concentration and investment			
	Low	69*	57*	-157*
	Medium	427*	650*	321
	High	-176	269	156
Black female heads	Complexity[d]			
	Low	552*	549*	260*
	High	499	587	691
	Uncertainty[d]			
	Low	660*	777*	549*
	High	464	484	181
	Tertiary sector complexity[d]			
	Low	267*	274*	73*
	High	775	874	543
	Crowding[d]			
	Low	434*	475*	450*
	High	680	708	250
	Firm growth[d]			
	Low	489*	627*	286
	High	343	171	210

[a] Three categories are used for status groups with the largest number of cases and when there is more variation in the distribution.

[b] Weeks worked and experience are controlled.

[c] Unless otherwise indicated weeks worked, experience, and six local, two industrial, and four occupational labor market variables, minus the variable in the interaction, are controlled.

[d] Concentration and investment had to be excluded as a control variable to obtain interpretable coefficients.

*$p < .05$.

nent role in the local market economic base. Among black male heads, however, payoffs to education are greater in local markets characterized by *low* manufacturing sector and tertiary sector health. For manufacturing health, it appears that introduction of controls for other labor market characteristics explains what positive influence residence in an economically prosperous local market has on earnings. The findings concerning both tertiary sector health and tertiary sector growth may be a function of the distribution of black males in jobs across markets. Since they tend to be employed in manufacturing, it may be that only in a manufacturing center (where manufacturing dominance is high) can positive payoffs to years of schooling be expected. Black females, in contrast, obtain higher returns from living in markets characterized by high tertiary sector complexity; in other words, areas that probably afford them job opportunities not open to black males. Finally, schooling pays off better for black females in markets where there is low racial crowding, once other labor market variables are controlled. Although racially crowded markets may also provide good job opportunities for black females, once the characteristics of these industrial and occupational positions are taken into account, competition may prevent these workers from obtaining the returns to schooling we expect; hence returns to education are stronger in markets with low crowding.

Looking at the *industrial* labor market interactions, for every status group except white male heads, there is a significant interaction between education and firm growth. The findings suggest that returns to schooling are stronger for women workers employed in industries with low growth rates. As indicated in Chapter 4, those industries that are growing (i.e., services and retail trade) are likely to provide jobs that fall into the secondary sector, and these jobs are not expected to provide strong returns to schooling. Among black male heads the patterns are more complex. The relationship appears curvilinear, with strong returns to schooling in industries with low growth rates as expected, but at least modest returns to schooling in high-growth industries as well. It may be that this difference reflects sex differentials in the types of jobs workers obtain, with black males more able than female workers to take advantage of whatever economic opportunities are presented by growth in these industries.

The findings regarding concentration and investment are less clear-cut. Among white female heads we find that returns to schooling are higher when concentration and investment are high, although this effect appears to be explained by the introduction of other labor market characteristics and was not particularly large to begin with. Among black male heads returns appear to be strongest in industries with moderate amounts of oligopoly power. It may be that those industries that score most highly on this index discriminate against black males in some way that hampers their obtaining the returns to schooling we expect. That there are no interactions between education and concentration and investment for white male heads and black female heads is contrary to our expectations.

It is, however, for precisely these two latter groups that there are education by *occupation* interactions. For both status groups the data clearly show a monotonic increase in the influence of education as task complexity increases. It will be remembered that high-complexity occupations are those requiring high intelligence and verbal, numerical, and spatial aptitudes, as well as directing and planning, general educational development, and specific vocational preparation. So, not only are various cognitive skills and educational credentials required for entry into high task complexity occupations, but also the incumbent's education will have a greater earnings return in these occupations. In short, white male heads are doubly advantaged when compared with the other status groups. Not only are they more often found in the high task complexity jobs, which have associated with them higher earnings, but when they are located in these jobs, years of schooling has a stronger positive influence on earnings than when they are located in the low task complexity jobs. Black women also receive this bonus of a stronger return to earnings, but as already shown, they seldom are high education achievers and seldom are they in high-complexity jobs. Thus, the label of "double negative" often attached to black women is found not to be entirely appropriate; those who are able to enter occupations characterized by high task complexity will receive higher returns to education. Nevertheless, the disadvantaged position of black women still is apparent; this return rate is about one-half the rate for white males in high-complexity occupations.

Physical dexterity interacts with education only for white male heads where we observe, after controls, that education exerts the strongest influence on earnings for those in occupations characterized by low physical dexterity demands. These are the high-level white-collar occupations in the upper tier of the primary labor market where we expect schooling to be rewarded. There also are strong returns to schooling at the highest level of physical dexterity. In this case education probably is acting as a proxy for skill level in the skilled blue-collar trades that employ mostly white males, are highly unionized, and pay well—jobs that Piore would describe as being in the lower tier of the primary labor market. We also find a significant education by uncertainty interaction for black female heads. The findings show that education has the strongest influence in occupations characterized by a low level of uncertainty (i.e., little change and variety). Jobs involving variety and change also are jobs requiring that decisions be continually made and actions often modified to adjust to the changing work environment. In such instances, it is reasonable to expect that it will be the person's actual performance on the job rather than years of schooling that will be rewarded monetarily.

To summarize the basic differences by race and sex, first, education by labor market interactions are more prevalent in the black than the white population. Second, except for the considerably higher number of education interactions with local labor market characteristics for blacks, no consistent patterns exist by race or sex. Third, education interactions with occupational labor market characteristics seem to characterize primarily the white male population. Generally speaking, then, the patterns of the observed interactions are pretty much status group-specific. The two exceptions to this are for areal manufacturing dominance and occupational task complexity, although the pattern of the exceptions does not suggest any ready explanation.

Interactions of Education with Class/Authority

Given the long research tradition that has demonstrated the importance of education in explaining earnings, it is not surprising that researchers interested in class/authority have investigated the possibility of education by class/authority interactions. Wright (1978) and Wright and Perrone (1977) found that the influence of education varies by class/authority position and that these differences are important in explaining race and sex differences in the earnings returns to education. In abbreviated form, Wright's argument is that a link between the legitimation function of education within hierarchies and the use of income as a control mechanism within authority hierarchies results in greater returns to education for supervisors and even greater returns the higher one is in the hierarchy. Thus, we would expect that the returns to schooling are higher in the supervisor than in the worker category and among supervisors, large span of control and large span of responsibility have associated with them greater returns to schooling. Wright argues that the commonly found low returns to education for blacks compared with whites are due to the higher proportion of blacks in nonsupervisory positions, where the returns are low regardless of race. Although Wright's theoretical discussion suggests no returns to schooling advantage for employers, his empirical findings lead us to expect a higher return for employers than for either supervisors or workers.

Examination of education by class/authority interactions involves creating multiplicative interaction terms for the interval-level measure of education with dummy variables representing employer, supervisor, and worker. For each of the four heads of household status groups these interactions were tested net of weeks worked, experience, education, class/authority, and the six local, two industrial, and four occupational labor market characteristics. Significant interactions were found only for white male and female heads.[6]

Table 7.4 displays unstandardized education slopes for several equation specifications. Regardless of specification, the pattern is the same for both men and women. Supervisors receive a greater earnings return than workers to each additional year of schooling. This difference is especially large for females; with all variables controlled, supervisors can expect an additional $668 for each year, whereas for workers the increment is $166. Among white male heads the education coefficient for employers is almost three times larger than supervisors'.

With one exception, these findings for the four status groups are consistent with the research of Wright and Perrone (1977). Whereas we find that white female supervisors benefit more than workers from increments in education, they find no significant difference. It must be remembered, however, that their analysis is not limited to female household heads and that they do not control for labor market characteristics. We should also comment on our findings with respect to Wright's (1978) work on race differences for males. Because the same data set is used, our findings should be essentially the same. Wright focused on workers and supervisors and what we have called the span of responsibility supervisory dimension. He found that the influence of education is essentially the same for black and white male workers and for black and white male supervisors with small spans of responsibility but that white males with large spans of responsibility receive a greater return to education than do black male heads. We controlled on the labor market variables and found, as did Wright, that white male supervisors with responsibility receive large education returns but their black male counterparts receive essentially zero returns (data not shown). For those with small spans of responsibility, however, our conclusions deviate somewhat from those of Wright. We found that the coefficient for white males is positive but not statistically significant, whereas for black males it is positive and significant. The same pattern also is observed when the span of control dimension is analyzed in a similar manner.

In sum, these data indeed indicate that education and class/authority interact in their influence on earnings, but more importantly, the data show that this interaction produces a cumulative advantage for the white but not the black population. White men and women can expect that as they move

[6]Because of the small number of cases in the employer category for both black and white female heads, tests were made only for differences in the education slopes of supervisors and workers for these two status groups.

Table 7.4

Education by Class/Authority Interactions

Status group and class/authority category	Unstandardized education coefficients after control for		
	No variables	Human capital[a]	Human capital and labor market[b]
White male heads			
Employer	2002* *	2138* *	1513* *
Supervisor	993*	1143*	596*
Worker	516	644	359
Black male heads	(Not significant)		
White female heads			
Supervisor	965*	1081*	668*
Worker	512	550	166
Black female heads	(Not significant)		

[a]Variables include experience and weeks worked.

[b]Variables include experience, weeks worked, and six local, two industrial, and four occupational labor market characteristics.

*$p < .05$.

up the class/authority hierarchy, not only will their earnings generally increase on the basis of the higher authority position alone, but the earnings return to their educational investment will increase. Black men and women will not experience the bonus of having their investment in schooling pay off more for them.

Interactions of Task Complexity with Local and Industrial Labor Market Characteristics

Thus far, the analysis in this chapter has been concerned with whether labor market variables interact with certain human capital variables and other personal characteristics of workers. We now consider possible interactions among the labor market characteristics themselves. In particular, we argue that the influence of local and industrial labor market characteristics varies across occupational labor markets.

As discussed in Chapter 1 and investigated in Chapter 3, areal labor market economic status may be viewed as a function of the industrial export base present in the community. According to Thompson (1965), however, workers do not benefit uniformly from a productive export sector and are not hindered uniformly by an unproductive one. Rather, the influence of local labor market characteristics on workers' earnings will vary depending upon their occupation. Recall that he poses the illustrative question: "Do the wage rates of medical technologists and retail clerks in Detroit reflect more the national demand and supply for these skills or the pay scales in the nearby automobile factories?" (1965:74–75). Stolzenberg's (1975) arguments concerning labor market fragmentation along occupational lines being a function of occupation-specific training undertaken in career preparation are relevant here. He suggests that the greater such a training investment, the less likely incumbents of that occupation will be to seek another line of work. Unskilled jobs or jobs for which they have only minimal skills would offer lower wages than the one for which the incumbents had trained. These factors produce segmentation along occupational lines. For example, workers with skills in plumbing would prefer to work in that field in order to maximize returns to their training investment as opposed to working in a field for which they have no training and where wages would therefore be lower (see Stolzenberg, 1975:647). He acknowledges, however, that among lesser skilled occupations, less segmentation of labor markets will occur. Hence, not all occupations constitute equally well-defined labor markets.

Thompson's analysis concurs. He suggests that the relatively skilled occupations do constitute occupational labor markets with wage levels set by national forces of supply and demand. For unskilled workers, however, these nationally defined labor markets do not exist. These workers will be most directly affected by export sector pay scales. Hence, the medical technologist is a member of a nationally formulated labor market and is likely to migrate to other areas to maintain that occupational affiliation, whereas the retail clerk will most likely change occupations if necessary so that housing investments and community ties are retained (Thompson, 1965:75). For skilled workers, then, occupational labor market characteristics will be more important to predicting earnings than areal labor market characteristics will be, whereas for unskilled workers the reverse should be true.

Although this idea has not yet received extensive testing, recent data provide some compatible evidence. Using data from a 1973 and a 1974 Bureau of Labor Statistics survey, Baldwin and Daski (1976) suggest that there is little areal variation in pay for office clerical and electronic data processing jobs, two skilled white-collar jobs, whereas there is greater areal variation for unskilled plant workers. They find that dummy variables representing broad U.S. Census regions in predicting interarea pay ratios are more likely to be statistically significant for lesser skilled workers than for those jobs with greater skill. However, since only four occupations were selected for analysis, additional studies are needed to evaluate this hypothesis.

Spilerman (1977) suggests a similar notion in his discussion of the importance of industry or firm characteristics as determinants of career lines. He argues that professionals' careers will be minimally affected by industry variables due to the national market in which these individuals become professionals and compete for advancement. He suggests that other skilled workers who are organized along occupational lines, such as those in crafts, will also be minimally affected by firm variables. For most other types of workers, however, industry variables play a major role in career advancement. Bluestone *et al.*'s (1973) classic argument regarding this issue is similarly structured. These authors suggest that for many workers, the firm with which they are affiliated may play a bigger role in promoting earnings attainment than the education that the worker has received and hence the relevant job characteristics.

Summarizing these arguments, we advance the following hypothesis: The influence of local labor market and firm (industry) characteristics upon earnings will be greater for low-skilled occupations than for high-skilled occupations. This hypothesis suggests that there is variation in the extent to which an occupation should be viewed as a distinct labor market. Although professionals and skilled workers will maintain their occupational identities at the expense of other ties, less skilled workers may change employers, industries, and even occupations in order to maximize returns to other commitments. Over time, these latter workers will be maximally affected by local labor market characteristics. Conversely, those workers with defined and continuing occupational identities will be maximally affected by characteristics of these occupational markets.

To test this hypothesis task complexity of an occupation is used as the measure of occupational skill level. We have opted not to use the basic U. S. Census classification scheme for this purpose because within each of the major categories there is considerable heterogeneity in skill requirements (see Chapter 5). In the analysis dummy variables were used to represent different complexity levels, and multiplicative interaction terms (the complexity dummies times the labor market variables) were created for the two industrial and six local labor market characteristics. Net of the three human capital and other three occupational labor market variables, statistically significant interactions were found only for white female heads and black male heads. In no instances do the data patterns for the significant interactions indicate support for the hypothesis (see Table 7.5). In fact, the data show support for the opposite effect: The influence of the labor market characteristics is the greatest for those in the high complexity jobs.

In sum, there simply is no evidence that local and industrial labor market variables have a stronger influence on the earnings of those in the less skilled occupations. In fact, the data indicate that there is no interaction for white male heads and black female heads, and for the other status groups the

Table 7.5

Task Complexity by Labor Market Characteristic Interactions

Status group and complexity level	Unstandardized coefficients for variable that interacts with complexity[a]			
	Firm growth	Concentration and investment	Manufacturing sector health	Manufacturing dominance
Black male heads[b]				
Low complexity	495*	160*	571*	-79*
High complexity	-1651*	1091	1640*	1115
White male heads	(None significant)			

Status group and complexity level	Firm growth	Crowding	Manufacturing sector health	Manufacturing dominance	Tertiary sector growth	Tertiary sector complexity
White female heads[c]						
Low complexity	-210	-146	249	-200	-3	-67
Medium complexity	109	-650	-293	249	356	-77
High complexity	484	1610	327	414	745	1317
Black female heads	(None significant)					

[a]Unless indicated otherwise the equations include experience, education, weeks worked, and six local, two industrial, and four occupational labor market variables.

[b]The interval-level measure of experience is used instead of the set of dummies. The cutting point for the complexity categories is -4.

[c]The interval-level measure of education is used instead of the set of dummies, and concentration and investment is excluded because of multicollinearity problems. The cutting points for the complexity categories are -4 and 7.

* $p < .05$.

influence of these labor markets is greater for those in the more complex occupations. From this we may conclude that not only will the earnings of black men and white women be increased if they are in an occupation high in task complexity (see Chapter 5), but when they hold these positions, local labor market factors exert the greatest positive influence on their earnings.

Interactions of Class/Authority with Labor Market Characteristics

As already documented, the past decade has witnessed a substantial upsurge of interest in both labor market and class/authority determinants of earnings. Little research, however, has been undertaken that explores whether labor market variables and class/authority interact in their influence on earnings. The objective in this section is to explore these interactions.

CLASS/AUTHORITY—CONCENTRATION AND INVESTMENT

Our initial interest in these interactions was spurred by the dual economy literature. Not only have scholars in this tradition argued that certain human capital resources vary in influence across core and periphery sectors (we have already examined interactions with education), but they also suggest that the nature of class/authority relations varies by economic sector (Braverman, 1974; Edwards, 1975). More specifically, Edwards proposes that the core sector is characterized by a bureaucratic system of control in which worker differentiation is based on job ladders, credentials, and complex authority systems. Within the periphery, firm size is smaller, there are fewer differentiated levels of control, and supervisory relations are less formal. In short, class/authority position should explain more variance in earnings in the core (monopolistic) sector than in the periphery (competitive) sector.

To test this hypothesis, industrial concentration and investment is used as a proxy for the core–periphery continuum, and multiplicative interaction terms of this with the employer–supervisor–worker dummy variables are created. Controlling for experience, weeks worked, education, the six local, four occupational, and the other industrial labor market variables, we found statistically significant interactions for both black and white male heads but not for black or white female heads.[7] To assess whether the patterns of these

---

[7] We acknowledge again that for the female status groups there exist nonrandom missing data for the concentration and investment variable. We refer the reader to Chapter 4 where this is discussed in detail.

interactions are consistent with the dual economy hypothesis, we have examined the net explained variance associated with class/authority for persons in industries with different levels of concentration and investment (see Table 7.6). These explained variance values may be viewed as estimates of the importance of class/authority in accounting for earnings differences within each of the categories.

If only the employer–supervisor–worker distinction is considered, the data for both black and white men are consistent with the hypothesis when all variables are controlled (see Column 2). Class/authority position is more important in explaining earnings in the industries with high concentration and investment ratios. However, although use of the more refined measure of class/authority still indicates for white males more class/authority influence for the medium and high categories relative to the low ones, the data

Table 7.6

Class/Authority by Concentration and Investment Interactions[a]

	R^2 increments (net of)			
	Employer/supervisor/worker		All dummies[d]	
Status group by concentration and investment	Human capital[b]	Human capital and labor market[c]	Human capital	Human capital and labor market
White male heads				
Low	.0046	.0032	.0979	.0906
Medium	.0106	.0108	.1502	.1439
High	.0341	.0285	.1226	.1151
Black male heads				
Low	.0182	.0067	.1557	.1355
Medium	.0352	.0047	.1328	.0186
High	.0194	.0435	.1319	.0782
White female heads	(No interactions)			
Black female heads	(No interactions)			

[a] Cutoff values of −1 and +1 were used to divide cases into low, medium, and high categories of concentration and investment.

[b] Four human capital variables are controlled: education, weeks worked, experience, and occupation.

[c] Variables controlled are: education, weeks worked, experience, firm growth and the four occupational and six local labor market variables.

[d] The full set of class/authority dummies is used for white males; the smaller set used for comparisons across all status groups is used for black males.

for black males show the opposite pattern. Translating this into the terminology of the dual economists, we may say that class/authority position will produce somewhat lower earnings differentials for white males if they are in the periphery sector. Black males, on the other hand, will find that it is in the periphery sector that their class/authority position will have the greatest impact on earnings. The substantial drop in net explained variance for the medium and high concentration and investment categories indicates that among black males the class/authority influence is partly spurious due to other labor market conditions or is mediated by these labor market conditions.

CLASS/AUTHORITY AND OCCUPATIONAL AND LOCAL CHARACTERISTICS

The various tests for class/authority interactions with the occupational and local labor market characteristics are, admittedly, more exploratory in nature. We do, however, expect that class/authority is more likely to interact with occupational than local labor market characteristics. It seems unlikely that the earnings gradient associated with the class/authority hierarchy will vary substantially from one locale to another, although if it does, this should be so for the black rather than white status groups. There very easily could be community and/or regional differences not only in a black person's access to class/authority positions but also in the reward structure associated with the class/authority hierarchy. It would seem, however, that class/authority and occupational characteristics are more integrally related. For example, physical dexterity would seem to be more strongly related to earnings among workers than it would among supervisors or employers. In addition, task complexity should be more important among supervisors and employers than workers; among workers there simply is less variation in the components (e.g., intelligence and verbal, numerical, and spatial aptitudes) underlying the complexity dimension.

The tests for interactions revealed several patterns. First, among white males the differences in the influence of labor market variables are for employers versus supervisors and workers, whereas for black males differences exist across all three class/authority categories. Second, a greater number of significant interactions exists for males than for females, although this may be due to our decision to exclude female employers from the analysis because of the small number of cases. Third, among blacks both occupational and local labor market characteristics interact with class/authority, whereas among whites the interactions exist primarily for occupational characteristics.

Table 7.7 provides the data necessary to identify the patterns of the signifi-

Table 7.7

Class/Authority by Labor Market Characteristic Interactions

Status group and class/ authority category			Unstandardized
	Complexity	Physical dexterity	Uncertainty
White male heads			
Employer	818*	1131*	-4628*
Supervisor/worker	256*	-18	-26
	Complexity	Physical dexterity	Uncertainty
Black male heads			
Employer[b]	-464*	-246*	-4019*
Supervisor[b]	-365*	-270*	-814
Worker	193*	-200	-300
	Complexity		
White female heads			
Supervisor	168*		
Worker	147*		
	Uncertainty	Tertiary sector health	Manufacturing sector health
Black female heads[c]			
Supervisor	-695	-305	-843
Worker	-228	-60	-64

[a]Unless indicated otherwise the equations include education, occupational labor market variables.

[b]Firm growth was automatically deleted by the SPSS program

[c]Because of multicollinearity, concentration and investment and

*$p < .05$.

cant interactions. The interactions with occupational labor market characteristics suggest that complexity interacts with class/authority for all status groups but black female heads. With one exception, black male heads, the patterns are as expected; that is, complexity is a stronger positive determinant of earnings the higher the class/authority position.

The analysis in Chapter 5 showed task uncertainty to have a significant negative influence for all status groups, but here the data suggest that it interacts with class/authority for all status groups but white female heads.

7.7 *(continued)*

coefficients for[a]		
Unpleasantness of work	Manufacturing sector health	
1218	494	
45	−54	
Manufacturing dominance	Manufacturing sector health	Tertiary sector growth
226*	147*	960
911	1401*	−151
−151	577*	−265

experience, weeks worked, six local, two industrial, and four

because of low tolerance.

firm growth were not controlled.

The interaction patterns are consistent across status groups. In particular, task uncertainty is more important the higher the person is in the class/ authority hierarchy. If we assume that responsibility, and consequently, impact of decisions on the firm's well-being increases from worker to employer, then it is not surprising to find that at the worker level earnings differences between those faced with a changing job environment will not be that much different from those whose jobs involve set activities and stable environments. At the supervisor or employer level, however, the importance of decisions and actions is greatly enhanced and earnings differentials can be expected to exist in part as a function of the degree of uncertainty in the work environment. The important point, however, is that persons in jobs characterized by task uncertainty earn less than those with well-controlled environments, *and* this differential increases the higher one is in the class/ authority hierarchy. Apparently, the person faced with variety and change (i.e., uncertainty) not only must confront any mental and physical stress this produces, but must also put up with lower wages.

As already indicated, the interactions of class/authority by local labor market characteristics were found primarily for the black status groups. Earlier analysis (Chapter 3) showed manufacturing dominance to be important only for black male heads, but the data here indicate that this effect exists only for black male supervisors. It may be that competition for supervisory personnel in local markets with strong demand for these skills contributes to the earnings bonus these workers achieve, whereas nonsupervisory personnel are unaffected by this aspect of market segmentation.

Several other significant interactions were found that were not expected on the basis of theory and for which we have not been able to offer meaningful post hoc explanations.[8] First, among black male heads increased physical dexterity has a significant negative effect on earnings only for supervisors and workers; among white males it has a strong positive effect for employers but no effect for supervisors and workers. It will be remembered (Chapter 5) that this variable had a significant net influence on earnings only for white male heads. However, the analysis here indicates that the effect exists only for employers. We have no explanation for this. Second, in Chapter 3 we found health of the manufacturing industries to have a significant positive effect for black males and a negative effect for black females. The data reported here lead us to qualify these earlier conclusions. The positive effect for black males is strongest for supervisors, but it also exists for workers. Among black females and white male heads, the data are suggestive of differences by class/authority position, but because none of the coefficients is significant across class/authority positions, we are reluctant to draw any inferences. Finally, although the interaction tests had shown tertiary sector growth interactions for black male heads and tertiary sector health interactions for black female heads, none of the coefficients across the class/authori-

---

[8]It is possible that we have underestimated the probability of Type I errors in the series of significance tests conducted in this chapter. Because the multiple significance tests are not independent of each other, the probability of rejecting the null hypothesis (no interaction) when it should not be rejected is higher than the .05 level used here (Bielby and Kluegel, 1977). This especially is a problem when the analysis is exploratory, as in this section. For this reason, we prefer to view these results as suggestive of interactions. Clearly, additional theoretical and empirical work will be needed to explore these interactions in more depth.

ty categories is statistically significant, and we are unwilling to attempt an interpretation.

Summary and Discussion

The series of interaction tests indicate that race rather than sex is the differentiating ascriptive characteristic; seldom were significant interactions found for one sex and not the other, but often significant interactions were observed for one race and not the other. In particular, it was the black status groups for whom the interactions more often were significant. The major findings follow.

We found that the inclusion of respondents with farm occupations did not alter the conclusions that would have been drawn if only the nonfarm population had been analyzed.

Age/cohort interactions with labor market and class/authority variables were expected and found almost exclusively for blacks. Generally speaking, it is the earnings of the older blacks that are more strongly affected by the the interacting variables; areal manufacturing dominance, firm concentration and investment, and physical dexterity requirements of the job all are more important for the older black workers. Older blacks, with the exception of the employer class, also are more likely to have the class/authority dimensions operate for them in the expected manner.

Based on results from other studies, we had expected the patterns emerging from these age/cohort interactions to support the argument that the attainment process for young blacks is more like that of the white population. We found mixed support for this, however. Although this may be true for certain labor market characteristics, the findings for class/authority suggest that it is the older blacks who are more like the white population. Since the class/authority differences are more "firm-determined" than the local, industrial, and occupational labor market influences, we can cautiously infer that firm adjustments directed toward equalizing race differences have been occurring less quickly than in the three more encompassing labor markets. An alternative explanation, of course, is that the greater earnings differentiation associated with class/authority for older blacks is the consequence of job experience and tenure, which were not captured by our measures of these variables; that is, it is an age effect rather than a cohort effect. We are reluctant to accept this alternative account, however, since it should also have been found for the white population.

The analysis of education by labor market characteristic interactions also showed a greater number of significant interactions for blacks than whites. In particular, interactions with the local labor market characteristics differentiated the races. This may be interpreted to mean that from one region or locale to another not only are the local labor markets different, but also black males can expect their investments in education to be rewarded differently. Thus, areal heterogeneity in returns to education exists for blacks but generally is not found for the white population. On the other hand, occupational labor market heterogeneity in returns to education characterizes white male and to some degree black female heads, but not black male or white female heads. In addition, industrial labor market heterogeneity in returns to education characterizes all status groups but white male heads. Finally, the analysis of differences in returns to education by class/authority position clearly demonstrated race differences. Not only do whites generally attain higher class/authority positions, but their returns to education increase as they move to the higher class/authority positions. Blacks receive the same returns at each level.

In two instances evidence inconsistent with theoretical reasoning was found. First, we were able to provide substantial literature support for our expectation that local and industrial labor market influences on earnings should be greater in the less skilled occupations, but no empirical support was found for this. In fact, some of the data indicated exactly the opposite effect. In the other instance we examined possible interactions of class/authority with local, industrial, and occupational labor market characteristics. Based on dual economy theory we hypothesized that a person's class/authority position would account for more variance in earnings if that person has an occupation in the high concentration and investment industries. We found, however, only partial support for this. Only for white male heads was there evidence that class/authority explains more variance in earnings in industries with the higher concentration and investment firms. We also examined class/authority interactions with occupational and local labor market characteristics. Although a number of interactions were revealed, only some were interpretable within our theoretical framework. In particular, for several status groups both task complexity and uncertainty have a greater influence on earnings as class/authority level increases.

CHAPTER 8

Summary and Conclusions

Introduction

In this chapter we summarize the theoretical arguments and empirical findings presented in previous chapters. We indicate what this study has shown that was not previously known and then use the findings to inform several theoretical issues in the field. We indicate what implications our findings have for the human capital and socialization and the structural perspectives of earnings attainment and discuss evidence for social selection as it suggests a "fit" between theories previously treated as disparate. We comment on the implications our findings have for other major arguments in the area of stratification including the issues of market imperfections, comparable worth, and Featherman and Hauser's (1978) discussion of changes associated with industrialism. Finally, we discuss what implications the analysis has for policy in the area of economic discrimination against blacks and women. Although such inferences are advanced with the usual cautions, we argue that "discrimination" is a multifaceted phenomenon that operates differently for different economic minorities. For this reason particular changes in economic policy would likely affect status groups differently, and the most effective avenues for promoting equality of economic opportunity for respective groups are likely to be distinct.

Summary

In Chapter 1 we outlined our problem as the explanation of individual earnings attainment in terms of both personal and structural characteristics.

We indicated that although the bulk of previous research had focused on individual-level determinants of earnings, there was ample theoretical guidance to construct hypotheses concerning the role of several types of labor market characteristics in the earnings attainment process. Furthermore, we indicated that there was a lack of systematic information concerning how these market characteristics would affect the earnings attainment of workers who varied by ascribed status. We reviewed several theories, most of which were constructed at the ecological level, in order to abstract the dimensions along which local labor markets, economic sectors or industrial markets, and occupational labor markets would vary. It was these dimensions that we hypothesized could aid in explaining earnings attainment generally and ascriptive status differences in earnings in particular. Following analyses by Thompson (1965) and O. Duncan and Reiss (1956) we suggested that the economic productivity of the manufacturing export sector and other economic characteristics defining local market functional specialization could affect workers' earnings. Dimensions of local labor market social organization, including residential segregation and racial competition, were also hypothesized to affect earnings attainment.

Our discussion of economic sectors or industrial labor markets relied heavily on work by Averitt (1968) and others regarding economic segmentation. Although we rejected the idea that the economy was necessarily divided into any number of distinct segments, we did accept the notion that firms do vary according to the criteria the dualists use to distinguish their segments. These criteria include degree of economic concentration, size in terms of accumulated capital and personnel, degree of capital intensity, productivity and profitability, degree to which a variety of products are produced, and whether the firms sell to local or national and international markets. Following discussion of Edwards (1975) concerning the correspondence between economic segmentation and work organization and by others concerning dual labor market theory, additional dimensions differentiating positions within firms were hypothesized as relevant. Although again we rejected the assumption that the labor market was necessarily divided into any number of distinct segments, we did accept the idea that jobs vary according to the safety and pleasantness of working conditions, the existence and extent of internal labor markets within firms, the degree of variety in work, the degree of job security, and the degree to which work rules are formalized and enforced through use of due process. Other literature concerning occupational segmentation (Stolzenberg, 1975) and differentiation (Spaeth, 1979; Kohn, 1969) suggested other dimensions along which occupations may vary including type of job skills, work orientations, and degree of complexity required in task performance. Degree of race and sex competition and segregation was also discussed, as were authority relations within the firm.[1]

Where possible we discussed for each of these dimensions how effects on labor earnings would vary by ascribed status. Although detailed predictions were not always possible, we argued that one manifestation of discrimination against economic minorities is reduced access to income-producing resources, such as authority positions in the firm, complex work, or jobs with firms characterized by oligopoly power and profitability. We considered the possibility that, independent of access to resources, women and blacks obtain inferior returns to the income-producing resources they do have. This chapter also included an overview of the book.

In Chapter 2 we discussed contextual analysis as a measurement strategy and presented arguments to show that the method would be useful in our study of labor market determinants of earnings. The criteria used to select an appropriate data source for individual workers were described, as were the samples selected from the Michigan Panel Study of Income Dynamics. We discussed the measurement of the basic individual-level variables and the sources for the local, industrial, and occupational labor market characteristics. For each of these sets of labor market characteristics, results were presented from factor analyses used to ascertain the central dimensions underlying the data and to aid in data reduction. In each case the findings allowed study of the structures of the respective markets prior to analysis of the effects that such structures would have on individuals. Key dimensions underlying the local labor market data were consistent with Thompson's (1965) and O. Duncan and Reiss' (1956) ideas concerning manufacturing export and tertiary sector specialization or were interpretable in terms of what is known about local labor market social organization. The factor solutions of economic sector and worker outcome characteristics produced di-

---

[1]As in any analysis, omitted variables limit the inferences we can derive. In this work, one key omission (due to data unavailability) is characteristics of employers. As Baron and Bielby (1980) have argued, there is likely to be interfirm variability in processes relevant to earnings attainment of individuals. Such variation is not likely to be fully captured by addition of occupational labor market characteristics and/or indicators of workers' class/authority positions. It is possible, for example, that employers differ in the extent to which they use educational credentials to screen applicants for jobs, and these variations are not well-reflected in the contextual characteristics we incorporate. It is also likely that the nature of job ladders within firms varies by employer, so that career patterns vary by employer or by employer characteristics. In future work it will be important to evaluate to what extent the conclusions we suggest here should be modified due to employer characteristics. One additional omission concerns network data relevant to the job search process. Although the 1978 Panel Study does contain some information on this issue, it could not be utilized in this analysis.

mensions consistent with dual economy and dual labor market characteristics, and the factor analysis of occupational characteristics produced six interpretable factors that covered work complexity, working conditions, and several skill and aptitude dimensions. For each factor solution we described the reliabilities of the resulting composites that varied from moderate to high and discussed the correlations among each set of composites in order to describe the respective structures of local labor market, economic sector and industrial labor market, and occupational labor market differentiation. Chapter 2 concluded with a discussion of the analytic strategy to be used in the remaining chapters.

In Chapter 3 we found strong racial differentiation in the pattern of the local labor market organization facing the respective status groups. Other descriptive data presented suggested race and sex differences in access to individual and labor market resources. The first multivariate equation presented estimated earnings as a function of years of schooling, weeks worked, work experience, and occupational status. This model (the basic equation) provided a baseline against which subsequent findings could be compared. A second equation added to this basic model the four local labor market characteristics used in a previous investigation of racial differences in earnings attainment of male workers (Parcel, 1979). The findings suggested that local labor market effects on earnings are stronger among blacks than among whites, particularly for manufacturing wage levels. Black males are especially affected by this characteristic, although the effect is also strong among white male heads.

Use of the composites in place of the four indicators used in prior research also revealed race and sex differences in the patterns and magnitudes of the findings. Black males' earnings continue to be influenced by manufacturing sector activity, and the remaining status groups' earnings levels were more influenced by tertiary sector characteristics. Effects of urban crowding are negative but limited to black male and female heads. Overall, the impact of local labor market characteristics on earnings is stronger among black male heads than among the remaining status groups. Use of regression standardization to decompose earnings differences between white male heads and black male heads, white female heads, and black female heads suggested that there were major differences in the operation of discrimination by race and by sex. Differences in composition and slopes and intercepts were of comparable importance among males, but cross-sex comparisons were more heavily influenced by the slopes and intercepts differences.

In Chapter 4 we added to the model by incorporating characteristics of economic sectors of industrial labor markets. In terms of descriptive analysis we found that the configurations of industrial resources faced by each status group were differentiated by sex, not by race, as had been the case concerning areal labor market resources. This pattern was due to industrial segregation, which was stronger among women than among men, and thus produced stronger correlations among the industrial resources for women than for men. Thus the patterns of labor market resources more closely resembled those that dualist theories would lead us to expect than did the data in Chapter 2 where each industry was given equal weight. The analytic findings suggested that industrial resources were statistically significant predictors of earnings net of human capital and socialization variables and local labor market characteristics. In particular, industrial concentration and investment influenced earnings for every group except white male heads. Additional regression decomposition reinforced the conclusions from Chapter 3 concerning the differential operation of discrimination by race and sex.

In Chapter 5 we continued to develop our model by incorporating indicators of both occupational labor markets and of class/authority position. Each set of variables added a statistically significant increment to explained variance across status groups. Our descriptive analysis replicated other research that (a) shows women to be underrepresented in craft, farm, and laborer occupations and overrepresented in clerical and service occupations, and (b) shows blacks to be underrepresented in professional and managerial positions but overrepresented in service and operative occupations. Our analysis went beyond earlier research, however, to document that the occupations of blacks and whites are differentiated primarily in terms of task complexity, pleasantness of work conditions, and physical activities, whereas for men and women, the differentiating characteristics are physical activity and interpersonal relations. These findings of race differences were viewed as consistent with dual labor market theory.

Our examination of the influence of task complexity, uncertainty, physical dexterity, and people–things net of human capital variables and local and industrial labor market characteristics showed complexity to have a positive influence and uncertainty a negative influence for all status groups. Finding white males to have greater access to highly complex occupations as well as receiving greater returns from these was viewed as consistent with the dualist perspective. Consistent with the competition argument, we also found that minority concentration in an occupation has a weak but significant negative effect on the earnings of both white male and female heads. The net effect of class/authority was especially important for white males, again serving to support the dual labor market theory. Finally, the regression standardization suggested that sex differences within the white population are due primarily to the manner in which the resources are translated into earnings. The earnings gaps between black and white men and between black women and white men are more a function of both compositional differences and differences in rates of return to these resources.

In Chapter 6 the goal was to subject the findings previously produced to two additional analyses. In the first case, we wished to rule out the possibility that the labor market effects we had discussed would be fundamentally altered by inclusion of several social psychological characteristics. Although popular theories posit the importance of such constructs in socioeconomic attainment, our findings suggested that several dimensions of social psychological functioning were only weakly associated with earnings attainment once the human capital and socialization variables in the basic equation and the labor market factors were controlled. Hence our inferences concerning the importance of labor market factors in earnings attainment remain intact.

The second investigation involved analysis of the problem of social selection. We explicitly acknowledged that there is matching between personal and structural characteristics such that workers with personal characteristics conducive to productivity are likely to have access to labor market positions with high productivity potential. If this is true, then the frequently used strategy of pitting the explanatory power of individual-level theories against structural theories is of limited utility. Evidence concerning the extent and pattern of social selection was produced by looking at bias in regression coefficients. The findings suggested that extent of social selection varied by race, with blacks, particularly black female workers, being more subject to selection than whites. Selectivity appeared extensive in access to industrial labor market positions, with years of schooling and experience being selected for. In addition, for female workers, biases in returns to job status are noticeable when industrial characteristics are omitted. Additional biases in returns to years of schooling are evident across status groups when occupational labor market characteristics are omitted, assuming job status is not controlled. Biases in returns to job experience are evidenced for males and white female heads when indicators of class/authority are omitted. These findings serve to sensitize us to both the pervasiveness of social selection and the variation in selectivity that the several status groups experience.

Chapter 7 provided an additional check on the findings by evaluating several hypotheses concerning statistical interaction. Throughout this book the analysis has been based on evidence concerning race and sex interactions with key variables in their influence on earnings; otherwise, however, the models presented thus far had been strictly additive. Evidence presented in Chapter 7 suggested that the assumption of additivity is generally, though not always, appropriate. There was no evidence of interaction on the basis of the farm/nonfarm occupational dichotomy. Interactions between age/cohort and several labor market variables were also minimal. A number of education by labor market characteristic interactions were statistically significant, but these were disproportionately concentrated among blacks. Similarly, interactions among the labor market characteristics themselves were found more often for blacks than for whites. Overall, however, findings indicate that although several of the findings produced in this portion of the analysis help to refine the conclusions discussed earlier, there is no basis for suggesting that the major conclusions drawn in previous chapters are misleading.

Discussion

IMPLICATIONS FOR HUMAN CAPITAL AND STATUS ATTAINMENT PERSPECTIVES

It is important to consider the implications of these findings for both the human capital and status attainment and the structural perspectives of earnings attainment. First, the human capital and status attainment variables— years of schooling, weeks worked, experience, and the Duncan SEI—are generally statistically significant predictors of earnings across status groups. To place this conclusion in perspective, it is important to recognize that both of these supply theories have been subjected to important criticisms in recent years. Coser (1975, 1976) has criticized the status attainment perspective for failing to incorporate relational aspects of class. Faia (1981) and Wilson (1978) have argued that models of status attainment have been seriously misspecified. In addition, researchers' interest has shifted from almost exclusive focus on the socialization and supply determinants of earnings to the myriad of theories and approaches that have been labeled as "structural". We believe, however, that these developments should not be allowed to obscure the fact that the supply variables are important in predicting earnings attainment. Although this argument should not be interpreted to suggest that none of the criticisms of these perspectives is legitimate, the findings indicate that despite the major contributions of the structural perspectives, it is inappropriate to ignore the supply variables when studying labor earnings of individuals.

Second, the degree of predictive success of these supply factors varies by ascriptive status. In particular, the findings in Table 3.6 indicate that the explained variance of these basic variables was lowest for white male heads and highest for black females. Although variations in explained variance by status have been reported before (R. Hall and Kasten, 1973; Treiman and Terrell, 1975; Blum, 1972; Featherman and Hauser, 1976a, in the more complete specifications), the implications of the patterns have not been fully appreciated. Despite the possible contribution of statistical explanations to this pattern, we do not believe that these factors completely explain these findings. (See Chapter 2, the note to the section, Michigan Panel Study of Income Dynamics, concerning nonlinearity. See also the discussion of "inflated" regression coefficients included in the section, Regression Standardization in Chapter 3.) It appears, then, that regardless of the criticisms leveled at these traditional theories, they have substantial effects on earnings for workers generally and for economic minorities in particular. They are therefore a useful basis on which to build a more comprehensive explanation of earnings attainment, a task we also address.

Finally, we observe status group variations in the extent to which the magnitudes of the basic variables are *maintained* when controls for other personal characteristics are introduced. As Chapter 6 suggested, introduction of controls for social psychological variables results in education and work experience becoming statistically nonsignificant for black male heads whereas these variables retain significance among white male heads. Black female heads evidence reductions in returns to years of schooling to the point of nonsignificance and some reductions in returns to experience, whereas there are no noticeable changes in these variables for white female heads. Thus the importance that some have placed on blacks' investments in years of schooling in particular may be misplaced.[2] Among whites, however, this investment appears to be worthwhile. Certainly, the overall importance of what we call supply variables is not diminished. Rather, the findings have specified *which* supply variables are most closely related to earnings for given status groups. It does appear that the human capital investment is more worthwhile for whites than for blacks. Such findings dictate that one cautiously interpret the initially produced findings concerning the relative importance of the basic variables across status groups. Failure to control for these additional personal characteristics can produce inflated estimates of the relative importance of the actual investment variables.

IMPLICATIONS FOR THE STRUCTURAL PERSPECTIVES

Turning to the structural perspectives, the findings provide important information concerning labor market structures and have major implications concerning the roles of these structures in the earnings attainment process.

[2]It is important to recognize that this conclusion is based on regression results generated from a sample whose experiences reflect the historical circumstances of a given period. Following Aigner (1970:252), it is possible that changes in the processes generating these variables would result in modifications to given conclusions. For example, changes in discriminatory hiring practices of blacks could, for a future cohort, result in stronger returns to investments in human capital variables relevant to hiring. Therefore it could be inappropriate to infer from this discussion that future generations of blacks should not make the types of human capital investments that have been financially rewarding for whites in the past.

First, it is important to recognize that the structures of these respective markets are multidimensional. Thus in the case of each of the three types of markets—local, industrial, and occupational—there is more than one dimension that is useful in describing the structure. Such multidimensionality suggests that these structures are complex, a notion that is inconsistent with perspectives that see these structures as dichotomous. Although this argument is most directly applicable to dual economy and dual labor market theories (see Wallace and Kalleberg, 1981, for similar discussion), it also helps to broaden the view of local labor market organization beyond the export–nonexport dichotomy suggested by Thompson (1965).[3] In addition, the findings help to tie together theories and research concerning the respective market structures, thus facilitating future theoretical and empirical investigation (see discussions of factor analyses in Chapter 2).

The second major finding concerning the markets is that the structures of local, industrial, and occupational labor market organization at the respective ecological levels differ from the structures of these markets as viewed from the perspectives of the several status groups. Nonrandom allocation of workers to contexts generally produces stronger relationships among dimensions of labor market organization in status group-specific correlation matrices than in matrices in which the given labor market is the unit of analysis. Residential segregation by race and industrial and occupational labor market segregation by sex produce these patterns of relationships. Thus, although the factor analyses of labor market characteristics performed at the respective ecological levels revealed several distinct dimensions for each type of market, in terms of the configuration of structural dimensions each group faces, these dimensions were often more closely related. For example, although the factor analysis of industrial characteristics suggested that profitability and concentration and investment were separate dimensions of economic segmentation, the close relationship between these two dimensions for several groups of workers precluded our using them simultaneously in multivariate analysis. A similar problem arose in studying the effects of dual economy and dual labor market variables on earnings and in analysis of local labor market social organization effects. These findings suggest that researchers should carefully consider the types of inferences they wish to draw when they study ecological data. Analyses of unweighted ecological relationships are useful in understanding the functioning of social structures, in this case, labor markets. However, whenever individuals are differentially dis-

---

[3]We recognize that all factor analytic solutions are importantly determined by characteristics of the input data. The greater the number of input variables and the more variety in "type" of input variables, the more likely the solution will contain more than one factor. Therefore, although we believe our conclusions regarding the multidimensionality of market structures to be useful and appropriate, they are not particularly surprising.

tributed within the structures, such unweighted relationships will not represent the environments that these individuals face.

The third major conclusion relevant to the structural perspectives concerns their role in predicting individual labor earnings. As was indicated in Chapter 5, Table 5.8, local, industrial, and occupational labor market characteristics often operate independently of each other. Labor market effects at the local labor market level, for example, are not explained by effects at other levels of economic and social organization (e.g., industrial and occupational markets). It was also found, however, that there were important status group variations in the magnitudes of the structural effects on earnings and that only some of these were consistent with theoretical predictions. For example, previous analysis of local labor market effects on earnings had been confined to male workers (Parcel, 1979); one of the goals in this analysis was to see whether there were comparable effects for women workers. Although previous analyses had supported the idea that manufacturing sector productivity and dominance were associated with reduced racial earnings inequality (Reder, 1955; Turner, 1951; Masters, 1975; Spilerman and Miller, 1976; Franklin, 1968) there were no comparable studies of sex inequality. On the basis of descriptive analysis by Bluestone *et al.* (1973) we reasoned that women should obtain weaker returns than men to manufacturing sector characteristics since women were less likely to be employed in manufacturing than men. This hypothesis was confirmed.

In addition, however, we found that returns to tertiary sector productivity were substantial for white male and white female heads and that tertiary sector growth was *negatively* associated with earnings for white male heads and black wives. It appears, then, that the local labor market characteristics tap "job opportunity" dimensions, although as analysis in Chapter 5 indicated, these local labor market effects are not eliminated when industrial and occupational labor market characteristics are controlled. The measures appear to tap particularly well the opportunities faced by black males. In addition, we also infer that the local market in which the worker is employed is of greater importance to a black male's earnings than to members of the remaining status groups and that this holds true particularly for older, as opposed to younger, black workers. If these findings represent cohort as opposed to age effects, over time there may be a weakening of these effects for black male heads to the point where the pattern more closely resembles that among white male heads. It appears, then, that young black workers are similar to their white counterparts not only in terms of returns to schooling (see Featherman and Hauser, 1978), but also in terms of the magnitudes of these local labor market effects.

The investigation of the effects of local labor market social organization on earnings was also centered around ascertaining the external validity of previously produced findings. In particular, we were interested in whether racial competition and residential segregation would evidence patterns for black and white female workers similar to those of black and white male workers. In this analysis, findings suggested that racial crowding hindered earnings attainment for both black male and female heads and had no significant effects on the remaining workers. White workers' and black wives' earnings levels are relatively indifferent to this factor.

The findings concerning the dual economy and dual labor market perspectives also are partly consistent and partly inconsistent with our expectations. On the basis of reasoning that economic minorities are disproporationately allocated to the periphery and to the secondary labor market, we anticipated differences in access to industrial labor market resources by race and sex. The data suggest that these differences exist by sex but not by race. On the basis of these findings there is no evidence to support the notion that black males are deprived of access to industrial resources conducive to earnings attainment. Similarly the evidence is inconsistent with the idea that white women can depend upon their racial status to obtain access to these resources. It would appear that devotees of the dualist model should revise their thinking concerning the distribution of industrial labor market positions since there do not appear to be important racial differences here; sex differences in these resources, which have received somewhat less attention, *are* readily apparent.

The findings regarding returns to dimensions underlying the dual economy are also not strictly consistent with our expectations. Although it was predicted that returns to these characteristics would be stronger for white males than for the remaining status groups, the findings suggested that returns to industrial concentration and investment were positive and statistically significant for all groups *except* white males. It appears that the degree of correspondence between investment and industrial resource variables contribute to these findings for white males; for this reason one should not conclude that concentration and investment *does not* influence earnings attainment for this status group. Concerning the remaining groups, even when "inflation" of these regression coefficients is taken into account (see discussions of regression standardization and missing data) the sizes of the concentration and investment effects are still substantial, although inferences concerning their relative magnitudes are probably ill-advised. We conclude that resources associated with the core of the economy *are* important to predicting workers' earnings, although in the case of white males they contribute no explanatory power net of the investment variables.

The theoretical discussion also raised the issue of the relationship between the dual economy and the dual labor market, or in terms of our analysis, the relationship between characteristics identified as differentiating industrial positions and jobs along "good–bad" or "productive–nonproductive" continua. All of the evidence points to considerable overlap between "core" and "primary" labor market characteristics and "periphery" and "secondary" labor market characteristics. Inspection of zero-order correlations across these characteristics suggests a high degree of congruence between relevant variables (e.g., firm profitability, worker benefits, etc.) for the several status groups. In regression analyses in which we included both indicators of economic sectors and of primary–secondary markets, the correspondence between these structural characteristics resulted in indicators of the dual labor market explaining variation previously attributed to characteristics of economic sectors. Inspection of correlations between these indicators and additional occupational labor market characteristics indicates positive correspondence between the complexity of occupations and whether the industry is profitable and negative correspondence with firm growth (see Appendix C). Thus, these data suggest that there is a substantial amount of overlap between characteristics of industries and occupations conducive to earnings attainment.

The findings involving occupational labor market characteristics suggest these variables are more important to white males' earnings levels than to those of any of the remaining status groups. Thus, although many of the variables in this category were statistically significant for several status groups, only among white male heads were the effects particularly strong. In particular, the substantial returns to occupational complexity and physical dexterity that are observed for white male heads are consistent with expectations derived from the dual labor market perspective. However, the uncertainty and unpleasantness of working conditions dimensions do not behave as the theory would suggest, thus indicating mixed support for the theory. Regarding class/authority, white males also obtain greater advantages from class/authority position than those in other status groups, another finding consistent with the dualist perspective.

On the basis of these findings it appears that although structural explanations are important in understanding workers' earnings, the relative importance of the several types of structural explanations varies by status group. It is not entirely clear why this should be true. There does not appear to be a systematic relationship between access to resources and their efficacy. In the case of occupational labor market characteristics and indicators of class/authority, white males have both high access and high efficacy. In the case of industrial labor market characteristics, women workers have low access but high efficacy. Concerning local labor market characteristics, although these variables are most effective for black male workers, their pattern of access to local labor market resources does not appear sharply differentiated from those of other status groups. Thus one cannot reason that given changes in the distribution of resources across status groups will necessarily result in similar changes in relative efficacy. These findings do suggest, however, that researchers who continue to investigate the role of structural determinants of earnings should recognize that the degree of explained variance they obtain may depend markedly upon the combination of structural variables and status groups they have chosen to study.

THE ROLE OF SOCIAL SELECTION

The approach in this monograph has been integrative in that the models have allowed for the operation of both supply and structural determinants of individual earnings. One advantage of this strategy is that it provides for a conservative test of the efficacy of both types of factors. Thus we do not overestimate the relative importance of either in explaining this outcome. In addition, however, we have argued that incorporation of both personal and structural determinants of earnings has allowed inferences concerning social selection in the earnings attainment process. We have found substantial evidence to support the notion that there are (usually positive) relationships between supply characteristics of individuals and structural variables describing industrial and occupational labor markets, as well as positions in the class/authority hierarchies of firms. For this reason it is not useful to think of the supply and the structural perspectives as juxtaposed. Rather, it appears more useful to think about the matching processes occurring throughout workers' careers that result in workers with high productivity potential being allocated to labor market positions with high productivity potential.

Although this analysis has provided general estimates of the magnitude of such selection, as well as some indication of which personal characteristics are selected for by which types of markets, we have only begun to study inequality in this light.[4] We know relatively little concerning the timing of selection over the course of workers' careers. In addition, since the structural characteristics we have used here have been measured at fairly high levels of aggregation (with the expection of class/authority), we have little knowledge of the inter- and intrafirm mechanisms through which selections are accomplished.

It does appear, however, that there are ascriptive status differences in the degree and patterns of the selection processes we have been able to chart.

---

[4]As might be expected, there is selection on the basis of a particular type of labor market characteristic only if that type of characteristic is significantly associated with earnings. Of course, this is not a sufficient condition since there must also be intercorrelations between the personal and structural variables in order for us to infer selection.

Black workers appear to be subjected to a higher degree of selection than whites. This leads to the suggestion that one manifestation of racial discrimination in our society is stricter allocation of workers to positions based on their accumulation of human capital.[5] For whites such allocation may be somewhat less systematic. Thus among whites, although human capital investments appear economically worthwhile, they do not seem to be essential to obtaining a favorable position in the labor market. On the other hand, such investment does not guarantee obtaining these favorable positions, despite the facts that whites are favored relative to blacks in access to occupational labor market resources and that white males are particularly favored in access to advantageous positions in the class/authority hierarchy. Among blacks, however, lack of investment in human capital is likely to result in deprivation to the limited structural resources to which blacks do have access. Blacks who do have favorable supply characteristics are likely to do well, relative to other blacks, in terms of obtaining labor market positions with productivity potential commensurate with their skills. We hope that the analysis of selection presented here will encourage other researchers to pursue this line of inquiry.

INFERENCES REGARDING MARKET IMPERFECTIONS AND
UNIVERSALISM

Implications that this analysis has for the conclusions suggested by other analyses of inequality are also of interest. Such discussion helps to integrate the findings reported here with those produced by others, thus furthering the cumulative nature of inquiry into inequality. Conclusions drawn by Jencks and his colleagues in *Inequality* (1972) and *Who Gets Ahead?* (1979) are particularly noteworthy. In the first analysis they argued that on-the-job competence and luck were important determinants of earnings. In the second analysis their emphasis changed to discussion of labor market imperfections that could produce variation in earnings independent of workers' personal characteristics. They explicitly recognize that workers with equal personal characteristics may not receive equal earnings due to "structural rigidities." Although these market imperfections could be removed, thus potentially diminishing inequality, they do not believe that the modest efforts reformers have made regarding performance on standardized tests

---

[5]This conclusion should not be interpreted to suggest that blacks necessarily obtain returns to these labor market resources that are equivalent to the returns whites obtain. The conclusion drawn here is a descriptive one involving differential allocation of positions by race and as such is independent of the economic worth that these positions have for incumbents.

and exposure to schooling are sufficient to convince employers that workers are equivalent (Jencks *et al.*, 1979:311).

Our arguments have not been formulated in terms of labor market imperfections, although our findings could be interpreted as evidence for the existence of labor market barriers. What is more important, however, is that our data provide a degree of specificity in the understanding of these structural forces that is highly desirable but not anticipated by Jencks' discussion. Instead of arguing that "institutionalization of work relationships" (Jencks *et al.*, 1979:309) constitutes a market imperfection, we have provided data that suggest the extent to which aspects of work organization such as job complexity and authority relations within the firm do or do not benefit specific groups of workers. Similarly, we move beyond the notion of the business cycle as a market imperfection to evaluate the extent to which several aspects of the economic climate in local labor markets do or do not affect the earnings attainment of workers who vary by ascribed status. Clearly it is this detailed knowledge of market imperfections that is most useful both to evaluating theory and for deriving implications for policy.

A second major theme in the stratification literature concerns the role of universalism in the status attainment process. Featherman and Hauser (1978) document a decline in the influence of status ascription and an increase in the role of universalism in the allocation of occupational positions between 1962 and 1973. Data concerning the decreasing association between educational attainment and socioeconomic background, a reduction in the magnitude of occupational status inheritance, improvement in the life chances of blacks and men of farm origin in terms of educational and occupational status attainment are all consistent with this conclusion (Featherman and Hauser, 1978:481). They indicate, however, that the inference concerning the increase in universalism should not be causally linked to the "thesis of industrialism" (i.e., to the changes that the U.S. economy has undergone in the shift from goods- to service-producing industries). They call for more direct investigation of industrial structures as they impact status allocation (Featherman and Hauser, 1978:482–484).

Certainly the inferences we can draw concerning universalism are of a different nature than those that Featherman and Hauser suggest, due to differences in their design and ours. In comparing the findings of their replication with the 1962 Occupational Changes in a Generation (OCG) survey, they derive inferences concerning changes in the operation of universalism over time. In contrast, our cross-sectional design sheds no direct evidence on temporal variations in universalism, but rather provides information concerning ascriptive status differences in the operation of universalism at a single point in time. In terms of access to resources, some of our findings are consistent with the notion that there are ascriptive status dif-

ferences in access to earnings-producing resources that favor majority group
workers. Although such differences concerning personal characteristics such
as years of schooling and job status are familiar ones, differences concerning
access to labor market resources are less well-known. Blacks as compared
with whites are less likely to be engaged in complex work and are more likely
to perform work involving physical activities in unpleasant environments.
Women as compared with men have reduced access to jobs with physical
activity requirements and increased access to jobs requiring social skills. In
addition, the data show expected race–sex differences in access to authority
positions, with white males being clearly more likely to occupy positions of
authority than the remaining status groups.

Findings regarding access to local and industrial market resources, however, do not fit as neatly. Although we find the expected sex differences in
access to industrial resources favoring males, there is no support for the idea
that blacks, relative to whites, are deprived of earnings-producing industrial
resources. Although we cannot rule out the possibility that more detailed
measurement of the industry categories would reveal more substantial racial
differences in these characteristics, it does not appear from our data that
there is a lack of universalism in the allocation of the races to industrial
positions. Concerning local labor market resources, the race–sex differences
are less clear-cut. Blacks are more likely to live in racially crowded areas
than are whites, and they also have somewhat greater access to tertiary
sector resources (which are not uniformly positively associated with earnings) than do whites. Wives have somewhat reduced access to manufacturing
resources than do heads of household, but in general the differences are not
large. Thus our inferences concerning ascriptive status differences in access
to resources do not suggest that economic minorities are uniformly deprived
of favorable labor market positions. Absence of racial differences in access to
industrial and some local labor market resources suggests that there is not a
lack of universalism in the allocation of these resources by race. In contrast,
differences in access to occupational resources and positions in the authority
structure, as well as sex differences in access to industrial resources, some
occupational resources, and authority positions, are more consistent with the
notion that there may be some lack of universalism in the allocation of these
resources.

Evidence of mean differences by race and sex in access to resources provides only very tentative information concerning the operation of universalism in the earnings attainment process. A more important type of evidence
consists of ascriptive status differences in the process of earnings attainment.
Although we have observed many differences in the process associated with
race, sex, and marital status, thus suggesting departures from equality, not
all of the findings suggest that economic minorities are the ones disadvan-

taged in returns to these characteristics. As indicated by the summary model in Chapter 5 (Table 5.7), returns to local labor market manufacturing characteristics are stronger for black males than for whites; all groups except white males obtain additional returns to industrial concentration and investment. Although comparisons are more difficult for the weeks worked construct, it appears that several status groups obtain stronger returns to this resource than do white males. Since there are also variables for which white males do obtain stronger returns than at least several of the other status groups—years of schooling, work complexity, job experience, tertiary sector productivity, and class/authority (not shown in Table 5.7)—there appears to be no single inference that can be drawn concerning universalism in the status attainment process. In some cases white males have an advantage in terms of the translation of resources into earnings, and these are the factors (listed earlier) that we most commonly think of as facilitating earnings attainment. However, economic minorities often obtain some returns to these factors as well; in other cases (also listed earlier) returns among economic minorities exceed those for white males. Thus inferences concerning universalism should be specific to particular personal and structural resources.

INFERENCES CONCERNING DISCRIMINATION AND
COMPARABLE WORTH

A central purpose in this analysis has been to better understand race and sex discrimination. Regression decomposition has consistently indicated that these two forms of discrimination are different in important ways (see Table 5.13). Racial discrimination among males is substantially a function of differential access to resources. Differential returns to resources are also important, and there is a positive interaction term that is nontrivial in size. Sex discrimination among whites is largely a function of differential efficacy of resources, with the difference in access to resources explaining relatively little and the positive interaction term being of trivial size. Although the actual percentages vary somewhat depending upon how completely specified our model is, the basic conclusion remains. It appears, then, that women are handicapped relative to men principally by their failure to obtain equivalent returns for the resources they do possess. In contrast, racial discrimination (among males) is only partly a function of unequal returns for equal resources. Here lack of access to desirable labor market positions accounts for a major proportion of the earnings difference. The positive interaction term suggests that additional earnings benefits would accrue to black males if some degree of equalization of access and efficacy occurred simultaneously. Such findings suggest that policy directed towards reduction in racial earnings differences should differ substantially from that directed towards reducing sex differences in earnings. Black males need greater access to the types of jobs white men hold as well as equal returns to the resources they do control. Women workers primarily need reduced discrimination in the translation of resources into earnings.

These ideas have important implications for current perspectives that view sex differences in earnings as strongly affected by the failure of employers to reward equivalent jobs held by men and women with equal pay. Although the Equal Pay Act outlaws discrimination in pay for equal work, proponents of *comparable worth* argue that jobs requiring similar levels of effort, skill, responsibility and having similar working conditions should also receive equal pay even if the jobs themselves are different (Treiman and Hartmann, 1981:2). If job evaluations place less value on one job as opposed to another, its incumbents earn less. Women have traditionally been disproportionately employed in jobs and occupations that have been less valued than those occupied by men, thus contributing to sex differences in earnings.

The findings we produce concerning returns to occupational characteristics and class/authority positions are clearly compatible with the notion that the jobs women hold are not evaluated equivalently to the jobs men hold. Our use of composites representing such factors as occupational complexity and working conditions, as well as indicators of span of responsibility and span of control taps dimensions relevant to the comparable worth notion, thus allowing inferences concerning whether jobs of comparable worth are equally rewarded. Evidence from regression standardization analysis indicating that sex differences in earnings are largely a function of unequal returns to labor market characteristics can also be interpreted to suggest that women fail to obtain equal earnings from occupational positions comparable to those that men occupy.

We believe, however, that there are two ways in which our analysis goes beyond what is explictly stated in the treatment of comparable worth. First, we demonstrate that women lack access to earnings-producing industrial resources and that these resources are important determinants of earnings for women, even when occupational and authority characteristics are introduced. Thus analysis of sex differences in earnings depends on knowledge of industrial as well as occupational segregation; industrial characteristics operate to affect earnings attainment independent of occupational and job characteristics. Second, our analysis provides additional detail concerning how status groups differ in the effects of structural variables on earnings. We are particularly struck by the unique economic position of black women. Findings from the regression standardization show that the relative importance of composition, slopes plus intercepts, and interaction components is intermediate between the race and sex comparisons just described. Policy directed at promoting earnings equality with white males for these workers would need to consider both access to and efficacy of resources.

Although writers of various intellectual and political persuasions have often classified black women workers as either primarily black or primarily female, on the basis of these findings we believe the economic position of this group is not well-captured solely by one or the other category. Both race and sex combine to influence their economic status. Therefore, policies directed towards reducing racial differences in earnings, without attention to sex, would help black males more than females, whereas policies directed towards reducing earnings differences based on sex, without sensitivity to black women as a racial minority, would help white women more than black women. In particular, despite the usefulness of the idea of comparable worth, one should recognize that increased emphasis on rewarding men and women equally for equivalent work *could* result in greater benefits for white than for black women. Such a conclusion assumes that attention would not simultaneously be devoted to equalizing access to resources for black women as compared with white men.[6] Nevertheless, the findings suggest racial differences in the importance of resource efficacy in the earnings attainment process for females.

It is important to remember that these conclusions are general ones derived from the summary of the operation of several variables. Implementation of programs designed to affect the distribution and efficacy of *particular* resources (e.g., class/authority or concentration and investment) might lead to somewhat different outcomes. One should also recognize the difficulty of the political issue raised by these findings. As Thurow (1980) argues, greater economic equality can only be achieved if some groups are willing to give up part of the economic benefits they currently enjoy, and this does not appear likely. For these reasons we view the conclusions from this portion of the analysis with additional caution.

Finally, in addition to providing evidence concerning the impact of labor market characteristics on individual earnings and information on discrimination, at a more general level we hope that our analysis will promote further interest in the relationship between social structure and the individual. Traditionally, this has been one of the major problems in sociology, with

---

[6]This conclusion also ignores the possibility that black female heads may not be a homogeneous subgroup with reference to socioeconomic attainment. It may be that the presence of children sharply differentiates the economic status of black women who head households, with childless women being more economically successful than those with children. Our analysis ignores this distinction. Conclusions regarding the importance of comparable worth versus access to resources should therefore be cautiously advanced in this case, since the importance of comparable worth may vary within the female heads subgroup.

analysis of the impact of labor market characteristics on individual earnings being one facet of this general issue. We have argued that contextual analysis is useful in the integration of structural and individual-level explanations of a phenomenon. Although the focus here is on economic inequality, in any subfield where there is a tradition of both individual-level and ecological-level research on a common outcome, it is possible to develop contextual models to aid in this integration. One purpose of this strategy can be to evaluate the relative effectiveness of structural and individual perspectives in predicting a given dependent variable. Alternatively, the strategy is useful in studying social selection. Although in this study we have been concerned with the nonrandom allocation of workers to labor markets, the process of social selection is a very general one. For this reason use of contextual analysis to integrate individual- and ecological-level explanations from other subfields should provide information concerning the operation of selection in other aspects of social life. We look forward to such research, as well as to further investigation of the relationship between social structure and the individual as it informs the problem of economic inequality.

Occupations and Industries Used in Matching Ecological and Survey Data[1]

1-Digit Occupational Categories
 Professional, technical, and kindred workers
 Managers, officials, and proprietors
 Self-employed businessmen
 Clerical and sales workers
 Craftsmen, foremen, and kindred workers
 Operatives and kindred workers
 Laborers, service workers, farm laborers
 Farmers and farm managers
2-Digit Occupational Categories
 Physicians and dentists
 Other medical and paramedical professionals
 Accountants and auditors
 Teachers—primary and secondary schools
 Teachers—college; social scientists; librarians; archivists
 Architects; chemists; engineers; physical, and biological scientists
 Technicians—includes designers, airplane pilots, surveyors, medical and
  dental technicians, and others
 Public advisors—includes clergymen, editors and reporters, personnel
  workers, social and welfare workers, and others
 Judges and lawyers
 Professional, technical, and kindred workers n.e.c.
 Not self-employed managers, officials, and proprietors (except farm)

---

[1]The following abbreviations are used in this appendix: n.e.c. means not elsewhere classified; NA means not ascertained.

Self-employed managers, officials, and proprietors (unincorporated businesses)

Secretaries, stenographers, and typists

Other clerical workers including library attendants, cashiers, bank tellers, receptionists, station agents, and others

Sales workers

Foremen, n.e.c.

Other craftsmen and kindred workers

Government protective service workers—firemen, police, marshals, and constables

Members of the armed forces

Transport equipment operatives

Operatives, except transport

Unskilled laborers—nonfarm

Farm laborers and foremen

Private household workers

Other service workers—includes beauticians, housekeepers, practical nurses, counter and fountain workers, attendants in physicians' offices and others

Farmers (owners and tenants) and managers (except farm laborers and foremen)

Industrial categories

  Agriculture, forestry, and fishing

  Mining and extraction

  Manufacturing Durables

    Metal industries

    Machinery, including electrical

    Motor vehicles and other transportation equipment

    Other durables

    Durables, NA what

  Manufacturing Nondurables

    Food and kindred products

    Tobacco

    Textiles, apparel, textile products, shoes

    Paper and allied products

    Chemical and allied, petroleum, coal, rubber, and plastic products

    Other nondurables

    Nondurables, NA what

  Manufacturing, NA whether durable or nondurable

  Construction

  Transportation

  Communication

Other public utilities
Retail trade
Wholesale trade
Trade, NA whether wholesale or retail
Finance, insurance, and real estate
Repair services
Business services
Personal services
Amusement, recreation, and related services
Printing, publishing, and allied services
Medical, dental, and health services, whether public or private
Educational services, whether public or private
Professional and related services other than medical or educational

Missing Data

Although we took care to minimize missing data problems by making reasonable assumptions concerning the assignment of individuals to areas, industries, and occupations, such steps could not completely eliminate the problem. Table B.1 lists the number of cases for which each variable is actually measured for each subsample. We present one figure for the sets of dummies (eg., education, weeks worked, work authority), since the figures are identical throughout each set.

Table B.1

Number of Cases by Variable Measured and Status Group

Variable	Male heads Whites	Male heads Blacks	Female heads Whites	Female heads Blacks	Wives Whites	Wives Blacks
Earnings	1870	768	297	349	817	356
Duncan SEI	1867	762	295	349	815	355
Years of schooling	1867	768	296	349	817	356
Weeks worked	1777	705	278	304	815	354
Experience	1867	767	292	344	813	355
Manufacturing dominance	1782	756	288	349	789	355
Manufacturing sector health	1742	751	285	349	777	355
Tertiary sector health	1863	768	296	349	813	356
Tertiary sector growth	1796	741	290	342	779	332
Tertiary sector complexity	1870	768	297	349	817	356
Urbanization	1099	446	184	193	482	192
Crowding	1823	768	293	349	792	356
Unemployment	1422	762	255	345	621	349
Segregation	832	520	150	247	372	231
Percentage black population	1870	768	297	349	817	356
Unemployment rate	1823	768	293	349	792	356
Wage per man-hour	1780	756	290	349	788	355
Profitability	1723	676	280	317	766	340
Concentration and investment	1453	576	176	190	491	210
Firm growth	1723	676	280	317	758	340
Work duration	1350	537	208	237	538	261
Benefits	1634	619	274	313	758	332
Sex discrimination	1366	539	208	237	539	261
Complexity	1867	762	295	349	815	355
Uncertainty	1867	762	295	349	815	355
Physical dexterity	1867	762	295	349	815	355
Physical activities	1867	762	295	349	815	355
People-things	1867	762	295	349	815	355
Unpleasantness of work	1867	762	295	349	815	355
Job authority	1753	697	276	299	807	351

Zero-order Correlations between Types of Labor Market Characteristics

In this appendix we inspect the zero-order relationships across the types of labor market characteristics we have been studying. The zero-order correlations between industrial and occupational labor market characteristics are of particular interest. If there is overlap between the dual economy and dual labor market such that the bulk of the primary labor market jobs are in the core of the economy and the bulk of the secondary labor market jobs are on the periphery, then there should be clear relationships between the industrial and occupational labor market characteristics. Inspection of the relevant matrices suggests that across status groups there are stronger relationships between the occupational and industrial variables than between occupational and areal or industrial and areal characteristics. For white male heads, 31 of 42 correlations exceed ±.10. Comparable ratios for the remaining status groups are: black male heads, 25:42; white female heads, 22:42; black female heads, 35:42; white wives, 27:42; black wives, 30:42.

Among the stronger correlations that portray systematic patterns across status groups are those involving complexity and people–things. There are always positive relationships between work complexity and firm profitability, findings that are consistent with our expectations concerning the location of primary labor market jobs in the core of the economy, but the comparable relationships are more variable for concentration and investment, with negative correlations evident among males and positive correlations among females, which is not entirely consistent with our predictions. There are always negative relationships between firm growth and these two occupational variables, which is consistent with our expectations that firms that are growing create jobs with only minimal degrees of occupational complexity; apparently the positions are also low in their requirements of social relations skills. The *generally* negative relationships between people–things and complexity, on the one hand, and work duration and benefits, on the other, speak to the complexity of the relationships between dual economy and dual labor market indicators. They suggest that jobs with high benefits and steady employment opportunities are likely to be low in work complexity and in the social relations skills they demand. These are most probably manufacturing jobs requiring little interaction with others in unionized establishments. They have a high degree of job security and good benefits but also entail relatively routine and repetitive work. This interpretation is consistent with our conception of manufacturing jobs in the core of the economy, in that it fits Piore's (1975) discussion of lower tier primary labor market positions. Certainly in the case of upper tier jobs we would expect positive relationships between these two sets of variables.

The generally positive relationships among people–things, complexity, and sex discrimination suggest that jobs that entail working with others may be more prone to sex discrimination than the manufacturing jobs just discussed. Recall that the sex discrimination composite consists of two variables, the percentage females employed and below average wages. Thus the positive relationship between people–things and sex discrimination undoubtedly reflects the tendency for women to be employed in jobs that require social relations skills but are poorly paid. The positive relationships between work complexity and sex discrimination are less easily explained, although it is plausible to suggest that the jobs for which women are hired that involve complexity are not well-paid either. The findings also suggest that work complexity by itself is no guarantee of high wages.

There are some sex differences evident in the relationships of physical dexterity and physical activity with the industrial indicators. Among males of both races, industries that are most profitable are not those that generally contain jobs requiring physical dexterity and physical activity. In these cases advanced technology is likely to facilitate productivity and hence profitability without requiring the physical skills more necessary when technology was more limited. Among women these relationships are somewhat weaker, although we can interpret the negative correlations between concentration and investment and physical activity in much the same way. We see, however, that among women there are positive relationships between concentration and investment and physical dexterity, thus indicating that the profitable firms that hire women workers do so for jobs that require some degree of physical dexterity. This is less true for men. The relationships between physical dexterity, physical activity, and sex discrimination also vary by sex. Among men the relationships are negative, thus suggesting that jobs requiring these physical work skills employ few women and pay relatively higher wages. Among women the relationships are variable and sometimes positive, thus suggesting that women are at times hired to perform jobs requiring some physical skills although these positions are not likely to pay well.

The relationships between task uncertainty and the industrial characteristics are often positive, thus suggesting overlap between positions described to be in the core of the economy and those described to be in the primary labor market. The relationships between unpleasant working conditions and the industrial labor market factors are generally weak for males and white female heads and often negative among the remaining female status groups. The negative relationships are compatible with expectations that jobs located in the core of the economy are jobs that workers perform in pleasant surroundings. The fact that the findings vary by status group is not easily explained. Finally, the relationships between the percentage male and the industrial variables are often positive, a finding consistent with expectations that males are disproportionately allocated to labor market positions in the core of the economy.

Although there is no clear theoretical basis for doing so, one can also inspect the correlations between areal and occupational labor market characteristics. Again we see that the correlations are usually small among white male heads: 39 of 42 are between ±.10. The same ratios for the remaining groups are: black male heads, 31:42; white female heads, 30:42; black female heads, 21:42; white wives, 29:42; and black wives, 19:42. As our discussion of the relationships between areal and industrial characteristics suggests, the correlations are strongest for black female workers, and they are weakest among white male heads. In terms of substantive relationships, across the groups there appear to be positive relationships between the complexity of work and the economic health of the tertiary sector, and there are negative relationships between this latter variable and physical activity of work and unpleasantness of working conditions. Such findings are consistent with expectations concerning jobs in the tertiary sector entailing work complexity if the jobs are located in the more technologically advanced areas of that sector and with the notion that these jobs necessitate little physical activity and are performed in pleasant surroundings. Jobs that are part of the less productive areas of the tertiary sector involve less complex work with greater physical activity and may be performed in unpleasant and/or unsafe surroundings. The observed negative relationships between physical activity and tertiary sector complexity are consistent with these ideas as well. Readers interested in the remaining relationships, which are generally quite variable across status groups, should consult Tables C.1a–C.1f.

Table C.la

Zero-Order Correlations Between Types of Labor Market Characteristics: White Male Heads

	Profitability	Concentration and investment	Firm growth	Work duration	Benefits	Sex discrimination
Manufacturing sector health	.009	-.014	.027	.030	.051	.004
Manufacturing dominance	-.064	-.026	.163	.195	.114	-.038
Tertiary sector health	.038	.016	-.011	.011	.084	.013
Tertiary sector growth	-.016	.011	-.020	-.053	-.002	.025
Tertiary sector complexity	.054	-.010	-.035	-.064	.000	.026
Crowding	.030	.027	-.032	-.066	-.025	.008
Uncertainty	.114	.016	.075	.021	.109	.130
Unpleasantness of work	-.086	.062	.146	.178	.111	-.058
Physical dexterity	-.242	.074	.053	.238	.119	-.234
Physical activities	-.107	.117	.086	.129	.042	-.430
People-things	.279	-.144	-.269	-.387	-.274	.394
Complexity	.230	-.085	-.352	-.239	-.143	-.185
Percentage male	-.166	.156	.153	.184	.132	-.327

	Manufacturing sector health	Manufacturing dominance	Tertiary sector health	Tertiary sector growth	Tertiary sector complexity	Crowding
Uncertainty	-.024	.044	.064	.015	.015	-.006
Unpleasantness of work	-.057	-.001	-.067	-.021	.000	-.005
Physical dexterity	.012	.030	-.036	-.017	-.048	-.013
Physical activities	-.095	-.021	-.171	-.028	-.069	-.037
People-things	-.018	-.091	.032	.006	.041	.035
Complexity	.107	-.095	.148	.008	.090	.050
Percentage male	.010	.005	-.057	.004	-.018	-.001

291

Table C.1b

Zero-Order Correlations Between Types of Labor Market Characteristics: Black Male Heads

	Profitability	Concentration and investment	Firm growth	Work duration	Benefits	Sex discrimination
Manufacturing sector health	.023	.043	.018	-.043	.061	-.097
Manufacturing dominance	-.080	-.015	.240	.148	.091	.097
Tertiary sector health	.017	.039	-.030	-.084	.073	-.101
Tertiary sector growth	.102	.105	-.148	.061	-.003	-.070
Tertiary sector complexity	.075	.071	.032	-.052	-.013	-.119
Crowding	-.067	-.096	.049	.022	-.082	.041
Uncertainty	.086	.211	.201	.325	.292	-.072
Unpleasantness of work	-.191	-.074	.005	-.066	-.019	.166
Physical dexterity	-.105	.005	.161	.132	-.079	-.250
Physical activities	-.217	.026	.012	-.066	-.053	-.364
People-things	.224	-.009	-.331	-.253	-.219	.399
Complexity	.341	-.253	-.424	-.307	-.253	.184
Percentage male	-.122	-.026	.092	.064	-.017	-.335

	Manufacturing sector health	Manufacturing dominance	Tertiary sector health	Tertiary sector growth	Tertiary sector complexity	Crowding
Uncertainty	-.007	.107	.060	.032	.078	-.100
Unpleasantness of work	.002	.049	.000	.041	-.080	.085
Physical dexterity	.080	.015	.069	-.093	.041	.023
Physical activities	-.124	-.026	-.171	.085	.026	.225
People-things	.007	-.155	.024	.088	-.001	-.081
Complexity	.073	-.116	.096	.094	-.032	-.131
Percentage male	-.038	-.023	-.072	.130	.120	.113

Table C.1c

Zero-Order Correlations Between Types of Labor Market Characteristics: White Female Heads

	Profitability	Concentration and investment	Firm growth	Work duration	Benefits	Sex discrimination
Manufacturing sector health	.001	.037	-.037	-.013	.030	-.085
Manufacturing dominance	-.136	-.089	.139	.033	.003	.010
Tertiary sector health	-.035	-.043	.016	-.018	-.005	-.107
Tertiary sector growth	.080	-.053	-.110	-.050	-.069	.045
Tertiary sector complexity	.047	-.027	-.009	-.002	-.019	-.180
Crowding	-.047	-.044	.057	-.114	-.072	.083
Uncertainty	-.010	-.036	.106	.049	.053	.071
Unpleasantness of work	-.041	-.075	-.075	-.035	-.053	.136
Physical dexterity	-.101	.105	.024	.071	.026	.021
Physical activities	-.121	-.243	-.017	-.059	-.139	.105
People-things	.219	-.018	-.284	-.414	-.206	.318
Complexity	.447	.188	-.336	-.094	-.019	.029
Percentage male	.124	.184	.109	.361	.270	-.334

	Manufacturing sector health	Manufacturing dominance	Tertiary sector health	Tertiary sector growth	Tertiary sector complexity	Crowding
Uncertainty	-.047	.087	.024	-.038	-.067	.105
Unpleasantness of work	-.047	-.021	-.138	-.038	-.085	-.086
Physical dexterity	-.039	.034	-.080	-.103	.094	-.010
Physical activities	-.080	.117	-.134	-.105	-.125	-.076
People-things	.068	-.023	.050	.105	-.044	.023
Complexity	.043	-.191	.132	.147	.105	.070
Percentage male	.010	-.073	-.047	.074	.019	.010

Table C.1d

Zero-Order Correlations Between Types of Labor Market Characteristics: Black Female Heads

	Profitability	Concentration and investment	Firm growth	Work duration	Benefits	Sex discrimination
Manufacturing sector health	.162	.011	-.170	-.086	.070	.010
Manufacturing dominance	.087	-.109	.100	.129	.096	.012
Tertiary sector health	.108	.290	-.078	-.056	.132	-.007
Tertiary sector growth	-.037	-.379	.034	-.005	-.196	.152
Tertiary sector complexity	.094	.097	.031	-.065	.059	-.058
Crowding	-.075	-.121	.160	-.061	-.092	-.057
Uncertainty	-.093	.279	.294	.339	.189	.111
Unpleasantness of work	-.109	-.174	-.147	-.154	-.132	.170
Physical dexterity	-.063	.311	.116	.482	.344	-.049
Physical activities	-.098	-.363	-.140	-.128	-.244	.086
People-things	.173	-.133	-.411	-.622	-.215	.188
Complexity	.358	.275	-.139	.070	.211	.102
Percentage male	.178	.542	.271	.586	.519	-.003

	Manufacturing sector health	Manufacturing dominance	Tertiary sector health	Tertiary sector growth	Tertiary sector complexity	Crowding
Uncertainty	.128	-.017	.196	-.021	-.048	-.053
Unpleasantness of work	-.238	.035	-.278	.110	-.028	.112
Physical dexterity	.020	.075	-.029	-.053	.024	-.041
Physical activities	-.081	.116	-.237	.153	-.128	.153
People-things	.032	-.088	.070	-.045	.113	.011
Complexity	.130	.081	.181	-.179	.129	-.197
Percentage male	.074	.130	.148	-.162	-.060	-.140

Table C.1e

Zero-Order Correlations Between Types of Labor Market Characteristics: White Wives

	Profitability	Concentration and investment	Firm growth	Work duration	Benefits discrimination	Sex discrimination
Manufacturing sector health	-.017	.090	-.067	-.040	.070	-.112
Manufacturing dominance	-.060	.052	.152	.185	.123	-.043
Tertiary sector health	.049	.123	-.072	-.051	.048	-.095
Tertiary sector growth	-.054	.007	.008	-.050	-.021	.051
Tertiary sector complexity	.092	.041	-.117	-.092	.010	-.045
Crowding	.072	.018	-.073	-.079	-.023	.044
Uncertainty	-.159	-.060	.242	.106	.072	.124
Unpleasantness of work	-.247	-.254	.106	.085	-.097	.071
Physical dexterity	-.081	.233	-.113	.209	.104	.066
Physical activities	-.110	-.208	.056	.141	-.114	-.013
People-things	.346	-.014	-.378	-.494	-.180	.052
Complexity	.392	.086	-.434	-.274	-.098	.139
Percentage male	-.176	-.129	.263	-.110	.001	.014

	Manufacturing sector health	Manufacturing dominance	Tertiary sector health	Tertiary sector growth	Tertiary sector complexity	Crowding
Uncertainty	-.048	.043	-.076	-.007	-.070	-.014
Unpleasantness of work	-.085	.134	-.159	.009	-.108	-.062
Physical dexterity	.042	.009	.065	.060	.042	-.037
Physical activities	-.110	.142	-.167	-.053	-.103	-.079
People-things	.046	-.159	.083	.014	.114	.084
Complexity	.048	-.160	.132	.018	.102	.113
Percentage male	-.081	.063	-.088	-.017	-.088	.015

Table C.1f

Zero-Order Correlations Between Types of Labor Market Characteristics: Black Wives

	Profitability	Concentration and investment	Firm growth	Work duration	Benefits	Sex discrimination
Manufacturing sector health	-.012	.154	-.215	-.346	-.005	.017
Manufacturing dominance	-.047	.133	.073	.135	.062	.238
Tertiary sector health	.047	.303	-.172	-.337	.066	.070
Tertiary sector growth	.081	-.327	.008	.081	-.159	-.187
Tertiary sector complexity	-.037	.049	.067	-.192	-.020	-.065
Crowding	.044	-.182	.055	.175	-.047	.088
Uncertainty	.071	.315	.302	.507	.388	.313
Unpleasantness of work	-.370	-.337	-.095	-.022	-.149	.304
Physical dexterity	.092	.329	.183	.448	.247	.159
Physical activities	-.448	-.601	-.038	-.140	-.292	.079
People-things	.373	-.045	-.598	-.607	-.250	-.142
Complexity	.633	.484	-.452	-.048	.062	-.227
Percentage male	-.021	.093	.097	.384	.177	.383

	Manufacturing sector health	Manufacturing dominance	Tertiary sector health	Tertiary sector growth	Tertiary sector complexity	Crowding
Uncertainty	-.173	.177	-.107	-.041	-.090	.036
Unpleasantness of work	-.131	.106	-.162	-.023	-.131	.091
Physical dexterity	-.022	.132	.041	-.155	-.071	.059
Physical activities	-.204	-.019	-.296	.159	-.107	.153
People-things	.257	-.153	.229	.021	.073	-.096
Complexity	.135	.005	.148	-.014	-.068	-.069
Percentage male	-.178	.200	-.153	-.015	-.193	.021

References

Aigner, D. J.
  1970 "A comment on problems in making inferences from the Coleman Report." American Sociological Review 35:249–252.
Aldrich, H. and J. Weiss
  1981 "Differentiation within the United States capitalist class: Workforce size and income differences." American Sociological Review 46:279–290.
Alexander, K. L., M. Cook and E. L. McDill
  1978 "Curriculum tracking and educational stratification." American Sociological Review 43:47–66.
Alexander, K. L. and B. K. Eckland
  1975 "Contextual effects in the high school attainment process." American Sociological Review 40:402–416.
Alexander, K. L., B. K. Eckland and L. Griffin, Jr.
  1975 "The Wisconsin model of socioeconomic achievement: A replication." American Journal of Sociology 81:324–342.
Alexander, K. L. and E. L. McDill
  1976 "Selection and allocation within schools: Some causes and consequences of curriculum placement." American Sociological Review 41:963–980.
Althauser, R. P. and A. L. Kalleberg
  1981 "Firms, occupations, and the structure of labor markets: A conceptual analysis." Pp. 119–149 in I. Berg (ed.), Sociological Perspectives on Labor Markets. New York: Academic Press.
Althauser, R. P., Sydney S. Spivak, in collaboration with Beverly H. Amsel
  1975 The Unequal Elites. New York: Wiley.
Althauser, R. P. and M. Wigler
  1972 "Standardization and component analysis." Sociological Methods and Research 1:98–134.
Alwin, D. F.
  1973 "The use of factor analysis in the construction of linear composites in social research." Sociological Methods and Research 2:191–214.
  1976 "Assessing school effects: Some identities." Sociology of Education 49:294–303.

Alwin, D. F., R. M. Hauser and W. H. Sewell
  1975   "Colleges and achievement." Pp. 113–142 in W. H. Sewell and R. M. Hauser (eds.),
          Education, Occupation and Earnings. New York: Academic Press.
Alwin, D. F. and C. W. Mueller
  1971   "Comment on 'Toward a temporal sequence of adolescent achievement variables'."
          American Sociological Review 36:503–508.
Andrisani, P. J.
  1973   "An empirical analysis of the dual labor market theory." Ph.D. dissertation, Ohio
          State University.
  1977   "Internal–external attitudes, personal initiative, and the labor market experience of
          white and black men." Journal of Human Resources 12:308–328.
  1981   "Internal–external attitudes, sense of efficacy, and labor market experience: A reply to
          Duncan and Morgan." Journal of Human Resources 16:658–666.
Atkinson, J. W. and D. Birch
  1970   The Dynamics of Action. New York: Wiley.
Averitt, R. T.
  1968   The Dual Economy. New York: Norton.
Bacon, L.
  1971   "Poverty among inter-regional rural-to-urban migrants." Rural Sociology 36:125–140.
Baldwin, S. E. and R. S. Daski
  1976   "Occupational pay differences among metropolitan areas." Monthly Labor Review
          May:29–35.
Baron, J. N. and W. T. Bielby
  1980   "Bringing the firms back in: Stratification, segmentation, and the organization of
          work." American Sociological Review 45:737–765.
  1982   "Workers and machines: Dimensions and determinants of technical relations in the
          workplace." American Sociological Review 47:175–188.
Barton, A. H.
  1968   "Bringing society back in: Survey research and macro methodology." American Be-
          havioral Scientist 12:1–9.
  1970   "Commentary and debate: Allen Barton comments on Hauser's context and consex."
          American Journal of Sociology 76:514–517.
Beck, E. M., P. M. Horan and C. M. Tolbert, II
  1978   "Stratification in a dual economy." American Sociological Review 43:704–720.
  1980   "Social stratification in industrial society; Further evidence for a structured alterna-
          tive." American Sociological Review 45:712–719.
Becker, G. S.
  1964   Human Capital. New York: National Bureau of Economic Research.
  1965   "A theory of the allocation of time." Economic Journal 75:493–517.
  1973   "A theory of marriage: Part I." Journal of Political Economy 81:813–846.
Becker, G. S. and B. R. Chiswick
  1966   "Education and the distribution of earnings." American Economic Review
          56:358–369.
Berg, I.
  1970   Education and Jobs: The Great Training Robbery. New York: Praeger.
Bergmann, B. R.
  1971   "The effect on white incomes of discrimination in employment." Journal of Political
          Economy 79:294–313.

Bibb, R. and W. H. Form
  1977   "The effects of industrial, occupational and sex stratification on wages in blue-collar
          markets." Social Forces 55:974–996.
Bielby, W. T. and J. R. Kluegel
  1977   "Statistical inference and statistical power in applications of the general linear model."
          Pp. 283–312 in D. R. Heise (ed.). Sociological Methodology 1977. San Francisco:
          Jossey–Bass.
Blalock, H. M., Jr.
  1956   "Economic discrimination and Negro increase." American Sociological Review
          21:584–588.
  1957   "Percent nonwhite and discrimination in the south." American Sociological Review
          22:677–682.
  1967   Toward a Theory of Minority Group Relations. New York: Wiley.
Blau, P. M.
  1977   Inequality and Heterogeneity. New York: Free Press.
Blau, P. M. and O. D. Duncan
  1967   The American Occupational Structure. New York: Wiley.
Blaug, M.
  1976   "The empirical status of human capital theory: A slightly jaundiced survey." Journal of
          Economic Literature 14:827–855.
Blaxall, M. and B. Reagan (eds.)
  1976   Women and the Workplace. Chicago: The University of Chicago Press.
Blinder, A. S.
  1973   "Wage discrimination: Reduced form and structural estimates." Journal of Human
          Resources 8:436–455.
Bluestone, B.
  1970   "The tripartite economy: Labor markets and the working poor." Poverty and Human
          Resources ■■:15–35.
Bluestone, B., W. M. Murphy and M. Stevenson
  1973   Low Wages and the Working Poor. Ann Arbor: Institute of Labor and Industrial
          Relations, The University of Michigan–Wayne State University.
Blum, Z. D.
  1972   "White and black careers during the first decade of labor force experience. Part II:
          Income differences." Social Science Research 1:271–292.
Bose, C. E.
  1973   Jobs and Gender: Sex and Occupational Prestige. Baltimore: Center for Metropolitan
          Planning and Research, Johns Hopkins University.
Bowles, S.
  1970   "Migration as investment: Empirical tests of the human investment approach to
          geographical mobility." The Review of Economics and Statistics 52:356–362.
Bowles, S. and H. M. Levin
  1968a   "The determinants of scholastic achievement—an appraisal of some recent evidence."
          Journal of Human Resources 3:3–24.
  1968b   "More on multicollinearity and the effectiveness of schools." Journal of Human Re-
          sources 3:393–400.
Boyd, Lawrence H., Jr. and Gudmund R. Iversen
  1979   Contextual Analysis: Concepts and Statistical Techniques. Belmont, California:
          Wadsworth.

Braverman, H.
1974   Labor and Monopoly Capital. New York: Monthly Review Press.
Brim, O. G. and S. Wheeler
1966   Socialization after Childhood: Two Essays. New York: Wiley.
Cain, G. G.
1976   "The challenge of segmented labor market theories to orthodox theory." Journal of
        Economic Literature 14:1215–1257.
Cain, G. G. and H. W. Watts
1968   "The controversy about the Coleman Report: Comment." Journal of Human Re-
        sources 3:389–392.
Cain, P. S. and D. J. Treiman
1981   "The dictionary of occupational titles as a source of occupational data." American
        Sociological Review 46:253–278.
Campbell, E. Q. and C. N. Alexander
1965   "Structural effects and interpersonal relationships." American Journal of Sociology
        71:284–289.
Chase, I. D.
1975   "A comparison of men's and women's intergenerational mobility in the United States."
        American Sociological Review 40:483–505.
Chow, G. C.
1960   "Tests of equality between sets of coefficients in two linear regressions." Econo-
        metrica 28:591–605.
Cohen, J. and P. Cohen
1975   Applied Multiple Regression/Correlation Analysis for the Behavioral Sciences. Hills-
        dale, New Jersey: Erlbaum.
Cohen, M.
1971   "Sex differences in compensation." Journal of Human Resources 6:434–447.
Coleman, J. S.
1968   "Equality of educational opportunity: Reply to Bowles and Levin." Journal of Human
        Resources 3:337–346.
Coleman, J. S., C. C. Berry and Z. D. Blum
1972   "White and black careers during the first decade of labor force experience. Part III:
        Occupational status and income together." Social Science Research 1:293–304.
Coleman, J. S., Z. D. Blum, A. B. Sorensen and P. H. Rossi
1972   "White and black careers during the first decade of labor force experience. Part I:
        Occupational status." Social Science Research 1:243–270.
Coleman, J. S., E. Q. Campbell, C. J. Hobson, J. McPartland, A. M. Mood, F. D. Weinfeld
and R. L. York
1966   Equality of Educational Opportunity. Washington, D. C.: U. S. Government Printing
        Office.
Collins, R.
1979   The Credential Society: An Historical Sociology of Education and Stratification. New
        York: Academic Press.
Coser, L. A.
1975   "Two methods in search of a substance." American Sociological Review 40:691–700.
1976   "Reply to my critics." The American Sociologist 11:33–38.
Cutright, P.
1974   "The civilian earnings of white and black draftees and non-veterans." American So-
        ciological Review 39:317–327.

Davis, J. A.
   1965   Undergraduate Career Decisions: Correlates of Occupational Choice. Chicago: Aldine.
   1966   "The campus as a frog pond." American Journal of Sociology 72:17–31.
Daymont, T. N.
   1980   "Pay premiums for economic sector and race: A decomposition." Social Science Research 9:245–272.
DeJong, P. Y., M. J. Brewer and S. S. Robin
   1971   "Patterns of female intergenerational mobility." American Sociological Review 36:1033–1042.
Doeringer, P. B. and M. J. Piore
   1971   Internal Labor Markets and Manpower Analysis. Lexington, Massachusetts: Heath.
Drew, D. E. and A. W. Astin
   1972   "Undergraduate aspirations: A test of several theories." American Journal of Sociology 77: 1151–1164.
Duncan, G. J. and J. N. Morgan
   1975   Five Thousand American Families: Patterns of Economic Progress. Ann Arbor: Institute for Social Research, University of Michigan.
   1981   "Sense of efficacy and subsequent change in earnings—a replication." Journal of Human Resources 16:649–657.
Duncan, O. D.
   1968   "Ability and achievement." Eugenics Quarterly 15:1–11.
   1969   "Inheritance of poverty or inheritance of race?" Pp. 85–110 in D. P. Moynihan (ed.), On Understanding Poverty. New York: Basic Books.
Duncan, O. D., D. L. Featherman and B. Duncan
   1972   Socioeconomic Background and Achievement. New York: Seminar Press.
Duncan, O. D. and A. J. Reiss, Jr.
   1956   Social Characteristics of Urban and Rural Communities, 1950. New York: Wiley.
Duncan, O. D., W. R. Scott, S. Lieberson, B. Duncan, and H. H. Winsborough
   1960   Metropolis and Region. Baltimore: The Johns Hopkins University Press.
Edwards, R. C.
   1975   "The social relations of production in the firm and labor market structure." Pp. 1–26 in R. C. Edwards, M. Reich, and D. Gordon (eds.), Labor Market Segmentation. Lexington, Massachusetts: Heath.
England, P.
   1981   "Assessing trends in occupational sex segregation, 1900–1976." Pp. 273–295 in I. Berg (ed.), Sociological Perspectives on Labor Markets. New York: Academic Press.
Faia, M. A.
   1981   "Selection by certification: A neglected variable in stratification research." American Journal of Sociology 86:1093–1111.
Farkas, G.
   1974   "Specification, residuals and contextual effects." Sociological Methods and Research 2:333–363.
Featherman, D. L.
   1972   "Achievement orientations and socioeconomic career attainments." American Sociological Review 37:131–142.
   1976   "Coser's 'In search of substance'." The American Sociologist 11:21–27.
Featherman, D. L. and R. M. Hauser
   1974   "Trends in occupational mobility by race and sex in the United States, 1962–1972,"

Working Paper 74–25. Madison: Center for Demography and Ecology, University of Wisconsin.

1976a "Sexual inequalities and socioeconomic achievement in the U. S., 1962–1973." American Sociological Review 41:462–483.

1976b "Changes in socioeconomic stratification of the races, 1962–73." American Journal of Sociology 82:621–651.

1977 "Commonalities in social stratification and assumptions about status mobility in the United States." Pp. 3–50 in R. M. Hauser and D. L. Featherman (eds.), The Process of Stratification. New York: Academic Press.

1978 Opportunity and Change. New York: Academic Press.

Firebaugh, G.

1979 "Assessing group effects: A comparison of two methods." Sociological Methods and Research 7:384–395.

Fisher, F. M.

1970 "Tests of equality between sets of coefficients in two linear regressions: An expository note." Econometrica 38:361–366.

Flanagan, R. J.

1973 "Racial wage discrimination and employment segregation." Journal of Human Resources 8:456–471.

Fligstein, N. and W. Wolf

1978 "Sex similarities in occupational status attainment: Are the results due to the restriction of the sample to employed women?" Social Science Research 7:197–212.

Form, W. and J. Huber

1976 "Occupational power." Pp. 751–806 in R. Dubin (ed.), Handbook of Work, Organization and Society. Chicago: Rand McNally.

Form, W. and D. C. Miller

1960 Industry, Labor, and Community. New York: Harper & Brothers.

Franklin, R. S.

1968 "A framework for the analysis of interurban Negro–white economic differentials." Industrial and Labor Relations Review 21:370–379.

Freedman, M. K.

1976 Labor Markets: Segments and Shelters. Montclair, New Jersey: Allanheld, Osmun.

Fuchs, V.

1971 "Differences in hourly earnings between men and women." Monthly Labor Review 94:9–15.

Glenn, N. D., A. Ross and J. Tully

1974 "Patterns of intergenerational mobility of females through marriage." American Sociological Review 39:683–699.

Gordon, D. M.

1972 Theories of Poverty and Underemployment. Lexington, Massachusetts: Heath.

Gordon, R.

1968 "Issues in multiple regression." American Journal of Sociology 73:592–616.

Granovetter, M.

1981 "Toward a sociological theory of income differences." Pp. 11–47 in I. Berg (ed.), Sociological Perspectives on Labor Markets. New York: Academic Press.

Greenwood, M. J.

1975 "Research on internal migration in the United States: A survey." Journal of Economic Literature 13:397–433.

Griffin, L.
  1976 "Specification biases in estimates of socioeconomic returns to schooling." Sociology of Education 49:121–139.
Griliches, Z. and W. M. Mason
  1973 "Education, income and ability." Pp. 285–316 in A. S. Goldberger and O. D. Duncan (eds.), Structural Equation Models in the Social Sciences. New York: Seminar Press.
Hadden, J. K. and E. F. Borgatta
  1965 American Cities: Their Social Characteristics. Chicago: Rand McNally.
Hall, D. T.
  1971 "A theoretical model of career subidentity development in organizational settings." Organizational Behavior and Human Performance 6:50–76.
Hall, R. E. and R. A. Kasten
  1973 "The relative occupational success of blacks and whites." Brookings Papers on Economic Activity 3:791–802.
Haller, A. O. and A. Portes
  1973 "Status attainment processes." Sociology of Education 46:51–91.
Hansen, W. L.
  1963 "Total and private rates of return to investment in schooling." Journal of Political Economy 61:128–140.
Hanushek, E. A.
  1973 "Regional differences in the structure of earnings." The Review of Economics and Statistics 55:204–213.
Hanushek, E. A. and J. E. Jackson
  1977 Statistical Methods for Social Scientists. New York: Academic Press.
Harrison, B.
  1972 Education, Training and the Urban Ghetto. Baltimore: The Johns Hopkins University Press.
Hauser, R. M.
  1974 "Contextual analysis revisited." Sociological Methods and Research 2:365–375.
  1980 "Comment on 'Stratification in a dual economy'." American Sociological Review 45:702–712.
Heckman, J.
  1974 "Shadow prices, market wages, and labor supply." Econometrica 42:679–694.
Heilbrun, J.
  1974 Urban Economics and Public Policy. New York: St. Martin's Press.
Heyns, B.
  1974 "Social selection and stratification within schools." American Journal of Sociology 79:1434–1451.
Hirsch, W. Z.
  1973 Urban Economic Analysis. New York: McGraw–Hill.
Hodge, R. W. and P. Hodge
  1965 "Occupational assimilation as a competitive process." American Journal of Sociology 71:249–264.
Hodson, R.
  1978 "Labor in the monopoly, competitive and state sectors of production." Politics and Society 8:429–480.
Hodson, R. and R. Kaufman
  1981 "Circularity in the dual economy: Comment on Tolbert, Horan, and Beck." American Journal of Sociology 86:881–887.

Hogan, D. P.

1978 "The variable order of events in the life course." American Sociological Review 43:573–586.

1980 "The transition to adulthood as a career contingency." American Sociological Review 45:261–276.

Horan, P. M.

1978 "Is status attainment research atheoretical?" American Sociological Review 43:534–541.

Iams, H. H. and A. Thornton

1975 "Decomposition of differences: A cautionary note." Sociological Methods and Research 3:341–352.

Institute for Social Research

1972 A Panel Study of Income Dynamics. Volumes 1 and 2. Ann Arbor: Institute for Social Research, University of Michigan.

Internal Revenue Service

1974a Statistics of Income–Business Income Tax Returns. Washington, D. C.: U. S. Government Printing Office.

1974b Statistics of Income–Corporation Income Tax Returns. Washington, D. C.: U. S. Government Printing Office.

Jencks, C., S. Bartlett, M. Corcoran, J. Crouse, D. Eaglesfield, G. Jackson, K. McClelland, P. Mueser, M. Olneck, J. Schwartz, S. Ward, and J. Williams

1979 Who Gets Ahead? The Determinants of Economic Success in America. New York: Basic Books.

Jencks, C., M. Smith, H. Acland, M. J. Bane, D. Cohen, H. Gintis, B. Heyns and S. Michelson

1972 Inequality: A Reassessment of the Effect of Family and Schooling in America. New York: Basic Books.

Jiobu, R. M. and H. H. Marshall, Jr.

1971 "Urban structures and the differentiation between blacks and whites." American Sociological Review 36:638–649.

Kain, J. F.

1968 "Housing segregation, Negro employment and metropolitan decentralization." Quarterly Journal of Economics 82:175–197.

Kain, J. F. and J. J. Persky

1969 "Alternatives to the gilded ghetto." The Public Interest 14:74–87.

Kalleberg, A. L. and L. Griffin

1980 "Class, occupation, and inequality in job rewards." American Journal of Sociology 85:731–768.

Kaufman, R., R. D. Hodson and N. P. Fligstein

1981 "Defrocking dualism: A new approach to defining industrial sectors." Social Science Research 10:1–31.

Kerckhoff, A. C.

1976 "The status attainment process: Socialization or allocation?" Social Forces 55:368–381.

Kerr, C.

1954 "The balkanization of labor markets." Pp. 92–110 in E. W. Bakke, P. M. Hauser, G. L. Palmer, C. A. Myers, D. Yoder, and C. Kerr (eds.), Labor Mobility and Economic Opportunity. Cambridge, Massachusetts: M. I. T. Press.

Kim, J. and J. Curry

1977 "The treatment of missing data in multivariate analysis." Sociological Methods and Research 6:215–240.

Kim, J. and C. W. Mueller
  1976   "Standardized and unstandardized coefficients in causal analysis: An expository note."
          Sociological Methods and Research 4:423–438.
  1978   Factor Analysis: Statistical Methods and Practical Issues. Volume 14 in Quantitative
          Applications in the Social Sciences. Beverly Hills: Sage.
Kluegel, J. R.
  1978   "The causes and cost of racial exclusion from job authority." American Sociological
          Review 43:285–301.
Kohn, M. L.
  1969   Class and Conformity: A Study in Values. Homewood, Illinois: Dorsey Press.
Kohn, M. L. and C. Schooler
  1978   "The reciprocal effects of the substantive complexity of work and intellectual flexibil-
          ity: A longitudinal assessment." American Journal of Sociology 84:24–52.
Lane, A.
  1968   "Occupational mobility in six cities." American Sociological Review 33:740–749.
Lazarsfeld, P., B. Berelson and H. Gaudet
  1968   The People's Choice. New York: Columbia University Press.
Lazarsfeld, P. F. and H. Menzel
  1969   "On the relation between individual and collective properties." Pp. 499–516 in A.
          Etzioni (ed.), A Sociological Reader on Complex Organizations. 2nd edition. New
          York: Holt, Rinehart & Winston.
Lipset, S. M., M. A. Trow and J. S. Coleman
  1962   Union Democracy. Garden City, New York: Doubleday.
Long, L. H. and L. R. Heltman
  1975   "Migration and income differences between black and white men in the North."
          American Journal of Sociology 80:1391–1409.
Maccoby, M.
  1976   The Gamesmen. New York: Simon & Schuster.
Masters. S. H.
  1975   Black–White Income Differentials. New York: Academic Press.
Mattila, J. M.
  1973   "A metropolitan income determination model and the estimation of metropolitan
          income multipliers." Journal of Regional Science 13:1–16.
Mattila, J. M. and W. R. Thompson
  1968   "Toward an econometric model of urban economic development." Pp. 63–78 in H. S.
          Perloff and L. Wingo, Jr. (eds.), Issues in Urban Economics. Baltimore: Johns
          Hopkins for Resources for the Future, Inc.
McClendon, M.
  1976   "The occupational status attainment processes of males and females." American So-
          ciological Review 41:52–64.
McDill, E. L., L. C. Rigsby and E. D. Meyers
  1969   "Educational climates of high schools: Their effects and sources." American Journal of
          Sociology 74:567–586.
Merton, R. and A. Kitt
  1950   "Contributions to the theory of reference group behavior." In R. Merton and P. F.
          Lazarsfeld (eds.), Continuities in Social Research: Studies in the Scope and Method of
          The American Soldier. New York: Free Press.
Meyer, J. H.
  1970   "High school climate and plans for entering college." Public Opinion Quarterly
          25:585–595.

Miller, A. R., D. J. Treiman, P. S. Cain and P. A. Roos

1980   Work, Jobs and Occupations: A Critical Review of the Dictionary of Occupational Titles. Washington, D. C.: National Academy Press.

Mincer, J.

1962   "Labor force participation of married women: A study of labor supply." Pp. 63–105 in Aspects of Labor Economics, National Bureau of Economic Research. Princeton, New Jersey: Princeton University Press.

1970   "The distribution of labor incomes: A survey—with special reference to the human capital approach." Journal of Economic Literature 8:1–26.

1974   Schooling, Experience, and Earnings. New York: National Bureau Economic Research.

Mincer, J. and S. Polachek

1974   "Family investments in human capital: Earnings of women." Journal of Political Economy 82:S76–S108.

Mooney, J. D.

1969   "Housing segregation, Negro employment and metropolitan decentralization: An alternative perspective." Quarterly Journal of Economics 83:299–311.

Morgenstern, R. D.

1973   "Direct and indirect effects on earnings of schooling and socioeconomic background." The Review of Economics and Statistics 55:225–233.

Mueller, C. W.

1974   "City effects on socioeconomic achievements: The case of large cities." American Sociological Review 39:652–667.

1977   "Socioeconomic achievements and city size." Pp. 249–269 in R. Hauser and D. Featherman (eds.), Occupational Stratification: The Analysis of Trends. New York: Academic Press.

Mueller, C. W. and B. G. Campbell

1977   "Female occupational achievement and marital status: A research note." Journal of Marriage and the Family 39:587–593.

Mueller, C. W. and H. Pope

1980   "Divorce and female remarriage mobility: Data on marriage matches after divorce for white women." Social Forces 58:726–738.

Oaxaca, R.

1973   "Male–female wage differentials in urban labor markets." International Economic Review 14:693–709.

O'Connor, J.

1973   The Fiscal Crisis of the State. New York: St. Martin's Press.

Oppenheimer, V.

1973   "Demographic influence on female employment and the status of women." American Journal of Sociology 78:946–961.

Oster, G.

1979   "A factor analytic test of the theory of the dual economy." Review of Economics and Statistics 61:33–39.

Osterman, P.

1975   "An empirical study of labor market segmentation." Industrial Labor Relations Review 28:508–523.

Parcel, T. L.

1979   "Race, regional labor markets and earnings." American Sociological Review 44:262–279.

1981   "The development and functioning of the American urban export sector, 1947–1972."

Pp. 187–217 in I. Berg (ed.), Sociological Perspectives on Labor Markets. New York: Academic Press.

Parcel, T. L. and C. W. Mueller
1983 "Occupational differentiation, prestige and socioeconomic status." Work and Occupations. Forthcoming.

Parnes, H. S., J. R. Shea, R. S. Spitz and F. A. Zeller
1970 Dual Careers. Volume 1. Washington, D. C.: U. S. Department of Labor, Manpower Research Monograph, No. 21.

Piore, M.
1971 "The dual labor market." Pp. 90–94 in David Gordon (ed.), Problems in Political Economy. Lexington, Massachusetts: Heath.
1975 "Notes for a theory of labor market stratification." Pp. 125–150 in R. C. Edwards, M. Reich, and D. M. Gordon (eds), Labor Market Segmentation. Lexington, Massachusetts: Heath.

Polachek, S. W.
1975 "Differences in expected post-school investment as a determinant of market wage differentials." International Economic Review 16:451–470.

Rao, P. and R. L. Miller
1971 Applied Econometrics. Belmont, California: Wadsworth.

Reder, M. W.
1955 "The theory of occupational wage differentials." American Economic Review 45:833–852.

Rees, A. and G. P. Schultz
1970 Workers and Wages in an Urban Labor Market. Chicago: University of Chicago Press.

Rehberg, R. A., W. E. Schafer and J. Sinclair
1970 "Toward a temporal sequence of adolescent achievement variables." American Sociological Review 35:34–48.

Reskin, B. F. and L. L. Hargens
1980 "Assessing sex discrimination in science." In R. Alvarez (ed.), Social Indicators of Institutionalized Discrimination. San Francisco: Jossey–Bass.

Robinson, R. and J. Kelley
1979 "Class as conceived by Marx and Dahrendorf." American Sociological Review 44:38–58.

Rosenfeld, R. A.
1978 "Women's intergenerational occupational mobility." American Sociological Review 43:36–46.

Scherer, F. M.
1970 Industrial Market Structure and Economic Performance. 1st edition. Chicago: Rand McNally.
1980 Industrial Market Structure and Economic Performance. 2nd edition. Chicago: Rand McNally.

Schultz, T. W.
1962 "Reflections on investment in man." Journal of Political Economy 60, Supplement Part 2:1–8.

Scott, W. R.
1981 Organizations: Rational, Natural, and Open Systems. Englewood Cliffs, New Jersey: Prentice–Hall.

Sewell, W. H., A. O. Haller and G. W. Ohlendorf
1970 "The education and early occupational attainment process: Replication and revision." American Sociological Review 35:1014–1027.

Sewell, W. H. and R. M. Hauser
  1972 "Causes and consequences of higher education: Models of the status attainment process." American Journal of Agricultural Economics 54:851–861.
Sewell, W. H., R. M. Hauser and D. L. Featherman (eds.)
  1976 Schooling and Achievement in American Society. New York: Academic Press.
Sewell, W. H. and V. Shah
  1967 "Socioeconomic status, intelligence and the attainment of higher education." Sociology of Education 40:1–23.
Shepherd, W. G.
  1969 "Market power and racial discrimination in white-collar employment." Antitrust Bulletin 14:141–161.
Siegel, P. M.
  1965 "On the cost of being a Negro." Sociological Inquiry 35:41–57.
  1971 "Prestige in the American occupational structure." Unpublished Ph.D. dissertation, Department of Sociology, University of Chicago.
Sjaastad, L. A.
  1962 "The costs and returns of human migration." Journal of Political Economy 70, Supplement:80–93.
Smith, A.
  (1789) The Wealth of Nations. New York: Modern Library.
  1937
Smith, D. M.
  1973 The Geography of Social Well-Being in the United States. New York: McGraw–Hill.
Smith, M. S.
  1968 "Equality of educational opportunity: Comments on Bowles and Levin." Journal of Human Resources 3:384–389.
Snyder, D. M., D. Hayward and P. M. Hudis
  1978 "The location of change in the sexual structure of occupations, 1950–1970: Insights from labor market segmentation theory." American Journal of Sociology 84:706–717.
Snyder, D. and P. Hudis
  1976 "Competition, segregation and minority income." American Sociological Review 41:209–234.
Sorensen, Aage B. and A. L. Kalleberg
  1981 "An outline of a theory of the matching of persons to jobs." Pp. 49–74 in I. Berg (ed.), Sociological Perspectives on Labor Markets. New York: Academic Press.
Sorensen, A., K. E. Taeuber and L. J. Hollingsworth, Jr.
  1975 "Indexes of racial residential segregation for 109 cities in the United States, 1940–1970." Sociological Focus 8:125–142.
Spaeth, J. L.
  1979 "Vertical differentiation among occupations." American Sociological Review 44:746–762.
Spenner, K. I.
  1979 "Temporal changes in work content." American Sociological Review 44:968–975.
  1980 "Occupational characteristics and classification systems: New uses of the Dictionary of Occupational Titles in social research." Sociological Methods and Research 9:239–264.
Spenner, K. I. and D. L. Featherman
  1978 "Achievement ambitions." Pp. 373–420 in R. H. Turner, J. Coleman and R. C. Fox (eds.), Annual Review of Sociology 4. Palo Alto, California: Annual Reviews, Inc.
Spenner, K. I., L. B. Otto and V. R. A. Call
  1980 Estimates of Third Edition DOT Job Characteristics for 1970 Census Occupation Industry Categories. Omaha, Nebraska: Career Development Associates.

Spenner, K. I. and L. V. Temme
   1977 "Spenner–Temme occupational variables for the 1970 Census occupation–industry classification." Unpublished paper.
Spilerman, S.
   1977 "Careers, labor market structure and socioeconomic achievement." American Journal of Sociology 83:551–593.
Spilerman, S. and R. E. Miller
   1976 "Community and industry determinants of occupational status of black males." Discussion paper #330. Madison: Institute for Research on Poverty, University of Wisconsin.
Stigler, G. J.
   1962 "Information in the labor market." Journal of Political Economy 70:94–105.
Stinchcombe, A. L.
   1974 Creating Efficient Industrial Administrations. New York: Academic Press.
Stolzenberg, R. M.
   1975 "Occupations, labor markets and the process of wage attainment." American Sociological Review 40:645–665.
   1978 "Bringing the boss back in: Employer size, employee schooling, and socioeconomic achievement." American Sociological Review 43:813–828.
Stolzenberg, R. M. and R. J. D'Amico
   1977 "City differences and non-differences in the effect of race and sex on occupational distribution." American Sociological Review 42:937–950.
Suleiman, E. N.
   1978 Elites in French Society: The Politics of Survival. Princeton, New Jersey: Princeton University Press.
Suter, L. E. and H. P. Miller
   1973 "Income differences between men and career women." American Journal of Sociology 78:962–974.
Sweet, J. A.
   1973 Women in the Labor Force. New York: Seminar Press.
Szymanski, A.
   1976 "Racial discrimination and white gain." American Sociological Review 41:403–414.
Taeuber, A. F., K. E. Taeuber and G. C. Cain
   1966 "Occupational assimilation and the competitive process: A reanalysis." American Journal of Sociology 72:273–285.
Taylor, P. A. and N. D. Glenn
   1976 "The utility of education and attractiveness for females' status attainment through marriage." American Sociological Review 41:484–498.
Temme, L. V.
   1975 Occupation: Meanings and Measures. Washington, D. C.: Bureau of Social Science Research.
Thompson, W. R.
   1965 A Preface to Urban Economics. Baltimore: The Johns Hopkins University Press.
Thurow, L. C.
   1969 Poverty and Discrimination. Washington, D. C.: The Brookings Institution.
   1980 The Zero-sum Society. New York: Basic Books.
Tolbert, C. M., II, P. M. Horan and E. M. Beck
   1980 "The structure of economic segmentation: A dual economy approach." American Journal of Sociology 85:1095–1116.
Treiman, D. J.
   1976 "A comment on Professor Lewis Coser's presidential address." The American Sociologist 11:27–33.

Treiman, D. J. and H. I. Hartmann (eds.)
  1981   Women, Work, and Wages: Equal Pay for Jobs of Equal Value. Washington, D. C.: National Academy Press.
Treiman, D. J. and K. Terrell
  1975   "Sex and the process of status attainment: A comparison of working women and men." American Sociological Review 40:174–200.
Turner, R. H.
  1951   "The relative position of the Negro male in the labor force of large American cities." American Sociological Review 16:524–529.
Tyree, A. and J. Treas
  1974   "The occupational and marital mobility of women." American Sociological Review 39:293–302.
U. S. Bureau of Census
  1970   Census of Population. Washington, D. C.: U. S. Government Printing Office.
  1975   Economic Censuses (1972). Washington, D. C.: U. S. Government Printing Office.
  1978   The County and City Data Book, 1977. Washington, D. C.: U. S. Government Printing Office.
U. S. Bureau of Labor Statistics
  1974   "Job tenure of workers, January, 1973." Monthly Labor Review 97:53–57.
  1977   Employment and Earnings Bulletin. Washington, D. C.: U. S. Government Printing Office.
  1978   Handbook of Labor Statistics, 1977. Washington, D. C.: U. S. Government Printing Office.
U. S. Department of Commerce—Bureau of Economic Analysis
  1977   National Income and Product Accounts of the U. S., 1929–1974. Washington, D. C.: U. S. Government Printing Office.
  1974, Survey of Current Business, February 1974 and July 1977. Washington, D. C.: U. S.
  1977   Government Printing Office.
U. S. Department of Labor
  1965   Dictionary of Occupational Titles. 3rd edition. Washington, D. C.: U. S. Government Printing Office.
  1977   Dictionary of Occupational Titles. 4th edition. Washington, D. C.: U. S. Government Printing Office.
U. S. Equal Employment Commission
  1975   Equal Employment Opportunity Report. Washington, D. C.: U. S. Government Printing Office.
Valkonen, T.
  1969   "Individual and structural effects in ecological research." Pp. 53–68 in M. Dogan and S. Rokkan (eds.), Quantitative Ecological Analysis in the Social Sciences. Cambridge, Massachusetts: M.I.T. Press.
Veroff, J., L. McClelland and K. Marquis
  1971   "Measuring intelligence and achievement motivation in surveys." Final Report to Office of Economic Opportunity, Department of Health, Education, and Welfare. Washington, D. C.
Wachtel, H. M. and C. Betsey
  1972   "Employment at low wages." Review of Economics and Statistics 54:121–129.
Wachter, M. L.
  1974   "Primary and secondary labor markets: A critique of the dual approach." Brookings Papers on Economic Activity 3:637–680.
Waite, L. J.
  1976   "Working wives: 1940–1960." American Sociological Review 41:65–80.

Waite, L. J. and R. M. Stolzenberg
1976 "Intended childbearing and labor force participation of young women: Insights from nonrecursive models." American Sociological Review 41:235–252.
Wallace, M. and A. L. Kalleberg
1981 "Economic organization of firms and labor market consequences: Toward a specification of dual economy theory." Pp. 77–117 in I. Berg (ed.), Sociological Perspectives on Labor Markets. New York: Academic Press.
Wanous, J. P.
1980 Organizational Entry: Recruitment, Selection and Socialization of Newcomers. Menlo Park, California: Addison–Wesley.
Weisbrod, B. A.
1966 "Investing in human capital." Journal of Human Resources 1:5–21.
Weiss, L. and J. G. Williamson
1972 "Black education, earnings and interregional migration." American Economic Review 62:372–383.
Wilson, K. I.
1978 "Toward an improved explanation of income attainment: Recalibrating education and occupation." American Journal of Sociology 84:684–697.
Winsborough, H. H. and P. Dickinson
1971 "Components of Negro–white income differences." Proceedings of the Social Statistics Section of the American Statistical Association.
Wolf, W. and R. Rosenfeld
1978 "Sex structures of occupations and job mobility." Social Forces 56:823–844.
Wright, E. O.
1978 "Race, class and income inequality." American Journal of Sociology 83:1368–1397.
Wright, E. O. and L. Perrone
1977 "Marxist class categories and income inequality." American Sociological Review 42:32–55.
Zucker, L. G. and C. Rosenstein.
1981 "Taxonomies of institutional structure: Dual economy reconsidered." American Sociological Review 46:869–884.

Index

QUANTITATIVE STUDIES IN SOCIAL RELATIONS
(Continued from page ii)

QUANTITATIVE STUDIES IN SOCIAL RELATIONS

Walter Williams and Richard F. Elmore, SOCIAL PROGRAM IMPLEMEN-TATION

Roland J. Liebert, DISINTEGRATION AND POLITICAL ACTION: *The Changing Functions of City Governments in America*

James D. Wright, THE DISSENT OF THE GOVERNED: *Alienation and Democracy in America*

Seymour Sudman, APPLIED SAMPLING

Michael D. Ornstein, ENTRY INTO THE AMERICAN LABOR FORCE

Carl A. Bennett and Arthur A. Lumsdaine (Eds.), EVALUATION AND EX-PERIMENT: *Some Critical Issues in Assessing Social Programs*

H. M. Blalock, A. Aganbegian, F. M. Borodkin, Raymond Boudon, and Vit-torio Capecchi (Eds.), QUANTITATIVE SOCIOLOGY: *International Per-spectives on Mathematical and Statistical Modeling*

N. J. Demerath, III, Otto Larsen, and Karl F. Schuessler (Eds.), SOCIAL POLICY AND SOCIOLOGY

Henry W. Riecken and Robert F. Boruch (Eds.), SOCIAL EXPERIMENTA-TION: *A Method for Planning and Evaluating Social Intervention*

Arthur S. Goldberger and Otis Dudley Duncan (Eds.), STRUCTURAL EQUATION MODELS IN THE SOCIAL SCIENCES

Robert B. Tapp, RELIGION AMONG THE UNITARIAN UNIVERSAL-ISTS: *Converts in the Stepfathers' House*

Kent S. Miller and Ralph Mason Dreger (Eds.), COMPARATIVE STUDIES OF BLACKS AND WHITES IN THE UNITED STATES

Douglas T. Hall and Benjamin Schneider, ORGANIZATIONAL CLIMATES AND CAREERS: *The Work Lives of Priests*

Robert L. Crain and Carol S. Weisman, DISCRIMINATION, PERSON-ALITY, AND ACHIEVEMENT: *A Survey of Northern Blacks*

Roger N. Shepard, A. Kimball Romney, and Sara Beth Nerlove (Eds.), MULTIDIMENSIONAL SCALING: *Theory and Applications in the Be-havioral Sciences*, Volume I — Theory; Volume II — Applications

Peter H. Rossi and Walter Williams (Eds.), EVALUATING SOCIAL PRO-GRAMS: *Theory, Practice, and Politics*

N

0